The Jewish Question

Historical Materialism
Book Series

The titles published in this series are listed at *brill.com/hm*

The Jewish Question

History of a Marxist Debate

By

Enzo Traverso

Translated by

Bernard Gibbons

BRILL

LEIDEN | BOSTON

Library of Congress Cataloging-in-Publication Data

Names: Traverso, Enzo, author. | Gibbons, Bernard, translator.
Title: The Jewish question : history of a marxist debate / by Enzo Traverso ;
    translated by Bernard Gibbons.
Other titles: Marxistes et la question juive. English
Description: Leiden ; Boston : Brill, [2018] | Series: Historical materialism book
    series, ISSN 1570-1522 ; volume 178 | Includes bibliographical references and
    index.
Identifiers: LCCN 2018037080 (print) | LCCN 2018038465 (ebook) |
    ISBN 9789004384767 (ebook) | ISBN 9789004301337 (hardback : alk. paper)
Subjects: LCSH: Communism and Judaism–History. | Jewish communists–History. |
    Jews–Europe, Eastern–History. | Jews–Russia–History.
Classification: LCC HX550.J4 (ebook) | LCC HX550.J4 T7213 2018 (print) |
    DDC 335.43089/924–dc23
LC record available at https://lccn.loc.gov/2018037080

Typeface for the Latin, Greek, and Cyrillic scripts: "Brill". See and download: brill.com/brill-typeface.

ISSN 1570-1522
ISBN 978-90-04-30133-7 (hardback)
ISBN 978-90-04-38476-7 (e-book)

What do you want with this particular suffering of the Jews? The poor victims of the rubber plantation in Putumayo, the Negroes in Africa with whose bodies the Europeans play a game of catch, are just as near to me. Do you remember the words written on the work of the Great General Staff about Trotha's campaign in the Kalahari desert? 'And the death-rattles, the mad cries of those dying of thirst, faded away into the sublime silence of eternity'. Oh, this 'sublime silence of eternity' in which so many screams have faded away unheard. It rings within me so strongly that I have no special corner of my heart reserved for the ghetto: I am at home wherever in the world there are clouds, birds and human tears ...

ROSA LUXEMBURG, letter to MATHILDE WURM (1917)

• • •

The puppet called 'historical materialism' is to win all the time. It can easily be a match for anyone if it enlists the services of theology, which today, as we know, is wizened and has to keep out of sight.

WALTER BENJAMIN, 'On the Concept of History' (1940)

• • •

The Jewish heretic who transcends Jewry belongs to a Jewish tradition. You may, if you like, see Akher as a prototype of those great revolutionaries of modern thought: Spinoza, Heine, Marx, Rosa Luxemburg, Trotsky, and Freud. You may, if you wish to, place them within a Jewish tradition. They all went beyond the boundaries of Jewry. They all found Jewry too narrow, too archaic, and too constricting. They all looked for ideals and fulfillment beyond it, and they represent the sum and substance of much that is greatest in modern thought, the sum and substance of the most profound upheavals that have taken place in philosophy, sociology, economics, and politics in the last three centuries.

ISAAC DEUTSCHER, *The Non-Jewish Jew* (1958)

• •
•

Contents

Acknowledgements

I wrote this book in Paris between 1985 and 1989 as a PhD thesis at L'Ecole des Hautes Études en Sciences Sociales. Its topic was conceived and discussed with Michael Löwy, my supervisor at the EHESS, who followed the different phases of my work until its completion: my intellectual debt to him is obvious in these pages. I wish to express my gratitude to John Bunzl, Nancy Green, Jutta Scherrer, Pierre Vidal-Naquet, Jean-Marie Vincent, and Claudie Weill, who read the manuscript and contributed their criticisms: their suggestions have proved most valuable. Thanks are also due to Bernard Gibbons and Peter Drucker for the English translation, as well as to Nathaniel Boling and Nicholas Bujalski for the final revision and many useful suggestions, not purely formal, that improved the quality of this second edition. Thanks, finally, to Sebastian Budgen for proposing to republish it, in a new, revised and expanded edition, in the Historical Materialism series by Brill. I owe very much to Jin ah, who was an inexhaustible source of encouragement for me when I wrote the first version of this book: I will never forget her intelligence and sensitivity. Finally, I wish to evoke the memory of my father, Beppino (1921–86). This book is dedicated to him.

Enzo Traverso

Historicising the Marxist 'Jewish Question': Preface to the Second Edition

This book was originally published in French in 1990. I had given the manuscript to the publisher one year earlier, a few months before the fall of the Berlin Wall. In a certain sense, it was one of the last pieces of the Marxist debate of the twentieth century. It was conceived as a critical reconstitution of a classical controversy and did not defend any orthodoxy – this time was over – but it belonged to that historical time, within its intellectual horizon. Its title – kept in the first English translation – mentioned 'the Marxists', the plural referring less to the doctrine than to its interpreters. It probably would have been more pertinent to speak of 'Marxisms', extending the plural to the theory itself, since thinkers as different as Karl Kautsky and Walter Benjamin did not simply suggest two distinct exegeses of the same 'canon', but rather two opposed conceptions of history. Reading this book, such a dichotomy appears evident, but it should have been specified in the title itself, in order to avoid any possible misunderstanding. The same matrix – Marx's thought – had produced a multiplicity of sometimes conflicting theories, and the debate on the 'Jewish Question' was an emblematic expression of such intellectual richness and diversity. In other words, the purpose of this book was not to propose a new 'Materialist conception of the Jewish Question'; it was to sketch an intellectual history of such a debate, exploring the multiple connections relating Judaism and Marxism, the Jews and socialism, ideas and historical experiences made by actually existing human beings.

During the 1990s, the collapse of communism and the emergence of Holocaust memorialisation in the public space of the Western world eclipsed this old controversy: on the one hand, Marxism became the strongest symbolic expression of an awful and deplorable 'century of ideologies'; on the other hand, the growing focus on the Judeocide favoured a parallel oblivion: the 'Jewish Question' ceased to belong to a century of 'questions' – national, colonial, etc. – and was finally interpreted, in almost ontological terms, as an anti-Semitic label, i.e. a problem lying in the existence itself of the Jews. Forgetting that for more than a century this formula had meant the oppression of a religious minority excluded from complete citizenship in many European states, a new wave of interpreters reduced it to its fascist definition. For the first time, Jean-Paul Sartre was posthumously accused of having reproduced the lexicon of the Vichy regime when, in 1946, he published his famous *Réflexions sur la question juive* (in English *Anti-Semite and Jew*), which seemed reminiscent of the infamous 'Commissariat général aux questions juives' created in 1941 by Marshal Philippe Pétain.[1] In fact, Sartre had different references in mind. A simple example allows us to refute this misinterpretation: Abram Leon, a Belgian Marxist thinker, wrote a remarkable essay on the 'Jewish Question' while hidden in Brussels under Nazi occupation, just before being arrested, deported and killed in Auschwitz.

Writing this book, I quickly understood that Marxism and the Jews were not two separate entities – a theory applied to an external object – but two intimately intertwined subjects interacting in different and changing ways for more than a century, from Marx to the Frankfurt School, from the Emancipation to the Holocaust and the birth of Israel. Thus, this book is both a history of ideas based on textual exegeses and the history of a symbiotic relationship between a theory and an intellectual minority. Since most of the Marxist thinkers writing on the Jewish Question were themselves Jewish, this book could be understood as both a study in Marxist self-criticism – a Marxist critique of Marxism[2] – and a history of Jewish self-interpretation. In other words, this book reveals a double dimension of the epistemological problem – already stressed by Georg Lukács – of the identity between the subject and object of historical knowledge. For a century at least, Marxism was an essential component of modern Jewish culture engendered by the tormented process of emancipation and secularisation that took place in Europe after the French Revolution; during this time, the Jews quickly became a crucial and irreplaceable actor in both revolutionary movements and Marxist theory. Of course, such a symbiotic relationship does not exhaust the entire trajectories of Marxism and Judaism. It would not be difficult to point out that the Jews played a marginal, almost insignificant role in the rich history of Italian, Latin American or Chinese and Japanese Marxism; in a similar way, one could easily point out that a classic like *Philosophies of Judaism* by Julius Guttmann (1933) does not include any reference to Marxism.[3] The symbiosis I refer to is mostly a story of crossing *heresies*: Marxists were heretics within the Jewish world and, symmetrically, the Jews mostly belonged to the heretic currents of Marxism. These double outsiders, nevertheless, have been at the core of the past century. The age of the October Revolution and Auschwitz, of communism and the Holocaust, of Stalinism and totalitarianism transformed them into both primary actors and designated targets, as both subjects and victims of history. If Emancipation had put them at the centre of the conflict between tradition and modernity, in the historical

---

1   See Suleiman 1995, pp. 201–18, and Traverso 1999.
2   Goldmann 1963, pp. 114–18.
3   Guttmann 1973.

constellation created by the First World War they became privileged witnesses and interpreters of the cataclysms that were devastating Europe. Marxism was thus one of the major dimensions of a turbulent epoch that, not accidentally, has been called 'the Jewish century'.[4]

The encounter between Marxism and the Jews did not take place in the etheric realm of ideas; it required a given space and time. This book suggests a large sequence: between the middle of the nineteenth century, when the young Karl Marx published his essay *Zur Judenfrage* (1843), and the Second World War, when the Holocaust destroyed, along with millions of European Jews, an entire generation of Marxist thinkers. The chronological frontiers of this debate are framed by the *longue durée* of Emancipation and the sudden, thunderous laceration of genocide. It also locates this intellectual debate in a cultural and geopolitical area: Eastern and Central Europe. In the West – notably in France, Italy and the United Kingdom – Emancipation created a layer of 'state Jews' who were socially and politically conformist, defenders of a form of conservative liberalism, faithful to the dominant order – both republican or monarchical – and who rejected any form of rebellion.[5] France produced republican Dreyfusards, the United Kingdom a champion of imperialism like Disraeli and Italy a monarchist chief of government like Sidney Sonnino. There, Jewish anarchists like Bernard Lazare were exceptions. In France, furthermore, the dogma of Jewish assimilation was strongly defended by the leadership of the Jewish community – the Alliance Israélite Universelle – and inscribed into the principles of Republican universalism. In the Tsarist Empire, where anti-Semitism was an endemic social practice and a codified system of laws until the Revolution of 1917, 'state Jews' could not exist. There, the Jews formed the leadership of all revolutionary movements. Between France and Russia, Germany was an intermediate space that combined legal emancipation and practical discrimination, with a large layer of Jewish *Bildungsbürgertum* and a pariah intelligentsia attracted by all sorts of avant-garde currents. In both Eastern and Central Europe, Marxism irresistibly attracted many Jews whose rejection of the faith of their fathers in the name of modernism was as strong as their exclusion from the political establishment, which was often shaped by a radical form of anti-Semitic nationalism. In such a context, Marxism became a fundamental tool of modernisation allowing them to overcome both traditional Judaism and nationalism. Abandoning their own religious legacy and being themselves rejected as Jews by all nationalist currents, they found in Marxism a solution to

---

4   See Slezkine 2004.
5   See Birnbaum 1996.

their identity dilemmas. Against Judaism and anti-Semitism, Marxism offered them a post-national, cosmopolitan and universalistic perspective. In Poland, where its introduction corresponded with the birth of a modern Yiddish culture, Marxism favoured the secularisation of the Diaspora, claiming national cultural autonomy for an 'extra-territorial' Jewish minority living in the middle of other ethnic and national groups (Russian, Polish, Ukrainian, Lithuanian, Byelorussian, German, etc.). Repudiating their religious heritage, the Jewish Marxists of the Tsarist Empire invented a modern form of citizenship for a national minority disconnected from a homogeneous territory. The Bund and the Poale Zion became the major expressions of a peculiar *Judeo-Marxism*, which offered solutions for a 'Jewish Question' conceived as the oppression of a national minority. Judeo-Marxism, nonetheless, is a label that can pertinently be applied to the Marxist Jewish intelligentsia of Central Europe as a whole, those who were certainly assimilated but also recognisable as a group with a well-defined social profile.

This book tried to conceptualise Judeo-Marxism – in my eyes, this remains one of its major achievements – but it probably did not pay attention enough to the dangerous affinities existing between such a definition and Nazi language, which was obsessively pervaded by the epithet 'Jewish Bolshevism' (*jüdischer Bolschewismus*). One could think – as I did – that the difference between both concepts is self-evident and does not need to be mentioned, but nonetheless this formal similarity cannot be denied and deserves a careful explanation.

In the Nazi *Weltanschauung*, 'Jewish Bolshevism' meant that the Russian Revolution was a malefic Jewish accomplishment. It stressed an identity between the Jews and Communism and was perceived as the last and most radical expression of the Enlightenment: the project of establishing the world rule of abstract reason against races and nations. In this view, the USSR appeared as a gigantic state in which a Jewish elite had gathered a Slavonic 'sub-humanity' (*Untermenschentum*) in order to threaten Western civilisation. The Jews were the brain of a proletarian state that gathered the wretched of the earth in the orders of battle against the West. In the eyes of Hitler, the struggle for conquering the German 'vital space' (*Lebensraum*), the destruction of the USSR and the extermination of the Jews were a single, coherent project.[6] He conceived of Operation Barbarossa – the war on the Eastern front, between 1941 and 1945 – as a secularised crusade against 'Jewish Bolshevism', the last step of a two-century conflict between the Enlightenment and its enemies, a kind of 'conservative revolution' or 'steel Romanticism' in which the poisonous fruits

---

6   On this form of Nazi 'syncretism,' see Mayer 1988, ch. 4, and Traverso 2003.

of modernity were fought with the instruments of modernity itself (powerful German technology). It is quite evident that this view was a distorting mirror of a real historical fact: Marxism was the inheritor of the 'radical Enlightenment'[7] and it is equally true that the emancipated Jews had become the most enthusiastic and creative representatives of this intellectual and political tradition. They easily identified with the abstract humanity posited by the French Declaration of Human Rights of 1789 until conceiving, theoretically with Marx and practically with Trotsky and Rosa Luxemburg, the project of a world revolution. They radicalised an idea of justice – extending it to the colonised peoples – that had been affirmed and violently contested since the French Revolution.

This association of the Jews with Enlightenment is also one of the keys for explaining the Marxist misunderstanding of the 'Jewish Question'. This book provides much evidence of the Marxist underestimation of the strength, persistence and depth of modern anti-Semitism, a phenomenon it mostly depicted as an anachronistic survival of backward, conservative social layers, a form of obscurantism inevitably condemned to disappear with the accomplishment of modernisation. Pogroms were a stigma of Russian primitivism and the Dreyfus Affair a late expression of French anti-Republicanism. Nazi anti-Semitism was the lethal disease of 'decaying' capitalism, not the ideology of a modern totalitarianism. In a similar way, Marxists held Judaism itself as a legacy destined to be dialectically 'sublated' (*aufgehoben*) in a socialist world, where a universal community of equals would have replaced present national and religious cleavages. In the *Communist Manifesto*, Marx and Engels clearly announced the economic and cultural unification of existing countries into a homogeneous supranational entity: 'The bourgeoisie has through its exploitation of the world market given a cosmopolitan character to production and consumption in every country ... In place of the old local and national exclusion and self-sufficiency, we have intercourse in every direction, universal inter-dependence of nations. And as in material, so occurs also in intellectual production. The intellectual creations of individual nations become common property. National one-sidedness and narrow-mindedness become more and more impossible, and from the numerous national and local literatures, there arises a world literature'.[8] According to such a diagnosis, a future, liberated world would inevitably forget what Rosa Luxemburg, in a significant parallel with Sigmund Freud, called the narcissism of 'minor difference'.[9] Marx

---

7   I am extending the concept elaborated by Israel 2001.
8   Marx-Engels 2012, p. 39.
9   Freud 2005, p. 108, and Luxemburg 1950, pp. 48–9.

had already identified 'the emancipation of the Jew with the emancipation of society from Judaism'[10] and, far from being horrified by such a statement, his disciples thought it was obviously shared by any reasonable person believing in Progress. Of course, both this underestimation of anti-Semitism and this perception of Judaism as an archaic vestige of a pre-modern world were deeply rooted in a teleological vision of history that, in spite of some isolated, critical questionings, shaped classical Marxism in the wake of the classical Enlightenment. This interpretation of the 'Jewish Question' applies, with few exceptions, from Marx to Abram Leon, covering the entire history of the debate reconstructed in this book. The first Marxist thinker who began to put it into question was Walter Benjamin, at the beginning of the Second World War, in his famous allegory of the Angel of History, which posits the equivalence between Progress and catastrophe.[11] After the war, Theodor W. Adorno and Max Horkheimer's *Dialektik der Aufklärung* (1947) was probably the first attempt to integrate the Holocaust into a Marxist vision of history that radically broke with any form of teleology. Taking into account certain formulations of this seminal book, one could suggest that they turned upside down the old teleology and presented Auschwitz as the dialectic accomplishment of civilisation. Instead of creating the premises of an emancipatory historical break, the conflict between productive forces and the social relations of production had increased class domination to the point of establishing a modern totalitarian form. Thus, the Nazi camps were the emblematic expression of a process of the 'self-destruction of the Enlightenment', deprived of its emancipatory potentialities and reduced to blind, purely instrumental *ratio*.[12]

Adorno and Horkheimer's book could be considered as the real conclusion – in the form of self-criticism – of the Marxist debate on the Jewish Question. For this reason, the second edition includes an additional chapter devoted to the Marxist confrontation with the Holocaust (whose first version was translated by Peter Drucker and published in English in 1999).[13] The periodisation suggested in the first edition – from 1843 to 1943 – is certainly pertinent insofar as it apprehends a sequence violently broken by the war and the Holocaust, the historical trauma that, by exterminating most of its actors, destroyed the conditions of such a debate. Nazi violence eliminated both Marxism and the Jews in Central Europe – the area Timothy Snyder has called the 'Bloodlands'[14] –

10   Marx 1994, p. 56.
11   Benjamin 2003, pp. 389–400.
12   Horkheimer and Adorno 2002, p. XVI.
13   A first version appeared in Traverso 1999, pp. 42–62.
14   Snyder 2010.

where the debate analysed in this book had taken place. After the war, this classical debate was virtually extinguished. Fifty years later, a famous French philosopher decided to devote essays to both Marx and Jewishness, but never thought to renew, in this way, the old Marxist debate on the Jewish Question.[15] Jacques Derrida was a Jew and a philosopher interested in Marxism, certainly not the inheritor of the theoretical controversies analysed in this book, which he completely ignored.

A Jewish intelligentsia permeated by Marxism, nevertheless, survived in exile, concluding a theoretical disputation outside of its original framework. One may suggest, applying to this debate the sharp observation of Peter Gay on Weimar culture, that the Judeo-Marxist intelligentsia found 'its true home' in exile.[16] Marx published his early essay on the Jewish Question in Paris, in 1843, in a small journal of German émigrés, the *Deutsch-Französische Jahrbücher*; Vladimir Medem, the theoretician of the Bund, published his memoirs in New York, where he had emigrated after the First World War; Leon Trotsky was exiled in Mexico when, interviewed by an American newspaper in 1938, he recognised the possibility of the extermination of the Jews in the event of a new world conflict; Abram Leon was a Polish immigrant who wrote his book *La conception matérialiste de la question juive* hidden in different boltholes between Brussels and Charleroi, in occupied Belgium; Adorno and Horkheimer wrote *Dialektik der Aufklärung* in California, during the war, and in 1947 gave their manuscript to an exile publisher reinstalled in Amsterdam: Querido Verlag. The 'Jewish Question' reveals to what extent Marxist theory was, in its classical age, a matter of *outsiders*.

A teleological vision of history – the philosophical background of an underestimation of the depth of European anti-Semitism – also explains the limits and ambiguities of most Marxist interpretations of Zionism until the end of the Second World War. This incomprehension was far from being a Marxist peculiarity, insofar as it shaped the attitudes and behaviours of almost all the actors of the Middle East, from the great powers to local national movements and political forces. Basically, until the end of the war nobody seriously took Zionism into account: neither the United Kingdom (the Balfour Declaration referred to a 'homeland' rather than to a Jewish state), nor the Jewish Diaspora (the overwhelming majority of the Jews who left Europe between the end of the nineteenth century and the Second World War went to the Unites States, Western Europe and Latin America, not to Palestine), nor even the Arabs, who were

---

15   Derrida 1993, and Derrida 1994.
16   Gay 2001, p. 145.

convinced that Zionism would disappear from the Middle East with decolon-
isation and the end of the British protectorate.[17] Marxists were certainly not
alone in underestimating the Zionist capacity to build a Jewish state.

Their approach lay more in a teleological vision of history than in geopolitical considerations. In their eyes Zionism was, first of all, an anachronistic
project, insofar as it was opposed to the 'forward march of history' and progress; it was yet another reactionary attempt to put the Jews inside the wall
of a ghetto. Nationalism had pushed the old world into a tragic impasse and
Zionism was nothing but a Jewish caricature of European nationalisms. Zionism, furthermore, tried to 'use' anti-Semitism as a chance for increasing Jewish
emigration to Palestine instead of fighting it. Since Herzl, the purpose of Zionism had been the creation of a Jewish state with the agreement of the great
powers, not the struggle of the Jews of Eastern Europe against tsarism, then of
the whole continent against anti-Semitic fascism. Nationalism united the Jews,
transcending their class divisions, and thereafter paralysed the class struggle
in the Diaspora. All Marxist currents generally shared these axioms, including those – like the Polish Bund – that recognised the legitimacy of a Jewish
national claim and even those – like the small minority of Marxist Zionists led
by Ber Borokhov – that associated the birth of a Jewish state with a national
liberation struggle and socialist revolution. It was only at the end of the 1930s
that the legitimacy of a Jewish national consciousness began to be recognised,
with a tangible taste of self-criticism, by a strongly Westernised, classical Marxist like Trotsky.[18]

In the middle of this force field, the Palestinian Question was rarely scrutinised. Of course, since the end of the nineteenth century – and more explicitly
since the first Arab revolt in 1929 – Palestinian national claims were recognised
and supported by the Comintern and, locally, by the almost entirely Jewish
Communist Party.[19] These political assessments, however, had a much more
empirical than theoretical character. Many voices – including some within the
Zionist movement – criticised the canonical, colonial vision of Palestine as 'a
land without a people for a people without a land', but the Palestinian nation-
building process engendered by the collapse of the Ottoman Empire never
became a central worry for European Marxism. At the end of the nineteenth
century, the colonial idea found many enthusiastic defenders among 'revisionist' Marxists: colonialism would have brought Western civilisation to backward

---

17   Cf. Mayer 2008; Khalidi 2010.
18   Trotsky 1970.
19   Cf. Budeiri 2010.

Palestine and Zionism could have become an instrument of historical Progress. From Edward Bernstein to Ber Borokhov, many Marxists stressed that
European Jewish settlers would develop the productive forces of Palestine, creating there the premises of socialism. In the nineteenth century, Marx thought
that, in spite of its violence, British imperialism was bringing progress to India,
where it acted as 'an unconscious tool of history'.[20] Why could the Jews not
play a similar role in Palestine? Fundamentally, this approach was nothing but
a dimension of a broader Eurocentric legacy that, in the middle of resistances
and contradictions, deeply shaped the tradition of classical Marxism. The peculiarities of Zionism – a colonialism trying to conquer territories and to expel
the Palestinians instead of subjecting and exploiting them – would come to be
understood (and became the object of Marxist analysis) only after the foundation of Israel.[21] At the edge of this crucial event – even after the massive arrival
in Palestine of the Jewish survivors of the Holocaust – the proposal for a bi-
national state never engendered a significant Marxist debate (as opposed to
cultural Zionism in which it found many supporters).

In emphasising the rupture produced by the war and the Holocaust – the
periodisation 1843–1943 symbolically assumed the uprising of the Warsaw
ghetto as a turning point – the first edition of this book probably *predated*
the conclusion of a debate whose epilogue took place after the war, in America and in Palestine. I had interpreted this epilogue as the beginning of a new
cycle rather than as the outcome of a previous debate. Probably it was both.
America and Palestine, however, indicate a geographical displacement that is
the mirror of the tragedies suffered in Europe by both Marxism and the Jews. In
other words, this book suggested a periodisation that could appear controversial for apprehending the features of an intellectual debate but clearly grasped
the collapse of its conditions: *genocide*. Differently from many other academic
quarrels, the Marxist disputation on the Jewish Question did not finish because
of 'natural' exhaustion, when all its actors had displayed their arguments. It was
destroyed in the Nazi concentration and extermination camps and suffocated
by Stalinism, throughout its multiple campaigns against communist heresies
and 'cosmopolitanism'. It reflects, in the most emblematic form, the wounds
inflicted by totalitarianism on twentieth-century critical thought. In the long
view, the war broke the symbiosis between Marxism and the Jews I mentioned
above. After the Holocaust, Jewish culture became less and less Marxist and,
conversely, Marxism became less and less Jewish. The axis of the Jewish World

---

20   Marx 1960, p. 41.
21   Cf. Weinstock 1970.

experienced a significant shift: just as the first half of the twentieth century was the age of Trotsky, the nomadic harbinger of world revolution, the second half became the era of Kissinger, the Cold War strategist of imperialism.[22]

According to Perry Anderson, Western Marxism was the product of a historical defeat of the workers' movement in inter-war Europe, which resulted in a double displacement, both geographical and theoretical: from Eastern and Central Europe to the West; from economy and politics to philosophy and aesthetics. He could also have added a Jewish dimension. Saying that until the 1930s Marxism had mostly spoken Russian and German implicitly means it had been written and spoken, to a very large extent, by Jewish Marxists. This objective assessment does not try to revisit the history of Marxism through an ethnic lens, simply to recall the social and cultural background of its rise and spread during its 'classical' period. When Anderson delivered his severe judgement on Western Marxism – 'method as impotence, art as consolation, pessimism as quiescence'[23] – he presented it as the result of a historical defeat, but did not mention the Holocaust, to which this defeat was inextricably bound. Perhaps impotence, consolation and pessimism were also the features of an unconscious work of mourning, a necessary *Trauerarbeit* – Adorno had qualified his Marxism as a 'melancholy science'[24] – waiting for new redemptive, emancipatory battles.

The first French edition of this book was released in 1990, but its first chapter was written five years earlier, i.e. thirty years ago.[25] It is certain that today I would not write the same book. I have updated the bibliographical references, revised some assessments and frequently introduced stylistic changes in order to improve its clarity and readability, but I did not rewrite it. Any book has its own trajectory and I think an author should be respectful of it. I am proud of this book, my first one, and I think it fulfilled its goal. It was the first critical reconstitution of an intellectual debate that took place over the course of a century and deserved significant consideration. This is its second English edition; it has known two editions in French and Spanish, as well as other translations into German, Japanese and Turkish. This means that this book answered a wide demand for knowledge. Even if today I would not write it in the same way, I certainly do not reject its results. Furthermore, studies devoted to this topic during the last 25 years have neither revealed new, fundamental sources nor changed

---

22   On this historical shift, see Traverso 2016.

23   Anderson 1976, p. 93.

24   Adorno 2005, p. 15.

25   See Pierre Vidal-Naquet's introduction to the original French edition in Vidal-Naquet 1996.

my vision. As a whole, the Marxist debate on the Jewish Question has not been the object of new investigations, even if some original works focusing on specific issues have been published.[26] Among the topics scrutinised in this book, the only two that have since deserved an extensive re-consideration are the Holocaust and Walter Benjamin's politics.[27] Even in this latter field, however, many of the rough intuitions outlined in this book do not seem obsolete to me. On the contrary, revisiting the writings of the author of the *Arcades Project* through a Marxist and a Jewish lens, setting aside the traditional codes of aesthetics, could prove to be a fruitful and refreshing exercise. Therefore, I hope that this new edition, almost a generation after the first one, will be useful for a younger readership.

Ithaca, NY, September 2015–Fall 2017

---

26   See in particular Jacobs 1992 and 2015, and Kessler 1993 and 1994.
27   On the Holocaust, see Geras 1998, Callinicos 2001 and Milchman 2003; on Benjamin, see Bensaïd 1990, Leslie 2000 and 2007, and Löwy 2006.

Introduction

Two works, written a century apart, constitute the prologue and the conclusion of the Marxist debate on the Jewish Question: *Zur Judenfrage* (*On the Jewish Question*), written in 1843 by the young (and not yet Marxist) Marx, and Abram Leon's *The Jewish Question: A Marxist Interpretation* (written during the Second World War and published in 1946).[1] This debate essentially took place in Central and Eastern Europe and experienced its 'classical' period between the end of the nineteenth century and the Russian Revolution of 1917. This chronological and geographical demarcation is not fortuitous but corresponds to a precise phase in the history of both Marxism and the Jews.

The reasons for this geographical demarcation are obvious enough: it was in Central and Eastern Europe that the great majority of the world's Jewish population was concentrated at the turn of the century; it was there that a Jewish proletariat and workers' movement took shape; it was there, too, where tradition and modernity, feudalism and capitalism, anti-Semitism and Emancipation were intertwined, that the features of a new Jewish Question, founded on the nationality-assimilation dialectic, were outlined.

It was in the countries of Eastern Europe and the Russian Empire alone that Marxists raised certain fundamental questions in approaching the Jews: What were the historic roots of the really-existing Jewish communities? Were the Jews a nation or a caste? Was there a historical future for the Jews or were they doomed to assimilate into the nations among which they lived? What was the nature of anti-Semitism? Neither in Western Europe (in France, England, or Italy) nor in the United States (where, nonetheless, there was a Jewish socialist current of some importance) did a Marxist debate develop around these problems.

It might be argued that French socialism did indeed concern itself with the Jewish problem, above all at the time of the Dreyfus Affair. However, the anti-Jewish tradition of Proudhonian and Blanquist socialism, which marked the history of the French workers' movement until the end of the nineteenth century, was outside Marxism. It is possible to find a consideration of the Jewish Question among certain French socialist or anarchist intellectuals who were influenced by Marx's thought, such as Jean Jaurès, Paul Lafargue, Georges Sorel, or Bernard Lazare, but their writings cannot be considered as contributions to a debate within French Marxism; they belonged instead to the ideological con-

---

1 See CW, vol. 3, p. 160; Leon 2010.

flicts of the Third Republic, in which they were opposed to anti-Semitic nationalism (like the polemics between Bernard Lazare and Edouard Drumont).[2] In
the United States, Jews were torn between national autonomy (an American
Yiddishkeit) and assimilation over a period of about fifty years, from 1880 to
1930. At the time of the great Jewish immigration – between the last quarter
of the nineteenth century and the First World War – the American working
class was multinational and its ethnic segments remained profoundly linked
to their own communities. In this context, the existence of a Jewish socialism
was considered as a completely normal phenomenon. Despite the prodigious
efforts of Engels, Daniel de Leon, and the Third International to 'Americanise'
Marxism, the latter remained almost invariably a vehicle of 'outsiders', a flag
of struggle for immigrant workers and a theory elaborated by marginalised,
heretical intellectuals.[3] Within this current, Jewish Socialists found their place
as Jews, without being obliged to declare their faith in assimilation.

On the chronological level, the caesura is inevitably marked by the Holocaust. During the war, Nazism would completely erase the *Yiddishland* and
Jewish socialism from the map of Europe – their last heroic manifestation being
the Warsaw ghetto uprising of 1943 – and, in the period following, the centre of
gravity of the Jewish problem shifted to Palestine. With the disappearance of
the Jewish communities of Central and Eastern Europe, Jewish identity was
redefined, globally, by the experience of genocide and by the birth of the state
of Israel. The war obviously represented a turning point for the Jewish question;
that is why our study ends in 1943.

The last quarter of the nineteenth century saw the Jewish Question reappear
under new forms. Alongside the birth, in Germany and Austria, of modern
anti-Semitism – no longer merely peasant but predominantly middle-class, no
longer simply religious but above all racial – the features of a Jewish national
question, linked in the first place to the development of Yiddish culture, took
shape in Eastern Europe, where tsarism oppressed the Jews through pogroms
and segregation in the Pale of Settlement. The formation of a Jewish workers'
movement obliged Marxists to come to terms with these new phenomena.

In this historical moment, the entire Marxist debate focused on a single
issue: *assimilation*. Marxist culture adopted a unilateral interpretation of Jewish history, inherited to a large extent from the Enlightenment, which identified Emancipation with assimilation and could conceive the end of Jewish

---

2 On the role of the Jewish Question in French socialism, see Green 1985; on Sorel's anti-
   Semitism, see Sand 1984; on Bernard-Lazare, see Wilson 1978.
3 See Buhle 1987, p. 101.

oppression only in terms of the abandoning of Jewishness. This interpretation emerged toward the end of the eighteenth century and seemed to be confirmed in the following period. In 1791, the Revolution granted civic rights to French Jews, and the Napoleonic conquests extended them to the Dutch, Belgian, and German Jewish communities. Despite the delays and setbacks imposed by the Restoration, Austria-Hungary granted emancipation in 1867 and Germany did the same between 1869 and 1871. As Pierre Vidal-Naquet has stressed, the French Revolution was taken as a model: Jews should no longer live as *a* nation but should become fully fledged citizens of *the* nation (in this case, France).[4]

Enlightenment culture perceived the Jews as a kind of *anomaly*, insofar as they escaped the political semantics of European modernity – the correspondence between state, nation and territory – and both the partisans of Emancipation and its opponents shared this view. The main divergences concerned the definition of the measures necessary to suppress this anomaly: the conservatives proposed segregation, to stop the Jews from contaminating the Christian world (then ethnically homogeneous national communities); the reformers envisaged the disappearance of Judaism through gradual assimilation (which obviously implied the granting of civic rights). The process of emancipation varied over time, assuming three distinct phases. The eighteenth-century rationalists supported the 'naturalisation' of the Jews, implicitly recognising their status as foreigners in the Christian world. Wilhelm von Dohm, in his famous work *Über die bürgerliche Verbesserung der Juden* (*On the Civic Reform of the Jews*), published in Berlin in 1781, had introduced the notion of 'improvement' (*Verbesserung*). This semantic change reflected a new perspective; the problem of Jewish emancipation transcended its theological basis and achieved a social and political dimension.[5] Nonetheless, the very use of the term *improvement* implied a pejorative judgment of the Jews, the idea that they remained shaped by socially negative features of which they must rid themselves. The project of emancipation elaborated by von Dohm thus found its point of departure in the anti-Jewish prejudices of the time.

The term *Emancipation* (*Emanzipierung*) appeared in the 1830s and was widely diffused after the 1848 revolutions. It was an emotionally charged concept but it did not change the old approaches; Emancipation was still seen as the means to help the Jews shed their negative dispositions. According to the historian John Bunzl, 'The declared objective of the policy of Emancipa-

---

4 Vidal-Naquet 1991, pp. 59–94.
5 Katz 1982.

tion was the assimilation of the Jews, the dissolution of their social and cultural identity'.[6] The Jewish intelligentsia itself internalised this attitude. Moses
Mendelssohn, the foremost figure of German-Jewish culture at the end of the
eighteenth century, fought for the linguistic assimilation of the Jews and for the
abandonment of Yiddish, which he despised as a 'jargon.' The *maskilim* – the
partisans of the *Haskalah*, the Jewish Enlightenment – led a heated struggle for
the integration of the Jews in the nation-state (the historian Heinrich Graetz
even opposed the translation into Yiddish of his own work).[7] In 1893, the *Zent-
ralverein deutscher Staatsburger jüdischen Glaubens* (the Union of German Citizens of the Jewish Faith) proposed to 'stimulate among Jews the sentiment of
their collective belonging to the German people ... Through the defense of our
equality, we struggle for the most elevated ideals of humanity – for the most
dear interests of our German fatherland'.[8]

Nationalism and the idea of progress transformed Jewish assimilation into
a sort of dogma. It is true that in Germany the emancipated Jews remained
in several respects 'outsiders' or, in Hannah Arendt's definition, *parvenus* who
still carried with them the traces of their past as *pariahs*.[9] The democratic and
liberal intelligentsia, however, tried to ignore this awkward reality. Gershom
Scholem bitterly observed that the process of assimilation meant that the Jews
struggled for Emancipation 'not for the sake of their rights as a people, but for
the sake of assimilating themselves to the peoples among whom they lived'.[10]
Nonetheless, the German-Jewish cultural symbiosis was not simply an illusion.
It produced works of an extraordinary richness in the fields of literature, music,
and the humanities. The historian Fredric G. Grunfeld, for instance, has depicted it as 'a golden age' that was surpassed only by the Italian Renaissance.[11]
In Central Europe, Emancipation effectively appeared as a process of Jewish
assimilation with the surrounding world, a world made up of nation-states, but
it would be wrong to see that as the loss of a peculiar identity, of any feeling of
belonging to a distinct group. It amounted, rather, to a complex phenomenon of
cultural integration. Although Jewishness underwent a deep cultural and social
metamorphosis during the process of its secularisation and modernisation, the
Jews did not disappear and continued to be perceived as Jews. In other words, a

---

6   Bunzl 1987, p. 27.
7   See Robin 1984, pp. 39–40.
8   Quoted by Goldscheider, Zuckerman 1986, p. 118.
9   Arendt 2007a, pp. 275–97. On this dichotomy between pariah and parvenu, see Traverso
        1995, ch. 2 and ch. 4.
10   Scholem 1976, p. 77. On this controversial issue, see Hess 2002.
11   Grunfelf 1979, p. v.

'Jewish Question' still existed. Poet Ludwig Börne described it in ironical terms: 'Some reproach me with being a Jew, some praise me because of it, some pardon me for it, but all think of it'.[12]

This picture synthesises the dominant psychological and cultural climate at the turn of the century. The Marxism of the Second International, shaped by positivism and evolutionistic determinism, welcomed the idea of Jewish assimilation as the inevitable and desirable result of the 'path of history.' This conception was implicit in almost the entire German and Austrian Marxist literature. The words of the young Marx, for example, who identified authentic emancipation with the 'liberation of society from Judaism'; of Victor Adler, who desired the 'death of the Wandering Jew'; and of Karl Kautsky, according to whom 'the Jewish nation can only triumph by disappearing', trace this theoretical journey.

Kautsky formulated a coherent socialist theory of assimilation in the framework of a positivistic-Marxist *Weltanschauung*. His interpretation of Jewish history in the light of the concept of *caste* was the link between the *Geldmensch* of Marx and the 'people-class' of Leon. The reduction of Jewish otherness to commerce, a socio-economic function that the Jews had fulfilled over several centuries, should have 'scientifically' explained the process of assimilation. The development of capitalism put into question and finally broke the isolation of the Jewish caste, 'de-Judaising' its members. Given that capitalism was the bearer of assimilation, those Jews who preserved their own particular consciousness were perceived as reactionary and anachronistic. To a certain extent, the theory of the people-class appeared as an objective description of the Jewish historical condition, but the explanation of the whole of Jewish history through an economic function inevitably obscured its cultural dimension, which was as much religious as secular.

The dissolution of the Jews in the surrounding nations was conceived as a sort of 'law' of the historic development of modern societies. It should be said that most Jewish Marxists – from Eduard Bernstein to Otto Bauer – shared this hermeneutic model. They found in the workers' movement the instrument of their own emancipation, i.e. a total assimilation, assumed and conscious, remote from the *Haskalah*'s axiom according to which emancipated Jews had to be 'Jews at home and men outside'. In socialist internationalism, they found as well a substitute for their denied or lost Jewish identity. In Germany and Austria, the paradigm of assimilation could correspond to the real assimilation

---

12   Quoted by Arendt 1976, p. 64. This phrase was written in 1832 but maintained all its topicality at the end of the century.

of the Jewish intelligentsia and did not have to confront a Jewish proletariat, with the exception of the *ostjüdisch* immigrants of Vienna and Berlin. In Eastern Europe, on the other hand, any assimilationist perspective came up against the existence of a Jewish nation and working class.

Under tsarist domination, civic rights were denied to the Jews. The fall of absolutism, Russian socialists thought, would bring emancipation of the Jews and, as in the West, their extinction as a particular group within the surrounding nations (notably in Russia). The Jewish world, however, remained completely foreign to the idea of assimilation. In Central Europe, the process of Jewish integration into German culture had both preceded and created the premises for Emancipation much earlier. This occurred in the context of what Jacob Katz has called a 'semi-neutral society',[13] i.e. the beginning of a dialogue and the tacit acceptance of Jews (or at least of certain amongst them, like the Court Jews) in the world of the Gentiles. Nothing similar happened in the East. There was a terrible resurgence of anti-Semitism in Poland, Lithuania, and Ukraine in the last twenty years of the nineteenth century, a period in which the assimilation of German and Austrian Jews appeared as an irreversible and accomplished fact. The century of German-Jewish symbiosis in *Mitteleuropa* was also the century of the modernisation of Yiddish, the language spoken by the overwhelming majority of the Jews of the Russian Empire. Between 1870 and the First World War, Yiddish literature reached its classic age, shaped by the works of Mendele Mocher Sforim, Sholom Aleichem, I.L. Peretz, and Sholem Asch. Obviously, there was a dialectical link between these two phenomena: the pogroms contributed to reinforce the isolation of the Russian Jews and erected a barrier against their assimilation. The capitalist development and the Westernisation of the Tsarist Empire broke down the walls of the ghetto, but at the same time the rise of anti-Semitism perpetuated the cleavage between Jews, Russians, and Poles. The breakup of the traditional Jewish world did not lead to assimilation but to the birth of a modern Jewish nation. The *Yiddishkeit* was the natural framework in which the Jews could appropriate the new ideas of democracy, socialism, nationalism, and so on. The social structure of the Jews of Eastern Europe consisted of a pre-industrial proletariat and an impoverished middle class that spoke Yiddish as a national language, perpetuated their religious practices, and kept an ethnic identity reinforced by a surrounding endemic anti-Semitism. The Jewry of Central Europe presented different features: a predominance of the bourgeois and middle classes, a very

---

13   Katz 1973, ch. 4.

high level of urbanisation, an accomplished process of linguistic and cultural assimilation and, finally, the abandonment of Yiddish language and religious orthodoxy.[14]

Consequently, in Eastern Europe, only a narrow nucleus of the intelligentsia could truly assimilate (and become assimilationist). Here the struggle for emancipation merged with the formation of a national consciousness. The Jewish workers' movement embodied this aspiration, combining it with the internationalism and universalism of the socialist tradition. The result was the elaboration of a plurality of theories and currents of thought that could be called *Judeo-Marxism*. Differently from the assimilationism of their German counterparts, the Marxists of the Tsarist Empire developed a wealth of approaches to the Jewish question: assimilationism (Russian and Polish Social Democrats), national autonomism (Bund), and Jewish nationalism (Zionists). For Lenin, Martov, Trotsky, and Rosa Luxemburg, assimilation remained the dominant historic tendency, whereas Vladimir Medem and Ber Borokhov demanded the right of the Jews of Eastern Europe to their own national existence. This latter position, nonetheless, was the point of departure of two distinct (and often opposed) trajectories. Borokhov essentially inverted the theory of Kautsky. According to the German theoretician (and Lenin, Stalin, and Rosa Luxemburg shared his point of view), the anomaly of a nation deprived of a specific territory and economy could be resolved only by assimilation. Borokhov, on the contrary, argued that the solution was the 'normalising' of the Jewish nation, giving it a territory, an economy, and a state (Palestine). For his part, Vladimir Medem thought that the development of capitalism tended to separate nation and territory, thus creating the conditions for a modern Jewish national community rooted in language and culture: *Yiddishkeit*. Medem criticised the abstract internationalism of the Bolsheviks in the following terms:

> Anybody who has the least familiarity with the national question knows that internationalist culture is not a-national. An a-national culture, neither Russian nor German nor Polish ... but a pure culture is an absurdity. In order to attract the working class, the internationalist ideas need to be adapted to the language spoken by the workers and to the concrete national conditions in which they live. Workers should not be indifferent to the condition and the development of their national culture, for it is

---

14   On the dichotomy between the Jewish communities of Eastern Europe and the assimilated Jews of the West, see Mendelsohn 1983, pp. 6–7.

only through it that they can participate in the internationalist culture of
democracy and the world socialist movement. It is obvious, but V[ladi-
mir] I[lyich] turns a deaf ear to all this.[15]

Before the October Revolution, the Russian Social Democrats (and the Bolsheviks in particular) neither understood nor supported the national demands of
the Jews. As David Meghnagi has correctly pointed out, they did not accept
'the idea that the Jew existed for himself, and not as a negativity of which he
must liberate himself'.[16]

In the interwar period, the Jewish Question experienced a historical turn.
The first great transformation took place in Eastern Europe. The Revolution
freed the Russian Jews and tried to extirpate anti-Semitism from the vast Slavic
countryside. In the course of the civil war, the Jewry rallied massively to the Red
Army (often the only existing defence against the pogroms) and its intelligentsia was in great number recruited into the Soviet state apparatus. No longer an
oppressed minority suffering discrimination, the Russian Jews were recognised
in the 1920s as a nation with a modern culture. Since the October Revolution, Yiddish culture – under all its forms, scientific, literary, and artistic – was
encouraged and experienced a great expansion, although, at the same time,
the pluralism of Jewish life almost disappeared. The Bund and different currents of socialist Zionism still existed in Poland, whereas in the Soviet Union
they rapidly joined the Bolshevik party. It did not amount to a 'liquidation', as
a certain historiography would contend,[17] but rather a self-dissolution of the
Jewish parties subjected to the powerful attraction of the October Revolution
(moreover the Poale Zion survived in the Soviet Union until 1928, at a time
when all opposition, even inside the Bolshevik party, was suppressed).[18] The
sole political expression of the Jewish world was reduced to the *Evsektsiia*, the
Jewish sections of the CPSU, whose initial 'enlightened despotism' on social
and cultural issues found its bitter conclusion in the bureaucratic farce of Birobidzhan.

In Western Europe, National Socialism put the Jewish Question on the
agenda again. Paralysed by the conflict between Social Democracy and the
Communist party, the German left was unable to understand the immense
danger Nazism represented and underestimated its anti-Semitism. Of course,
in Weimar Germany, nobody could predict Auschwitz, but neither the social

---

15   Quoted by Ertel 1982, p. 164.
16   See Meghnagi 1985, p. 181.
17   See, for example, Marienstras 1977, p. 75.
18   See Gurevitz 1974.

democratic nor the communist left was able to perceive the qualitative difference that existed between the Russian pogroms, the religious prejudice of Vienna's Mayor Karl Lueger, and the redemptive anti-Semitism of Adolf Hitler and Alfred Rosenberg. This brand of racist anti-Semitism necessarily implied different practices, which manifested once it was transformed into a state ideology in an advanced capitalist country such as Germany. The Holocaust was the product of the combination of a racist ideology with the instrumental rationality of capitalism. But it was impossible to envisage such a combination if one interpreted history as a linear development of the productive forces, and the source of uninterrupted social progress. Teleological Marxism, therefore, was unable to understand either anti-Semitism or fascism.

At the end of the nineteenth century, the German and Austrian Socialists had largely underestimated the danger of anti-Semitism, considering it as an embryonic stage in the development of the anti-capitalist consciousness of the exploited masses. In 1923, during the period of the French occupation of the Ruhr, the German Communists had repeated the same error. The irresponsible illusion that anti-Semitic demagogy was in the last analysis useful to the anti-capitalist mobilisation of the workers only resulted in the hindering of the comprehension of the immense menace represented by Nazism.

The Christian origins of the anti-Semitic phenomenon were hardly ever mentioned in Marxist literature, and the passage from religious anti-Judaism to the *völkisch* conception of the Jews as a foreign and dangerous race was never studied in any satisfying fashion. The attitude of the Socialists, in general, was to consider anti-Semitism as a tactic employed by the dominant classes to divide the mass of workers and exploit the prejudices of the middle class. Of course, this was true to a large extent, but such an analysis was far from an understanding that grasped the phenomenon in all its historic complexity.

In the 1930s, Trotsky tried to rethink the Jewish Question in terms that challenged the assumptions of classical Marxism (assimilation conceived not only as historic tendency but also as programme), while avoiding the errors of Zionism and Stalinism. His reflection was rich – he understood the modernity of the Jewish Question and its national dimension in the Yiddish-speaking diaspora – but limited. His innovations were taken up only partially by Abram Leon, who put the finishing touches on the Marxist conception of the Jewish Question while remaining in the methodological and conceptual framework established by Kautsky: the caste became a people-class, a broader but fundamentally analogous notion.

The problem of assimilation was then at the heart of this debate. The emphasis on assimilation – desired, encouraged, indicated as a task of historic development – essentially concealed a constant attempt to suppress the Jewish

Question. Rosa Luxemburg explained this attitude in very clear terms, writing that 'for the disciples of Marx and for the working class a Jewish question as such does not exist'.[19]

Indeed, it is necessary to recognise that this suppression has continued until today. In the post-war period, Marxists have produced some remarkable analyses of Zionism but have rarely tried to assess the history of the debate on the Jewish Question inside the left. The available literature on the history of Jewish socialism, which has grown significantly in the past fifteen years, represents an ethnic revival (the rediscovery of a cultural identity by the Jewish communities of the Diaspora) rather than a re-appropriation by the left of a segment of its history. Those historians who have concerned themselves with the Bund and with socialist Zionism – their works are often cited in this book – are almost entirely Jewish historians and not Marxists, or, in other words, historians of the Jewish Question and not historians of socialism.[20] There are, certainly, some partial studies devoted to the analysis of the Jewish Question in the thought of certain Marxist writers or to some particular aspect of the relationship between socialism and Jews. There exists, then, a 'scattered' and fragmentary literature. The rare attempts at a global historic reconstruction of this debate are questionable. There is an abundant anthology edited by Massimo Massara, which is one-sided in its choice of texts and inspired by an apologetic concern with regard to the writings of Stalin.[21] Equally contestable appear Edmund Silberner's efforts to reduce any Marxist idea on the Jewish Question to a variant of anti-Semitism.[22] The synthesis attempted by Roberto Finzi is much more interesting and creative, but nonetheless it does not go beyond the limits of an essay.[23] At the outset of my research, thus, I was aware of this historiographical lacuna. I have tried to reconstruct a debate, putting together its pieces. Jewish socialism has been erased from the map of Europe; it is necessary to prevent it from being erased from history.

---

19   Luxemburg 1974, pp. 147–8.

20   See Bunzl 1975, and Weinstock 1984–6.

21   See Massara (ed.) 1972.

22   See Silberner 1962 and 1983.

23   See Finzi 1981, vol. 3/2, pp. 897–936.

CHAPTER 1

Marx, Radical Enlightenment and the Jews

Marx and Engels's approach to the Jewish Question has always been the object of historiographical controversies, which can be summed up in three fundamental interpretations. The first is theological and deals with Jewish Messianism as being one of the pillars, albeit subterranean and hidden, of Marxism; the second considers Marx – or at least the young Marx – as an anti-Semite; the third, on the contrary, sees *Zur Judenfrage* (1843) as the point of departure for a scientific analysis of the Jewish Question. Highly controversial, these three positions de-historicise or unilaterally stress some contingent assumptions by the founders of historical materialism.

The vision of Marx as a thinker deeply shaped by his Jewish origins is widely held, especially among historians of philosophy. The most notable representative of this interpretation is undoubtedly Karl Löwith. In his *Meaning in History: The Theological Implications of the Philosophy of History* (1949), he claimed to have discovered, beyond the 'ideological' conception of history as the history of class struggle, the traces of a 'transparent messianism' that had its 'unconscious root in Marx's own being, even in his race'.[1] Löwith established a series of formal correspondences between Marxism and monotheist Judeo-Christian theology: a) between the bourgeoisie/proletariat antagonism and the Christ/Antichrist conflict as the foundation of history; b) between the concept of the proletariat and the idea of the chosen people, i.e. between the perspective of a revolutionary liberation and the expectancy of a resurrection-redemption; c) between the conception of communism as the transition from the kingdom of necessity to the kingdom of freedom and the theological vision of the advent of the kingdom of God as the passage from the *Civitas terrena* to the *Civitas Dei*.[2] These correspondences prove, according to Löwith, that Marxism shares the same teleological conception of history as Hebrew and Christian theology.

Many scholars who are in a number of ways culturally and politically very different from each other – among them Arnold Toynbee, Nikolai Berdiaev, Franz Borkenau and Martin Buber – defend this vision, which sees Marx's thought as a socialist secularisation of Jewish eschatology.[3] The most fascin-

---

1 Löwith 1949, p. 44.
2 Ibid., pp. 44–5.
3 See Toynbee 1974, p. 403; Berdiaeff 1975, p. 38 and 1933, p. 28; Borkenau 1956, pp. 35–6; Berlin 1980, p. 356; finally, Buber 1967, p. 24.

ating attempt to 'Judaise' Marx was that of Bernard Lazare, a revolutionary Jew who for a whole period of his life shared the same point of view as the author of *Zur Judenfrage*. In his controversial essay *Anti-Semitism: Its History and Its Causes* (1894), he wrote:

> This descendant of a line of rabbis and of doctors inherited all the logical strength of his ancestors: he was a clear and lucid Talmudist, who would not be hampered by the foolish minutiae of the practice, a Talmudist who practiced sociology and applied his native qualities as exegete to the critique of political economy. He was animated by this old Hebrew materialism that dreamed perpetually of a paradise realized upon earth and always rejected the distant and problematic hope of an Eden after death; but he was not only a logician, he was also a rebel, an agitator, a biting polemicist and he took his gift for sarcasm and invective, like Heine, from Jewish sources.[4]

A typical representative of this current is the American critic Murray Wolfson. In his opinion, Marx's philosophical trajectory went through three fundamental stages between 1843 and 1845: a first phase, rationalist and *aufklärerisch*, in 1843 (*Critique of Hegel's Philosophy of Right*); a second, materialist humanist phase, shaped by the influence of Feuerbach (*Economic and Philosophical Manuscripts, On the Jewish Question*), in 1844; and finally a dialectical materialist phase opened by the *Theses on Feuerbach* (1845) and ended by *Capital* (1867). According to Wolfson, these three philosophical stages find their religious analogies in the scepticism of the Enlightenment thinkers, in Christian humanism as opposed to Judaism, and, finally, in Jewish monotheism. Essentially, historical materialism was only the expression of Marx's return, in his maturity, 'to Jewish monist conceptions ... that reflect the profound ideological heritage bequeathed by his father despite himself'.[5]

This theological interpretation is highly controversial: not only does it not find any support in the cultural formation of the author of *The Communist Manifesto*, but above all it completely ignores his critique of religion as the expression of human alienation (which was not abandoned after 1844 and which can be found in many of the texts of his maturity).[6] It is possible to recog-

---

4 Lazare 1969, p. 170; quoted also in Wilson 1978, p. 97. Later, Bernard Lazare modified his appreciation of the young Marx's essay, pointing out that his cultural formation had been completely unaffected by Judaism (see Wilson 1978, p. 317).

5 Wolfson 1982, p. xiii.

6 See Parinetto 1980.

nise some formal affinities between the Marxist vision of the role of the proletariat in capitalist society and the messianic vision of the Jews as the chosen people, the subject of redemption; or between the idea of socialist revolution and the Jewish conception of the Apocalypse as the necessary transition from the historic present to the Messianic future (the reestablishment of the kingdom of God on earth).[7] There is, however, no doubt that Marx never developed this parallel and founded his theory on the analysis of the capitalist mode of production, for which he never had to borrow from the sources of Judaism. In other words, these structural homologies between Marx's theory and Jewish Messianic thought do not reveal any elective affinity (*Wahlverwandschaft*) such as that established by Max Weber between the Protestant ethic and capitalism, which implies a form of symbiosis, if not a veritable fusion, between the two related elements.[8] Explaining historical materialism through Marx's Jewish unconscious is pure speculation, an interesting hypothesis, but not an interpretation supported by convincing evidence.

A Marxist (romantic) current nourished by reference to Jewish Messianism will appear only at the beginning of the twentieth century, in the writings of Ernst Bloch, the young Lukács, and, above all, Walter Benjamin: the coarticulation of theology and Marxist materialism one finds in his 'On the Concept of History' (1940) is absent throughout Marx's work. One could share the point of view of Shlomo Avineri, according to which the 'eschatological element' detectable in Marx should not be attributed to the Judeo-Christian tradition but rather treated as the consequence of his 'Hegelian antecedents'.[9] Born into a Jewish family that had converted to Lutheranism, Marx received no religious education and grew up, under the influence of his father, in a liberal and *aufklärerisch* environment. He considered himself a German, an atheistic communist and recognised himself as neither a Jew nor a converted Jew. He was, in Isaac Deutscher's definition, a 'non-Jewish Jew'.[10] A similar attitude character-

---

7   For a definition of Jewish messianism see Scholem 1971, pp. 1–36.

8   See Löwy 2013, ch. 3.

9   Avineri 1968, p. 4. See also Wistrich 1976, pp. 3–4.

10   Deutscher 1968. Marx's ancestors included entire generations of rabbis. His paternal grandfather, Marx-Levy, was rabbi at Trier until his death, like his son Samuel, Karl's uncle. Herschel, Marx's father, became a lawyer and married Henriette Presborck, the descendant of a family of Dutch rabbis. A cultivated man open to the rationalist ideas of the Enlightenment, he converted to Protestantism toward the end of 1816 or at the beginning of 1817, changing his Jewish first name Herschel to Heinrich. This conversion was imposed by necessity: it was an indispensable condition for practising as a lawyer after the introduction of the laws that barred Jews from access to public functions. It was also probably a painful decision if it is true that before adopting this extreme solution, which

ised a whole generation of revolutionaries and Jewish Marxists at the turn of the twentieth century, from Rosa Luxemburg to Otto Bauer, from Karl Radek to Leon Trotsky.

The second interpretation of Marx's approach, which is as scattered as it is contestable, portrays him as an anti-Semite. According to Edmund Silberner, who devoted an article to this topic in 1949 in the journal *Historia Judaica*, Marx was a 'declared anti-Semite'.[11] In the wake of Silberner, many others have seen Marx as a victim of so-called 'Jewish self-hatred' (*jüdische Selbsthaß*).[12] In his monumental *History of Anti-Semitism* (a work as historically erudite as it is methodologically weak), Léon Poliakov depicted Marx as the initiator of 'Jewish anti-Semitism'.[13] For his part, Robert Misrahi saw *Zur Judenfrage* as an 'appeal to genocide'.[14] Avoiding this radical assumption, more recently Pierre Birnbaum wrote that Marx constantly borrowed his arguments from 'the lexicon and an imagination of anti-Semitism'.[15]

This interpretation is often based on the extrapolation of certain phrases wrenched out of context and completely de-historicised. It retrospectively projects onto Marx's text a century of later history and recasts it as a necessary landmark in the road to genocide. It amounts to an ahistorical reading – this controversial article was written in 1843 and not in 1943 – that confuses

broke with a secular tradition, he addressed a petition to the governor general of the lower Rhine demanding civic rights for the Jews and protesting against the 'infamous decree' – promulgated by Napoleon I in 1808 and remaining in force in the Rhineland after its annexation to Prussia – that considerably reduced the measures of emancipation adopted by the French Revolution (see Feuer 1972). Franz Mehring's judgment, which attributed to Herschel Marx's conversion primarily to his modern and progressive culture, should then be treated with caution. See Mehring 2003, p. 4.

11   Silberner 1949a, p. 50.

12   See Lamm 1969, p. 60; Künzli 1969; Rubel 1957, p. 88. The concept of *jüdisches Selbsthaß* originated with Theodor Lessing, who published a book with this title in Berlin in 1930 (see Lessing 1984), although he did not relate the concept to Karl Marx. According to Sander Gilman, who devoted to this topic a classical study, Marx's Jewish self-hatred appeared in his attempt to 'project onto the figure of Lassalle all of the negative qualities ascribed to the Jew by contemporary society. Thus he could define himself as different from this "black Jew" ... Marx was a convert, not to Protestantism, but to a world view where even the external signs of the Jew would vanish'. See Gilman 1986, p. 207.

13   Poliakov 1981, vol. 2, pp. 227–37.

14   Misrahi 1972, p. 62. The most radical representative of this 'school' remains Dagobert D. Runes, who sees in Marx's thought the 'bloodthirsty dream' of a 'world without Jews'. See Runes 1960, p. xi.

15   Birnbaum 2004, p. 76. Birnbaum devotes to Marx a chapter of his book in which, beside traditional arguments, he reveals a letter sent from Breslau to Marx in 1877 by Heinrich Grätz, the most important Jewish historian of the nineteenth century, pp. 41–2.

the literature of the nineteenth century on the Jewish Question with Nazi anti-Semitism. As Detlev Claussen has pointed out, this method arises from a Judeocentric vision of history, which eternalises anti-Semitism by considering it as the only possible relation between Jew and non-Jew. In this way, 'the non-Jewish Jews are transformed automatically into traitors, the French *Lumières* into a form of anti-Jewish atheism, German idealism into Lutheran anti-Semitism and Karl Marx into German Radical'.[16]

Without falling into such simplistic (or ideological) traps, Istvan Meszaros compares the attitude of Marx to that of the French utopian socialists.[17] The anti-Semitism of Alphonse de Toussenel, author of *The Jews, Kings of the Epoch* (1845), or of the philosopher Pierre Joseph Proudhon, who supported the closure of all the French synagogues and the deportation to Asia of the Jews, not only reproduced some stereotypes on the Jewish usurer, banker, or speculator, but explicitly rejected their emancipation. George L. Mosse pertinently observed that Marx's argument 'was opposed to all forms of racism, because it was favorable to the complete assimilation and the abolition of conflicts between men. Marx definitively distanced himself radically in his conclusions from the French socialists who wished to expel or annihilate the Jews'.[18]

Apart from these two interpretations – Marx as Jewish theologian and Marx as anti-Semite – there is a third, symmetrically opposed to the second but similarly ideological. It seeks to incorporate *Zur Judenfrage* into Marxism as a canonical text, ritualistically quoted and similarly de-historicised. For several generations of Marxist intellectuals, this essay offered the key for resolving the Jewish historical enigma. In 1902, in his preface to a selection of Marx's early writings, Franz Mehring confirmed the value and contemporary relevance of *Zur Judenfrage*, which in his view constituted a 'decisive step' that went beyond the ambiguities of Feuerbach and the Young Hegelians through the discovery of the 'earthly foundation' of the Jewish problem, namely, that 'bourgeois society continually produces the Jews from its entrails [*Eingeweiden*]' and that 'Judaism realizes itself in bourgeois society that, in turn, realizes itself in the Christian world'.[19] For her part, Rosa Luxemburg wrote in 1910 that Marx, in his 1843 polemic against the 'Hegelians' Bauer and Feuerbach, had arrived at an acute understanding of the 'social base' of the Jewish Question, the recognition that Judaism was nothing other than the 'spirit of the usurer and the trickster', which belonged to each society founded on exploitation and thus also

---

16   See Claussen 1987, pp. 61–2.
17   Meszaros 1970, p. 72.
18   Mosse 1978, ch. 9.
19   Mehring 1923, p. 356.

to 'Christian' society.[20] In 1931 the Stalinist Otto Heller wrote that in his essay, Marx had found 'the key to the explanation of the entire history of the Jews, of their particular situation inside society, as well as the means of putting an end to it'.[21] Fundamentally similar judgments, although more sober and nuanced, have been expressed by Antonio Gramsci, Abram Leon, and Isaac Deutscher and, more recently, by Daniel Bensaïd.[22] The Bundist Vladimir Kossovsky was one of the few, at the beginning of the twentieth century, who criticised Marx's youthful study as being foreign to the materialist conception of history.[23]

1   Marx: the Jew as *Geldmensch*

Most interpretations of *Zur Judenfrage* forget its fundamental premise: Marx demanded the emancipation of the Jews, in opposition to Bruno Bauer who denied them this right, considering them as inferior to Christians and incapable of becoming free (in his opinion, the Jews were demanding that the Prussian state abandon its Christian nature and grant them civic rights while themselves refusing to renounce Judaism, that is, their own religious prejudice). Nonetheless, in Marx's view, the conquest of civic rights would not 'resolve' the Jewish Question. Quite simply, it would place Jews and Christians on equal footing in the face of a more general problem of human emancipation: 'Therefore we do not say to the Jews as Bauer does: you cannot be emancipated politically without emancipating yourselves radically from Judaism. On the contrary, we tell them: because you can be emancipated politically without renouncing Judaism completely and incontrovertibly, *political emancipation* itself is not *human emancipation*'.[24]

Marx examined the different forms taken by the Jewish Question in Europe and the United States. In Germany, where the Prussian state recognised itself as Christian, the problem took on a theological character, establishing a religious conflict between Jews and Christians, with citizenship being reserved to the latter. In France, it was on the contrary an essentially constitutional problem, because of the incompleteness of political emancipation. Under the Restoration and the July Monarchy, the state maintained a religious character and

---

20   Luxemburg 1974a, p. 144.
21   Heller 1933, p. 19.
22   See Gramsci 1996, pp. 173–4; Deutscher 1968, p. 32; Leon 1970, p. 66; Bensaïd 2006.
23   Quoted by Heller 1977, pp. 109–10.
24   *MEW*, vol. 1, p. 361; *CW*, vol. 3, p. 160. On the debate sparked off by Bruno Bauer's work in 1843, see Rotenstreich 1959.

the Jewish Question thus seemed to be invested with a theological aspect, but this was only an appearance. In fact, discrimination against the Jews was limited and purely formal. As for the United States, there secularism prevailed from its inception. However, the secular nature of the state did not eliminate the existence of religion as a social phenomenon. This demonstrated, according to Marx, the limits of political emancipation. The state could free itself of religion, without this meaning an authentic liberation of humanity. Political emancipation constituted a great 'progress' in Marx's eyes but inevitably led to a split (*Spaltung*) between public man and private man (*Öffentlichen* and *Privatmenschen*), between secular state and the real religiosity of man.[25] Religion could only be transcended through *human* emancipation, and political emancipation, once accomplished, would only reveal its intrinsic limits: 'The emancipation of the state from religion is not the emancipation of the real man from religion'.[26] The Jews could, then, emancipate themselves politically – something Bauer denied – while preserving their Judaism that, like all religion, was the expression of human alienation. Paraphrasing Feuerbach, Marx criticised the theological method with which his opponent had approached the question: 'Bauer considers that the *ideal*, abstract nature of the Jew, his *religion*, is his *entire* nature ... Let us consider the actual, worldly Jew, not the *Sabbath Jew*, as Bauer does, but the *everyday Jew*. Let us not look for the secret of the Jew in his religion, but let us look for the secret of his religion in the real Jew'.[27] In *The Holy Family*, he takes this concept up again in the following terms: 'Judaism preserved itself and develops *through* history, *in* and *with* history'.[28]

The materialist approach clearly shaped by Feuerbach – religion seen as a form of anthropological projection – opened the second part of the 1843 essay where, having abandoned his philosophical reflection on the difference between political and human emancipation, Marx sought to develop a definition of Judaism, its nature and historic significance. His ideas were nothing new: he took up certain themes already present in Feuerbach – Judaism as the religion of egoism – and more generally in the Young Hegelians, for example, the Jew-money equation established by Moses Hess. Marx wrote: 'What is the secular basis of Judaism? *Practical* need, *self-interest*. What is the worldly religion of the Jew? *Huckstering*. What is his worldly God? *Money*. Very well then! Emancipation from *huckstering* and *money*, consequently from practical, real

---

25   *MEW*, vol. 1, p. 356; *CW*, vol. 3, p. 160.

26   Ibid., p. 361; p. 160.

27   Ibid., p. 372; p. 169.

28   *MEW*, vol. 2, p. 116; *MEW*, vol. 1, p. 147.

Judaism, would be the self-emancipation of our time'.[29] The constitutive elements of 'practical, real' Judaism – money and trade – had become the foundations of bourgeois society. The 'chimerical nationality' (*chimärische Nationalität*) of the Jew, of the 'man of money' (*Geldmensch*) dissolved itself in the world of capital; therefore, the Jews had emancipated themselves to the extent that the Christians had 'become Jews'.[30] Since the values of Judaism were rooted and widespread in bourgeois Christian society, human emancipation, the suppression of capitalism, and the transcending of Judaism merged in the same process. Once 'trade' is suppressed, Judaism would lack its *raison d'être*:

> Once society has succeeded in abolishing the *empirical* essence of Judaism – huckstering and its preconditions – the Jew will have become impossible [*ist der Jude unmöglich geworden*], because his consciousness no longer had an object, because the subjective base of Judaism, practical need, has been humanised, and because the conflict between man's individual-sensuous existence and his species-existence has been abolished. The *social* emancipation of the Jew is the *emancipation of society from Judaism*.[31]

Of course, Marx's arguments belonged to the philosophical battle of the radical Enlightenment. He saw in money and trade not only the very nature of Judaism but also the features of modern bourgeois society. Consequently, Jewish and human emancipation coincided with the transcending of reified social relations. The final result of this process could only be the disappearance of Judaism, not rejected but *sublated* and absorbed into universalism. Far from being anti-Semitic, this approach was rooted in the tradition started two centuries earlier by Spinoza.[32]

Let me come back to the two works that inspired Marx's essay: Ludwig Feuerbach's *Essence of Christianity* (1841) and Moses Hess's *Essence of Money* (1843). Hess became a close friend of Marx in Paris, and his article, although only published in 1845, was originally written for the same issue of the *Deutsch-Franzözische Jahrbücher* in which *Zur Judenfrage* appeared.[33] The Feuerba-

---

29   *MEW*, vol. 1, p. 372; *CW*, vol. 3, pp. 169–70.

30   Ibid., p. 373; p. 173.

31   Ibid., p. 377; p. 174.

32   Cf. Bensaid 2006, p. 77.

33   On the relationship between Marx and Moses Hess, see Cornu 1958, vol. 2, pp. 322–30; Löwy 1970, pp. 66–8; Hirsch 1963, p. 29, and, more recently, Sperber 2013, pp. 127–41.

chian vision of religion as the expression of human alienation, as a reversed image of the world wherein men project onto a divine sphere their own material desires, was the premise of Hess's essay, which pointed to, along with religious alienation, a social alienation symbolised by money. According to Hess, the function of money within society corresponded to that of God in religion: 'Money', one reads in the seventh thesis of *Über das Geldwesen*, 'is the product of men who have become strangers to one another, that is, alienated man [*der entaüsserte Mensch*]'.[34] Transcending Feuerbach's definition of Judaism as 'egoism in the form of religion',[35] Hess equated Judaism, Christianity, and bourgeois mercantile society. The future spiritual father of socialist Zionism saw the egoistic men of bourgeois society 'as beasts of prey, as vampires, as Jews and wolves starved of money [*als Raubtiere, als Blutsauger, als Juden, als Geldwölfe*]'.[36] It is not astonishing that, in this intellectual context, Marx drew equally from Bauer's essay itself, particularly its conception of the chimerical nationality of the Jew.[37]

Criticising Marx's *The Jewish Question* means, first of all, to historicise it, i.e. to see it as a moment in the formation of his thought and as a product, however particular, of a specific cultural context: that of Germany in the first half of the nineteenth century. Thus historicised, Marx's youthful work reveals both a pre-Marxist conception of capitalism and many commonplaces of the democratic radicalism of his time. It also includes the premise of a future idea of assimilation, which is a link between his juvenile left-Hegelianism and his mature communism. The limits of his essay deserve careful scrutiny that can be synthetised in a few points.

a. Marx claimed civic rights for Jews as a condition to the solution of the fundamental problem of human emancipation, but he completely ignored the historical fact of the oppression suffered by the Prussian Jews in the first half of the nineteenth century. *The Jewish Question* does not contain any reference to the discrimination that affected them: namely, a whole set of restrictions (on movement, on residence, on the exercise of certain professional activities, on access to the civil service, and so on), not to speak of the pogroms that took place in Germany up to 1819. Discrimination – one could add – that had affected Marx's family itself.

b. Identifying Judaism, trade and bourgeois society, Marx had not yet recognised the proletariat as the subject of universal human emancipation and

---

34   Hess 1921, p. 167.
35   Feuerbach 1881, p. 114.
36   Hess 1921, p. 183.
37   Bauer 1958, p. 63.

was inclined to see in commerce and circulation, rather than in production, the peculiar features and the fundamental structure of the capitalist system.[38] In this sense, his 1843 text appears much closer to Hess's *Essence of Money* than to *Capital*, that is, closer to a purely moral denunciation of capitalism than to a historical analysis of it. In *The Jewish Question*, as in *Über das Geldwesen*, the Jew is a symbolic figure of alienated humanity in the bourgeois world, the incarnation of a man who, according to Elisabeth de Fontenay, has become a stranger to himself.[39] As Daniel Bensaïd has pertinently pointed out, Marx strongly denounced the fetishism of money but had not yet understood that it simply symbolised 'commodity fetishism and reification'.[40]

c. The image of the Jew sketched by Marx, and summed up in the definition of the chimerical nationality of the *Geldmensch*, was nothing but the transformation into a philosophical category of certain aspects of the historical situation in which most Jews of Central and Eastern Europe lived in the early nineteenth century. At that time, according to Julius Carlebach, small traders and hawkers constituted 66 percent of the Jewish working population in Prussia,[41] whereas in Eastern Europe the overwhelming majority of Jews fell into these categories.[42] This was the background for the definition of the Jews as *Geldmenschen*, which later Marxists transformed into 'caste' (Kautsky) and 'people-class' (Leon). Marx himself occasionally reproduced this vision in *Capital*, describing the 'commercial people of antiquity' who lived 'like the gods of Epicurus, in the *intermundia*, or rather like the Jews in the pores of Polish society'.[43] Here the Jews no longer appear as the symbols of modern capitalism but rather as the representatives of pre-capitalist market economy, which was much closer to reality.

d. The long process of the transition from feudalism to capitalism, displayed in Western Europe between the fourteenth century and the industrial revolution, did not produce a symbiosis between the Jews and the ascendant bourgeoisies; on the contrary, it engendered a durable socioeconomic decline of the Jews. In the fourteenth and fifteenth centuries, they were expelled from many Western European countries and forced to seek ref-

---

38   See Löwy 1970, 68.
39   Fontenay 1973.
40   Bensaid 2006, p. 107.
41   See Carlebach 1978, p. 56.
42   See Leon 1970, p. 195.
43   *MEW*, vol. 23, p. 93; *CW*, vol. 35, p. 325.

uge in petty trade and usury or to emigrate, mostly to the Ottoman Empire and Eastern Europe. Representatives of a monetary economy in feudal society, the Jewish traders seemed to have exhausted their historical function in the period of emerging capitalism and were pushed out by the nascent bourgeois classes. A significant layer of Jewish industrialists would appear only in the second half of the nineteenth century, after emancipation had been achieved. Of course, a prosperous elite of Jewish bankers – the 'Court Jews' – favoured the first globalisation of the European economy, but its cosmopolitan and transnational network felt much more comfortable with the Old Regime than with modern nation-states. Court Jews, nevertheless, were a tiny elite among a mass of Jewish peddlers. The central thesis of *Zur Judenfrage* should at least be nuanced: the 'Judaisation' of Christian bourgeois society coincided, historically, with the economic decline and social uprooting of the Jews.

e. Marx's economic schema led to a mythical vision of Judaism. In spite of his repeated references to history, he posited his Judaism/capitalism equation as an *a priori*, supra-historical axiom. He perceived the Jew as a figure inseparable from money and identified the suppression of capitalism with the disappearance of Judaism. In his eyes, the Jews were a 'uniform entity'.[44] In his later works, however, Marx abandoned this position. In the *Grundrisse*, written fifteen years after *The Jewish Question*, there is a passage in which the contemptible features of the *Geldmensch* are attributed no longer to Judaism but to Christian Lutheranism: 'The cult of money has its asceticism, its self-denial, its self-sacrifice – economy and frugality, contempt for mundane, temporal and fleeting pleasures; the chase after the *eternal* treasure. Hence the connection between English puritanism, or also Dutch Protestantism, and money-making [*Goldmachen*]'.[45] This formulation, which one could call Weberian *ante litteram*, demonstrates that for Marx – at least in his maturity – the 'cult of money' was not a Jewish specificity and that his argument was not inspired by an anti-Semitic prejudice.

---

44 See Carlebach 1978, p. 184. Ilan Halevi has offered a clarification on this point: 'The idea that Judaism could be anything other than a simple function of bourgeois society, *a fortiori* that it could itself contain contradictions – that is to say deprived of a unique essence – was as foreign to the young Marx as to the old Bauer. From whence the common and systematic usage of the singular: "the" Jew. From whence Marx's idea that Judaism was a pure product of bourgeois society, and would disappear with it: an anti-historic and anti-Marxist idea if ever there was one'. See Halevi 1981, p. 158.

45 Marx 1953, p. 143; Marx 1973, p. 232.

f.   Marx expressed an 'assimilationist' disposition in fairly clear terms: the
     Jew would become 'impossible' when trade, his reason for existence, had
     been eliminated, and true human emancipation would lead to the extinc-
     tion of Judaism. Of course, this approach ignores the link – at the core
     of Jewish history – between a religion and an ethnic group, a link that
     was perpetuated, one could say *by, with, and in history*, transformed and
     renewed throughout the ages. But this approach was common to nearly
     all the currents of thought favourable to emancipation, and was con-
     sidered in general as the way to eliminate the Jewish 'anomaly.' Far from
     being, as Robert Misrahi wrote, 'one of the most anti-Semitic works of the
     nineteenth century',[46] this article by the young Marx reflected in reality
     an attitude very widespread in Germany among the partisans of eman-
     cipation.[47] As Gareth Stedman Jones pertinently observed, his essay was
     a 'direct continuation and extension of the republican discourse about
     "regeneration", which had characterized the French Revolution'.[48] Ger-
     shom Scholem observed that Emancipation cost the Jews 'a resolute dis-
     avowal of Jewish nationality – a price the leading writers and spokesmen
     of the Jewish avant-garde were only too happy to pay'.[49] Marx belonged
     to a generation of German Jewish intellectuals who certainly had tran-
     scended (or recused) the *Haskalah* but whose existence was one of its
     legacies. He conceived human emancipation as also meaning emancip-
     ation from Judaism, whereas Mendelssohn wished to preserve a Jewish
     identity while Germanising and modernising it. Marx's article belongs to
     a precise historical moment, between the first emancipatory laws in Ger-
     many, which saw the emergence of a 'pariah' Jewish intelligentsia – Marx
     and Heinrich Heine were among its most brilliant representatives – and
     the survival of a layer of 'Court Jews', the bankers who financed the Prus-
     sian regime. *Zur Judenfrage* was the product of this time: it could not be
     understood, in the words of Hannah Arendt, 'except in the light of this
     conflict between rich Jews and intellectual Jews'.[50]

---

46   Misrahi 1972, p. 101.
47   David McLellan has correctly pointed out that in his youthful study, Marx seemed to judge
     'the political maturity of a state by the degree of Jewish emancipation which had been
     attained and he considered as incoherent a civil society which denied equality of rights to
     Jews'. See McLellan 1970, p. 141. A similar point is made by Bloom 1942, p. 6; Avineri 1964,
     p. 450; Davis 1967, pp. 71–2; Arvon 1978, pp. 105, 111. The most developed and convincing
     criticism of the thesis of Marx's anti-Semitism probably remains Draper 1977.
48   Stedman Jones 2016, p. 167.
49   Scholem 1976, p. 75.
50   Arendt 1976, p. 64.

One final question concerns Marx's silence on the situation of the Jews of Eastern Europe, who were the great majority of the Jewish population at the time. Certainly, Marx had no in-depth knowledge of the problem, but it is difficult to believe that he would have altered his radical critique of the Jewish religion if he had studied Hassidism. The secularisation and modernisation of *Yiddishkeit* would take place only at the end of the nineteenth century; when Marx wrote his article, the Eastern European Jews still knew the reality of the ghetto, living as an 'ecologically' enclosed and separated community. In the years of Emancipation, the Jews of Central and Western Europe saw in the *Ostjudentum* only a negative model, the image of their own past. Marx was a son of his epoch and shared this point of view.[51]

2   Engels: the Jews as a 'People without History'

Friedrich Engels's assessments of the Jewish Question did not differ from Marx's, but belonged to a later period and were supported by historical arguments mostly related to the national questions put on the agenda by the revolutions of 1848. In their writings of this period, nations are presented as historical formations – economic, political, and cultural – created by the rise of capitalism.[52] Marx and Engels did not identify nations and states, but saw the latter as fundamental instruments of the creation and delimitation of both national markets and bourgeois political rule. In their view, only the 'vital' nations could achieve a state existence, whereas the 'non-historic' nations were ineluctably condemned to assimilation. In *The German Ideology* (1845–6), they presented the development of capitalism as a dialectical process of creation and negation of nations. Capitalism engendered modern nation-states only in order to overcome them. One can read in this text that large-scale industry 'produces for the first time world history', by unifying the different nations in an international economic system, and 'creating a class for which nationality is already annulled'.[53] For Marx, capitalism was a world economic system, not the sum

---

51   Moreover, the Jews did not always appear as usurers in Marx's writings. During the Crimean War, he published a long article in the *New York Daily Tribune* on the historic precedents of the Eastern Question, in which he denounced 'the poverty and the suffering of the Jews of Jerusalem', forced to live 'despised by the Orthodox and persecuted by the Catholics' but capable of putting up a stiff resistance 'to Muslim oppression and intolerance'. It amounts to a few phrases only, curiously forgotten by those who accuse Marx of anti-Semitism. See *MEW*, vol. 10, p. 176.

52   See Rodinson 1968, p. 133.

53   *MEW*, vol. 3, p. 60.

of different national segments but a supranational organic totality, a system unitary by its very nature, hegemonic over the planet, and doomed to supplant all archaic social formations (primitive, feudal, 'Asiatic', etc.). Marx and Engels conceived of socialism as a socio-economic system superior to capitalism that could be built only through a supranational process. Therefore, socialism carried on a cosmopolitan tendency already existing under capitalism. *The Communist Manifesto* enthusiastically points out the historical role of capitalist cosmopolitanism, the product of a world economy that created 'a universal inter-dependence of nations', unifying thus not only material production but also intellectual life ('the intellectual products of individual nations become a common patrimony').[54] In the internationalist utopia of Marx and Engels, the future world appeared as a universal community. The theory of peoples 'without history' (*geschichtlosen Völker*) developed by Engels in 1848 has to be inscribed in the context of this vision of capitalism as an immense ethnic and cultural crucible and as a powerful factor acting towards the assimilation of nations.

Borrowed from Hegel, this conception was never explicitly defended by Marx in his writings. During the revolutions of 1848, he distinguished between 'revolutionary nations' and 'counter-revolutionary nations' on the basis of a descriptive classification that carried no judgement on the national 'vitality' of different peoples. But it was a primarily terminological distinction and it would be difficult to disassociate completely the positions of Marx and Engels on this topic.[55] Throughout the second half of the nineteenth century, the two German revolutionaries supported unconditionally the Polish national movement, rejecting at the same time all the claims for autonomy and national independence of the Slavic nations of Central and Southern Europe, which they thought were doomed to be erased by the 'march of history'. In January 1849, Engels developed his arguments in the following terms:

> There is no country in Europe that does not have in some corner or other one or several fragments of peoples (*Völkerruinen*), the remnants of a former population that was suppressed and held in bondage by the nation that later became the main vehicle for historical development (*Trägerin der geschichtlichen Entwicklung*). These relics of a nation, mercilessly trampled under the course of history (*von dem Gang der Geschichte*), as Hegel says, these residual fragments of peoples (*Völkerabfalle*), always

---

54   *MEW*, vol. 4, p. 446. See Rosdolsky 1965, p. 336, and Löwy 1981a, pp. 11–12.

55   See Haupt and Weill 1974.

become fanatical standard-bearers of counter-revolution and remain so until their complete extirpation or loss of their national character, just as their whole existence in general is itself a protest against a great historical revolution.[56]

The great nations of Central and Western Europe, Engels explained, had fought the revolutions of 1848–9, whereas the Slav peoples – except for the Poles – had revealed themselves as 'counter-revolutionary' nations because of their support for Tsarist Russia. Engels did not try to give a sociological or political explanation of the counter-revolutionary role of these national movements in 1848 but deduced it quite simply from their supposed 'counter-revolutionary essence', or rather from their character as peoples 'without history'.

Usually, Marxist scholars interpret the failure of the revolutions of 1848 through their historical context, that of an epoch where the bourgeoisie had exhausted its revolutionary potentialities (it had been capable of resolving neither the national nor the agrarian questions) and where the proletariat was still not ready to take power. It was at the same time too late for a bourgeois revolution and too early for a socialist one.[57] In Central Europe, the 1848 revolutions revealed deep contradictory tendencies, insofar as the Polish and Hungarian national movements claimed political independence regardless of the many ethnic and national minorities living in their own territories. The leading social force of the Polish and Hungarian movements was the landowning aristocracy, which exploited and oppressed many peasant nations. For instance, Ukrainians could not support the cause of Polish independence because they were engaged in building their own national identity, which expressed itself, among other ways, in a class antagonism against Polish landowners. The same relation existed between, on the one hand, Serbs, Croats, Romanians, and Slovaks, and on the other, Magyars and Germans. Instead of analysing the social nature of these national movements, Engels drew a map of Europe on the basis of two categories: 'historic nations' and 'peoples without history'.[58]

Within this schema – an essentially German revolution in Central Europe and an essentially Polish one in Eastern Europe – Engels placed the Jews in the category of *geschichtlosen Völker*. His analyses principally concerned Posnania, a Polish province of the Prussian state, and Hungary. As a minority tradition-

---

56   *MEW*, vol. 6, p. 172.

57   See Löwy 1981b, p. 27 and 1974, pp. 373–4.

58   See Rosdolsky 1979, pp. 114–28. As an analysis of the positions of Engels on the 1848 revolution, this work, written in 1948, is irreplaceable.

ally allied to the dominant nations, the Jews of Posnania were pro-German; in Congress Poland, pro-Russian; in Bohemia, pro-Austrian; in Ukraine, pro-Polish; and so on. For example, Engels considered the Jews of Posnania as an instrument of Prussian domination over the Polish majority. In the *Neue Rhein-ische Zeitung* of 9 June 1848, he argued:

> Throughout Poland, the Germans and the Jews form the nucleus of the nation, active in commerce and in industry; these are the descendants of immigrants, having for the most part fled their homeland because of religious persecutions. They have built the towns of Poland and, for some centuries, shared the destiny of the Polish kingdom. The Jews and the Germans, a consistent minority in the country, try to exploit the contingent situation of the country to impose their power. The Jews perceive themselves as Germans, but in reality they are very little so, like the American Germans. They are considered as Germans in order to oppress the language and the nationality of the Poles, who constitute more than half of the population of Posnania.[59]

The following year, Engels adopted an openly anti-Semitic rhetoric in defining the Jews of Posnania as 'the dirtiest of all races' (*die schmutzigste aller Rassen*).[60]

In general, Marx and Engels perceived the Jews of Central and Eastern Europe as anachronistic vestiges of a previous age, communities of small traders lacking any cultural identity but fiercely opposed, because of their small economic activities, to any process of assimilation. Their language, Yiddish, was 'a horribly corrupted German' (*ein schauderhaft verdorbenes Deutsch*).[61] Although they did not form a peasant nation, the Eastern Jews were not considered as a community bearing a specific national culture but as a people without history, as an ethnic group coinciding with a caste of traders who had survived in the interstices of the most backward social formations of Europe. The revolution of 1848 had tried to wipe out this relic from the past. Such a brutal diagnosis was obviously related to a conception of capitalism as the crucible for the fusion of nations. According to *The Communist Manifesto*, the capitalist system produced the enslavement of the 'barbarous and semi-barbarous' countries by the 'civilised' countries, by making dependent 'the peasant peoples on

---

59   *MEW*, vol. 5, p. 56.
60   *MEW*, vol. 6, p. 448.
61   Ibid., p. 170.

the bourgeois peoples, the East on the West'.[62] This enslavement certainly took place, but instead of causing assimilation it exacerbated many national conflicts.

3 The Struggle against Anti-Semitism

Engels came back to the Jewish Question in 1890, when *Arbeiterzeitung*, the daily socialist newspaper of Vienna, asked him to analyse the rise of Austrian anti-Semitism. In his article, he vigorously condemned any form of hostility toward Jews, who, for the first time, he no longer identified with capitalism but considered as possible allies in the struggle for socialism. It was a crucial turn, because the struggle against anti-Semitism was finally seen as one of the priority tasks of the international workers' movement. According to Engels, hatred of the Jews represented 'the reaction of the feudal, declining social layers [*mittelalterlicher, untergehender Gesellschafts-schichten*] against modern society, composed essentially of capitalists and wage workers'.[63] Under a demagogic façade, which did not hesitate to sometimes adopt an apparently socialist language, lurked a reactionary movement that Engels qualified as 'a variant of feudal socialism', with which the Social Democrats should have 'nothing in common'.[64] In his eyes, anti-Semitism expressed the economic backwardness of Eastern and Central Europe, but was disappearing in the 'civilised' West. ('If one wished to promote anti-Semitism in England or America, one would provoke only laughter'.)[65] Its social base was those sectors of the traditional petty bourgeoisie that had been ruined and impoverished by capitalist development: the feudal caste of Junkers in Prussia and the 'craftsmen and secondhand dealers' in Austria.[66]

The turn was significant, but Engels's assessment revealed a blind faith in Progress that simply excluded the possibility of a modern anti-Semitism and was fed by the contradictions of a modern, advanced capitalist society. A few years later, when the Dreyfus affair took place in France, most Austrian and German socialists expressed their incomprehension. Engels ended his article with the recognition of the role played by the Jews in the workers' movement: 'We owe very much to the Jews. Without mentioning Heine and Börne, Marx

---

62 *MEW*, vol. 4, p. 466. See in relation to this the remarks of Finzi 1983, pp. 129–40.
63 *MEW*, vol. 8, p. 50.
64 *MEW*, vol. 22, p. 50.
65 Ibid., p. 49.
66 Ibid., p. 50.

was of pure Jewish blood (*war Marx von stock jüdischem Blut*), Lassalle was Jewish, very many of our best comrades are Jewish'.[67] He cited Victor Adler – who probably did not appreciate being included in the list – Eduard Bernstein, and Paul Singer, and mentioned almost with pride that he had himself been considered to be Jewish by the anti-Semitic German press. In 1887, probably under the influence of Eleanor Marx, Engels discovered the existence of a workers' circle created in London's East End by Jewish immigrants from Eastern Europe, and in 1891, according to the testimony of the American Jewish socialist leader Abraham Cahan, he planned to write the preface to a Yiddish edition of *The Communist Manifesto*.[68]

These elements show that Engels changed his views on the Jewish Question at the end of his life. His legacy, nevertheless, remains ambivalent: on the one hand, he clearly denounced the rise of anti-Semitism in Germany and Austria; on the other hand, he nourished the illusion that anti-Semitism was condemned to disappear, to be inevitably erased by modernity and progress.

---

67   Ibid. On the circumstances in which Engels wrote this letter, see Massing 1985, pp. 188–90.
68   See Silberner 1949b, p. 337.

CHAPTER 2

The Jewish Marxist Intelligentsia

The presence of Jewish intellectuals on the left in Eastern and Central Europe at the turn of the twentieth century cannot be explained by the sum of individual trajectories; it should rather be studied as a large-scale tendency affecting a social group and a generation as a whole. Of course, significant differences separated the Jewish intellectuals of the Tsarist Empire from those of Germany or Austria, but their political radicalisation was almost simultaneous. A typological and sociological analysis of the Jewish Marxist intelligentsia in these cultural and geopolitical areas – the *Kaiserreich* and two multinational empires – must take into consideration the differences as much as the similarities.

The relationship between the Jews and Marxism can be interpreted through Yuri Slezkine's metaphor of the Jews as a minority of Mercurians (foreign and mobile, producers of concepts) in a world of Apollonians (indigenous, sedentary, producers of gods).[1] The more radical the opposition between them was, the more the Jews transcended ethnic identities towards cosmopolitanism: this was the path followed by the Jewish intellectuals of Central Europe and the assimilated Jews of the Russian Empire, bearers of a post-national, universalist Marxism. In the Pale of Settlement, where the latter appeared as a current of thought carried on by a Mercurian elite organically connected to an Apollonian society – the *shtetl* – Marxism took a national form, becoming a sort of Judeo-Marxism.

1 Central Europe

Jewish socialists were especially numerous in Berlin, Vienna, and Budapest. They represented about 10 percent of the German socialist movement, according to Eduard Bernstein's estimate.[2] In his classic 1911 study on the sociology of political parties, Roberto Michels had already underlined the 'particularly significant presence of Jews among the revolutionary and socialist leaders', estimating that 20 to 30 percent of Jewish intellectuals were Social Democrats.[3] Differently from the so-called 'Austro-Marxists' of Vienna, who kept a

---

1 Slezkine 2006, ch. 1.
2 Bernstein 1921.
3 Michels 1957, pp. 250–5.

substantial continuity until the end of the 1930s, in Germany and Hungary they experienced a radical break as a consequence of the Great War and the following revolutionary upheavals – the Berlin insurrection of January 1919, and the Bavarian and Hungarian socialist republics of 1919–20 – in which they played a leading role. After the First World War, the Jews joined in large numbers the communist parties of Central Europe.

In pre-war German social democracy, the Jews belonged to all political currents: they were representatives of the Kautskyan centre, which in 1917 created the USPD (Oskar Cohn, Hugo Haase, Josef Herzfeld, Kurt Rosenfeld, and Emmanuel Wurm) and the principal spokespersons of the revisionist current (Eduard Bernstein, Josef Bloch). In Vienna, they formed the leadership of the socialist party and nearly all the theoreticians of Austro-Marxism (with the remarkable exception of Karl Renner): Victor Adler, the founder of the party; his son, Friedrich Adler, future secretary of the Second International; Friedrich Austerlitz, the director of *Arbeiterzeitung*; Robert Danneberg, one of the creators of the urban project of 'Red Vienna;' and finally, Otto Bauer, Rudolf Hilferding, and Max Adler, three towering figures of Marxist thought of their time. Among the principal leaders of the Bavarian revolution were Kurt Eisner, head of the first government after the fall of the Kaiser, and the founders of the Soviet Republic of April–May 1919: Eugene Leviné, Eric Mühsam, Ernst Toller (head of the army), and Gustav Landauer (people's commissar for culture). In the government of the contemporaneous Hungarian Soviet Republic, eighteen out of twenty-nine people's commissars were Jewish. Intellectuals formed the leadership of the revolution, and the Jews were the great majority amongst them (between 70 and 95 percent, according to several scholars):[4] Béla Kun, the charismatic leader of the revolution, Josef Revai, and Matias Rakosi, without forgetting the philosopher and literary critic György Lukács, people's commissar for culture. The leaders of the German Spartakist movement were also Jewish (Rosa Luxemburg, Leo Jogiches, Karl Radek, Paul Frölich, Rosi Wolfstein), as were the leaders of the communist party (KPD) that emerged from the 1920 Halle congress, in which the Spartakus group merged with the USPD (Paul Levi, August Thalheimer), and the two intellectuals who took the head of the party after the defeat of the insurrectionary attempt of 1923 (Ruth Fischer and Arkadi Maslow). It could be added that toward the end of the 1920s, Jewish Communists were very numerous inside the anti-Stalinist opposition, which, in Germany, rejected the suicidal concept of 'social fascism' and fought for a

---

4   Cf. Deak 1968, p. 138. Ezra Mendelsohn has pointed out that throughout Central Europe 'the most Jewish' Marxism was found in Hungary; see Mendelsohn 1983, p. 96.

united front on the left against the rise of Nazism (in addition to those already mentioned should be added Werner Scholem and Arthur Rosenberg, one of the most important German historians under the Weimar Republic).[5]

Many Jewish activists of the Central European left were intellectuals, who were for the most part journalists or writers and often university educated. It could be said without exaggeration that they represented the breeding ground for the social democratic intelligentsia, and among them were – as the list above clearly shows – some of the most important figures of the Marxism of the Second International. In general, they belonged to the high or upper middle classes: they were the sons of merchants or industrialists, the Jewish elite who had become prosperous after Emancipation. Significant exceptions were Friedrich Austerlitz, who came from a very poor Jewish family; Eduard Bernstein, son of a railway worker; and Hugo Haase, son of a shoemaker. Very often, their adherance to socialism took place before the war and, as can be seen, they were found in all the socialist currents, from the revisionist and reformist right to the radical left, through the Kautskyan and Austro-Marxist centre. Some of them had an *ostjüdisch* ancestry. Integrated first into German social democracy and then the Spartakist movement, they were the leaders-in-exile of organisations active inside the Tsarist Empire, which constituted the framework in which they developed culturally and politically. This was the case with, for example, the militants of the Social Democratic Party of the Kingdom of Poland and Lithuania (SDKPiL): Leo Jogiches, Rosa Luxemburg, and, for several years, Karl Radek.

How did they become socialists? In a few decades, a profound metamorphosis had brought the Jews from the ghetto – still a reality at the beginning of the nineteenth century in Germany and in Austria – to emancipation and assimilation. Despite the emergence of a new anti-Semitism from the end of the 1870s onwards, which revealed the limits and the contradictions of this process, the social achievements of the Jews were impressive. Political emancipation had two immediate social effects: a general improvement of economic conditions and widespread urbanisation, which was reflected rapidly by a concentration in the big German and Habsburg cities. Around 1910, the Jews constituted 5 percent of the population of Prague and Berlin, 10 percent in Vienna, and 20 percent in Budapest.[6] The emancipated Jews did not abandon the old professions – above all trade – in which they had specialised for several centuries and

---

5   One can find extensive information on the biographies of these Socialists and revolutionaries in Weber 1969, vol. 2 (exclusively devoted to the biographies of the leaders of the KPD); Broué 1971; Lazitch and Drachovich 1973; Bourdet 1971.

6   See Karady and Kemeny 1978, p. 30.

which they could now practice with more freedom, but they began to practice other activities, such as industry, leading to the emergence of a fairly significant layer of Jewish businessmen. Social improvement produced a combination of preindustrial and advanced capitalist forms inside the economic structure of Jewry.[7] Additionally, a Jewish intelligentsia of a modern type was created, concentrated in the liberal professions: lawyers, journalists, doctors, and so on.[8] The process of assimilation did not, however, bring with it an abandonment of cultural identity: an urban layer, the Jews were concentrated in certain quarters of the big cities, and showed a clear propensity for endogamy and maintaining a strong group identity. Their adoption of German culture was enthusiastic and complete and, in most cases, they wished to be respectable citizens of one empire or another. This 'policy of assimilation' was then neither linear nor devoid of contradictions: citizens of the 'Jewish faith', they were part of the *Kulturgemeinschaft*, but they remained excluded from the German or Austrian *Volk*. Even in Hungary, where a rich Jewish bourgeoisie shared economic power with the landowning Magyar aristocracy, normally jealous of its noble privileges but not particularly anti-Semitic, linguistic and cultural assimilation did not prevent the continuance of Jewish identity. Citizenship (*Staatsangehörigkeit*) and 'nationhood' or 'ethnic belonging' (*Volksangehörigkit*) did not merge, but rather fixed an invisible but tangible separation.

At the turn of the twentieth century, the social structure of the Central European Jewish communities was shaped by the presence of a hypertrophic intellectual layer, proportionally very much more significant than that of the nations in which the Jews lived. Some figures suffice to give an idea of the breadth of this phenomenon: in 1895 Jews represented 10 percent of the students in higher education in Germany (where they were only 1 percent of the total population) and 23.6 percent in Vienna (10 percent of the population).[9] This Jewish intelligentsia faced anti-Semitism, finding no openings in public institutions, and was rigorously excluded from university teaching.[10] The formation of a Jewish financial, industrial, and commercial bourgeoisie was not accompanied by the birth of a Jewish academic elite. Anti-Semitism was preached in the universities and shaped the ideology of all conservative polit-

---

7   See Mosse 1976, p. 81. See also Mosse 1987.
8   According to Victor Karady and Istvan Kemeny, in 1920 in Budapest, Jews represented 50.6 percent of lawyers, 46.8 percent of doctors, and 43.3 percent of journalists (Karady and Kemeny 1978, p. 42). Between 1870 and 1910 in Vienna 11.3 percent of economically active Jews worked in the liberal professions: see Rozenblit 1983, pp. 49–50.
9   See Rosenthal 1944, p. 257. On Vienna, see Barkai 1970, p. 36.
10   Gay 1975, pp. 32–3. According to Gay, the rare Jewish academics were very often converts.

ical forces; to a certain extent, it was a component of 'national identity'. The Jewish intelligentsia remained marginalised and discriminated against. One could say, to use an expression of Hannah Arendt, that emancipation created, besides a Jewish parvenu bourgeois, a Jewish *pariah* intellectual.[11] Jews were brilliant public intellectuals, but very rarely were they recognised scholars (*Gelehrte*), i.e. accepted inside academic institutions. A physician like Albert Einstein and a philosopher like Edmund Husserl were exceptions. Among pre-war socialists, however, these exceptions did not exist. Thus, the entire social context objectively pushed the Jewish intelligentsia to think and act against the current, to become critical of the established order. Inevitably, socialism benefited greatly from this situation.

For this social layer emerging out of the new Jewish bourgeoisie, the revolt against capitalist society and its system of values took the form of a conflict of generations, of a rupture with the world of their fathers, who had behaved as perfect German or Austrian bourgeois citizens but who, as Joseph Roth put it, 'did not have the courage to convert, preferring to water down the entire Jewish religion'.[12] One of the components of this revolt was 'Jewish self-hatred' (*jüdische Selbsthaß*), a formula that reflected the internalisation of anti-Semitic prejudice by the young intellectuals in revolt against bourgeois society and their family background (that of the assimilated Jewish middle classes).[13] The 'assimilationism' of the Viennese Jewish bourgeoisie, who were completely integrated on a socio-economic plane, created a very acute crisis of identity in the Jewish intelligentsia, sometimes leading to a global rejection of Jewish identity (Karl Kraus), if not to a veritable form of Jewish anti-Semitism (Otto Weininger). Arthur Schnitzler's novel *Der Weg ins Freie*, published in Vienna in 1905, remains the best literary representation of this social phenomenon.[14]

'Jewish self-hatred', nonetheless, does not explain such an attraction to socialism. It pertinently describes the case of Victor Adler – who converted to Lutheranism as an adult, founded the Austrian pan-German movement, was opposed to a socialist involvement in the struggle against anti-Semitism, and was even capable of rejecting a motion of protest against the Beilis trial in 1913[15] – but it does not allow us to understand the political and intellectual

---

11   See Arendt 2007, pp. 275–97.

12   Roth 1984, p. 384.

13   See Hellige 1979, p. 483.

14   See Gilman 1986.

15   See Wistrich 1974; Silberner 1963, pp. 234–7. The thesis of Victor Adler's Jewish anti-Semitism is not accepted by his biographer (and leader of Austrian social democracy), see Braunthal 1965a, p. 138, and Braunthal 1965b.

itinerary of Ernst Toller or Gustav Landauer, writers and revolutionaries who were conscious of their own Jewishness. In short, this symbiotic relationship between Jews and socialism could not be reduced to a form of 'self-hatred'; it deserves a careful investigation of its multiple roots. Born out of the recent emancipation, this Jewish intelligentsia was at the same time assimilated, nourished by German culture and rejected by anti-Semitism. It was alienated both in relation to its own tradition (abandoned or denied) and in relation to the society in which it lived. The sense of rootlessness it experienced was well-expressed by Kafka, in 1918, in a letter to Max Brod in which he defined himself as the man of the *westjüdische Zeit*, deprived of historic memory, cut off from his own past, and obliged to live in an alien world. Many Jewish socialists shared a similar cultural dilemma.[16]

But this picture is not complete. Jewish immigration from Eastern Europe confronted the assimilated German-speaking Jews of Berlin or Vienna with another Jewish community, poor and oppressed, reminding them of the ghetto, but also the bearer of a culture, the *Yiddishkeit*, which marked it as a nation. Upon their arrival, the *Ostjuden* – not only the tens of thousands who established a presence in the *Leopoldstadt* in Vienna, or in the *Scheunenviertel* in Berlin, but also the millions who crossed Germany and Austria en route to the United States – faced the anti-Semitic reaction of nationalism and engendered a deep trouble among the Jewish population: assimilation was no longer a *fait accompli* but rather seemed to be a fragile acquisition, contested by the rise of anti-Semitism and the presence of a distinct Jewish nation, transplanted to an area where Jewish and German cultures appeared to have established a complete symbiosis.[17] In other words, Eastern Jews destroyed all their efforts to appear like 'authentic' Germans or Austrians.

This contradiction was one of the sources of Zionism. Jewish identity was rediscovered and claimed by a sector of the liberal assimilated Jewish elite, suddenly confronted with the reality of anti-Semitism (Theodor Herzl) or fascinated by the cultural and spiritual values – in most cases idealised – of the *Ostjudentum* (Martin Buber). But this same contradiction also motivated the commitment to social democracy of many Jewish intellectuals, who thus expressed their double rejection of anti-Semitism and Jewishness. On the one hand, the socialist movement resolutely defended democracy and fought against all forms of anti-Semitism; on the other, it made no distinction in its

---

16   See Baioni 1984, p. 3. On Kafka, Jewishness and anarchism, see Löwy 2004.

17   On the problem of Jewish immigration to Germany from Eastern Europe, see Wertheimer 1981, and above all Aschheim 1982. On the conflict between *Ostjuden* and assimilated Jews in Vienna and Berlin, see also Roth 1985, pp. 39–53.

ranks between Jews and Gentiles. For the Jewish intelligentsia, the workers' movement represented both a shelter against racism and the privileged place of its assimilation. This was at the root of the assimilationism of the Jewish Socialists.

This psychological attitude was moreover favoured by the socialist culture of the time. At the turn of the twentieth century, Marxism was, in its dominant currents, a variant of positivistic evolutionism. It saw history as a linear process of development of the productive forces and as a society's unending march toward 'progress', which inevitably implied Jewish assimilation. In 1916, Eduard Bernstein wrote: 'Assimilation is a social and cultural necessity. A discussion that wishes to arrive at a fruitful conclusion must not pose the problem of whether assimilation can or should be completed, but rather seek the best means of completing it'.[18]

For the Central European Jewish intellectuals, becoming socialist meant first and foremost a break with their ethnic group of origin, and a social and psychological break with their Jewish background. If in Poland, Lithuania, or Ukraine Jewish revolutionaries could at the same time be the representative of a proletarian class and an oppressed nation, in Central Europe, on the contrary, class-consciousness and ethnic identity were divided. In 1884, Bernstein wrote to Engels that in German social democracy, many leaders of Jewish origin felt virtually obliged to display anti-Semitism so as to dispel any suspicion in the party that they were 'favouring Jewish interests.' A remarkable exception were the SPD deputies Georg Davidsohn, Oskar Cohn, and Emmanuel Wurm, who, despite their atheism, registered themselves in the Reichstag as Jews [mosaisch], to show their solidarity with the German Jewish community, which was subject to discrimination and the object of racist hatred.[19] One could also recall the intellectuals who played a major role during the Bavarian revolution, such as Kurt Eisner, Erich Mühsam, Gustav Landauer, and Ernst Toller, who were both assimilated and conscious of their Jewishness despite their hostility to Zionism; but with the exception of Eisner, they could be characterised as 'anarchist-Bolsheviks' rather than Marxists.[20] For most Jewish revolutionaries, Marxism transcended, in an internationalist perspective, the Jewishness/anti-Semitism antinomy: Jewishness conceived as the heritage of a past made of oppression and obscurantism (according to the traditional *aufklärerisch* vision), anti-Semitism as the ideology of nationalism and the ruling classes.

---

18   Bernstein 1916, pp. 247–8.
19   Quoted by Wistrich 1982, pp. 76, 80.
20   On 'anarcho-Bolsheviks,' see Löwy 1981c, pp. 5–47.

The combination of anti-Semitism, generational conflicts, and *ostjüdisch* immigration produced a kind of identity crisis inside the assimilated Jewish intelligentsia, who had a strong sentiment of being part of German culture – in contrast to the *Ostjuden* – but who were also marginalised and rejected as alien by German society. Many Jews must have shared the sentiment expressed by Ernst Epler in these words: 'To what extent am I Jewish? The Jewish religion is indifferent to me. Only the remnants of Jewish tradition remain living in me. I grew up between the *Arbeiterzeitung* and the Heroic German Legends, and at school I gorged myself on profound humanism, Germanism and visceral anti-Semitism. And all this added up finally to give as its result: Ernst Epler is Jewish'.[21]

Excluded from university chairs, the state bureaucracy, and the army, the Jewish intellectuals were, to employ a Gramscian typology, neither 'traditional' nor 'organic' intellectuals; they were neither the expression of old, conservative elites, nor the organisers of the ideological hegemony of the new ruling classes. They lived in a neutral space, in a sort of no-man's-land where they perfectly embodied a 'freely floating' or 'socially unattached intelligentsia' (in Karl Mannheim's definition); hence, their predisposition toward avant-garde movements.[22]

Socialism represented one possible road among others for the Jewish intellectual. There was also the possibility of literary or artistic expression that was not directly political. One has only to think of the explosion of Jewish creativity in Berlin, Vienna, and Prague that corresponded with the rise of Marxism. A different issue was the rediscovery of specifically Jewish cultural themes (like Messianism) reinterpreted in the light of German anti-capitalist romanticism (Walter Benjamin, Ernst Bloch, Gustav Landauer, Gershom Scholem, and others).[23] These political and cultural orientations were not alternatives, but could sometimes cross over, as in the case of György Lukács between 1918 and 1923, or as in the case of Walter Benjamin after 1923.

In the wake of the revolutionary hopes aroused by the birth of Soviet Russia, the situation of Jewish leftist intellectuals was no longer exceptional but did retain certain specificities. As Eric Hobsbawm has stressed, in this moment the Jewish cultural milieu found itself 'under the triple impact of the collapse of the pre-1914 bourgeois world, the October Revolution and anti-Semitism'.[24]

---

21 Epler 1986, p. 75.

22 On this concept of *freischwebende Intelligenz*, see Mannheim 1936, pp. 137–8.

23 See Löwy 1992.

24 Hobsbawm 1973, pp. 250–1. According to John Bunzl, 'Every Jew who joined the workers'

Since a young Jewish intellectual could not join one of the bourgeois nationalist parties – for the most part confessional or anti-Semitic – there remained only two alternatives: Zionism ('our own version of the nationalism of blood and soil') or communism. And until the end of the Second World War, the second option appeared to the majority of such intellectuals to be incomparably more attractive.

2   Eastern Europe

In Eastern Europe, the Jewish Marxist intelligentsia grew up in a completely different context, shaped by the social geography of the Tsarist Pale of Settlement and by the existence of a Jewish national community with its own class conflicts. Toward the end of the nineteenth century a Jewish workers' movement and a Marxist intelligentsia appeared, speaking Yiddish along with Russian, Polish, and German. In 1905, the Jews, who formed only 4 percent of the total population of the Tsarist Empire, accounted for 37 percent of the political activists arrested during the Revolution; the Bund – the Jewish Workers' League of Poland, Lithuania, and Russia – were an organised force comparable to that of the Bolsheviks and the Mensheviks, among whom Jews were also numerous (respectively 11 percent and 23 percent of party members).[25] A great number of these Jewish activists were intellectuals. What was the road that led them to revolutionary commitment? What ideological orientation did their radicalisation take? Any attempt to answer such questions should start from the chronological frontiers that framed this historical experience: 1881 and 1918. 1881 marked a significant increase of anti-Semitism, which was institutionalised as a governmental practice after the coronation of Alexander III; 1918 means the end of the First World War, the independence of Poland, and the Russian Revolution, a turning point that would profoundly shake the life of the Jewish communities.

During the last two decades of the nineteenth century, the Eastern European Jewry experienced the disintegration of its traditional structures. It remained a nation *sui generis* – dispersed, deprived of territorial unity in spite of its cultural and linguistic homogeneity – but religion had ceased to be its exclusive foundation. The social reorganisation of the Jewish world came out of the process

---

movement did so also, consciously or unconsciously, in order to transcend a specifically Jewish alienation'; see Bunzl 1987, p. 34.

25   See Brym 1978, p. 54.

of industrialisation of the Tsarist Empire, and was launched by the economic
reform of 1861 (with the abolition of serfdom). In fact, the process of social and
economic modernisation of the Jewish world had started earlier and had created a significant managerial layer. In the first half of the nineteenth century,
for instance, they played a significant role in the birth of the Russian railroads;
in Ukraine the Jews owned more than one-fourth of the factories, controlled 30
percent of the textile industry and represented almost 90 percent of the trades-
men, but the anti-Semitic waves of the 1880s and 1905–6 reduced their influence, pushing a growing number of Jews to emigrate to Western Europe and the
United States.[26] Alongside this assimilated bourgeoisie (less significant, in economic terms, than its Central European equivalent), a Jewish proletariat also
developed that was at the same time excluded from large-scale industry and
ethnically separated from the rest of the Russian or Polish working class. The
division of labour coincided with the ethnic division of the proletariat: the Jewish workers were concentrated in certain 'Jewish' branches (the manufacture of
clothing and tobacco, tannery, and so forth) and were scattered in a multitude
of small workshops. They were close to a large sub-proletarian layer of *luftmenshn* (literally 'men of air'), hawkers or unemployed, Chagallian figures floating
into air, who constituted nearly a quarter of the active population of the Jewish
community in 1897.[27] Finally, following the reforms of Alexander II, who had
partially suppressed the restrictions on residence in the towns and access to the
universities, a modern Jewish intelligentsia came into existence. In 1840 there
were fifty Jewish high school and almost no university students, whereas in 1886
the Russian universities already contained 1,700 Jewish students.[28] From the
1880s onward, nevertheless, the tsarist regime introduced discriminatory laws
that progressively impeded this trend and stimulated a strong wave of Jewish
intellectual emigration to Germany and Switzerland. Between 1894 and 1902,
the rate of Jewish students in the Russian universities dropped from 13.3 percent to 7 percent.[29]

This new intellectual generation differentiated itself from the *maskilim* of
the first half of the nineteenth century like the disciples of Moses Mendelssohn and the defenders of the *Haskalah*, I.B. Levinson and M.A. Ginsburg,
whose admiration for German culture was coupled with a total isolation from
Russian spiritual life. The Jewish intelligentsia that grew up in the 1880s was

---

26   See Budnitskii 2012, p. 12.
27   See Schwarz 1951, pp. 18–21. According to Salo Baron, in several communities the number
       of *luftmenshn* was as high as 40 percent of the population; see Baron 1964, p. 114.
28   See Shapiro 1961, p. 149.
29   Budnitski 2012, p. 30.

Russian speaking and was familiar with, in addition to Marx and Darwin, Herzen and Chernyshevskii. Régine Robin has stressed the phenomenon of the 'crossing languages' among the Eastern Jews: the traditional Yiddish/Hebrew bilingualism was replaced by new forms of Yiddish/Hebrew/Polish or Yiddish/Hebrew/Russian trilingualism, and joined often by a fourth language: German.[30] Thus, the wave of pogroms of the 1880s shook a Yiddish speaking intelligentsia that had been deeply transformed by both mass emigration and urban concentration. Between 1880 and the 1920s, about three million Jews fled Eastern Europe toward the West, mostly to the United States, Germany and France, without any corresponding diminution in the size of the Jewish population in the Pale of Settlement, which rather experienced a constant demographic expansion (from about five million in 1897 to more than seven million on the eve of the Second World War). Urbanisation – aided by a series of laws forbidding Jews from living in certain regions and in small villages – displaced the axis of community life from small- and medium-sized centres – *shtetl* originally meant village – to towns and cities. Overall, the Jews took on a clearly urban character. Between 1850 and 1925, the number of Jews rose from 41,000 to 322,000 in Warsaw, from 2,800 to 156,200 in Lodz, from 17,000 to 153,000 in Odessa, and from 3,000 to 140,200 in Kiev.[31]

These years gave birth to modern Yiddish, which transformed the old 'jargon' of the street into a literary language. In 1908, the Jewish intellectual elite, at a conference in Czernowiz, recognised Yiddish as a 'national language' alongside Hebrew, which they characterised as a 'national language of the past'.[32] Yiddish literature experienced a veritable flowering. The *Haskalah*, which a century earlier had led to assimilation in Germany, in the Tsarist Empire became, despite its original goals, a vehicle for the adaption and absorption of modern international culture inside the *Yiddishkeit*, which corresponded with a process of secularisation and politicisation of the Jews.[33] In other words, it took a 'romantic' character and powerfully contributed to reshape the Jewish self-perception in national terms.[34] These social and cultural changes took place in a context shaped by the rise of a violent and murderous anti-Semitism, no longer a widespread prejudice but a permanent hostility threatening Jewish life on a daily basis. The anti-Semitism of the tsarist regime raised a wall

---

30   Robin 1984, p. 17.

31   See Della Pergola 1983, p. 88.

32   See Robin 1984, pp. 122–7, and Dinse and Liptzin 1978, pp. 110–12.

33   See Ertel 1982, pp. 148, 171.

34   See Litvak 2012.

against assimilation and pushed Jewish culture toward political radicalism. Pavel Aksel'rod described in these terms the enormous psychological impact that the pogroms of the 1880s had on the first Jewish socialist circles:

> The pogroms obliged the socialist intelligentsia to understand that the Jews as a people found themselves in a unique situation in Russia, when they were targets for the hatred of the different sectors of the Christian population; and that they, the socialist Jews, were wrong in neglecting the actual condition of the Jews as a people different from the others. It was then that the revolutionaries understood that they must not abandon the masses in the name of cosmopolitanism. The 'indigenous masses' were not only deprived of cosmopolitan sentiments, they had not even accepted the idea of solidarity with the poorest classes of the different nationalities of Russia.[35]

In the context of tsarism, no Yiddish writer could aspire to academic or official recognition. The Jews were gradually expelled from the universities and, between 1887 and 1905, their rate fell from 14.4 to 7 percent.[36] Many revolutionaries were intellectually shaped in the socialist émigré circles of Germany or Switzerland where they had gone to study.[37] To a society of *luftmenshn* there now corresponded a *déclassé* intelligentsia. The impossibility of assimilation, legal discrimination, and the fact of belonging to an oppressed culture favoured the radicalisation and the politicisation of the Yiddish-speaking intellectuals.

Until the 1880s, populism exerted a strong attraction for rebellious Jewish youth. Two Jews, Mark Natanson and Aaron Zundelevich, were members of the executive committee of Land and Liberty, a populist-terrorist Russian movement; Pavel Aksel'rod and Lev Deutsch, who would found the Emancipation of Labor group (the first Russian Marxist organisation) in Geneva with Plekhanov and Vera Zasulich, had been *narodniki* at the beginning of their revolutionary careers. The Jewish presence inside the populist movement was significant but in no way comparable to that which would shape the left from the 1880s onward. Despite its affinities with Western intellectual tendencies like Marxism and socialism, populism was basically a current of Russian thought. Jewish intellectuals, because of their cultural heritage, could not identify with the peasants (*moujiks*) and still less idealise traditional values. Their revolt

---

35   Quoted by Talmon 1970, p. 37. See also Wistrich 1976, p. 13.
36   See Brym 1978, p. 55.
37   Weill 1996.

against religious orthodoxy and the obscurantism of the ghetto could not find an outlet in the Russian countryside. They recognised in populism an instrument of struggle against tsarist absolutism and even accepted, up to a certain extent, its indifference toward peasant anti-Semitism (this led the populists to take a very ambiguous position toward the pogroms of 1882), but their adhesion to populist ideology remained only superficial and transitory. Aaron Aptekman, a Jewish *narodnik* from Karkhov, openly recognised his troubles: 'I did not know the Russian people, because I was born and grew up in a town without ever having seen a village in my life. Apart from this, I was foreign to the Russian people by race and blood. I knew very little Russian history and, speaking frankly, I did not like it'.[38]

The birth of a specifically Jewish working class toward the end of the nineteenth century allowed this Jewish intelligentsia to find a social anchorage, a class point of reference, through adopting a Marxist orientation. This was the context in which, in Lithuania and Poland, the Bundists and the socialist Zionists became the 'organic intellectuals' (in the Gramscian sense of the term) of the Jewish workers' movement. In Ukraine, the Jewish intellectuals were often assimilated and constituted a veritable breeding ground for the Russian Social Democratic Labor Party (RSDLP). Sometimes the double impact of anti-Semitism and the rise of a Jewish workers' movement pushed many assimilated intellectuals toward a new Jewish national identity (such was the case with Vladimir Medem), but it could also lead to a political engagement negating the very concept of Jewish nationality – an attitude encouraged by Russian Marxism – or to a kind of revolutionary cosmopolitanism rejecting any classification of the national type. These different currents shared nonetheless a universalistic 'red utopianism', in that they all – including the Zionists – invoked the concept of proletarian internationalism.[39]

Roughly speaking, one can sketch a typology of the Jewish Marxist intelligentsia in Eastern Europe by distinguishing between five categories:

a. the Bundists: Raphael Abramovich, Samuel Gojansky, Arkadi Kremer, Vladimir Medem, John Mill; or socialist intellectuals close to them, like Chaim Zhitlovsky;

b. the socialist Zionists: Ber Borokhov and Nachman Syrkin;

---

38   Quoted by Patkin 1947, p. 87. See also Kiel 1970, pp. 295–310.

39   As Alain Brossat and Sylvia Klingberg have pointed out, 'the voluntarist universalism of a Trotsky ... and the revolutionary spirit of the leaders of the Bund at the turn of the century ... are they not two branches of the same tree? Do not both these attitudes have as their source the same Utopia that, at the beginning of the century, rose like a red sun in Eastern Europe?' See Brossat and Klingberg 1983, pp. 26–7.

c.   the assimilated Jews of Russian social democracy: Pavel Aksel'rod, Fedor
      Dan, Lev Deutsch, Lev Borisovich Kamenev (Rosenfeld), Moishe Ouritski,
      Lev Martov (Iulii Osipovich Tsederbaum), Leon Trotsky (Lev Davidovich
      Bronstein), Lakov Sverdlov, Gregory Zinoviev (Radomyl'skii), Adolf Joffe,
      Mark Liber (Mikhail Isaakovich Goldman), David Riazanov (Golden-
      dakh);
d.   the red (and rootless) 'cosmopolitan' Jews: Karl Radek (Sobelsohn), Alex-
      ander Parvus (Izrail' Lazarevich Gel'fand), Charles Rappoport;
e.   the (assimilated) Jewish leaders of Polish social democracy: Leo Jogiches,
      Rosa Luxemburg, and Adolf Warski.

Whereas the members of the first two categories were Marxists claiming their
Jewishness, those of the last three can be defined through Isaac Deutscher's
definition of 'non-Jewish Jews': intellectuals who participate in the Jewish
tradition of denying and transcending Judaism itself.[40] According to Isaac
Deutscher, the 'non-Jewish Jews' embodied a modernist and secular, not to say
heretical and atheistic, tendency belonging to Jewish history from Spinoza to
Freud and Trotsky. In the Russian Empire, it affected the youth of the big cities, outside of the Pale of Settlement. In Moscow, St. Petersburg and Odessa, the
young Jewish intellectuals longed for Western modernity, the first step of which
was the adoption of the Russian language and literature, the second exile. In
Poland and Lithuania, on the contrary, they were plunged into a Jewish community – economically, socially and culturally homogeneous – in which secularisation took the form of Yiddish language and literature. In Moscow and St.
Petersburg, they became Bolsheviks and Mensheviks; in the Pale of Settlement,
Bundists; Socialist Zionists swung between these two poles. Their relation to
Jewishness was radically antithetical: the first group rejected it in the name of
cosmopolitanism and universalism and the second could not think modernity
outside of its national dimension. In all cases, they passed through a generational conflict. Becoming Russian, Yuri Slezkine explains,

> meant leaving the parental home. If the Russian world stood for speech,
> knowledge, freedom, and light, then the Jewish world represented silence,
> ignorance, bondage, and darkness. In the 1870s and 1880s, the revolution
> of young Jews against their parents reached Russia – eventually in the
> form of Marxism but most immediately as Freud's family romance. The
> Jews who shared Mandelstam's reverence for the 'clear and pure Russian
> sounds' tended to share his horror of the 'Judean chaos' of their grand-
> mother's household.[41]

40   See Deutscher 1968.
41   Slezkine 2006, p. 136.

The Bund, the principal political force inside the Jewish community of the Pale, was born from the fusion of the first organised workers' circles with this radicalised intellectual elite. In order to speak with the Jewish workers, socialists were compelled to adopt their language, which led gradually them to conceive a political project based on both class and nationality, in which the liberation of the proletariat as an exploited class was intermingled with the liberation of the Jews as an oppressed nation. The tool for this symbiosis was Yiddish, which found in the Bund one of its stronger defenders.[42] In his memoirs, Hersch Mendel sums up his motivation for joining the Bund when he was a young Jewish worker in Warsaw: 'It seemed to me that I could find there the synthesis between international socialism and the Jewish Question. I was very grateful toward the Bund, which allowed me to be at the same time a proud Jew and an ardent socialist'.[43]

Vladimir Medem, the Bund's theoretician, was born in Minsk in 1879 into a Jewish family converted to Lutheranism but was baptised in the Orthodox Church. His parents led a comfortable life – his father was a state counsellor – in a typically assimilated milieu, which was rather exceptional in the heart of the Pale of Settlement. He went to a Russian school, where he also learned French and German, but at home he often overheard his mother talking Yiddish with the maids. At high school, confronted with the reality of anti-Semitism, he began to spend time in an exclusively Jewish environment. Entering into contact with the socialist circles of Kiev, he joined the Bund in 1899. In exile in Switzerland, he became a leader of the party and devoted himself to the study of the national question. He wrote his first articles in Yiddish only in 1912 (his theoretical works of the previous years were written in Russian), and the Bundist workers of Kiev affectionately referred to him as the 'goy'. Vladimir Medem's itinerary mirrors the process of a recovery of Jewish identity by an assimilated intellectual at the beginning of the twentieth century, confronted with anti-Semitism and the development of the workers' movement. In his memoirs he describes the discovery of his Jewishness: 'This was not a sudden change, a leap, nor even a conscious decision ... Everything happened spontaneously and gradually, without my perceiving it. I can only grasp the two extremes: childhood, when I considered myself Russian, and maturity, when I considered myself Jewish. Between these two poles, several years passed during which I changed slowly, imperceptibly'.[44] Medem defined his Jewishness as

---

42   On the role played by the Bund in the modernization of Yiddish, see Fishman 2005, ch. 4.

43   Mendel 1982, p. 73.

44   Medem 1979, p. 129.

a 'Diaspora feeling', deeply rooted in the values of the *Yiddishkeit* and foreign to Zionism (always rejected by the Bund).[45]

Ber Borokhov, the ideologue of Marxist Zionism, came to Yiddish only in his maturity and wrote a good part of his works on the national question in Russian. He was born in 1881 in the area of Poltava, in Ukraine. His family was assimilated and his mother tongue was Russian. In 1900 he joined the RSDLP, and, after having been expelled for Zionism, he joined the Poale Zion, the Marxist Zionist party for whom he developed a theoretical framework in his 1906 essay 'Our Platform'. Differently from most Zionists, Borokhov rejected a purely instrumental use of Yiddish, which he recognised as the modern national language of the Jews. He even devoted himself to learning Yiddish philology, although he did not reject Hebrew: 'Yiddish and Hebrew', he wrote, 'are like the body and the spirit, each can choose according to his ideas to be solely body, or solely spirit. What seems necessary to me is their link'.[46]

On the other hand, the figure of Chaim Zhitlovsky appears strictly unclassifiable in the milieu of Jewish socialism. Born into a family of Hassidim in a *shtetl* near Vitebsk, he grew up on the classic texts of Judaism. He soon became a Populist and plunged himself into Russian culture, to the point of changing his Jewish name to the very much more Russian Yefim Ossipovich. But his activity among the Ukrainian *narodniis* was only a brief interlude and in 1883 he returned to Yiddish. Rejecting both Zionism and assimilationism, he was one of the first Jewish intellectuals in Eastern Europe to elaborate a concept of Jewish national autonomy in the Diaspora. In 1896, in Berne, he translated and published in Yiddish *The Communist Manifesto*. He was a fellow traveller of the Bund until 1904 when, shaken by the Kishinev pogrom, he adopted a 'territorialist' attitude. He then joined the Jewish Socialist Workers party (SERP), the Jewish version of the Russian Socialist Revolutionaries, who demanded territorial national autonomy. In 1908, he played an important role at the Czernowiz conference, where Yiddish was recognised as a national Jewish language. He considered Hebrew to be an archaic tongue that could only survive alongside Yiddish like Latin in the feudal period, used by scholars, whereas the modern national languages were in the process of developing themselves. A non-Marxist, he rejected the economic determinism of Plekhanov and, probably because he remained imbued with the subjectivist voluntarism of his youthful populist experience, Zhitlovsky participated in the Russian Revolution as a Socialist Revolutionary. In the interwar period, faced with the rise of National

---

45   Ibid., p. 179.
46   Quoted by Robin 1984, p. 107.

Socialism in Germany, he became a critical partisan of the Soviet Union. He always remained an outsider to Jewish socialism or, in the words of the historian Jonathan Frankel, a sort of 'ideological nomad'.[47]

Pavel Aksel'rod was a transitional figure between the Bund and Russian Marxism. In fact, his whole political life was shaped by a permanent tension between Jewishness and universalism, socialism and nation. Born into an orthodox Jewish family, at the age of twenty he wished to devote himself to the study of the *Haskalah*, but in 1872 he became an agnostic after reading the works of Lassalle and Herbert Spencer. In 1883, after a brief anarchist and populist phase, he set up the first Russian Marxist circle in Geneva along with Plekhanov. When the first wave of pogroms broke out, Aksel'rod, who was still a populist, could not conceal his disquiet at the extremely ambiguous position taken by the *narodniki* in relation to anti-Semitism. In his opinion, the pogroms did not express simply the revolt of the Russian peasants against Jewish traders but were directed against all Jews, without exception, as a group. He even decided to write a pamphlet on this problem, but unhappily he did not finish it. The Dreyfus affair, which, as he wrote to Plekhanov, absorbed him completely ('head, heart and entire being'), reawakened his Jewish consciousness.[48] He was angered by the indifference with which the French socialist left observed the trial and proposed that the Russian 'colony' of Zurich and Geneva write a letter to Émile Zola to acknowledge his support for Dreyfus. After the October Revolution, Aksel'rod definitively abandoned the hypothesis of assimilation and became sympathetic to Zionism. In Aksel'rod, who remained throughout his life a leader of the Menshevik current of Russian social democracy, one can find the traces of a Judeo-Russian identity, the product of the coexistence of different cultures and experiences.

We join now a wide gallery of assimilated Russian Marxists. Iulii Osipovich Tsederbaum (Martov) was born in 1873 in Constantinople, where his father directed a Russian navigation company. He was a 'grandson of the *Haskalah*' as his biographer, Israel Getzler, has put it.[49] When he was four years old, his family moved to Odessa, where in 1881 he experienced a pogrom that was to mark him throughout his life. A little later, the Tsederbaum family moved to Saint Petersburg, outside the Pale of Settlement. Thanks to the connections of his grandfather, he was able to enrol in university despite the *numerus clausus* that limited Jewish students. In 1892 he was arrested for the first time and drew close to the Emancipation of Labor group. The following year, he was exiled to Vilnius

---

47   See Frankel 1984, p. 258. On Zhitlovsky, see Goldsmith 1987, ch. 7.
48   Quoted by Ascher 1965, p. 260.
49   See Getzler 2003, pp. i–ii.

in Lithuania. In this industrial town, which was also at the time the spiritual and cultural capital of the *Yiddishkeit*, Martov discovered his Jewishness, learned Yiddish and threw himself completely into the activities of the workers' circles. On 1 May 1895, he organised a conference at which he proposed the establishment of an independent Jewish workers' party (he thus contributed to the birth of the Bund, which took place in Vilnius two years later).[50] Returning to Saint Petersburg, he reverted to a Russian – or, better, pan-Russian – understanding of the class struggle, which distanced him from the Jewish specificity he had perceived in Lithuania. At the second congress of the RSDLP, held in Brussels and London in 1903, Martov was one of the principal critics of the Bund, which he attacked not only for organisational federalism but also for national particularism. However, Martov never became an unreserved assimilationist and his attitude often retained a residue of Jewish identity. In 1913, for example, he was wholeheartedly involved in the campaign against the Beilis trial, and after his return to Russia thanks to amnesty, he chose to live a clandestine existence in Saint Petersburg – a town in which Jews could live in limited numbers – rather than accept a formal conversion to Lutheranism.

In 1929 Trotsky wrote in his autobiography that he had never been influenced by his Jewish origins. Indeed, the political and cultural formation of the founder of the Red Army was completely exterior to the Yiddish-land. Born in 1879 to a family of Jewish farmers at Ianovka, in the Ukrainian countryside, he studied at Odessa in a Lutheran German technical institute. He was sympathetic to populism at Nikolaev, where he participated in the foundation of the first socialist circles, although he never entered into contact with the Jewish workers' movement or Yiddish Marxist literature. In 1903 he was, with Martov, the principal critic of the Bund during the RSDLP congress. He claimed to have as much right to represent the Jewish proletariat as the Bund, which drew a sarcastic comment from Mark Liber, who defined him as the spokesperson of a Jewish proletariat 'in which he had never worked'.[51] Subsequently, Trotsky participated in the organisation of self-defence groups against the pogroms, of which he gave an impressive description in the pages of *1905*, and was actively involved in the struggle against anti-Semitism (during his exile in Vienna, he intervened on the question of the Beilis trial and the condition of the Jews of Romania).[52] It always amounted, however, to an attitude assumed by a Russian revolutionary, that is, someone outside the Jewish community. During the civil war after October 1917, the counterrevolution constantly used anti-Semitism to attack the

---

50   Ibid., ch. 3.

51   See Tobias 1972, p. 211.

52   See chapter 5.

Jewish chief of the Red Army, as did Stalin, from the end of the 1920s onward, in his struggle against the Left Opposition inside the Bolshevik party. Yet this did not divert Trotsky from his vocation as a true 'non-Jewish Jew'. Odessa, Saint Petersburg, Moscow, London, Paris, Vienna, New York, Mexico: these were the cities that formed the backdrop to his life. 'My life in so many countries, my acquaintance with so many different languages, political systems and cultures', he wrote in his autobiography, 'helped me to absorb internationalism in my very flesh and blood'.[53] In the mid-1930s, under the impact of Nazism in Germany, the Russian revolutionary abandoned the dogma of assimilation to adopt a perspective of territorial autonomy for Yiddish-speaking Jews.[54] It was a significant shift that indicated an attempt at a critical reflection on the traditional Marxist conception of the Jewish Question.

Trotsky and Martov emerged from Russian socialism and maintained this point of reference through the entire period of their exile prior to the October Revolution. The 'rootless cosmopolitans' were a different category of the Jewish Marxist intelligentsia. It is true that this definition derives from Stalinism, but it nonetheless can be useful if freed from any negative connotation. A condition of complete rootlessness effectively shaped quite a significant number of assimilated or semi-assimilated Jewish intellectuals, who had fled the *Yiddishkeit* to find themselves nationless, in many cases literally stateless, in the sense of Arendt's 'pariah'. One can apply to these revolutionaries the literary metaphor of Peter Schlemil, the character of Chamisso, wandering the world in search of his own lost shadow, or that of Roth's clown, 'the man divided in two, leaving his own center of gravity and thus falling outside of himself'.[55]

Karl Radek was the most authentic representative of the 'rootless cosmopolitan'. Strictly speaking he could be considered neither Polish nor Russian nor German, but, assuredly, he was Jewish. The historian Werner Lerner defines him as *vaterlandslos* ('nationless').[56] His real name was Sobelsohn and he was born in 1885 at Lemberg (Lvov), the capital of Habsburg Galicia. He was brought up as an 'emancipated' Jew, which in the Austrian empire meant the adoption of German language. In Galicia, where social and ethnic divisions seemed to coincide – Polish landowners, Ukrainian peasants, Jewish traders, and a German bourgeoisie – assimilation normally meant 'Germanisation.' He learnt German at the insistence of his mother, but this constraint led him rapidly, as a reaction, to the discovery of Polish culture. At thirteen, he read Adam Mick-

---

53   See Trotsky 1970b, p. 340.
54   See Nedava 1971, pp. 218–19.
55   See Magris 1979, p. 71.
56   Lerner 1970, pp. VII, 174.

iewicz with passion. He wrote in an autobiographical note: 'At school, I soon fell under the influence of Polish history and literature. I was fascinated by Polish nationalism, despite its Catholic trappings. And I made it my own'.[57] Radek, his pen name throughout his political life, was taken from a Polish novel. Radek's political itinerary was that of an outsider. From Polish nationalism, he progressed to the social democracy of the Kingdom of Poland and Lithuania (SDKPiL), led by Rosa Luxemburg, whose intransigent internationalism led her to oppose the demand for Polish independence. In 1911, he joined the German social democracy, where he became one of the leading figures of the 'Bremen left' (one of the components of the future Communist party). During the war, in Switzerland, he participated in the Zimmerwald movement and engaged in a long polemic with Lenin on the national question. He rejected the slogan of national self-determination, based in his opinion on a 'total incomprehension of the character of a socialist community', which he conceived as a supra-national universe.[58] The October Revolution brought Radek to Russia; he became a Bolshevik and moved to Moscow, where he worked as secretary of the Communist International. Before being devoured by Stalinism, Radek's life was identified completely with the revolutionary movements of Poland, Germany, and Russia. An assimilated Jew and *vaterlandslos*, he sublimated his lost identity by dissolving it in the world revolution.

Some years after his death in 1924, Parvus became one of the favoured targets of Nazi propaganda: as a Jew, a speculator, and a Marxist, he could be made better than anybody else to incarnate the demonic image of the *Jude* painted by Hitler. Izrail' Lazarevich Gel'fand was born at Berezin, in the province of Minsk, in 1867. He lived with his family in Odessa until the age of twenty, then went to Switzerland to study and, finally, moved to Germany, where he made his name as a brilliant socialist journalist. While maintaining his links with the Russian Marxists – he was a collaborator of *Iskra* – he did not consider himself a *émigré*. Considered dangerous by tsarism, a disagreeable guest for the Prussian authorities, a radical Marxist who was often a thorn in the flesh of the social democratic bureaucracy, Parvus moved tirelessly from one German city to another until the outbreak of the First World War. In a series of articles published in 1900 in the *Neue Zeit*, he analysed imperialism as a system dominated by the historic crisis of the nation-states, henceforth in conflict with the supra-national development of the productive forces.[59] From this vision of capitalism as a global system stemmed his idea of a transcending of national realities. The

---

57   See Radek's autobiography in Haupt and Marie 1969, p. 321.
58   See Lerner 1970, pp. 45–7.
59   See Zeman and Scharlau 1965, pp. 65–6.

controversy between Parvus and Nachman Syrkin, which took place in 1890 at a conference of the Russian-Jewish Society of Berlin, reveals the conflicting orientations dividing the Jewish intelligentsia: 'Alexander Helphand: "Today, nationalism no longer makes sense. Even the making of my jacket shows the overcoming of national divisions in the world; the wool comes from the sheep of Angora, spun in England and woven in Lodz, the buttons come from Germany, the yarn is Austrian ..." Nachman Syrkin: "And the rip in your sleeve comes from the Kiev pogrom"'.[60]

Torn between Poland and Germany, Rosa Luxemburg was the paradigm of the 'non-Jewish Jew', a revolutionary intellectual in which all trace of Jewish identity seemed to be effaced. Her intransigent internationalism, which rejected the right of nations' self-determination, was the theoretical outcome of a vision of the world in which the idea of nationality could no longer find any place. In reality Luxemburg, a Polish Jew integrated into German social democracy, was concerned with the fate of Polish nationality and culture, of which she was a part, despite her violent hostility to Polish nationalism. Even she could be defined as a granddaughter of the *Haskalah*. She was born in 1871 in Zamosc, a town in the heart of the Pale of Settlement, where a third of the population was Jewish. Her middle-class family had been assimilated for two generations, and her father showed a certain inclination toward Polish nationalism. According to Paul Frölich, her biographer and companion in struggle, 'the house of the Luxemburgs was filled with Polish and German culture'.[61] Rosa did not know Yiddish. As a leader of the Polish left, she was always opposed to the Bund. The rare references to the Jewish Question in her writings reveal an assimilationist attitude that never wavered. In a letter to her friend Mathilde Wurm, written from the Wronke prison in February 1917, she characterised herself openly as somebody foreign to the world of the Jews: 'What do you want with this theme of the "special sufferings of the Jews"? I am just as much concerned with the poor victims of the rubber plantations of Putamayo, the Blacks in Africa with whose corpses the Europeans play catch'. She concluded that there was no 'special place' in her heart for the ghetto: 'I feel at home in the entire world, wherever there are clouds and birds and human tears'.[62] And yet it is clear that this declaration of love for the whole of oppressed humanity had a typically Jewish component, namely a universalism that could only be internalised thoroughly by those who had made their lives a meeting point for the cultures of different nations.

---

60   Quoted by Levin 1977, p. 380.
61   Frölich 2010, p. 4. On Rosa Luxemburg's Jewish origins, see also Nettl 1966, vol. 1, pp. 52–3.
62   Luxemburg 2013.

Another figure among the rootless cosmopolitans – although not deprived of a Jewish consciousness – was Charles Rappoport. Born in 1865 in Dakszy, in Lithuania, he frequented both the traditional Jewish primary school and the Yeshiva, the higher school of rabbinical studies. His parents wanted him to be a rabbi, but the *Haskalah* produced in him a profound 'internal revolution', linked to his discovery of German and Russian culture. At Vilnius, he was part of the Jewish revolutionary circle created by Leo Jogiches and, in 1887, wanted by the tsarist police, he decided to emigrate to France. He then went to Switzerland, where he completed his university studies and founded, with Chaim Zhitlovsky, the Union of Russian Revolutionary Socialists (to be distinguished from the orthodox Marxist group of Plekhanov and Aksel'rod). He became a Marxist in Paris in 1903, after his integration in the French socialist movement and his participation in the campaign in defense of Dreyfus. In 1920 he was among the founders of the French Communist party. Unlike the other Russian exiles, who 'lived in their own world and had no contacts with the political life of the surrounding milieu', Rappoport became profoundly integrated in the French workers' movement, considering himself an 'internationalist' and a 'cosmopolitan'. But at heart he remained Jewish. In his memoirs, written in Yiddish, he wrote: 'First, I worked among the Russian intelligentsia, then among the French proletariat, including the Jewish workers of Paris. I have spoken ten languages, but all with a Yiddish accent'.[63]

It is necessary to stress the general indifference shown by the Jewish Marxists of Eastern Europe toward religion, which deeply permeated the whole life of the Eastern Jews. Most of the leaders of the Bund – for example Kossovsky, Abramovich, Kremer, Mill, and Gojansky – were educated in the Jewish higher schools, the Yeshivas, where they learned Hebrew and received a religious training. The discovery of socialism and the pursuit of their studies (often unfinished) in Russian or Western universities signified for them a break with traditional religion and culture and an adhesion to a Marxist, atheist, and *aufklärerisch* worldview. There remained, however, a fundamental link to their community of origin: Yiddish. Unlike the anarchists, who were partisans of an iconoclastic atheism and organised banquets during Yom Kippur, the Bund saw religion as one of the components of Jewish national identity. Messianic references to the struggle for the 'redemption of humanity' were not unusual at its meetings, and its militia defended the entire Jewish community, including synagogues, against the pogroms.[64] To a great extent, this meant nonetheless

---

63   Rappoport 1951, p. 236.
64   Nathan Weinstock has pointed out that despite their atheism, the Bund always avoided 'leading any campaign against the Jewish religion'; see Weinstock 1984, vol. 1, p. 140.

an instrumental attitude, insofar as it was simply the product of an adaptation of orthodox Marxist conceptions to the social and cultural conditions of a Jewish proletariat whose mentality remained strongly shaped by religion. The revolutionaries of Eastern Europe were all rigorously atheist. The young Isaac Deutscher, for example, was compelled to give a proof of his atheism by eating a ham sandwich on the tomb of a rabbi on the eve of Yom Kippur.[65] Vladimir Medem read the Bible at the age of twenty, impelled by an 'aesthetic' but not religious interest, as he put it in his memoirs.[66]

Among these intransigent atheists, a significant exception was Nahman Syrkin (1868–1924), an eclectic Zionist figure midway between Marxism and populism, a fellow traveller of several revolutionary Zionist organisations, a partisan of the Soviet Union and the Third International (without abandoning Zionism) at the beginning of the 1920s, a brilliant writer and propagandist in Yiddish but an advocate of Hebrew as the 'sole national language' of the 'people of Israel'. As Jonathan Frankel has stressed, Syrkin saw in Zionism a 'new version of the old Jewish Messianism'.[67] In 1902 he characterised the classic works of Judaism as a 'literary memorial of the class war between the possessors and the disinherited' and in 1918, in New York, he added that 'the Jewish people is socialist not by necessity, but because the revolution was declared on Mount Sinai'.[68] However, Syrkin seems to be the exception that confirms the rule. Born into a rich family in Mogilev, he combined an orthodox religious education with studies in the German universities (where he was influenced in particular by Dilthey and Simmel) without ever establishing any deep links with the workers' movement of the Yiddishland.

3   Hypotheses

A comparative analysis of the Jewish Marxist intelligentsia in Central and Eastern Europe reveals both common features and significant cleavages, which were related to the political, social, and cultural contexts sketched out above. The homogeneity of the Marxists of Central Europe – assimilated and assimilationist, of bourgeois origin, *Aufklärer*, for the most part indifferent not only to religion but also to the Jewish cultural heritage – contrasts with the heterogeneity and differentiations of the Eastern Marxists. The latter were assimilated

---

65   See Tamara Deutscher's introduction to Deutscher 1968, and Farber 2014.
66   Medem 1979, p. 131.
67   Frankel 1984, p. 306.
68   Ibid.

and Yiddish speaking; assimilationists, partisans of Jewish national autonomy, and even Zionists; the offspring of rich families but in most cases of lower middle class extraction; finally, cosmopolitans, because of tsarist persecution or displacement through Jewish emigration.

As can be seen through some of the above biographical references, all the Jewish Marxists of Eastern Europe were confronted with the reality of anti-Semitism and the dilemmas stemming from their origin. Some fragments of Jewish identity would reappear even among those intellectuals who adhered to Russian socialism after their flight from a *Yiddishkeit* whose horizons were too narrow for them. Yet they would always remain foreign to the influence of the Jewish religion. In Central Europe, on the other hand, in the aftermath of the October Revolution, Marxism became attractive to a nucleus of Jewish intellectuals of romantic background, permeated with a revolutionary messianic spirit. Both Ernst Bloch, the author of *Geist der Utopie* (1918) and *Thomas Münzer* (1921), and Walter Benjamin, whose thought was basically a fusion of Judaism – conceived as a religious and not an ethnic category – and historical materialism, were emblematic of this tendency. Benjamin's syncretic Jewish Marxism rehabilitated Jewish theology, which he evoked in his theses 'On the Concept of History' (1940) with the allegory of the 'little hunchback' who comes to the aid of Marxism in the chess game of history.[69] Benjamin's communist and anarchist Messianic thought, so profoundly shaped by a Jewish theological dimension, presupposed assimilation and, to a certain extent, constituted a reaction to the crisis into which the Jewish-German symbiosis had historically entered. It amounted, in Michael Löwy's definition, to a process of 'cultural anamnesis or religious an-acculturation'.[70] In Eastern Europe, where the Jewish question appeared in its national dimension, the Jewish intelligentsia displayed an absolute indifference to the religious faith of its fathers. It rebelled against religion, which appeared in its eyes in the form of rabbinical obscurantism rather than in a rebellious and spiritual dimension. The result was that inside a community still linked to tradition and respectful of the Torah, the Jewish Marxists were all atheists and *Aufklärer* (none of them experienced the ideological evolution of a S.N. Bulgakov or engaged in the quest for a synthesis of Marxism and religion).[71] One could quote in this respect the Marxist Zionist Moishe Zilberfarb, who proposed to replace 'the principle of the separation of church and state by that of the separation of religion and nation'. He explained that such a measure was necessary to free the Jewish masses

---

69   See Benjamin 1969.

70   See Löw 1985, p. 56.

71   See Scherrer 1976 and 1977.

from the 'vision of the traditional world'.[72] However, the political radicalisation of the Jewish intellectuals was nourished by a common factor in Central and Eastern Europe: anti-Semitism. Obviously enough, Vienna and Berlin did not experience the pogroms of Poland and the Ukraine, but, throughout Central and Eastern Europe, Jewish intellectuals experienced discrimination and marginalisation that favoured their revolutionary engagement. At the turn of the twentieth century, alongside the stereotypes of the Jewish banker and usurer appeared that of the Jewish communist, anarchist, and revolutionary. Often these contradictory figures merged in the arsenal of counterrevolutionary and anti-Semitic propaganda.

Politicization and revolutionary commitment were common features of the Jewish intelligentsia in Central and Eastern Europe. In Western Europe, on the other hand, Jewish Marxists were very much more rare. In France, despite a significant anti-Semitic tradition – it is enough to think of the extraordinary sales of Edouard Drumont's *La France juive* – and the explosion of the Dreyfus affair at the end of the last century, the Jewish community enjoyed full rights and was well established in the institutions. In the general consistory of the Jewish community, one could find industrialists and bankers, but also officers, ministers, and academicians. The French Jewish intellectuals were not pariahs. Under the Third Republic, according to the historian Michael Marrus, 'far from being revolutionaries, Jews considered themselves model citizens, devoted to the cause of the maintenance of the existing order'.[73] Thus, there was no Jewish socialist intelligentsia comparable to that of Germany, Austria, Poland, or Russia.

---

72   Quoted in Suchecky 1986, pp. 393–4.

73   See Marrus 1981. On the attitude toward socialism of the Jewish intellectuals in Western Europe and in the Austro-Hungarian Empire, see Hobsbawm 1979, pp. 77–79.

CHAPTER 3

The German and Austrian Marxists (1880–1920)

Unsurprisingly, in Central Europe the Marxist debate on the Jewish Question turned on two major themes: anti-Semitism and Zionism, which were often approached, especially in the theoretical works of Otto Bauer and Karl Kautsky, in the light of a Marxist theory of nation and nationalism. The transformations of Eastern Jewry were usually neglected or limited to a few general articles on the Bund – in most cases written by Russian Jewish émigrés – published by *Die Neue Zeit*. Zionist socialism, by contrast, was represented in the pages of *Sozialistische Monatshefte*, the journal of the revisionist current of German social democracy led by Joseph Bloch. The most authoritative voice, nevertheless, was that of Karl Kautsky, the 'Pope' of the German social democracy, who codified and vulgarised Marxism as the official ideology of the Second International. Adapting it to evolutionism and social Darwinism, he interpreted historical materialism as a 'positive science' of society.[1] Within this intellectual framework, the idea of a natural, necessary, and linear direction of historical development – a long but unfailing road culminating in socialism – deeply influenced the Marxist attitude toward the Jewish Question. Consequently, the disappearance of anti-Semitism and Jewish assimilation were perceived as ineluctable results of the natural evolution of society.

1   Anti-Semitism

At the end of the nineteenth century, Germany and Austria experienced neither the violence of the Russian pogroms nor the street demonstrations that accompanied the Dreyfus affair in France (in 1898), in which crowds cried 'death to the Jews!' It is Central Europe at the turn of the century, nevertheless, that gave birth to modern anti-Semitism. It amounted for the first time to a genuine mass movement that obtained a stable political representation in Austria (notably in Vienna, under the social Christian municipality of Karl Lueger) and an ephemeral electoral success in Germany in 1893. Anti-Semitism – this term was coined by a Hamburg journalist, Wilhelm Marr, in a successful pamphlet titled *Der Sieg des Judenthums Über das Germanenthum*

---

1   See Hobsbawm 2011, and Andreucci 1979.

(1873) – was first of all a reaction to the process of intensive industrialisation and modernisation that deeply affected the German and Austrian societies. Emancipation had led to a significant economic improvement for the Jews, whereas the old ruling classes (the Junkers) and many traditional professions – artisans, traders, shopkeepers, and peasants – felt threatened and marginalised, as declining groups that had lost their security and social status. In the popular imagination, the Jews represented capitalism and liberalism. They were perceived as the symbol of industrial modernity – the hated *Manchestertum* – that incarnated the collapse of a golden age and an entire system of values. Anti-Semitic agitation started with the financial scandals that broke out in Germany after the crash of the Vienna stock market in 1873, in which some Jewish bankers were involved.[2]

Anti-Semitism codified in ideological terms the transition from traditional, religious Judeophobia to a new, racist form of hostility against the Jews. The anti-Semitic works of authors as different as Wilhelm Marr, Heinrich von Treitschke, Eugen Düring or Georg von Schönerer shared a vision of the Jew as unassimilable, a foreigner in the Germanic *Volk*. Although virulent, the writings of Adolf Stöcker and August Rohling, a German Lutheran predicator and a Catholic theologian at the University of Prague, did not break with the tradition of Christian anti-Judaism, which still allowed the Jews a chance of 'purification' through baptism. But very rapidly anti-Semitism slid toward racism. For Treitschke, the Jews were 'Orientals', a foreign body and a danger to German culture. For Georg von Schönerer, the best-known propagandist of pan-Germanism in Vienna, baptism was absolutely useless when 'the filth is in the race' (*in der Rasse liegt die Schweinerei*). The ideas of Düring were well summed up by the title of his 1880 book: *The Jewish Question as a Problem of Racial Character and the Damage it Causes to the Existence, the Morality and the Culture of the Peoples.*[3]

The birth of modern anti-Semitism was intimately linked to the development of racism as an imperialist ideology. In the anti-Semitic mentality, the Jew appeared as a dangerous being, a bearer of terrible diseases. As defended by social Darwinism, racial biology justified the pillage of Africa and Asia and the subjection of the non-European peoples by the great powers. But, unlike the colonised peoples, whose otherness and inferiority were recognised by the law, the Jews were emancipated. If emancipation had given them the status of citizen, if the colour of their skin, their language, or their culture made them

---

2   See Volkov 2006.
3   On anti-Semitism in Central Europe see Pulzer 1988, and Berding 1988.

indistinguishable inside the nation in which they lived, this simply reinforced the danger related to their negative essence. They appeared as an interior menace, a poisonous agent that had breached all security borders. At the turn of the twentieth century, the *Protocols of the Elders of Zion* symbolised this vision of Judaism as international conspiracy. This is the general context in which the debate of the German and Austrian socialists on anti-Semitism took place.

Victor Adler was one of the first social democratic leaders to open the discussion when, in 1887, he published an article titled *Der Antisemitismus*. In his eyes, Jewish emancipation had been a consequence of the victory of the bourgeoisie over feudalism: as a social system dominated by the 'free competition' of economic forces, capitalism could not continue to enclose into a ghetto a people that had specialised in commerce ('by heredity and by tradition') for several centuries. However, he did not consider the Jews as being at the origin of bourgeois society, because, in his opinion, it was capitalism that had 'created the Jews'.[4] The artisan and the shopkeeper could not understand the laws of the world economy and found a scapegoat in their Jewish competitor: this was the origin of anti-Semitism. In this social conflict, nonetheless, socialism had to remain neutral: anti-Semitism remained basically a 'private' affair of the dominant class. The conflict between Jews and anti-Semites was a problem internal to the bourgeoisie, and socialists should rigorously avoid compromising themselves. Their task, Adler affirmed, did not consist in 'drawing chestnuts from the fire' for one or the other, but in struggling for socialism, which, by eliminating private property and the power of money, 'would finally lead the Wandering Jew to his tomb'.[5]

Two years later, he reaffirmed this position in very clear terms: 'The Austrian workers desire neither "Jewish" nor "Christian" exploitation and nobody could ever mobilise them either for or against the Jews'.[6] To take up the defence of the Jews against anti-Semitic reaction would mean taking the side of one fraction of the bourgeoisie against another, and such a policy was repugnant to the leader of the Habsburg Empire's socialists. In 1891, at the Brussels congress of the Second International, Adler succeeded in forcing a motion that condemned anti-Semitism and 'philo-Semitism' without distinction, despite the protests of American Jewish socialists.[7] His attitude revealed an ideological adaptation to endemic anti-Semitism, and also, without any doubts, the mark of the 'Jew-

---

4   Adler 1929, vol. 8, pp. 346–7.

5   Ibid., p. 348.

6   Adler 1929, vol. 6, p. 73.

7   Adler 1929, vol. 7, pp. 65–6. On Victor Adler's attitude toward anti-Semitism, see Barkai 1970, and Silberner 1963, pp. 234–7.

ish self-hatred' mentioned in the previous chapter. A former pan-Germanist converted to socialism, Victor Adler defended the most radical version of this form of neutralism. At the 1897 congress of the Austrian Socialist party, many delegates (including, notably, Jakob Brod) criticised his attitude,[8] but this discrepancy never seriously affected his leadership.

Adler was not alone. In 1891, an editorial in *Die Neue Zeit* significantly entitled *Anti und Philosemitismus* defended a point of view very similar to his own. Like most editorials in this journal, it was unsigned, but historians generally attribute it to Franz Mehring (although it was not included in his *Werkausgabe*). According to the article, anti-Semitism expressed a romantic, feudal, and hence reactionary form of anti-capitalism. On the other hand, 'philo-Semitism', of which it gave no concrete example, was only a variant of capitalist ideology, the specular image of anti-Semitism. In other words, the Jews represented a superficial, obvious target for the anti-Semites in their struggle against capitalism, waged in the name of the feudal past; the philo-Semites, on the contrary, defended capitalism by disguising themselves as saviors of the oppressed and persecuted Jews. In such a conflict, nevertheless, anti-Semitism was fundamentally less dangerous than philo-Semitism, because the first was opposed to the Jews 'more in words than in deeds', whereas the second was a defence 'in deeds and not in words' of capitalism.[9] Its conclusion joined that of Adler: 'For the conscious worker, the opposition between anti-Semitism and philo-Semitism has never had any meaning'.[10] What is remarkable in this analysis, not devoid of erudite references to young Marx's theory identification of the Jews with money, is simply its date. Barely one year earlier, the aged Engels had written his letter to the *Arbeiterzeitung*, widely reprinted by the social democratic press, in which he vigorously condemned anti-Semitism. *Die Neue Zeit* (Mehring) clearly wished to distinguish itself from Marx's friend, the spiritual leader of the Second International.

The position put forward by Eduard Bernstein in this debate was much more nuanced. An assimilated Berlin Jew, he admitted a certain sympathy for his 'co-religionists' while stipulating that this amounted neither to adulation for the 'Judaism of money' (*Geldjudentum*) nor adhesion to a form of 'Jewish chauvinism'.[11] In his opinion, criticism of the negative aspects of Judaism had nothing to do with anti-Semitic propaganda. Whereas Engels had perceived the social base of anti-Semitism in the petty bourgeois layers affected by the

---

8   See Wistrich 1982, pp. 263–4.
9   Mehring 1891, p. 587.
10   Ibid., p. 588. With regard to this, see also Wistrich 1977, pp. 35–54.
11   Bernstein 1893, pp. 233.

development of capitalism – small traders, landowners, peasants – Bernstein paid attention to the role played by the 'members of the liberal professions': intellectuals, journalists, scholars, employees, in short the representatives of those professional categories who, because of Emancipation, saw the Jews as unwelcome competitors. According to Bernstein, anti-Semitism was not only 'the socialism of fools', to recall a traditional socialist formula, but also the 'lifeline of threatened privilege'.[12] The bastion of this specific form of anti-Semitism was the German academy and its target was neither the 'usurer' nor the *Geldmensch*, but the modern Jewish intellectual.

Almost ignored when it was first formulated, this analysis became, nearly forty years later, the starting point for Arthur Rosenberg's study on the 'sociology of German university reaction.' Rosenberg analysed Treitschke as a typical representative of German scholarly anti-Semitism in the 1880s. A fierce defender of the values of Germanic Christianity against *Zivilisation*, which was considered as an intrinsic feature of the Jewish 'soul', Treitschke expressed the romantic, conservative, and aristocratic reaction to the rise of industrial capitalism. According to Rosenberg, this form of anti-Semitism, widespread in the milieu of German universities at the turn of the twentieth century, had a purely ideological connotation. 'At the time of Treitschke', he wrote, 'and up until the First World War, the German university circles were hardly affected, on the economic plane, by Jewish competition. Under the *Kaiserreich*, the number of Jews, or even people of Jewish descent, among the high-ranking officials, the judges and professors, was very small'.[13] In spite of their prejudices, the Junkers, the true German aristocracy, were accustomed to collaborate with them, insofar as their power benefited from the financial support of the 'Court Jews'. Treitschke's anti-Semitism, on the contrary, was typical of a social layer of parvenus, who cultivated an ideal of aristocratic life. The authentic aristocracy, Rosenberg emphasised, had no need of such an 'ideological corset [*ideologische Korsettstange*]'.[14]

This 'ideological corset', nonetheless, was never carefully scrutinised. Marxists stressed the social roots of German academic anti-Semitism, without criticising its philosophical or historical discourse. They did not engage in the polemics by opposing two outstanding scholars like Heinrich von Treitschke and Theodor Mommsen. Rosenberg simply pointed out the traditional Christian character of this kind of academic anti-Semitism, but neglected its pecu-

---

12   Ibid., p. 234.
13   Rosenberg 1930, p. 81.
14   Ibid., p. 82.

liarities. In fact, Treitschke was not openly racist; he had proposed neither the expulsion of the Jews from Germany nor the withdrawal of their recently granted full citizenship, but his attitude clearly transcended a canonical form of Christian anti-Judaism. He saw the Jews as a foreign body within the German nation (in which religion and stock were inseparable) and a powerful obstacle to its evolution. In depicting the Jews as 'unassimilable', precisely at the moment in which they had achieved their cultural assimilation, Treitschke established a link between old anti-Judaism and modern anti-Semitism.[15] Bernstein and Rosenberg's interpretations were complementary. Treitschke's anti-Semitism mirrored a German intellectual tradition at least two centuries old, and at the same time expressed the fears of the Prussian academy. The Jewish intelligentsia was not a competitor and did not threaten the privileges of the German 'mandarins' as long as it remained excluded from the academy: the roots of anti-Semitism were both social and ideological.

The report made by August Bebel at the Cologne congress of German social democracy in 1893 was undoubtedly the most significant statement against anti-Semitism before the First World War. The anti-Semites had just scored an electoral success assuring them representation in the Reichstag, an event that nobody could ignore. In his report, nevertheless, Bebel went well beyond contingencies and approached the problem in broader terms, establishing 'scientific' criteria for the understanding of Jewish history: 'When a race is persecuted and forced to live in segregation for several generations, when it is separated from its environment, then it is more than natural, on the basis of the hypotheses of Darwin on heredity and the different forms of adaptation, that the original characteristics of this same race will accentuate and develop with time. The persecutions have left an indelible mark on the Jews contributing to the forging of this people that we know today'.[16] Bebel compared the Jews to the Gypsies (causing some hilarity among the congress delegates) and showed an authentic respect for these two persecuted peoples (the persecutions they had suffered, he pointed out, being much worse than anything that had happened as a result of Bismarck's anti-socialist laws). Borrowing his arguments from positivistic evolutionism, Bebel defined the Jews as a race, even if this characterisation was not charged with a negative connotation, and their survival was explained in the light of a socioeconomic determinism conceived

---

15   On Treitschke, see Kampmann 1981, pp. 265–79. See the pieces of the polemic between Treitschke and Theodor Mommsen in Bölich 1965.

16   Bebel 1906, p. 8. On the anti-Semitism of the students in Germany, see Kampe 1985, pp. 10–23.

as a natural – almost biological – law of heredity. Bebel was a talented propagandist, not a theorist, but his analysis reflected perfectly the culture of German social democracy at the end of the nineteenth century.[17]

Anti-Semitism, Bebel argued, was particularly widespread among the small peasants, the shopkeepers, and civil servants, especially after the financial crash of 1873–4. But in Germany it was also widespread among students who, because of 'intellectual overproduction', came into conflict with the Jewish youth that had 'invaded' the Prussian universities. Bebel defined anti-Semitism as a reactionary anti-capitalist movement, 'seeking to hinder the natural evolution of society', which it was necessary to fight in the name of 'progress'. It was a movement without a future but – that was his astonishing conclusion – it could favour the rise of social democracy. Once a certain degree of development was reached, anti-Semitism would 'necessarily, and against its own will, transform itself into a revolutionary movement, working thus for our interests, the interests of the Social Democratic party'.[18] History was advancing toward progress, and anti-Semitism could not obstruct the rise of social democracy.

The analysis of the *Sozialistische Monatshefte* hardly differed. For Wilhelm Ellenbogen, leader of the Austrian Socialist party, anti-Semitism was the 'deformed class movement of a declining social layer, the petty bourgeoisie', and represented a 'feudal-clerical' resistance to the development of industry and capitalism.[19] He attributed its growth in Austria to urbanisation: a mass of Catholic and uncultivated peasants moved to the cities, where they became easy prey to prejudice and demagogy. But Ellenbogen considered anti-Semitism as a 'necessary phase of transition [*eine notwendige Durchsgangsperiode*] in the development of social relations'.[20] Once again, in an evolutionistic and deterministic perspective, anti-Semitism was reduced to a problem of social backwardness, not only transitory but also 'necessary'. In *Die Neue Zeit*, Philip Scheidemann drew the same conclusion: 'The fact that the big anti-Semitic parties can still survive', he wrote, 'proves the extent to which the petty bourgeois and peasant layers in Germany remain backward'. With social and economic progress, anti-Semites would become conservatives or consistent anti-capitalists, like the Social Democrats.[21]

Karl Lueger, leader of the conservative, populist Social Christian party in Austria and mayor of Vienna between 1897 and 1910, confirmed this vision of

---

17   See Steinberg 1979.
18   Bebel 1906, p. 27.
19   Ellenbogen 1899, p. 419.
20   Ibid., p. 425.
21   Scheidemann 1905–6, p. 636.

anti-Semitism. According to the socialist leader Friedrich Austerlitz, Lueger summed up the whole 'petty bourgeois psychology', consisting in the transformation of politics into an exercise in demagogy. An authentic incarnation of the 'small people' with all its prejudices, Lueger 'had not invented anti-Semitism, he had only exploited it'.[22] The historical conditions that engendered this kind of demagogue – very popular among the lower middle class who he won over with his violent campaigns against Jewish banking and finance – were peculiar to Austrian capitalism. In the Habsburg Empire a symbiosis between the industrial bourgeoisie and the old aristocracy had taken place, Austerlitz explained, in terms that recall Arno J. Mayer's concept of the 'persistence of the Old Regime'. This intertwining of bourgeois and feudal forms explained both the weakness of liberalism and the survival of Austrian 'provincialism', the major source of Lueger's electoral triumphs. But the Viennese Jews themselves, Austerlitz added, were also in part responsible for the spread of anti-Semitism. In the Habsburg capital, liberalism from the beginning had a 'particular Jewish flavour', insofar as some 'Jewish cliques' controlled the artistic, cultural, scientific, and financial milieus. He claimed that the Jewish monopoly of the Viennese press had inevitably aroused a widespread hostility toward the Jews. In speaking of 'Jewish domination' (*Judenherrschaft*), Austerlitz – himself the editor of a socialist newspaper, *Arbeiterzeitung*, and himself of Jewish descent – sought not only to draw attention to the great number of Jewish journalists, but above all to 'the subservience of the press to specific Jewish interests. It was a kind of Jewish conspiracy, the legend of the solidarity of the people of Israel was realising itself'. According to Austerlitz, Lueger simply echoed this widespread animosity toward the Jews, the magnates of the press and finance. But Lueger's propaganda was inoffensive in practice: he wished neither to expel the Jews nor to deprive them of civil rights. He restricted himself to 'fighting' them.[23] In other words, in denouncing Lueger's provincial demagogy, Austerlitz reproduced a vision of the 'Jewish conspiracy' that was directly borrowed from the traditional arguments of anti-Semitism.

It is against these ambiguities that the principal Marxist theorists of the Second International, Karl Kautsky and Otto Bauer, positioned themselves in this debate. In an article written in 1903, after the Kishinev pogrom, Kautsky distinguished between Russian and Western anti-Semitism: the aim of the former was to preserve Absolutism from modernisation, whereas the latter was a reaction against accomplished modernity. Thus hatred of the Jews took on a very

---

22   Austerlitz 1900–1, p. 40.
23   Ibid., p. 43.

much sharper and more violent character in Russia, because it was directly carried out by the regime, which used the Jews 'as a lightning conductor during the storms that gather over the autocracy'.[24] Only the workers' movement, by bringing together Jews and non-Jews in a common struggle, could fight this obscurantist reaction.

The argument put forward by Otto Bauer was similar: in the West, where the Jews were often part of the bourgeois class, anti-Semitism was the 'first naïve form of anti-capitalism' (*der erste naïve Ausdruck des Antikapitalismus*); in the East, where a Jewish proletariat existed, anti-Semitism was harmful because it took on a nationalist connotation and divided the workers by engendering a form of nationalism, including among the Jewish workers. Thus, Russian socialism had to fight against this reactionary ideology while rejecting 'Jewish nationalism', which led to the separation of the Jewish workers from 'their Slavic brothers'.[25] The concept of 'Jewish nationalism' is vague here, but, as we will see later, it referred, far beyond Zionism, to any idea of a Jewish cultural autonomy.

This was the intellectual background of the German and Austrian Socialists' reaction to the Dreyfus affair. In 1899, Wilhelm Liebknecht expressed his point of view in an article for *Die Fackel*, the Vienna magazine of Karl Kraus. He was clear: 'I do not believe in the innocence of captain Dreyfus'.[26] He found it simply inconceivable that an officer could be condemned solely because he was Jewish. Such a thing could not happen in Germany, and then still less in Republican France, the country of Jewish emancipation. An officer from a good family could not be accused of spying and of treason against his country without reason. The trial had not proved Dreyfus's guilt, but neither had it proved his innocence; and as a rule in espionage trials proof did not exist, because the incriminating evidence was in the hands of the enemy. Consequently, the campaign in defence of Dreyfus based itself on a 'monstrous presumption', that of his *a priori* innocence. 'That the Jew Dreyfus', he wrote, 'has been sent to Devil's Island solely because of anti-Semitism (*aus blossem Judenhaß*) is a supposition that contradicts all psychology and all common sense'.[27]

---

24   Kautsky 1902–3, p. 306. On Kautsky and anti-Semitism see Jacobs 1992, ch. 1.

25   Bauer 1910–11, p. 94.

26   Liebknecht 1899, p. 1.

27   Ibid., p. 3. On Liebknecht, see Silberner 1963, pp. 208–11. His position was not shared by the whole of the workers' movement, neither in Germany nor in France. It nonetheless reflected a mentality that was fairly widespread at the time, even inside social democratic circles.

Rosa Luxemburg did not share this naïve confidence in the institutions of the Third Republic. In her commentaries of 1898–9 on the affair – published in Dresden on the basis of information drawn from the French press and the letters of numerous correspondents living in France (C. Rappoport, B. Cricevsky, I. Urbach) – she openly took up the defence of the captain. However, this did not mean support for the bourgeois *dreyfusarde* campaign. In relation to this, the attitude of Jaurès appeared to her to be timid and weak. In her opinion he should have seized the opportunity of this trial that had captured the attention of the whole of France to intensify anti-militarist propaganda. In Luxemburg's eyes, the Dreyfus affair could be explained neither as the aberration of some reactionary circles nor as the sudden upsurge of archaic forms of anti-Semitism; it was, on the contrary, the symptom of a deep crisis, of a veritable decomposition of French society: 'Four social factors are manifested in the Dreyfus case that make it an interesting question for the class struggle: militarism, chauvinism/nationalism, anti-Semitism and clericalism'.[28] Rosa Luxemburg did not interpret Anti-Semitism as an expression of social backwardness, but rather as one of the aspects of the ripeness of capitalism in a country where 'bourgeois society is declining not too slowly but too rapidly'.[29] The Dreyfus affair, however, primarily revealed the dangers of militarism, in relation to which anti-Semitism was reduced to something of little importance. Kautsky shared this assessment. His support for the *Dreyfusards* was unambiguous – he gave to Jaurès the merit of having saved the honour of French socialism and he affirmed his conviction that the working class should not remain neutral – but this battle was directed against militarism and political reaction, not against anti-Semitism.[30]

In short, Central Europe's Marxists shifted from the initial identification of anti-Semitism and philo-Semitism (Adler and Mehring) to a clearer position against anti-Semitism (Bebel). All of them interpreted anti-Semitism as a form of social backwardness that was doomed to disappear with economic development. It extolled a romantic and reactionary ideology, but its roots were economic, brought about by the fear of Jewish competition.

In fact, the positivistic clichés of the Marxism of the Second International excluded the possibility of a modern anti-Semitism. 'The current anti-Semitism', Kautsky wrote in 1890, 'is an ephemeral and narrow [*ephemere und bornierte*] movement, locally and temporally limited'.[31] In his eyes, anti-Semitic

---

28   Luxemburg 1971, p. 82.
29   Luxemburg 1972, p. 268.
30   Kautsky 1899, p. 1.
31   Kautsky 1890, p. 23.

ideology was medieval, retrograde, and reactionary, and he neglected or misunderstood the consequences of the transition from religious anti-Judaism to
racial anti-Semitism: the first sought the conversion of the Jews; the second was
directly opposed to Emancipation. He persisted in considering as an archaic
prejudice a movement and an ideology that were the product of modernity.

2   **Zionism**

Political Zionism was born, at the turn of the twentieth century, in response
to the crisis of Jewish Emancipation. It embodied the reaction of a sector
of the (assimilated) Western Jewish intelligentsia to the rise of modern anti-
Semitism, and the echoes that this reaction had within Eastern Jewry, which
had been deeply transformed by a process of modernisation and secularisation
(the *Haskalah*). Some basic assumptions of the Zionist ideology, in particular
the vision of anti-Semitism as an eternal and immutable historical reality, were
not completely new, but differed from those of a pre-Zionist intellectual like
Leo Pinsker, the author of *Auto-emancipation* (1881), who conceived of Jewish
liberation as an aspect of a process of emancipation of the whole of oppressed
humanity. Theodor Herzl, the founder of modern Zionism, abandoned this universalist perspective to develop a typical nationalist movement, seeking the
construction of a Jewish state. A Viennese journalist, Herzl was a completely
assimilated Jew of Hungarian origin who had converted to Zionism in Paris as
a result of the impact of the Dreyfus affair. His vision of Zionism had neither the
socialist dimension of Moses Hess nor the spiritual dimension of Nathan Birnbaum, but was rooted in imperialism and conservative liberalism. For Herzl,
the Jews should accomplish the historical mission of bringing Western civilisation to Palestine. Imbued with a strong colonialist and Eurocentric spirit, his
Zionism secularised the biblical image of *Eretz Israel* in the form of a modern
Jewish state – a kind of Jewish copy of the German Empire – superimposed
onto the historic reality of Arab Palestine.[32]

In general, Marxists interpreted the birth of political Zionism as a new, somewhat bizarre form of Jewish nationalism. For German-speaking Jewish Marxists, it only echoed a world they had left behind and of which they no longer
wished to be part. 'A movement that wishes to support a modest philanthropic
work, whose premises completely contradict reality and whose goals are from

all points of view utopian, can only fail':[33] published in 1913 in the *Arbeiterzeitung*, this sentence perfectly summed up the socialist vision of Zionism.

In 1893, Julius Ignatieff (Parvus) analysed in *Die Neue Zeit* the birth of Jewish nationalism and a Jewish workers' movement in Russia. Probably referring to a May Day demonstration in Vilnius, in Lithuania, he observed that two socialist leaders had harangued the crowd and criticised Zionism in Yiddish (*im jüdische Jargon*). Under the pressure of anti-Semitic persecutions in the Tsarist Empire, the nationalists had elaborated a project for the 'redemption of Judaism' through the colonisation of Palestine or Argentina, where the Jews could build 'an independent national economy'. But the capitalists would not cease to be capitalist in Palestine and the Jewish workers had no interest in emigrating there to be exploited by a Jewish boss. The solution to the Jewish question, he suggested, lay in a class struggle 'without distinction of race or religion ... for the redemption of humanity (*für die Erlösung der Menscheit*)'. According to Parvus, the Jewish workers, nonetheless, had developed a 'national sentiment' rooted in cultural values. Instead of denying their 'ethnic belonging' (*Volksangehörigkeit*), they should cultivate 'a nationalism of light and not of shadows, of culture and not of barbarism, a nationalism that is not xenophobic but the bearer of fraternity between peoples'.[34]

Ignatieff emphasised three fundamental points: a) there was in Russia a Jewish proletariat that had developed a consciousness of its class interests and organised itself; b) the Jews of the Eastern Europe represented an oppressed nation; c) the Jewish Question would find a solution through the class struggle in the Diaspora and not by the colonisation of Palestine or another country. These conceptions mirrored the strategic assumptions of the Bund but certainly were not unanimous. Once again in the pages of *Die Neue Zeit*, in 1895, B. Emmanuel considered Zionism to be a product of Emancipation, which had led to the formation of a Jewish bourgeoisie at odds with the old dominant classes now confronted with 'competitors emerging from the ghetto'.[35] This conflict had engendered a renaissance of Judaism, of which Zionism constituted one of the most remarkable and significant aspects. Emmanuel foresaw a growth of Zionism in Eastern Europe, where it could also attract the impoverished petty bourgeoisie. Excluded from nascent industries, the small traders and artisans were turned into *luftmenshn* and, seeking an alternative to their decline, were attracted by the myth of the colonisation of Palestine. Emmanuel certainly did not deny the obstacles facing Zionism – in his opinion Palestine,

---

33   Quoted by Wistrich 1981, p. 124.
34   Ignatieff 1893, pp. 176–9.
35   Emmanuel 1895, p. 599.

'a strip of land between the sea and the desert', was 'to a great extent unsuitable for colonisation'[36] – but recognised its virtues. This point of view, nevertheless, was unacceptable to the Jewish Socialists of Galicia. For them, Zionism was nothing but the political movement of a layer of assimilated Jewish intellectuals – their failure to publish a newspaper in Yiddish proved their marginality. In Galicia, where the proletariat formed 30 percent of the Jewish population, Zionist propaganda could only serve as a diversion from the class struggle and, consequently, it had to be fought in the same way they fought the rabbis, 'the kosher pots and the *tephilims*'.[37] In 1896, the publication of Herzl's *Der Judenstaat* provoked in *Die Neue Zeit* a brief, ironic, and piquant review by Jakob Stern, who depicted as 'bizarre' and 'utopian' the idea of creating a Jewish state in Palestine. The Jewish capitalists felt themselves well protected by the 'civilised countries' and Zionism had no interest for them.[38] A more closely argued criticism was put forward by Johann Pollak at the first World Zionist Congress held in Basel in 1897, where he criticised the Zionist vision of the Jews as a nation. In his eyes, the Jews of Western Europe were very different from their co-religionists in Russia or Poland: 'The English, French, or German Jew has nothing in common with the Russian or Polish Jew, and the difference in their perceptions (*Empfindungsweise*) is not overcome through religion. On the contrary, the religious feeling modifies itself according to the particular cultural conditions of the country'.[39] A common language spoken by the Jews did not exist, and even Yiddish, this Judeo-German (*judendeutsch*) 'dialect' that was postulated as a language, varied considerably between Russia, Poland, and Galicia. Thus, because they were differentiated on the cultural, linguistic, and religious levels, the Jews were not a nation. The concept itself of a 'Jewish people' was mistaken because, in reality, it was divided into classes with different social interests. The proletariat was hostile to Zionism, which, in the best case, could only represent an embryonic response to oppression by the more backward sectors of the Jewish working class. Finally, he saw Zionism as an 'ephemeral manifestation', a movement created by a nucleus of romantic intellectuals 'by which a nation that is no longer living presents itself for the last time on the scene of history, before disappearing definitively'.[40] There was no alternative to assimilation, and Zionism was only the last historical expression of Judaism before its disappearance from the stage of history.

---

36   Ibid., pp. 602–3.
37   Häcker 1895, p. 760.
38   Stern 1896–7, p. 186.
39   Pollak 1897–8, p. 598.
40   Ibid., p. 600.

The attitude toward Zionism of the *Sozialistische Monatshefte*, the journal of the revisionist current of the SPD, was much more benevolent. In 1897, Sergei Njewsorow canonically interpreted Zionism as a product of anti-Semitism and stigmatised the project of a 'Jewish state' as a 'bourgeois fiction' (*eine bürgerliche Fiktion*). In his eyes, however, Zionism was not a reactionary but a 'democratic and progressive' movement that contributed to 'the moral advancement of Judaism'.[41] Behind this statement there was a positive vision of both colonialism and the Jewish identity. The intellectual father of revisionism, Eduard Bernstein, was fairly close to Njewsorow. His scepticism concerned the feasibility of a Jewish state in Palestine, a province of the Ottoman Empire where the Jews formed a small minority of about an eighth of the population. Zionism illustrated the 'despair' (*Verzweiflung*) into which anti-Semitism had plunged the Jews of Europe,[42] not the harmful character of colonialism. On the latter, he had already explained very clearly his position in 1897: 'We will condemn and struggle against certain methods of repression of the savage peoples, but not against the fact that they are subjected in order to impose on them the law of a superior civilization'.[43]

During the First World War, Bernstein reaffirmed his feeling of belonging to the German nation – 'I am not a Zionist, I consider myself above all as German' – but appreciated in Zionism a 'value for cultural life', insofar as it was not a form of Jewish chauvinism. Zionists could also be 'authentic cosmopolitans [*echter Weltbürger*]' involved in the creation of 'the great family of the peoples'. Bernstein distinguished three complementary types of Jewish identity: the feeling of belonging to the nation in which they live (*Landespatriotismus*); the solidarity for their people (*Stammespatriotismus*); and finally what he called 'cosmopolitan patriotism [*weltbürgerlichen Patriotismus*]'. Nations defined themselves, in Bernstein's view, in relation to international culture, which they could enrich with their specific contribution. As a consequence of their history, the Jews were 'born pacifists',[44] that is, the natural bearers of cosmopolitanism and the spirit of conciliation between the nations.

It was a leader of Poale Zion, Leon Chasanowich, who illustrated in the *Sozialistische Monatshefte* the more orthodox arguments of Zionist socialism. He criticised the abstract cosmopolitanism of Western Marxism, which led to the 'nebulous utopia' of a homogeneous humanity 'without flesh or blood'. For him, internationalism implied a 'progressive and defensive nationalism of the work-

---

41   Njewsorow 1897a, p. 648.

42   Bernstein 1913–14, p. 745. On Bernstein and the Jewish Question, see Jacobs 1992, ch. 2.

43   Bernstein 1897b, p. 109. See also Haupt and Rebérioux 1967, and Andreucci 1979.

44   Bernstein 1917, pp. 32–49.

ing class' within the perspective of a free cultural development of any single national community.[45] In Eastern Europe, only a narrow Jewish elite was assimilated, whereas the proletariat, the great majority of the Jewish population, developed its own national language and culture. According to Chasanowich, the colonisation of Palestine was necessary for the national renaissance of Judaism, but it could not exhaust the 'life will' of the Jewish people, which was tangible even in the Diaspora. 'The Poale Zion', Chasanowich stated, 'does not share the pessimistic vision of bourgeois Zionism on the Diaspora'.[46] His arguments in defence of Palestine combined a kind of Marxist Physiocracy with a more classical form of colonialism. On the one hand, he posited that the crisis of capitalism could only be overcome through a 'return to agriculture', an economic field historically neglected by the Jews; on the other hand, Zionism could fulfil a 'civilising mission' in an economically and culturally backward country through the introduction of Western culture and techniques. This Jewish settlement, wrote the Poale Zion leader, was not opposed to the indigenous Arab population. Zionism, he wrote,

> cannot deny the existence of an indigenous population in Palestine (as is the case throughout the world!). The methods of culture introduced by the Jews and unknown to the Arabs would permit mass settlement but at the same time pave the way for the cultural and economic ascent of the Arabs ... It would be simply ridiculous to speak of a Jewish colonial policy conducted through violence and rejected by social democracy. The Jews would carry out a civilising mission in the best sense of the term [*eine im beste Sinn des Wortes zivilisatorische Aufgabe*] opening Palestine to modern culture.[47]

In the course of time, however, the Jews would at last form the majority of the Palestinian population. Following a kind of historical, natural law, an inferior nation had to be replaced by a superior one.

If one puts aside Chasanowich's theory of the 'return to agriculture' conceived as a 'necessity of the epoch', what is most striking in his argument is his Eurocentric view of the world, which identifies 'progress' with the 'civilising mission' of the West. The Jewish settlers, bearers of a superior culture, would enlighten the Arab fellahin of Palestine. At that time, Chasanowich did not imagine that a Palestinian nation might enter into conflict with Zionism. He saw

---

45   Chasanowich 1914, p. 963.
46   Ibid., p. 967.
47   Ibid., p. 971.

the world outside Europe as a tabula rasa, peopled by non-historical nations, as an area open to colonisation. In short, Poale Zionists thought the Jewish settlers could educate – 'assimilate' – the Palestinian Arabs in the same way in which the German and Austrian Marxists like Kautsky and Bauer believed in Jewish assimilation in Eastern Europe. Colonialism was the common ground between the Zionist Marxists of the Russian Poale Zion and the revisionist current of German social democracy, which opened to the former the columns of its theoretical journal. In 1920, after the Balfour Declaration, the *Sozialistische Monatshefte* would characterise the Zionist project in these terms: 'Like any form of colonization, the Zionist-Jewish colonization of Palestine aims to develop the productive forces of the country and is then a factor of cultural progress'.[48]

To sum up the broad lines of this debate, orthodox Marxists criticised Zionism for three main reasons. First of all, it was a chimerical project, insofar as Palestine did not possess the objective conditions for the construction of a modern state and was inhospitable to the point of rendering vain any project of Jewish mass immigration. Second, it represented a historically anachronistic idea because it obstructed the dominant tendency to assimilation and wished to revive a Jewish nation that had disappeared at the end of the Middle Age. Finally, it was a reactionary form of Jewish nationalism, the reflected image of anti-Semitism. At least up until the Balfour Declaration in 1917, the German and Austrian Marxists considered Zionism as a nationalist current animated by a narrow intellectual elite, supported by some philanthropists from the big Jewish bourgeoisie, but deprived of a mass base and, above all, without a future. Besides this clearly dominant position, there were also the revisionists and the Zionist Socialists, who on the contrary stressed two positive aspects of the Zionist movement: its cultural function inside the Diaspora and its 'civilising mission' in Palestine.

Despite their differences, these two approaches shared the same Eurocentric prejudices: they were inspired by the idea of Progress and rooted in a conception of history that assumed Western Europe as a paradigm. Thus – as we shall see in detail – for Bauer and Kautsky, assimilation, once realised in Western Europe, would inevitably follow in Eastern Europe with the force of a 'natural law'. And even the Zionists, for whom assimilation would take place in Palestine under the form of a Westernised Jewish state, strongly claimed a Eurocentric view. In both cases it was a question of eliminating the Jewish 'anomaly', that of a minority transgressing the political semantics of Western modernity: sovereign state, homogeneous nation, and unified territory.

---

48   See Wistrich 1976, pp. 126–7.

3   The Paradigm of Assimilation: Otto Bauer

A chapter of Otto Bauer's famous book *The Question of Nationalities and Social Democracy*, published in Vienna in 1907, is devoted to the Jewish Question. His criteria for defining the national phenomenon were as much cultural as socioeconomic, insofar as he reformulated in Marxist terms an idea of 'community' (*Gemeinschaft*) initially forged by the German romantic sociologist Ferdinand Tönnies. Bauer defined the nation as a 'community of destiny' (*Schicksalgemeinschaft*), stipulating that community did not mean homogeneity or identity.[49] The core of this conception was the common culture, which acted as a historical legacy within a collective body (the 'historic element within us'). Conceived as the cultural dimension internalised by each individual, the nation was not necessarily linked to territory but could also be 'extraterritorial'. On this basis, the Austro-Marxists – Karl Renner already before Bauer – viewed national-cultural autonomy as a proper answer to the centrifugal pressures that then traversed the Habsburg Empire. The principle of national autonomy had been inserted into the programme of social democracy at the 1899 Brünn congress (in the sense of territorial and not personal autonomy), in the context of a policy seeking the 'conservation and development of the national individuality of all the Austrian peoples'.[50] In this perspective, the nation, crystallised in a community of culture but not necessarily circumscribed into a territory, could survive and develop in a world without borders, classes, or states. Despite appearances, however, it was not a nationalist conception. Bauer did not reject cosmopolitanism, which he considered as inherent in modern society; he thought, rather, that international culture (linked to the ever-more rapid diffusion of technical, scientific, and literary novelties in the world) was absorbed by the different nations according to their specific 'national perception [*Wahrnehmung*]'. International culture was susceptible to reinforce and enrich national particularities instead of suppressing them, which implied a conception of the nation as a living historical entity. Such a theory, which recognised the possibility of an extraterritorial nation, was perfectly fitted for the Eastern Jewry, and it is not astonishing that the Russian Bund enthusiastically adopted it. Bauer, however, denied to the Jews the status of a nation, at least in the modern sense of the term. In his opinion, Jews had lived for some centuries in the interstices of feudal society, as the sole representatives of monetary exchange inside a natural economy in which com-

---

49   Bauer 1975–80, vol. 1, p. 172. See Davis 1967, pp. 149–57; and Weill 1987, pp. 23–46.
50   The Brünn program is reproduced in Haupt, Löwy, and Weill 1974, pp. 204–7.

modity production was very limited. In Bauer's view, this socio-economic function – the foundation of their ethnic specificity – had been preserved in Eastern
Europe, where the Jews remained intermediaries (as small traders or hawkers)
between the peasants and the urban market. Under feudalism, the Jews had
formed a nation, founded not only in a common culture (language and traditions) but also on a 'community of blood' (*die Gemeinschaft des Blutes*).[51]
From that time, 'race' and culture had coalesced in a specific Jewish destiny,
different from that of other nations. Nonetheless, the rise of capitalism – an
economic system founded on generalised commodity production – broke the
Jewish monopoly of commerce; monetary circulation developed and the Jews
thus merged with the surrounding peoples. Deprived of their specific destiny,
they assimilated to other cultures, but this process was not finished yet.[52] The
emancipated Jews of Central Europe had abandoned their traditional clothing but remained recognisable because of their gestures; they had dismissed
religious orthodoxy but had replaced it with Reform Judaism; finally, they had
established normal relations with non-Jews but conserved their endogamic
practices and retained a 'strong consciousness of the community to which they
belonged'.[53] Assimilation was the dominant tendency but was not yet concluded: 'Whatever the rhythm of the process of assimilation, one cannot doubt
that it will be accomplished everywhere: capitalism and the modern state are
working worldwide to destroy the old Judaism [*das alte Judentum*]'.[54]

The definition of the Jews as a 'community of blood' was a commonplace at
the beginning of the twentieth century (including among the Jews themselves),
but Bauer did not emphasise it, and paid attention instead to assimilation as
a cultural process. In Eastern Europe, the Jews still constituted a nation, but
they were a 'non-historical nation' (*einer geschichtlosen Nation*), that is, a community deprived of a national literature, which retained only a culture in a
state of collapse and a 'degenerate' language.[55] If they were progressively losing
their national character, it was because of the inconsistency and immobility of
their culture, which could not resist assimilation, and not only because of their
extraterritorial status. In the eyes of Bauer, the renaissance of Jewish culture in
the Tsarist Empire and in Habsburg Galicia was an ephemeral phenomenon.
Consequently, the claim for Jewish national autonomy was simply anachronistic, insofar as it meant the creation of Jewish schools in places where Jewish

---

51　　Bauer 1975–1980, vol. 1, p. 416.
52　　Ibid., p. 418.
53　　Ibid., p. 419.
54　　Ibid., p. 420.
55　　Ibid., p. 421.

children were already learning the language of the majority nation. His argument, one could observe, was quite contradictory: would an education in their mother tongue, Yiddish, have prevented Jewish children from also learning German, Russian, or Polish? Why then was Bauer in favour of the creation of Czech schools in Vienna? After having devoted a whole chapter of his book to the reawakening of the 'peoples without history' and to the demonstration of the right of the Czechs to belong to the community of modern nations, Bauer suddenly changed his mind when it came to the Jewish Question. In the face of the renewal of Yiddish culture, the reaction of this very sophisticated Marxist thinker did not differ very much from that of an ordinary Viennese Jew.

This appeared quite clearly when Bauer discussed the 'mistrust' felt by Christian workers toward the Jews. In his view, this was not a symptom of anti-Semitism but only of intolerance in the face of the 'foreign appearance' of the Jews:

> Inasmuch as their accent, their gesticulations, their clothes, their customs hurt [*verletzen*] the feelings of their Christian class comrade, their foreman, their boss, the old economic opposition between peasant and Jewish merchant transmits itself again under the form of instinctive aversion, of aesthetic displeasure [*eines ästhetischen Mißfallens*], to the descendants of the one and the other, although the descendant of the Christian peasant has now become a worker in the same way as that of the Jewish merchant.[56]

In order to bring about class unity between the Christian and Jewish workers, the latter should adopt the 'customs' of the former. In conclusion, Bauer defended the right of the Czechs to national autonomy – not only in Bohemia, but also in Austria – and refused it to the Galician Jews, for whom he prescribed assimilation.

Bauer paid attention to the Galician Jewry – 800,000 people, which was 11 percent of the population at the beginning of the century – in an article written in 1912 for the journal *Der Kampf*. For the most part 'poor petty bourgeois' (*arme Kleinbürgeren*), the Galician Jews constituted 'still a particular nation with its own language – what could be called a jargon – customs, and traditions'.[57] Unlike their assimilated Western co-religionists, they still remained a 'foreign people' here, but they could not escape assimilation: 'This particularity

---

56   Ibid., pp. 431, 391.
57   Bauer 1975–80, vol. 8, p. 588.

of the Judaism of Eastern Europe', wrote Bauer, 'is a consequence of the backwardness of the regions where they settled. Capitalist development will also lead the Jews of Eastern Europe to assimilation. Any attempt to artificially block assimilation and to cultivate inside Judaism an ideology opposing assimilation goes against progress, is reactionary'.[58]

Still in 1912, Bauer wrote a long study on the problem of the assimilation of ethnic minorities, which he defined as a 'necessity corresponding to a natural law' (*eine naturgesetzliche Notwendigkeit*).[59] Thus, he formulated four 'laws of assimilation'. The first concerned *number*, the principal factor of resistance of a minority threatened by assimilation. The small national minorities assimilated themselves rapidly and easily, except in the case of the 'peasant linguistic islands' (for example, the Germans in Galicia or the Croats in lower Austria), the 'linguistic islands of the small towns' (the German villages of Hungary and Bohemia), and the Jewish ghettoes of Eastern Europe. The second law dealt with *residence*: assimilation was easier where the minority lived intertwined with the majority, without forming an ethnic concentration or a linguistic island. The third law concerned *race* and *culture*. Racial and cultural proximity between the minority and the majority was an important factor in the process of assimilation. The Jews, like the Chinese and the blacks in the United States, did not assimilate very quickly because of their 'racial specificities'.[60] The fourth law, finally, was related to *social integration*: ethnic minorities could assimilate themselves more easily when they were no longer identified with a profession or a specific social function. The Jewish bourgeoisie, for example, tended to assimilate because it had been able to join the dominant classes of the dominant nations.

Number, place of residence, race, culture, and class identity constituted for Bauer the indispensable objective conditions for assimilation,[61] outside of which any attempt at forced or artificial assimilation was doomed to failure. He gave the negative example of the *Marranos*, who remained crypto-Jews (*Kryptojuden*) until the eighteenth century, when the development of capitalism activated the law of social integration and consequently the others followed.[62] In a similar way, the Jews of Eastern Europe had resisted assimilation

---

58   Ibid., p. 589.

59   Ibid., p. 596.

60   Claudie Weill observed that in Bauer's book, 'the concept of race remains fluid: sometimes it is a community of limited ancestry that undertakes no communication with the exterior, sometimes it is individuals united by common physical characteristics' (the Jews); see Weill 1987, pp. 30–1.

61   Bauer 1975–80, vol. 8, pp. 597–603.

62   Ibid., p. 620.

because of their number (six million at the turn of the century), spatial concentration (the Jewish villages, or the Jewish districts of the big cities), culture
and religion (Yiddishkeit) and economic structure (small traders and artisans),
but their assimilation remained a historic goal. The backwardness of Eastern European Jewry could only delay assimilation, not impede it. The Jews of
Vienna showed the road to follow.[63]

The Marxist Zionists promptly reacted to Bauer's book in the pages of the
Sozialistische Monatshefte. In 1908–9, Maxim Anin devoted a series of articles
to the analysis of the socio-economic structure of the Eastern Jews, concluding that assimilation was objectively impossible. Shattered by the penetration
of capitalist social relations, they were facing an economic impasse that transformed many impoverished artisans and small traders into *luftmenshn* or compelled them to emigrate, and at the same time obstructed their assimilation.
The development of capitalism in Eastern Europe might perhaps bring the
emancipation of the Jews (as in the West) but also built 'the ever higher walls of
a socioeconomic ghetto' (*eines sozialökonomischen Ghettos*),[64] which rendered
completely vain any hypothesis of assimilation. But Anin also criticised Bauer
because of his negative vision of the cultural dimension of Jewish life in Eastern
Europe: 'When Bauer, like the great majority of European comrades, speaks of
Judaism, he thinks of the assimilated Jewish bourgeoisie or the orthodox Jewish
fanatics. But there also exists another Judaism – the enormous majority of the
Jewish people – which is neither assimilated nor the prisoner of religious orthodoxy, which struggles energetically and courageously for the creation of new
forms of national self-determination'.[65] In a sharp conclusion, he denounced
the absurdity of Bauer's position, which 'preached national suicide' to the Jews,
and put it bluntly: 'But is it not a psychological nonsense to advocate assimilation as a program, as a goal of action?'[66]

Bauer's theory, which corresponded to the general orientation of the Austro-
Marxists, had a strong impact on the socialist debates of the Habsburg Empire.
The Jewish Social Democratic party of Galicia, founded in 1905, demanded
the right to be recognised as a national section of the unified party (*Gesamt-
partei*) and, at the same time, cultural national autonomy for the Galician Jews.
Despite their references to the congresses of Vienna (held in 1897, which reor-
ganised the party into six autonomous national federations) and Brünn (1899,
which adopted a national programme), the Jewish Socialists had been expelled

---

63   See Pfabigan 1986, p. 109.
64   Anin 1908, p. 618.
65   Anin 1909, p. 235.
66   Anin 1911, p. 397.

by the (Polish) Galician social democrats and stigmatised as separatists by the whole party.[67] In 1906, Jindrich Grossmann, secretary of the Galician Bund, had answered in advance to all the arguments of Bauer's book: 'For us, Jewish nationality is a reality founded on the experience of life and not of metaphysical speculations. It is because of this that we want our individuality to be taken into account like that of others'.[68] The Jewish Socialists had created a party in Galicia, where there was a Jewish nation, not in Austria or Bohemia, where the Jews were assimilated. After all, Grossmann added, it was up to the Jews themselves to decide if they constituted a nation or not, something that should be an elementary principle for Marxists. He defended Yiddish as a modern and living language with the following words:

> The Poles do not consider the 'jargon' as a language, because of its German, Polish, and Hebrew elements! But can a language spoken by eight to nine million people not be a language? A language in which the loftiest ideas of the revolution are learned, in which it is possible to read the classics of modern literature, in which one can read Marx's *Communist Manifesto* and *Capital*, Kautsky's *Erfurt Program* and *Social Revolution*, and so on, all this does not suffice to define our idiom as a language?[69]

In relation to the definition of the Eastern Jews as a *geschichtloses Volk*, Grossmann recalled that Marx had included even the Czechs in this category. The Austrian Marxists had rectified this erroneous judgment and recognised the Czechs as a nation: why not the Jews?[70]

It should be added that the Galician Bund was born because the Jewish workers' movement could not identify with the social democracy of the region, which displayed the Polish flag and considered the Jews as Polish citizens of the Mosaic confession. Initially disavowed and accused of separatism, the Galician Bund succeeded at last in imposing its presence. In 1911 it annexed the Jewish federation of the Polish Social Democratic party of Galicia (PPSD), which recognised its complete legitimacy as the representative of the Jewish proletariat (as there was no longer a unified party, the Viennese Austro-Marxists were exempted from the ratification of this accord).[71] It is curious to observe that the only Austrian socialist leader willing to recognise the Jews' right to a 'national exist-

---

67   See Löw 1984, pp. 61–6.
68   Grossmann 1984, p. 221.
69   Ibid., pp. 223–4.
70   Ibid., pp. 224, 227.
71   Wistrich 1982, p. 322.

ence', Engelbert Pernerstorfer, was not Jewish. Moreover, it is significant that he expressed his point of view, in 1916, not in the party press but in Martin Buber's Zionist journal, *Der Jude*. He recognised the 'right to national existence' of the Jews of the East, because they represented a nation with its 'own spirituality [*Geistigkeit*]' like any 'nation of culture [*Kulturnation*]'.[72]

4 The Paradigm of Assimilation: Karl Kautsky

Karl Kautsky analysed the Jewish Question in an article entitled 'Das Judentum', published in 1890 in *Die Neue Zeit*. His approach was both sociological and historical: he studied anti-Semitism as a phenomenon dating from Antiquity and sought its origins in the Diaspora, which had not transformed the Jews from farmers into settlers but, rather, into traders. In the towns, they had created their own communities (*Judenkolonien*), but they still considered Palestine as their country, and, consequently, their settlement in the Diaspora had a 'provisional' character.[73] According to Kautsky, the Jews were the only people who had succeeded in preserving their own 'nationality' during the process of Hellenisation and, subsequently, under Byzantine domination. In the Middle Ages, they formed a nation coinciding with a specific social layer of traders and usurers: 'To be Jewish in the Middle Ages did not mean only being a member of a particular nation but also of a particular profession. To be Jewish meant to be a usurer (*Wucherer*) and vice versa; the Jewish character became that of the usurer and that of the usurer the Jewish'.[74] But capitalism undermined the socioeconomic foundation of the Jewish nation, eliminating the segregation of the Jews into a sole professional branch and transforming them into workers, artisans, and intellectuals. Capitalism had initiated a new Diaspora, which scattered the Jews into different economic activities and would lead in the end to the disappearance of Judaism.

In 1908, Kautsky depicted the Eastern Jews as a community of small traders or hawkers who spoke their own language, Yiddish, or as he put it, 'not Hebrew but a corrupted German (*ein verdorbenes Deutsch*) that separated them from their surroundings'. Kautsky was thus inclined – like Max Weber – to characterise the Jews as a 'caste' (*Kaste*) rather than a nation.[75] In defining the nation as a primarily linguistic and territorial community, he conceived of the Jews of

---

72 Pernerstorfer 1916–17, vol. 1, p. 313.

73 Kautsky 1890, p. 26.

74 Ibid., p. 28.

75 Kautsky 1908, p. 7. See the criticisms of Ratner 1911, pp. 1340–1. On the definition of the Jews

the Diaspora as the vestiges of a former nationality. They possessed no territory and spoke a 'non-language', and thus did not constitute a nation in the modern sense of the term: their historic decline was inevitable, although delayed by their economic function, which contributed to their preservation as a distinct ethnic group.

In his book on *The Origins of Christianity* (1910), Kautsky again wrote about the Jewish nation of the Diaspora ('a nation without peasants, formed exclusively by the urban population', a nation of 'traders'),[76] but he added that it was a nation henceforth deprived of its fundamental constitutive elements, race and language. In *Rasse und Judentum* (1910), Kautsky's analysis was codified in the following formula: 'All that which forms the essence of a nation, they are losing: the territorial community as well as the community of language'.[77] The Diaspora thus marked the end of the Jewish nation. If Judaism had conserved itself through the centuries despite losing its national character, it was thanks to the survival of a 'residue of the former national life', namely religion.

Rasse und Judentum achieves the theoretical elaboration of Second International Marxism on the Jewish Question. Most of the book was devoted to the criticism of 'scientific' theories of race, whose legitimacy was rarely contested at the time. Drawing his inspiration from the ethnologist Ratzel and, more probably, from the Italian positivist anthropologist Cesare Lombroso, Kautsky argued that human races changed continually because of crossbreeds and fusions, adaptation to the surrounding environment (itself evolving), and, finally, social and technical progress that modified the conditions of life of human beings. It was impossible to distinguish inherited racial features from those that had been acquired: 'Racial determination, which appears so evident among the animals, increasingly disappears among men'.[78] On this basis, Kautsky rejected the concept of a Jewish race. The criteria normally adopted to define a race – often very debatable, he admitted – did not correspond to the characteristics of the Jews, as he emphasised by sketching a Lombrosian classification:

a.   only a small minority of Jews, 13 to 14 percent, possessed what could be called the 'Jewish nose';

b.   one could observe a certain resemblance in the form of cranium between the Jews and the other peoples of Eastern Europe;

---

as a 'caste', quite widespread in German sociology at the turn of the twentieth century, see Momigliano 1980.

76   Kautsky 1910, pp. 232–3.

77   Kautsky 1921, p. 55.

78   Ibid., p. 34. See Lombroso 1894. See also Knepper 2013, pp. 171–86.

c.   one found in general the same demographic dynamic among the Jews as
      among the nations in which they lived;
d.   it was not possible to speak of specific Jewish illnesses;
e.   finally, the Jewish accent was the product of the environment of the 'par-
      ticular' life of the Jews and not an inherited characteristic.

Thus, there was no Jewish race: the 'Jewish spiritual type' was the product of two
millennia of urban life. Neither race nor nation, for Kautsky the Jews formed a
caste. In pages that seemed drawn from a manual of social Darwinism, he formulated his theory in these terms:

> It is necessary to ask if natural selection, under the form of the conserva-
> tion of the fittest, has not had a great influence on development. Nonethe-
> less, it is obvious that it has exerted a constant and powerful influence on
> the formation and preservation of the species through the elimination of
> the unfitted to a particular environment … By a constant selection and a
> conscious adaptation to the conditions of life, the Jews have succeeded in
> making up for the baneful consequences of the urban environment with
> more success than the urbanized peasants. In the course of several gen-
> erations, the Jews transformed themselves into an urban people.[79]

In the cities, their commercial specialisation became a 'distinct hereditary trait'
of the Jews. Capitalism, however, had broken down the walls of the ghetto (both
ethnic and economic), and allowed them to accede to other productive activities. Once the socio-economic framework was modified, assimilation became a
natural law. Kautsky described assimilation as a complete disintegration of the
Jewish community, implying the loss of any ethnic and cultural peculiarity. This
process would happen in three phases: linguistic assimilation, conversion and
exogamy. His conclusion was the following: 'It is only in the ghetto, in segregation and under political oppression, in illegality and hostility that the Jew can
survive among the other peoples. On the other hand, he dissolves, he melts
into the surrounding environment, he disappears where he is treated as free
and equal'.[80]

The three steps indicated by Kautsky – linguistic assimilation, conversion
and exogamy – certainly were not the dominant tendencies either in Central or
in Eastern European Jewry, but they remained a horizon of historical progress.[81]

---

79   Ibid., p. 63.
80   Ibid., p. 64.
81   Ibid., p. 73.

Since he conceived of assimilation as a natural tendency of social development, Kautsky was obviously opposed to Zionism, a movement he considered
an objective accomplice of anti-Semitism in that its goal was to 'distance the
Jewish community from today's nations'.[82] The project of colonising Palestine
seemed to him concretely unfeasible and politically reactionary, for several
reasons:

a.   the *Ostjuden* could put an end to their situation of poverty and oppression
      through a revolution in Russia, certainly not by creating a Jewish state in
      Palestine;
b.   the Jews, an urban people for some centuries, could not suddenly trans-
      form themselves into an army of rural settlers;
c.   Palestine was a very poor territory, where the conditions for industrial
      development did not exist (lack of material resources and raw materials,
      non-existence of an internal market capable of supporting local produc-
      tion, deficiency of lines of communication, etc.).

Kautsky defined Zionism as a 'sport for philanthropists and men of letters', seeking to conquer Palestine 'as a world ghetto for the isolation of the Jewish race'.[83]
In 1921, three years after the Balfour Declaration, in a new edition of *Rasse
und Judentum*, he added these significant lines to his critique of Zionism: 'It
is labor that gives a people the right to the land in which it lives, thus Judaism can advance no claim on Palestine. On the basis of the right of labor and
of democratic self-determination, today Palestine does not belong to the Jews
of Vienna, London, or New York, who claim it for Judaism, but to the Arabs of
the same country, the great majority of the population ... In their argument,
the Zionists ignore completely the Arab population or treat it as a negligible
factor'.[84] Unlike most Marxist critiques, which confined themselves to the 'utopian' character of Zionism and its harmful effects on the class struggle in the
Diaspora, Kautsky also took into account the existence of an Arab nation in
Palestine, which would inevitably come into conflict with the project of con-
structing a Jewish state.

Rasse und Judentum ended by celebrating assimilation. In Kautsky's view,
there was a deep discrepancy between the growing engagement of Jews in
avant-garde movements, which made them an 'eminent revolutionary factor',
and the increasingly conservative role of Judaism, which he defined as the 'rope
around the neck of the progressive Jew, one of the last relics of the feudal

---

82   For conceptualising Jewish 'assimilation,' cf. Sorkin 1987, and the case studies gathered in
      Frankel and Zipperstein 1992.
83   Kautsky 1910, p. 84.
84   Ibid., p. 96.

Middle Ages'.[85] In his enlightened and positivist spirit, he identified assimilation with progress: 'We will not have completely emerged from the Middle Ages as long as Judaism still remains among us. The more quickly it disappears, the better it will be for society and for the Jews themselves'.[86]

This attitude was moreover consistent with the Kautskyan version of internationalism. For the editor of the *Neue Zeit*, as we have seen, the pillars of the nation were language and territory. In his critique of the Austro-Marxists, he stressed the importance of centralisation in the capitalist economy, which came into conflict with any idea of national autonomy. Unlike Bauer, who foresaw a growing differentiation between nations under socialism, he formulated the hypothesis of their fusion. Because the nation was a linguistic-territorial community, produced by capitalism and thus transitory, its disappearance under socialism should be accomplished through the transcendence of linguistic pluralism, leading to one or several universal languages, which would impose themselves in a 'Darwinian' fashion through a process of natural selection among the existing languages. This hypothesis, advanced for the first time by Kautsky in his study *Die moderne Nationalität* (1887), was taken up again in 1917 in another text, *Die Befreiung der Nationen*, wherein he wrote that 'the goal is not the differentiation, but the assimilation of nations'.[87] This vision of a 'happy end' to history, in which the destiny of the nations was their dissolution into a universal melting pot, inevitably implied the extinction of Judaism. In this perspective, Jewish national autonomy became 'reactionary', that is, opposed to the march of history and to progress.

---

85   Ibid., p. 93.
86   Ibid., p. 108.
87   Kautsky 1917, quoted by Rosdolsky 1979, p. 204; see also Kautsky 1887, p. 448. On Kautsky's theory of the nation, see in particular Weill 1987, pp. 9–22.

CHAPTER 4

Russian Marxism (1900–20)

To Russian Marxists, the debate between the Bund and socialist Zionism always appeared either useless or incomprehensible. For them, the Jewish Question was not a National Question. Obsessed by the idea that Russia, semi-feudal and semi-Asiatic, had to make up the gap that it had accumulated with the West, they saw both anti-Semitism and Jewish culture as nothing but a legacy of tsarist backwardness. Strangers to both Yiddish language and culture, they identified progress and modernity with assimilation. In this chapter, we shall investigate the assessments of Russian (Lenin, Stalin, and Trotsky) and Polish (Rosa Luxemburg) Marxists.

1 Lenin

Although approached pragmatically, the Jewish Question appears across Lenin's writings, mostly in polemical interventions against the Bund. The Bund's decision to consider itself as an independent Jewish socialist party, as well as its call for a federal reorganisation of both social democracy and the Russian Empire, met with a hostile reaction from Lenin. In the pages of *Iskra*, he denounced the 'nationalism' and 'separatism' of the Bund, which was guilty in his view of undermining the strength and unity of the Russian workers' movement, and stigmatised the project of cultural national autonomy as the product of an 'unfortunate penetration of nationalism'.[1] Recalling the statutes approved by Russian social democrats in 1898, he stressed that, far from being an independent party, the Bund was simply its specific organisation for propaganda among the Jewish workers.[2]

Lenin never abandoned this general approach, but his arguments changed over time. In the articles published in *Iskra* at the beginning of 1903, he constantly depicted the Russian Jews as a distinct nationality. He praised their 'national culture' and, at the same time, rejected Bundist separatism as an attempt to 'erect a Chinese wall around their nationality, their national work-

---

1 *LCW*, vol. 6, p. 422.
2 Ibid., pp. 328–33.

© KONINKLIJKE BRILL NV, LEIDEN, 2019 | DOI:10.1163/9789004384767_006

ing-class movement'.[3] After the second congress of the Russian social democracy, where the split with the Bund took place, Lenin changed his attitude and
strongly denounced federalism. In a new article for *Iskra* in October 1903, the
concept itself of Jewish nation had become a 'Zionist idea absolutely false and
essentially reactionary'.[4] He quoted the 'eminent Marxist theorist Karl Kautsky' for whom, as we have already seen, language and territory were the constitutive characters of the nation. Thereafter, he characterised the 'idea that the
Jews form a separate nation' as politically dangerous and 'absolutely unten-
able scientifically'.[5] Not only did the Jews not possess any territory, but even
their language, Yiddish, despite the prodigious efforts of the Bund to ennoble
it, was not worthy of a civilised nation, as proved by its abandonment by the
emancipated Jews of Western Europe one century earlier. In Lenin's opinion,
the idea of a Jewish nation could only hold back assimilation and preserve a
'spirit of the ghetto' among the Jews.[6] Two years later, however, Lenin's polemical tone had softened considerably. In 1905, the Bolsheviks published a complete account in Yiddish of their last congress: Lenin wrote a brief preface in
which he defined the Jews as a 'nationality deprived of all rights', victims of a
political and economic oppression rooted in the absence of 'elementary civic
rights'.[7] This contradictory oscillation between recognition and negation of the
national character of the Russian Jews also shapes his later writings. In 1913 he
again quoted Kautsky, according to whom the Russian Jews were a 'caste' rather
than a nation, but, at the same time, he criticised Otto Bauer, who did not wish
to extend his concept of cultural national autonomy to the Jews, the 'only extraterritorial nation'.[8] Finally, in his famous 'Critical Notes on the National Question', which appeared in the same year in the theoretical journal *Prosveshchenie*
[*Enlightenment*], he again referred to the Jews as 'the most oppressed and persecuted nation'.[9] This permanent oscillation probably means, as Eddy Kenig
has observed, that Lenin did not consider the Jews as being part of the Russian
nation, but at the same time he strongly called for their assimilation.[10] Pragmatically, he tended to accept the idea of a Jewish nation during periods of
collaboration with the Bund (before the 1903 split and, in 1905, when the Bund

3   Ibid., 518–19.
4   *LCW*, vol. 7, p. 99.
5   Ibid., p. 100.
6   Ibid.
7   *LCW*, vol. 8, p. 495.
8   *LCW*, Vol. 19, p. 506.
9   Lenin 1976, p. 14.
10   See Kenig 1976, p. 6.

and the Bolsheviks jointly called for a boycott of the Duma) and to deny it in phases of conflict (after the 1903 split and, after 1912, when the Bund joined the 'August bloc' created by the Mensheviks).

Taking up a theme already advanced by Anton Pannekoek in *Nation and Class Struggle* (1912), Lenin defended an intransigent internationalism that denied the 'bourgeois' principle of national culture. Socialists should not defend national culture, but rather struggle for an international socialist and democratic culture, which meant to struggle against both Great Russian and Jewish nationalism. In practical terms, that amounted to a claim for assimilation without coercion. 'Jewish national culture', wrote Lenin,

> is the slogan of the rabbis and the bourgeoisie, the slogan of our enemies. But there are other elements in Jewish culture and in Jewish history as a whole. Of the ten and a half million Jews in the world, somewhat over a half live in Galicia and Russia, backward and semibarbarous countries, where the Jews are *forcibly* kept in the status of a caste. The other half live in the civilized world, and there the Jews do not live as a segregated caste. There the great world-progressive features of Jewish culture stand clearly revealed: its internationalism, its identification with the advanced movements of the epoch (the percentage of Jews in the democratic and proletarian movements is everywhere higher than the percentage of Jews among the population). Whoever, directly or indirectly, puts forward the slogan of Jewish 'national culture' is (whatever his good intentions might be) an enemy of the proletariat, a supporter of all that is *outmoded* and connected with *caste* among the Jewish people; he is an accomplice of the rabbis and the bourgeoisie.[11]

From here emerged the idea – subsequently taken up by Kautsky – of a dichotomy between 'progressive Jews' and 'reactionary Judaism': the former were opposed to the latter and could contribute to 'progress' through assimilation. Lenin never paid attention to the existence of a modern and secular Jewish national culture. He identified Jewish culture with either Zionism or religion, and perceived it exclusively as the heritage of a medieval superstition conserved by the rabbis. Isolated and persecuted, the Eastern Jews formed a caste, whereas in Western Europe they had joined the 'civilised world' through Emancipation. Thus, the assimilation of nations was an objective historical tendency brought about by capitalism: could the Jews remain attached to their cultural-

---

11   Lenin 1976, pp. 14–15.

ethnic particularism when capitalism, the universal melting pot, ceaselessly broke down national frontiers? Lenin argued in the name of progress, invariably identified with the West, and claimed that only the 'petty bourgeois reactionary Jews' could be opposed to assimilation. 'No one liberated from nationalist prejudices', he continued, 'can fail to perceive that this process of assimilation of nations by capitalism means the greatest historical progress, the breakdown of hidebound national conservatism in the various backwoods, especially in backward countries like Russia'.[12] To oppose assimilation meant then 'to turn back the wheel of history', not pointing Russia and Galicia in the direction of Paris and New York, but vice versa. He depicted the American 'melting pot' as a model, portraying New York as a kind of mill that 'grinds down national distinctions', and argued that 'what is taking place on a grand, international scale in New York is also to be seen in *every* big city and industrial township'.[13] Ignoring or hiding that New York, precisely at this time, had become one of the capitals of Yiddish culture, Lenin described Jewish assimilation as synonymous with progress: those who supported the idea of a Jewish national culture wished to stop the 'wheel of history'. Seen through the eyes of a Russian Marxist who had affirmed the necessity of a Western-type development of capitalism in Russia (against the Populists), the Jewish world of Eastern Europe with its rabbis and *luftmenshn* appeared as a symbol of cultural backwardness, poverty, and obscurantism. Lenin's insistence on Jewish assimilation was, in the last analysis, only one aspect of his struggle against the archaism of Russian life.

On the other hand, the Bolshevik leader always condemned anti-Semitism as one of the most odious aspects of the backwardness and barbarism of Tsarist Russia. It certainly had very deep roots in Russian society, but its nature and its manifestations stemmed above all from Absolutism. In 1906, Lenin stigmatised those responsible for the Bialystok pogrom:

> The old familiar picture! The police organize the pogrom beforehand. The police instigate it: leaflets are printed in government printing offices calling for a massacre of the Jews. When the pogrom begins, the police are inactive. The troops quietly look on at the exploits of the Black Hundreds. But later this very police go through the farce of prosecution and trial of the pogromists. The investigations and trials conducted by the officials of the old authority always end in the same way: the cases drag on, none of

---

12   Ibid., p. 18.
13   Ibid.

the pogromists are found guilty, sometimes even the battered and mutilated Jews and intellectuals are dragged before the court, months pass –
and the old, but ever new story is forgotten, until the next pogrom.[14]

This was the normal dynamic of a pogrom. To combat anti-Semitic violence,
Lenin proposed the creation of workers' self-defence militias. If the pogroms
amounted to state violence against the Jews, one could obviously not demand
that the state protect the Jewish population from the assaults of the Black Hundreds. When a wave of pogroms broke out in 1903 – notably in Kishinev –
Lenin praised the common response organised by the Russian, Ukrainian, and
Jewish workers of Odessa,[15] stressing that the struggle against anti-Semitism
directly concerned all the labouring masses of the Russian Empire. In 1914,
Lenin wrote that it was a question of honour for the Russian workers to support the draft legislation against anti-Semitic discrimination introduced into
the Fourth Duma by the social democratic parliamentary group.[16] Five years
later, when the pogroms were an everyday reality in the Ukraine during the
Russian Civil War, the Bolsheviks widely distributed an appeal by Lenin on
phonographic record against anti-Semitism, which they defined as an 'abysmal
ignorance' and an 'ancient survival of feudal times, when the priests burnt
heretics on the stake'. Emphasising the class nature of this reactionary movement, he described it as a scapegoat policy: an attempt by the landowners and
the bourgeoisie to 'divert the hatred of the workers and peasants who were tor-
tured by want against the Jews'; an attempt to foment 'hatred against the Jews
in order to blind the workers, to divert their attention from the real enemy of
the working people, capital'.[17]

Lenin saw another form of anti-Semitism in the plans for the nationalisation of Jewish schools, proposed by an educational civil servant in 1913 and
greeted favourably by the government. Far from wishing to enhance Jewish
national culture – Yiddish was prohibited in Tsarist Russia – this project sought
to separate Jewish children in special schools, thus excluding them from all the
other educational institutions. Lenin protested vigorously against this measure, which took as its model the 'dark centuries of the Middle Ages, with
their Inquisition'.[18] In light of this plan, he reinforced his criticism of the theory of national cultural autonomy, which proposed to transfer the manage-

---

14   *LCW*, Vol. 10, p. 509.
15   *LCW*, vol. 6, pp. 518–19.
16   *LCW*, Vol. 20, pp. 172–3.
17   *LCW*, Vol. 29, p. 252.
18   *LCW*, Vol. 19, p. 307.

ment of education from the state to various nations. It should be stressed that while opposing the creation of separate Jewish schools, Lenin considered it an elementary democratic right for national minorities (including the Jews) to receive an education in their mother tongue. The public schools could, where it was necessary, permit 'the hiring, at state expense, of special teachers of Hebrew, Jewish history, and the like, or the provision of state-owned premises for lectures for Jewish, Armenian, or Romanian children, or even for the one Georgian child'.[19] Of course, this assessment attenuated to a great extent his negative judgment of the potentialities of the Yiddish language and culture, but did not change his vision of anti-Semitism as a barrier against assimilation. The pogroms were responsible for the survival of the ghettoes where, as a by-product of anti-Semitism, Yiddish culture was born. The suppression of anti-Semitic discrimination, the conquest of civic rights, in short, Emancipation, would break down the walls of the ghetto, and the Jews would at last mix with the surrounding populations, as had already happened in the West. In some texts, Lenin recognised the Jewish right to local and regional, but not national, autonomy.[20]

In fact, the Jewish Question mirrored a broader problem. Putting in front of the non-Russian peoples of the Tsarist Empire before the choice between assimilation or self-determination, the Bolsheviks did not satisfactorily answer the claims of many extra-territorial minorities, who rejected the first solution but, at the same time, for objective reasons could not realise the second one. In short, Lenin simply reproduced the old approach of Engels from 1848, prescribing on the one hand the assimilation of the 'nations without history' and, on the other hand, the separation of the 'historic nations'.[21] This attitude amounted, in the case of the Jews, to demanding their equality before the law while also favouring their cultural assimilation. The theory of national autonomy was an attempt to go beyond this contradiction and found an immediate reception among the socialists of many other national minorities of the Russian Empire, from the Armenian to the Georgian, from the Latvian, Lithuanian, and Estonian to the Ukrainian socialists.[22]

---

19   Lenin 1976, p. 33.
20   See Low 1958, pp. 29, 62. For a synthesis of Lenin's thinking on the Jewish Question, see also Shukman 1970, pp. 43–50; Kriegel 1977, pp. 181–202, and, Silberner 1983, pp. 72–93.
21   Weill 1987, p. 141.
22   See Ratner 1911, p. 89.

2   Stalin

The Bolsheviks gave to Stalin, a Georgian, the task of codifying their theory of assimilation. After having been sent to Vienna by Lenin, he published in 1913 *Marxism and the National Question*. Essentially, he only reproduced the arguments already advanced by Lenin against the Bund, denouncing the struggle for a Sabbath holiday as an apology for the Jewish religion, and the campaign for the development of Yiddish as a 'specific purely nationalist aim'.[23] In his view, the policy of the Bund came down to 'keeping all that which is Jewish, conserving all the national particularities of the Jews, up to and including those that are manifestly damaging to the proletariat, to isolate the Jews from all that which is not Jewish'.[24] Thus, the existence of Jewish trade unions did not result from the economic structure of the Pale of Settlement but were the product of the separatist tendencies of the Bund, the consequence of a national sectarianism.

According to Stalin, the Jews had never been a nation. In fact, he defined the concept of nation in a rigid way, virtually reducing it to a mechanical correlation of elements: 'A nation is a historically constituted, stable, community of people, formed on the basis of a common language, territory, economic life and psychological makeup, manifested in a common culture'.[25] Moreover, this correlation was a normative criterion, insofar as 'it is only when all these characteristics are present together that we have a nation'. According to Georges Haupt, Stalin fused concepts drawn from Kautsky, Bauer, and Medem in his theory, and developed a 'coherent, but rigid and scholastic system'.[26] For his part, Michael Löwy has observed a difference between the idea of nation elaborated by Lenin and that of Stalin. The first had never spoken of the 'common psychological makeup' and, in general, his definition was much more flexible.[27] It is obvious that on the basis of Stalin's criteria, the Jews could not form a nation. Deprived of a territory and a common economy, they could only keep 'certain relics of the national character' on the basis of their origins and religion,[28] and their 'petrified religious rites and fading psychological relics' could not prevail over the cultural, social, and economic life of the people among whom they lived. For Stalin, Jewish assimilation was developing rapidly in the Tsarist Empire. He wrote:

---

23   Stalin 1973, p. 56.
24   Ibid., p. 60.
25   Ibid., p. 60.
26   Haupt 1974, pp. 60–1.
27   Löwy 1974, pp. 386–7.
28   Stalin 1973, p. 63.

Thus encrusted as national minorities, in regions peopled by other nationalities, the Jews serve principally the 'foreign' nations, as manufactur-
ers and traders, or in the liberal professions, and they adapt themselves
naturally to the 'foreign nations' in respect of language, and so on. All
this, with the growing displacement of the nationalities, proper to the
developed forms of capitalism, leads to the assimilation of the Jews. The
suppression of the 'zones reserved for the Jews' can only accelerate this
assimilation.[29]

Given this dominant tendency, the Bundist project of cultural national autonomy was only an attempt to artificially conserve an ethnographic residue.

Differently from Lenin, who saw it as the core of the Jewish Question in
Russia, anti-Semitism seemed almost non-existent for Stalin. His 1913 study
mentions it only once, where hatred for the Jews was classified as a 'form of bel-
licose nationalism' alongside Zionism and Armenian nationalism.[30] In other
words, Stalin did not clearly distinguish between dominant and dominated
nations, and put their nationalisms on the same plane. His theoretical indifference towards anti-Semitism, however, coexisted with practical prejudices.
In 1905 he addressed the Georgian workers of Baku in these terms: 'Lenin is
outraged that God has sent him comrades like the Mensheviks! Who are these
people, anyway? Martov, Dan, Aksel'rod, circumcised Yids! You can't go into
a fight with them and you can't have a feast with them!'[31] It was not an isolated episode. All his biographers relate an incident in 1907, during the London
congress of the Russian social democracy: as most of the Bolshevik delegates
were Russian, whereas there was, among the Mensheviks, a significant Jewish
minority, Stalin was fond of repeating a sinister joke according to which the
Bolsheviks would have to organise a pogrom to get rid of the 'Jewish faction'.[32]

3   Trotsky

Before October 1917, Trotsky generally shared Lenin's attitude to the Jewish
Question. During the second congress of the Russian social democracy, in
1903, he had criticised Bundist separatism; then, in 1905 and 1913, he was fully
engaged in the struggle against anti-Semitism. In spite of his multiple oscilla-

---

29   Ibid., p. 90.
30   Ibid., p. 56.
31   Quoted by Montefiore 2008, pp. 130–1, and Wolfe 1984, pp. 524–5.
32   See Montefiore 2008, p. 173.

tions in defining the Jewish nation, unlike Lenin or Stalin he never transformed the idea of assimilation into a dogma. In 1904, he implicitly recognised the existence of an extraterritorial Jewish nation when he wrote that 'the field of action of the Bund is not the state, but the nation. The Bund is the organization of the Jewish proletariat'. This did not prevent him from seeing in the Bund the 'stamp of militant provincialism and the parish pump outlook'.[33] He criticised its 'nationalist deviations', without ever doubting its legitimacy as a representative of a section of the working class of the Russian Empire. When it came to understanding the basic causes of the split between the Bund and social democracy, his analysis was less abstract than that of the Bolsheviks. At the founding congress of the Russian social democracy, the autonomy of the Bund had been purely technical, but he observed that little by little the 'particular' had gained ground over the 'general': from representing the social democracy inside the Jewish proletariat, the Bund had become the representative of the Jewish workers to the Social Democratic party. In essence, the congress of 1903 had only recorded a split that already existed in reality.

Criticising Zionism, nevertheless, the young Trotsky had praised the role of the Jewish workers' movement. In January 1904, he published an article in *Iskra*, 'The Decomposition of Zionism and Its Possible Successors', devoted to the Zionist Congress at Basel, where a significant conflict had broken out between the two wings of the movement: the secular current of Herzl and Nordau and the religious current of Ussishkin. Unitil that moment, the unity of Zionism had been preserved thanks to concessions made by Herzl, but its future and credibility seemed seriously compromised. Trotsky described the 'decomposition' of Zionism which, torn between the Machiavellian tactics of its leader (Herzl was described as a 'repulsive figure' and a 'shameless adventurist') and 'the hysterical sobs of the romantics of Zion', had transformed the congress into a 'spectacle of impotence'.[34] Trotsky predicted an inevitable decline of this movement whose social base, the liberal democratic intelligentsia, after having abandoned the Palestinian mirage, would understand that the priority was the struggle against tsarism as the fundamental cause of anti-Semitism. All at once, the 'nationalist orientation' of the Bund revealed itself in a new light, as an attitude capable of stimulating the political evolution of the Zionist left: 'Zionism will not disappear without leaving successors. But these successors may well prove to be the Bund'.[35] This prediction was not borne out by reality – the crisis of Zionism did not prove to be insurmountable, and the Zionist left, instead

---

33   Trotsky 1980.
34   Quoted by Nedava 1972, p. 197.
35   Ibid., p. 199.

of joining the Bund, created a series of revolutionary organisations without renouncing its basic aims – but it indicates a relatively flexible approach to the idea of Jewish nationality. In 1919, now head of the Red Army, Trotsky accepted the proposition from Poale Zion to create Jewish 'national battalions' to organise the defence of the Jewish population against the pogroms and to win their allegiance to the new Soviet regime.[36]

We have already mentioned that Trotsky was actively engaged, in Nikolaev, Kiev, and St. Petersburg, in the organisation of self-defence groups against the pogroms. The pages of *1905* give us a very striking description of a pogrom, probably that of Odessa. He stressed the meticulous preparations of the tsarist authorities: first, the rumour was spread that the Jews were going to mount an assault on an Orthodox church; then, the local press accused the socialists of having destroyed sacred icons. All was planned to incite the crowds to hatred against the Jews. On the planned day, there was a patriotic procession, preceded by a military fanfare, playing the 'hymn of the pogroms', 'God Save the Tsar'.[37] An imposing deployment of police prevented any response by the Jewish population, while bands of the Black Hundreds proceeded to devastate the Jewish neighbourhood through pillage and murder. He concluded his description with the following words: 'During this black October bacchanalia, compared with which Saint Bartholomew's night looks like the most innocent piece of theatre, three thousand five hundred to four thousand people were killed and as many as ten thousand maimed in one hundred towns'. The material waste, estimated at some tens, if not hundreds of millions of rubles, 'was several times greater than those suffered by the landowners as result of the agrarian riots. Thus did the old order avenge its humiliation!'[38]

In 1913, while exiled in Vienna, Trotsky wrote an article for the *Neue Zeit* devoted to the Beilis affair – the last big 'ritual murder' trial of the last century – that represented in his eyes a 'line of cleavage between two epochs'.[39] This trial reflected, directly or indirectly, all 'the contradictions and the cultural conflicts' of Russian society. In the background, pulling the strings of this shameful anti-Semitic parade, was the tsarist autocracy. The chauvinist press, the pogroms' bands, and reaction as a whole had organised a 'medieval trial' with the support of the regime that exhumed the myth of a world Jewish conspiracy to overthrow the Christian order. Trotsky developed a comparison between the Beilis trial and the Dreyfus affair, so as to understand the difference between

---

36   Ibid., p. 114.
37   Trotsky 1971a, ch. 12.
38   Ibid.
39   Trotsky 1913–14, pp. 310.

anti-Semitism in Russia and in France: 'Doubtless, a certain analogy exists. But between these two events there is at least as great a distance as that which exists between the Jesuits' anti-Semitism in France and the violence of the pogroms in Russia'.[40] The accusation of treason pronounced against an officer and that of ritual murder launched against a 'simple Jewish worker' appeared to Trotsky as two completely different things that could not be reduced to a question of style. 'We know of no trial', he wrote, 'in which the lumpen-bureaucratic abjection [*die lumpenbureaukratische Niedertracht*] of a clique that dominates a people of one hundred and sixty million should show itself impudently before all the world as in the Kiev trial ... The Beilis affair consequently takes on the aspect of a monstrous stage parade organized by the state against a weak and defenseless Jewish worker, which embodies the absence of civic and political rights'.[41] He did not even accept the thesis of the spontaneous and popular character of Russian anti-Semitism because, in his opinion, unless incited and supported by the regime, the pogroms would never have taken place. Moreover, one could mention that during the 1930s, the exiled Russian revolutionary evoked the Dreyfus and Beilis affairs as historical precedents for the Moscow trials.[42]

Again in 1913, during a long stay in the Balkans as a war correspondent for a liberal Kiev daily, Trotsky wrote a series of articles on the Jewish Question in Romania, another country afflicted by an endemic anti-Semitism. There also, as in Russia, anti-Jewish hatred was a part of the official ideology and a government practice. It had become, according to Trotsky, a new 'state religion, the last psychological cement holding together a feudal society that is rotten through and through, and covered over with the gilt tinsel of a constitution essentially based on privilege'.[43] These two 1913 articles depict anti-Semitism as a feudal survival in Eastern Europe, once more contrasted to the Western countries like France, where the Jesuits 'alone' remained to perpetuate this obscurantist tradition. Diametrically opposing East and West, he explained that in the countries that had experienced a bourgeois revolution, a 'Jewish Question' no longer existed.

Trotsky did not deny the right of peoples to determine their own future but, far from defending this democratic right in abstract terms, he inscribed it in the context of the historical crisis of nation-states in the age of imperialism. The development of the productive forces had broken the framework of national

---

40   Ibid., p. 316.
41   Ibid., p. 319.
42   See Trotsky 1982, vol. 12, p. 116.
43   Trotsky 1980, p. 414.

states and demanded the creation of supranational structures.[44] Differently than Kautsky and Stalin, Trotsky defended a fundamentally cultural-historical conception of the nation. He distinguished between nations, made of multiple and variable elements like territory, language, culture, and history of a people, and nation-states, the specific form, historically determined and transitional, that the bourgeoisie and capitalism gave to the national phenomenon. During the First World War, he put the problem in this way: 'The nation is an active and permanent factor of human culture. The nation will not only survive the current war, but also capitalism itself. And, in the socialist regime, the nation, freed of the chains of economic and political dependence, will for a long time be called upon to play a fundamental role in historical development'.[45] Some almost identical formulations could be found in the writings of Vladimir Medem. But Trotsky, an assimilated and cosmopolitan Jew, did not see a nation and a national culture in the world of the Eastern Jews. As we will see in Chapter 7, his thinking on the Jewish Question would experience a significant evolution during the 1930s, when he admitted the existence of a living Jewish nation in Eastern Europe that had to be defended against the Nazi threat.

4   Rosa Luxemburg

As we have seen in a previous chapter, Rosa Luxemburg looked at the Jews as a Polish or a German Jew. At first hostile to the demand for national independence, from the beginning of the 1890s – a period of exacerbation of national oppression through the Russification of the entire educational system – the socialists embarked on a nationalist turn. National liberation became a central goal of the Polish Socialist party (PPS) and found a theoretical justification in the writings of Boleslaw Limanowski and Kazimierz Kelles-Krauz.[46] Opposed to all forms of national separatism, in 1893 Rosa Luxemburg founded the Social Democracy of the Kingdom of Poland and Lithuania with Leo Jogiches and Adolf Warski. Roughly speaking, they considered the right to national self-determination as abstract and sterile in general and concretely useless for Poland, which was economically integrated into the Tsarist Empire. By supporting this demand, they feared, the socialists risked becoming an instrument of nationalism (the ideology of the landed aristocracy and the small bourgeois intelligentsia). Finally, they viewed separatism as a historic anachronism,

---

44   Trotzki 1918, p. 20. See also Mandel 1980, p. 48.
45   Trotsky 1975, p. 48.
46   See Waldenberg 1983, pp. 81–114.

which tried to build new national states in the age of cosmopolitanism.[47] In spite of her opposition to the idea of nation-states, however, Rosa Luxemburg, did not reject nationality as an essentially cultural phenomenon. Maria-José Aubet has pertinently pointed out that in Luxemburg's writings, the concepts of 'nation' and 'nationality' never appear as equivalents of 'economic community' or statehood but designate rather a spiritual and cultural entity unified by a common language, religion, literature, etc.[48] Opposed to Polish independence, Luxemburg recognised the necessity of fighting 'for the defense of national identity, as a cultural legacy, specific and distinct, that has its own right to exist and flourish'.[49] Thus, the nation and capitalism could be separated: capitalism determined the future of the nation-states, but not that of the nation as cultural communities. Unlike Lenin and Kautsky, who predicted the extinction of nations under socialism through a universal process of assimilation, Luxemburg conceived the principle of national self-determination as an 'idea that in bourgeois society is completely non-existent and can be realized only on the basis of a socialist regime'.[50]

The SDKPiL had adopted a programme of cultural national autonomy (on a territorial basis) for Poland. In *The National Question and Autonomy* (1909), Luxemburg defined 'modern national autonomy' as a form of 'self-government of a certain nationality territory',[51] stipulating that national culture did not exist 'in the air or in the theoretical void of abstraction, but in a definite territory, a definite social environment'.[52] In short, while defending a cultural-historical conception of the nation, she rejected the idea of an extraterritorial national autonomy. This means that her favourable attitude toward Jewish assimilation stemmed neither from an abstract internationalism, negating the idea of the nation, nor from a conception of socialism as the abrogation of national differences.

Usually, the Polish socialists praised Jewish assimilation as a symptom of progress, which would lead almost naturally to emancipation. This fierce claim

---

47   On Rosa Luxemburg and the national question, see in particular Haupt 1980, pp. 293–341, and Aubet 1977.

48   Aubet 1977, p. 111.

49   Luxemburg 1976, p. 97. In 1900, Rosa vigorously denounced the policy of Germanisation directed by the Prussian government against the Poles of Posnania, reflected in the introduction of German as an obligatory language in the primary schools. See Luxemburg 1972, vol. 1/1, pp. 810–28.

50   Luxemburg 1976, pp. 139–40.

51   Ibid., p. 265.

52   Ibid., p. 253.

for Jewish assimilation was both a mark of nationalism and a response to the Bund, which refused to come out clearly for Polish independence. The only remarkable exception inside the party was Kelles-Krauz, who looked favourably on the idea of a modern Jewish nation, one that would be created not 'by the economic factor ... but by cultural and ideal factors': in his opinion, Jewish emancipation should also include the 'right to possess one's own nationality'.[53] But Kelles-Krauz was an isolated voice inside Polish Marxism. The leaders of the SDKPiL, most of them Jewish intellectuals, were unequivocally in favour of assimilation.[54] In the middle between the PPS and Kelles-Krauz, Luxemburg defined the Jews as a 'nationality' but, at the same time, she was sceptical about any form of national autonomy. She wrote that 'Jewish national autonomy, not in the sense of freedom of school, religion, place of residence, and equal civic rights, but in the sense of the political self-government of the Jewish population with its own legislation and administration, as it was parallel to the autonomy of the Congress Kingdom, is an entirely utopian idea'.[55] The Jews were not a territorially homogeneous population, and autonomy could not be realised 'in the air ... without any definite territory'.[56] At the economic level, the Jews were inserted in the productive structure of the Tsarist Empire and had no particular 'capitalist interests': the development of capitalism would not lead to the 'separation of Jewish bourgeois culture, but acts in an exactly opposed direction, leading to the assimilation of the Jewish bourgeois, urban intelligentsia, to their absorption by the Polish and Russian people'.[57]

As the Jewish bourgeoisie was assimilated, the national Jewish culture had no perspective of development and Luxemburg interpreted the widespread bilingualism (or even trilingualism) of the Jewish intelligentsia as a tendency toward assimilation. Indifferent to the Yiddish culture, she saw Jewishness only as a combination of social backwardness and religious tradition. Consequently, 'Jewish national individuality' did not have the aspect of an urban bourgeois culture, as was the case for all modern nations, but rather the 'form of a small-town lack of culture'.[58] She considered as completely insignificant the efforts

---

53   Quoted by Waldenberg 1983, p. 104. On the general attitude of the PPS toward the Jewish question see Hanstein 1969, pp. 240–52.

54   See Merchav 1976, p. 187. On the SDKPiL and the Jewish Question, see Silberner 1983, pp. 212–17.

55   Luxemburg 1976, p. 266.

56   Ibid., p. 267.

57   Ibid. Karski, another significant leader of the SDKPiL, defended a similar position in 1913. See Schumacher and Tych 1966, pp. 91–3.

58   Luxemburg 1976, p. 267.

deployed by a 'handful of publicists' to develop Yiddish and saw in the workers' movement the only modern cultural expression of Judaism in Eastern Europe. Nonetheless, by its very nature socialism was the bearer of an internationalist culture that could not fill 'the historical lack of bourgeois culture among the Jews'.[59] Her attitude was, thus, quite contradictory. On the one hand, she rejected the demand for Polish independence because of the integration of the Polish bourgeoisie into the Russian economy, but this did not prevent her from opposing attempts at Russification and defending the development of Polish culture. In the Jewish case, on the other hand, she thought that the assimilation of a bourgeois economic elite was an insuperable obstacle to the flourishing of a national Jewish culture. Her definition of the *Yiddishkeit* as 'plebeian lack of culture' was an *a priori* rather than the result of careful argumentation. According to the Bundist leader John Mill, she 'hated Yiddish as only an assimilationist Polish Jew could'.[60] Rosa Luxemburg's foreignness to the *Yiddishkeit* went back to her childhood in Zamosc, where she grew up in an assimilated Jewish milieu of Polish culture, but was also certainly reinforced by her emigration to Germany. Seen from Berlin, the Jewish life of the Tsarist Empire appeared as a world not only a few hundred kilometers away but, perhaps, some centuries distant as well. This world, into which she was born but without being a part, was completely foreign to her, and she was incapable of perceiving the changes taking place within it.

Luxemburg assigned to the proletariat the task of leading the process of assimilation: 'The progressive element, in the first place the proletariat, will understand sooner or later that it must adapt itself to Polish language and culture, for it lives among the Polish people and, at the same time, it cannot develop Jewish culture'.[61] She did not want a forced assimilation of the Jews, who would choose freely to abandon their own national identity by 'conforming to the influence exercised on their consciousness by cultural and economic development'.[62] Assimilation, then, was conceived as both a goal and a historical tendency. Like most socialists of her time, Rosa Luxemburg also adopted the history of Western Europe as a model: the Jews of Lodz and Warsaw should assimilate as their co-religionists in London and Paris had already done. It is fairly astonishing to note that, in order to illustrate the tendencies to Russi-

---

59   Ibid.

60   Mill 1949, Vol. 1, pp. 179–80. On the relationship between Rosa Luxemburg and John Mill, see Nettl 1966, vol. 1, pp. 253–4. See also Bensussan 1985, p. 659.

61   Luxemburg 1974, p. 138.

62   Ibid.

fication or to Polishization of the Jews of Lithuania, she gave the example of Vilnius, where 82 schools out of 227 were Jewish.[63] The dogma of assimilation was internalised to the point that she accepted it against the evidence of historical reality.

This attitude inevitably implied a suspicion of any specifically Jewish cultural manifestation, and Rosa Luxemburg did not conceal her hostility toward the Bund. In 1894, she and Leo Jogikhes had depicted the Jewish socialist circle of Vilnius, which would give birth to the Bund, as 'one hundred percent separatist' and as the Jewish version of the PPS.[64] Her correspondence with the Russian and Polish socialists was replete with strongly critical allusions to Bundist federalism and separatism. In a 1901 letter, she wrote that

> for their political behaviour in relation to our party as well as their general methods of operation – what they deserve at the least is to have any upstanding, respectable person throw them down the stairs the minute they open the door (and for this purpose it is best to live on the fourth floor). For years I have known both John and Alexander [John Mill and Arkadi Kremer] personally; they are individuals who are made up of two elements: stupidity and cunning. They are incapable of speaking two words to anyone without having the concealed intention of robbing them (in a moral sense). The entire policy of the 'Bund' is based on this system.[65]

In 1903, however, Rosa Luxemburg expressed a much more sober judgment, in which she recognised the Bund as the sole force capable of organising the Jewish proletariat in Poland and Lithuania. In a letter to Adolf Warski, she proposed a close collaboration between the SDKPiL and the Bund, with the purpose of building a mass mobilisation against the Kishinev pogrom. But this recognition of the role of the Jewish workers' movement never changed her basic hostility toward the Bund.

Of course, her condemnation of all forms of nationalism did not exclude Zionism, a movement she thought all the more guilty in that it was the expression of a 'people without history'. In her celebrated study *The Russian Revolution* (1918) she rehabilitated this Engelsian category to explain the nationalist

---

63   Luxemburg 1976, p. 273.
64   See Frankel 1981, p. 198.
65   Luxemburg 2013. On Luxemburg's attitude toward the Bund, see Nettl 1966, vol. 1, pp. 272–
     3.

wave that had swept Europe during the war. In this text, her critique of Zionism was not only directed against its politics, but more generally, against the idea of a Jewish nation:

> Nations and semi-nations announce themselves everywhere and affirm their right to establish states. Putrefied corpses come out of hundred year old tombs, animated by a new springlike vigor, and peoples 'without history', who have never constituted autonomous state identities feel the violent need to set themselves up as states. Ukrainians, Byelorussians, Lithuanians, Czechs, Yugoslavs, the new nations in the Caucasus ... The Zionists are already building their Palestinian ghetto, for the moment in Philadelphia ... it is currently *Walpurgisnacht* on the nationalist Brocken.[66]

In 1910 Rosa Luxemburg wrote a series of articles on anti-Semitism for the weekly *Mlot* (*The Hammer*), published legally by the SDKPiL in Warsaw. They were not theoretical analyses but rather polemical interventions related to contemporary events. The defeat of the 1905 revolution had plunged Poland into a state of 'psychological collapse' that nourished anti-Semitism and was exploited by the reactionary press.[67] Anti-Semitism replaced the old anti-Russian and anti-tsarist slogans and, as Jews were numerous among socialists, it had become synonymous with anti-socialism. Thus, the anti-Semitic campaign of the nationalist press in reality concealed an offensive by the Polish bourgeoisie against the workers' movement. Anti-Semitism had become the banner of the clerics and the nationalist intelligentsia, the 'common mask of the political downturn', but behind this mask, there was a 'deadly hatred for self-determination and for the liberation of the workers'.[68] This campaign, which eventually culminated in pogroms, was the bourgeoisie's revenge for the workers' conquests of 1905. In short, Rosa Luxemburg defined anti-Semitism as a form of 'racial hatred' that revealed the level of tension reached by the class conflict within capitalist society.[69]

Unlike the Austrian, German, or Russian Marxists, who generally interpreted Polish anti-Semitism as a medieval legacy, Rosa Luxemburg saw it also as a bourgeois political manifestation, the product of class antagonisms within a modern capitalist society. She considered anti-Semitism as a phenomenon

---

66   Luxemburg 1963, p. 82.
67   See Haupt and Korzec 1975, p. 187.
68   Luxemburg 1974, p. 131.
69   Ibid., p. 148.

both modern and archaic, the product of the particular combination of anti-worker bourgeois reaction and an 'age-old' oppression of nationalities by Russian Absolutism. In the *Junius Pamphlet*, her internationalist manifesto written during the First World War, she saw anti-Semitism as a symbol of the barbarism which capitalism, in the absence of a socialist revolution, was bringing to humanity. She described the wave of nationalism that had swept Europe at the beginning of the conflict through the allegory of a pogrom:

> The atmosphere of ritual murder, the Kishinev air where the crossing guard is the only remaining representative of human dignity ... Violated, dishonored, wading in blood, dripping filth – there stands bourgeois society. This is it [in reality]. Not all spic and span and moral, with pretense to culture, philosophy, ethics, order, peace, and the rule of law – but the ravening beast, the witches' sabbath of anarchy, a plague to culture and humanity. Thus it reveals itself in its true, its naked form.[70]

Faced with the immense carnage of the war, Luxemburg launched the slogan 'socialism or barbarism!' Anti-Semitism was the most hideous face of capitalist barbarism.

5   Conclusion

We have tried to reconstruct the attitude of the Russian and Polish Marxists to the Jewish Question through the writings of Lenin, Stalin, Trotsky, and Rosa Luxemburg (respectively a great Russian, a Russified Georgian, a Russian-Ukrainian Jew, and a Polish Jew). From their writings emerge, albeit with differing inflections, some common elements:

a.   a firm and intransigent criticism of anti-Semitism (with the exception of Stalin), shorn of the ambiguity and reticence that, as we have already seen, shaped a great number of German and Austrian Marxists;

b.   a refusal – despite uncertainty and wavering on definitions – to approach the Jewish question in Russia in its national dimension;

c.   finally, the idea of assimilation, conceived both as a political strategy and as a natural tendency of historical development. The *a priori* character of this orientation was purely negative. The Russian and Polish Marxists never posed, in their writings, the question of whether the Jews of the

---

70   Luxemburg 1970, pp. 53–5.

Tsarist Empire wished to assimilate and to what extent this process was practical. Assimilation was proposed quite simply by taking the model of the history of Western Europe.

What is most striking in all these writings is their almost complete lack of references to the concrete life of the Jewish communities of Russia. For the Russian and Polish Marxists, Jewish culture was circumscribed within the limits of the feudal ghetto and the synagogue; it remained an aspect of the backwardness and the 'Asiatic barbarism' of absolutist Russia. In such a suffocating atmosphere, assimilation appeared to Russian and Polish Marxists as deliverance.

CHAPTER 5

Jewish Marxism

Has Jewish Marxism ever existed? In Central Europe, as we saw in a previous chapter, many Jews were actively involved in the socialist movement and deeply shaped the debates of *German* Marxism. In Eastern Europe – where, at the end of the nineteenth century, Yiddish was the mother tongue of nearly 97 percent of the Jews of the Czarist Empire – the intellectual landscape was different, because of the existence of a living Yiddish culture and a vigorous Jewish workers' movement. This was the historical background of a specific form of 'Judeo-Marxism', whose most significant expressions were socialist Zionism (Ber Borokhov) and Bundism (Vladimir Medem). Besides the assimilated Jewish intellectuals who joined the Russian or Polish social democracy, movements or parties emerged that defined their own theoretical and political identity in relation to specifically Jewish concerns. This inevitably crystallised a theoretical and political separation from Russian (and Polish) Marxism, resulting in conflict between Lenin and the Bund.

1   Russian Marxism and Jewish Marxism

The bases of Russian Marxism were established in 1883 in Geneva, when a circle of populist exiles (Georgy Plekhanov, Pavel Aksel'rod, and Vera Zasulich) founded the Emancipation of Labor Group. Two years previously, the assassination of Tsar Alexander II had marked the apogee and started the decline of *narodniki* terrorism, signalling the end of the era of tsarist liberal reforms. Russian Marxism, whose philosophical profile carried the imprint of Plekhanov, arose as an attempt to respond to the crisis of populism, with which it established a clear theoretical frontier. The Populists argued that Russia could, because of its particular historical situation, experience a socialist transformation by 'skipping' the capitalist phase of economic development. They idealized the *obshchina*, the peasant community still predominant in the Russian countryside at the end of the nineteenth century, considering it as a lever capable of regenerating the whole of Russian society. Thus, they depicted the future of Russia as a sort of agrarian socialism, the product of a peasant revolution that they would have first stimulated and then set off through a series of exemplary actions (above all terrorist attacks). Russian Marxism originated precisely out of the radical rejection of this perspective. According to Plekhanov and his disciples, Russian capitalism was an inescapable reality and would inevitably pass through all the phases of economic development already experienced by the West. Of course, this process implied the dissolution of the rural communes (implemented by the abolition of serfdom in 1861) and a shift of the axis of the political opposition to Tsarism from the land to the cities. Thus, the political subjectivism of the populists had to be replaced by the organisation and mobilisation of the working class. The conclusions that Plekhanov drew from this critique were simple and clear: the socioeconomic conditions of a bourgeois revolution were in the process of being created in Russia and the socialist revolution would follow the historically unavoidable stage of capitalism.[1] As emphasised by many scholars, this position was very distant from that of Marx, whose writings show that, a few years earlier, he had shared the hypothesis of a direct transition from the *obshchina* to communism[2] (it seems closer to that of the old Engels, who nevertheless declined to openly criticise the populists – despite pressures from his Russian socialist friends).

The point of departure of Russian Marxism was the idea that the Tsarist Empire could not escape a complete phase of capitalist development. From its origins until the 1905 revolution, it remained imbued with objectivism and positivistic evolutionism. In 1894, Petr Struve's *Critical Notes on the Economic Development of Russia* marked the birth of 'legal Marxism', with which Marxism took form in Russia as a theory of capitalist development. The economist Alexander Gershenkron has sharply observed that at the end of nineteenth century, Marxism realised in Russia 'a late and precarious reconciliation between the intelligentsia and industrial progress'.[3] From this point of view, a work such as Lenin's *Development of Capitalism in Russia* (1899), with its vision of a linear and organic economic growth, represented a further contribution from within the theoretical coordinates fixed by Plekhanov, Struve, and Tugan-Baranovskii. It is only after the 1905 events that Trotsky broke with this vision, opposing

---

1   For the history of the debate between Marxism and Populism in Russia, see Walicki 1969; Venturi 1980; and Battistrada 1982.

2   In a letter addressed to the Russian review *Otecestvennye Zapiski* in 1877, Marx warned his readers against the danger of transforming his 'historical sketch of the genesis of capitalism in Western Europe into a historico-philosophic theory of the general development, imposed by fate on all peoples, whatever the historical circumstances in which they are placed'. See *MEW*, vol. 19, p. 111; *CW*, vol. 24, pp. 200–1. He reaffirmed the same concept in a letter to Vera Zasulich, dated 3 March 1881, which was not published by the Geneva-based group of Russian Marxists and which was discovered by David Riazanov only in 1911. The writings of Marx and Engels on this question are collected in Shanin 1984.

3   Gerschenkon 1965, p. 177.

to it his theory of 'permanent revolution'.[4] In *Results and Prospects* (1906), he studied Russian social and economic development from the perspective of the international capitalist economy conceived as a totality. He saw the urban proletariat – produced by Russia's recent and intensive industrial growth – as the central subject of a socialist transformation excluding the 'historic necessity' of a long phase of capitalist development, as well as rejecting the dogma (shared by all socialist currents) of the 'bourgeois' character of the Russian Revolution. In this sense, Trotsky's theory was the dialectical sublation of the conflict between Marxism and populism.

The genesis of Jewish Marxism took place outside of this problematic that had so profoundly shaped the origins of Russian Marxism. In Poland, Lithuania, Belorussia, and more generally throughout the Pale of Settlement, the Jewish intelligentsia was receptive to Marxism neither as a theory of capitalist development nor as a theory of permanent revolution. Both strategic orientations identified the Russian proletariat as their social subject, whereas one of the principal features of the Jewish Eastern world was the exclusion of its working class from advanced, mechanised industry. There, the socialist circles were rather confronted with the contradictions of social development in Russia, which combined economic backwardness with cultural modernisation, exclusion from Russian industrialisation and dissolution of the old Jewish community. The result was the birth of Jewish Marxism as a theory of the national question.[5] The social background of Judeo-Marxism – this term avoids confusing it with the assimilated Jews participating in Russian Marxism – was a structurally marginal and ethnically homogeneous proletariat with the cultural background of an extraterritorial national minority. Using the concept *Judeo-Marxism* to refer to the particular form assumed by Marxist thought in the Yiddish-speaking Jewish world does not mean presenting it as a monolithic phenomenon, or underestimating its internal differences. It simply helps to grasp its specific genesis, inside the Russian Empire, within the framework of the Jewish Question seen as a National Question. As we have seen, Russian Marxism had a very strong Jewish dimension, but the numerous young Jewish intellectuals who wrote for socialist Russian journals and participated in the polemics between Bolsheviks and Mensheviks, or in the ideological conflicts between Marxists and Populists, came from the big cities of the Tsarist Empire, not from the Pale of Settlement. According to Yuri Slezkine, the Bund

---

4   On the genesis of Trotsky's theory of permanent revolution, see Löwy 1981b.
5   This remark is also valid, to a certain extent, for the Polish, Georgian, and Armenian Marxists. On this question, see Weill 1987, pp. 89–95. On the extremely influential role played by Marxism in the process of the modernisation of the Yiddish-speaking Jewry, see Stern 2018.

'prospered briefly in the least urbanised and Russified parts of the Pale, where it tended to appeal to the secularised Jews who had not yet entered the all-Russian youth culture'[6] and where, consequently, Marxist universalism took a national rather than a cosmopolitan form. Despite their methodological and strategic differences, both Vladimir Medem's and Ber Borokhov's theories dealt with the liberation of the Russian Jews from their national oppression.

The definition of the *Yiddishkeit* as nation essentially distinguished Judeo-Marxism from Russian Marxism. This discrepancy became clear in 1905, the year in which the Fourth Congress of the Bund adopted a programme of cultural national autonomy as well as the year of the birth of socialist Zionism. The trajectory of Judeo-Marxism was ephemeral, because of the transformations produced within the Jewish world of Eastern Europe first by the Russian Revolution, then by the rise of anti-Semitism and finally by the Holocaust. Its ideas, nevertheless, transcended its short existence.

2   The Jewish Workers' Movement

Between the annexation of the Kingdom of Poland by the Tsarist Empire (1795) and the end of the nineteenth century the Jewish population of Russia experienced an intense period of demographic growth, going from one to five million people[7] in spite of a mass emigration – a true exodus – that took place from the 1880s onward.[8] In the Pale of Settlement (Poland, Lithuania, Byelorussia, Ukraine, and some Baltic areas), the Jews were concentrated in small market towns – the traditional *shtetlakh*, where they often accounted for a majority of the population – or in cities, where they often represented between 10 and 50 percent of the urban population. Half of Russian Jews – in some regions as many as two-thirds – lived in the big cities, and they constituted less than three percent of the rural population inside the Pale of Settlement (at a time when the overwhelming majority of Russians were peasants).[9] In 1897, 54.4 percent of economically active Jews were traders, hawkers, or people without a clearly defined occupation – the *luftmenshn*; 18.4 percent were artisans and 25 percent wage workers, only 10 percent of these being non-manual.[10] These figures

---

6   Slezkine 2004, p. 148.

7   See Ertel 1982, p. 147, and Schwarz 1951, pp. 10–11. For a more general analysis, see Della Pergola 1983.

8   For a general overview, see Howe 1976; for France, see Green 1986.

9   See Schwarz 1951, p. 11, and Della Pergola 1983, pp. 82–6.

10   Schwarz 1951, pp. 18–20.

corresponded to half a million artisans, autonomous or independent, and fifty thousand factory workers.[11] The composition of the Jewish working class was as follows: 52 percent in the clothing sector (tailors or cobblers), 19 percent in building (carpenters, joiners, blacksmiths, painters, and so forth), 9 percent in food and the manufacture of tobacco, and the rest in a multitude of secondary activities.[12]

Some important specificities of the Jewish proletariat deserve to be emphasised. Unlike the Russian working class, which was of peasant origin, the Jewish working class came from crafts. Its first trade unions did not take the model of the *obscina* but that of the *khevroth*, the Jewish crafts cooperatives.[13] Its main feature was its exclusion from large-scale industry and its atomisation in a great number of small factories that employed an exclusively Jewish labour force and survived on the margins of economic development. The Jewish workers could celebrate the Sabbath, whereas the big factories, which employed a Russian or Polish workforce, closed on Sunday.[14] Their cultural specificities, rooted in their religion and language, were reinforced by their structural separation from the Russian proletariat. This concentration of Jewish workers in a kind of socioeconomic ghetto was the material origin of a specific socialist movement,[15] insofar as clear ethnic and cultural barriers separated them from the Russian or Polish workers. Inside the Jewish community, on the other hand, the class cleavage was much more fluid: the large category of *luftmenshn* was at the crossroads of the different social layers, and absorbed the pauperised traders and the unemployed workers during periods of crisis. Consequently, for the Jewish workers, class consciousness was identified with national identity. Sometimes, in the small workplaces, the Jewish workers were in contact on a daily basis with their (Jewish) boss, without ever having the opportunity to meet Russian or Polish workers.

The Jews did not work in big factories. Abram Leon emphasised the metamorphosis of the 'Jewish pre-capitalist merchant into artisan worker' when he stressed the combination of this process with the 'elimination of the Jewish worker by the machine'.[16] According to the socialist press, the religious prescription of the Sabbath was the principal cause of the exclusion of the Jews

---

11   See Brym 1978, p. 31.
12   See Bunzl 1975, pp. 32–5, and Suchecky 1986, pp. 61–2.
13   According to Nathan Weinstock, 'There was no break of continuity between the religious organizations of craftsmen (*Khevroth*) and the first embryonic workers unions,' see Weinstock 1984, vol. 1, p. 24.
14   See Levin 1977, p. 40.
15   Bunzl 1975, p. 37.
16   Leon 2010, p. 204.

from industry, because Christians took their holiday on Sunday.[17] It is in this Jewish working class of Lithuania and Poland that the Bund was created. In 1894, Arkadi Kremer (with the help of Iulii Martov) wrote *On Agitation* in Russian, a pamphlet that marked a significant turn in the life of the Jewish socialist circles of Vilnius and Bialystok by the shift from clandestine propaganda activity to agitation. The transition from narrow circles of a few dozen workers to the organisation of thousands of workers necessitated the adoption of Yiddish, and this instrumental change led to the birth of a Yiddish socialist intellectual elite.

There was a fairly rapid passage from pamphlets, leaflets, conferences, and songs to the birth of a genuine Yiddish socialist literature. It was a spontaneous mutation, the implications of which the Bund's precursors did not entirely recognise. Martov and Kremer had conceived the adoption of Yiddish as a technical expedient necessary to approach the Jewish proletariat, but they had no intention of creating a Yiddish Marxist literature. This was, rather, the product of an empirical orientation, which nonetheless took place very rapidly: already in 1897 the first Yiddish translation of *The Communist Manifesto*, by Chaim Zhitlovsky, had appeared. The foundation of the Bund took place at Vilnius, in October of the same year, at a congress gathering thirteen delegates from different towns within the Pale of Settlement (Vilnius, Vitebsk, Bialystok, Minsk, etc.).[18] The programmatic document approved by the congress recognised the specific oppression suffered by the Jewish proletariat, both as class and as national minority, but did not explicitly reject the perspective of assimilation (for example, it did not claim that Yiddish would be taught in the public schools). At the beginning, the Bund struggled *against* anti-Semitism and legal discrimination, not *for* the recognition of a Jewish nationality. The following year, during the Minsk congress that set up the RSDLP where three out of nine delegates were Bundists, the new party characterised itself as 'pan-Russian' so as to refer to the proletariat of the Tsarist Empire as a whole and not simply to the Russian-speaking part of it.[19] Suggested by the Bund, this definition implicitly recognised the multinational character of the workers' movement in Tsarist Russia, but the Jews were still a long way from being considered a nationality like the others. The Bund took this step in 1901, when it put the national question at the centre of its fourth congress. Under the influ-

---

17   See Mendelsohn 1970, pp. 19–20.
18   On the formation of the Bund, see Tobias 1972, pp. 22–69, as well as Weinstock 1984, vol. 1, pp. 33–154 and Levin 1977, pp. 236–79. On the 'prehistory' of the Bund, see Menes 1955, vol. 2, pp. 355–68.
19   See Tobias 1972, p. 78.

ence of the Austro-Marxists, who had developed (at the 1899 Brünn congress of the PSO) a project of cultural national autonomy for the different national components of the Habsburg Empire, the Bund defined the Jews as a nationality. Following the orientations of the South Slav Federation of the Austrian Socialist party, which had proposed at the Brünn congress an extension of the concept of cultural national autonomy to the extraterritorial minorities, the Bund approved a programme centred on three demands: a) the transformation of the Russian multinational empire into a federation of peoples; b) the right to national autonomy for each of them, regardless of their territory; c) the recognition of the Jews as a nation. Of course, the priority remained the struggle for civic rights and the suppression of anti-Semitic legislation, but the turn was significant.[20] The national programme, however, did not mean nationalism: the Bund stigmatised Zionism as a 'bourgeois' reaction to anti-Semitism and as an instrument to divide and disorientate the working class.[21]

Because of its new character as a Jewish workers' party, the Bund came quickly into conflict with Russian social democracy. The split took place during the famous second congress of the RSDLP, held in 1903 in Brussels and London. The Bund – represented by five delegates: Kossovsky, Medem, Eisenstadt, Liber, and Portnoy – did not submit its new programme to the congress for discussion, but confined itself to presenting the organisational conditions that it considered indispensable to its remaining within the RSDLP: on the one hand, to be recognised as the sole representative of the Jewish proletariat, and, on the other, the transformation of the social democracy into a federation of national organisations, on the model of the Austrian socialist party. These conditions gave rise to a sharp debate and were in the end rejected (the Bund motion obtained only the five votes of its own delegates). The congress voted for a res-

---

20   The resolution on the national question approved by the fourth national conference of
      the Bund affirmed that 'a state such as Russia, consisting as it does of many nationalit-
      ies, should, in the future, be reconstructed as a federation of nationalities with complete
      national autonomy for each nationality, independent of the territory in which it is located.
      The conference holds that the term "nation" is also to be applied to the Jewish people. In
      the light of existing circumstances, however, it is still too soon to put forth the demand for
      national autonomy for Jews and hence ... for the time the struggle is to be carried on only
      against all discriminatory laws directed against Jews ... [and] against any suppression of
      the Jewish nationality, but at the same time care must be taken not to fan national feel-
      ing into a flame, for that will only obscure the class consciousness of the proletariat and
      lead to chauvinism' (quoted by Levin 1977, p. 277). For the history of the Bund's debate
      on the national question, see Tobias 1972, pp. 160–76. On the influence of the Austro-
      Marxists, whose Brünn congress was reported by the Bund's reviews in 1899, see Kazdan
      1960, pp. 184–6. See also Mill 1949, pp. 66–7.
21   See Hertz 1960, pp. 339–54.

olution on the 'right of nations to self-determination', but rejected an amend-
ment put forward by Medem that proposed to establish 'institutions capable of
assuring the full liberty of cultural development' for all national minorities.[22]
A split became inevitable when two opposed motions were put forward, one
by Martov and the other by Liber: the first defined the Bund as a section of the
RSDLP intervening among the Jewish workers, a task posing specific linguistic
problems; the second, on the contrary, wished to extend the Bund's autonomy
to all questions concerning the life of the Jewish proletariat. In other terms:
was the Bund a Jewish workers' party or a segment of the RSDLP, concentrating
on propaganda among the Yiddish-speaking workers? Trotsky summed up the
Russian position: 'The efforts that they [the Bundists] have expended on this
narrow terrain of the Jewish Pale of Settlement could, if the work was carried
out in a larger area, yield tenfold results ... The organizational isolation of the
Bund has penned up the revolutionary energy of its militants in a narrow reservoir and has mercilessly narrowed – and for some time, it seems – the political
horizons of its leaders'.[23]

Oriented toward the creation of an action party under the tsarist autocracy –
according to Lenin and the Bolsheviks, it was necessary to create a strongly
centralised organization of professional revolutionaries – the Russian Social
Democrats saw in the Bund's federalism the danger of a nationalist deviation
and organisational fragmentation, which would have weakened the workers'
movement. For Lenin, tsarism was not the Habsburg Empire and the adoption
of an Austrian model by the Russian party would have been a serious mis-
take.[24] It is obvious that such organisational discrepancies hid two different
approaches to the national question, which the Bund's fifth congress in 1905
would definitively codify.[25] The split, only finally resolved in 1906, was deeply
traumatic for the Bund. In his memoirs, Medem described it as 'a genuine
catastrophe. To us it seemed as though a piece of flesh had been torn from a
living body'.[26] Rather than the result of opposed sectarianisms, as some historical interpretations would seem to suggest, this split was the product of
the structural-economic and national separation of the Jewish and the Russian workers in the Pale of Settlement. According to Plekhanov, however, the
Bundists were no more than 'Zionists with seasickness'.[27]

---

22   See Levin 1977, p. 298.
23   Quoted by Weinstock 1984, vol. 1, p. 189.
24   See Löw 1984.
25   See Tobias 1972, p. 331.
26   Medem 1979, p. 290.
27   Plekhanov said that during an interview with Vladimir Jabotinsky in 1905; see Nedava

The 1905 revolution showed the strengths and the limits of the Bund. Inside the Jewish community, its hegemony was incontestable, but on a global scale, its role was fairly marginal. Despite its organisational power, it was isolated by a revolution whose epicentres were St. Petersburg and Warsaw and which found its core in the proletariat of the big factories. In 1905, the Bund's intrinsic weakness, linked to the fragmentation and the structural fragility of the sector of the working class that it represented, became evident. During the Revolution, the Bund revealed itself to be, in Nathan Weinstock's words, a 'colossus with feet of clay'.[28] In 1905, however, the Bund was no longer only a workers' party; it had also become a national party seeking a dialectical synthesis between socialist internationalism and the defence of an oppressed national culture. There was no contradiction between Jewish liberation and world socialist revolution.

3 National Autonomy: Vladimir Medem

Vladimir Medem's long study, *The National Question and Social Democracy*, published in Russian and Yiddish in 1904, summed up a wide-ranging debate that had developed in the Bund since its foundation. This text revealed the influence of Austro-Marxism, but it was not a simple adaptation of the Brünn's theses to the Jewish-Russian context (Otto Bauer's book would be published only three years later). Medem's task was, first of all, to give a theoretical foundation to the action of the Bund and, secondly, to clarify the nature of its differences with the Russian social democrats.

Medem defined modern nationality as a creation of the bourgeoisie, a class that had historically been able to support both imperialist nationalisms and national liberation movements. In the Austro-Hungarian Empire, the German bourgeoisie tried to assimilate the Czechs (an oppressed nation) in order to extend its own national market, whereas the Czech bourgeoisie, deprived of any political power, defended itself by demanding independence and trying to assimilate the Germans of Bohemia.[29] In its bourgeois meaning, the idea of the nation was nothing but a disguised form of class collaboration (national

---

      1973, p. 45. In 1906, however, the Bund participated in the reunification congress of the
      RSDLP in Stockholm. A resolution approved by the congress recognised the Bund as the
      only representative of the Jewish proletariat without territorial limitations to its activity
      and considered the national question as still 'open' (in fact, the delegates did not have the
      time to discuss it); see Bukhbinder 1931, pp. 362–3.

28   Weinstock 1984, vol. 1, p. 207.

29   Medem 1943, pp. 180–1. For a study on the formation of Medem's thought on the national
      question, see Pinson 1945, pp. 233–64; Patkin 1947, pp. 198–212.

unity above class divisions). But nationalities, Medem argued, could also exist as cultural communities beyond and against their bourgeois form within the framework of capitalism. Language, literature, culture and national consciousness should not be mechanically reduced to economic structures. Of course, nations were not closed and immutable entities: 'a national culture as an independent essence, as a closed circle with its own content, has never existed. The nation is the particular form in which the universal human content expresses itself (*der algemein mentshleker hinalt*). The foundation of cultural life, which generally is the same everywhere, takes different colorings and national forms to the extent that the different groups, among which specific social relations are established, adapt themselves to them. These social relations – the context in which class conflicts are born and intellectual and spiritual currents develop – confer on the culture a national character (*a natsionaln shtempl oif der kultur*)'.[30] In other words, 'a-national' cultures did not exist.

There are clear affinities between this conception and Otto Bauer's theory of 'national apperception' – the particular way in which each nation internalises and assimilates the contents of international culture – which the Viennese Marxist would develop three years later in *Die Nationalitätenfrage und die Sozialdemokratie*. Unlike Bauer, however, Medem considered language as a pillar of the nation. If culture inevitably took national forms, it needed particular languages. The consolidation of Yiddish, Medem wrote, was 'the principal task in the field of cultural creation'.[31] Unlike the defenders of Hebrew, partisans of a completely abstract conception of the nation, who considered Yiddish to be a 'dirty street jargon' (*a shmutsikn gas-zshargon*), Medem took this idiom for a 'national language', profoundly rooted in 'the life, the hopes, and the aspirations' of the Jewish masses.[32] In spite of some formal affinities, this conception of the nation was very different from Kautsky's. For Kautsky, language was instrumental to the establishment of economic and social relations, and the development of the productive forces would lead to the transcendence of linguistic pluralism; whereas for Medem, language was above all the source and the laboratory of national culture. In his view, the Jews and the Armenians proved that national cultures could exist without separated national economies: 'national oppression elevates cultural life'.[33] In the case of the Jewish minority, moreover, language and literature could not be the superstructure of a national economy simply because they did not constitute the culture of

---

30   Medem 1943, p. 188.
31   Medem 1943, p. 341.
32   Ibid., pp. 342–3.
33   Medem 1943, p. 191.

a dominant class: they were the crucible of the political consciousness of the working class. Another passage of this 1904 study defined the nation as a 'particular psychology' (*eigentumlekhe psikhologie*) without, however, developing this concept and without perceiving all its implications.[34]

Finally, the Bund leader denied any organic, necessary relationship between a nation and a homogeneous territory. The right to self-determination and the creation of new independent states – he stressed in *National Movements and National Socialist Parties in Russia* (1908) – were not a panacea for resolving the national question. This principle belonged to the bourgeois nationalist tradition, the source from which Marxists had derived their theory of the nation as an entanglement of market and state, but in many cases nations, states cultures and territories did not mechanically correspond. The Poles of Lithuania or the Lithuanians of the Ukraine were part of living nations, although settled outside of Polish and Lithuanian territories. The Polish nationalists used the terms *land* and *nation* as synonyms, but it was a misunderstanding. This is why the Bund conceived Jewish autonomy in national-cultural (*natsional-kultureler*), not in territorial terms. When nations formed 'islands on a foreign territory (*bildn hinzlen oif a fremder territorie*)',[35] personal autonomy prevailed over the territorial principle. For the Jews, personal autonomy – a concept taken from Karl Renner – meant the creation of organs (*kehilah*) charged with managing Jewish national life (education, public affairs) inside a multinational Russian federation, which kept sovereign power.[36] To sum up, Medem saw the nation as an almost hierarchical structure based on two principal elements, language and culture, and a secondary one, the economy, in which territory did not play any significant role. This conception appeared within the Bund in 1899, when the first echo of the resolutions at the Austrian Brünn congress reached Russia. In *Der yiddisher arbeter*, John Mill welcomed the theses of Austro-Marxism as the 'overthrow of the old law, according to which a nation is its territory, by another, namely that a nation is its culture'.[37] In 1904, Vladimir Kossovsky argued that territory had played a role in Western Europe, whose nations had passed through three distinct stages – 'nation-race', 'nation-territory', and 'nation-state' – and where capitalism had developed within the pre-existing framework of national states. In Eastern Europe, on the contrary, a belated capitalism had led to the creation of hybrid bourgeois-feudal forms inside a system of multinational states. There, the 'nation-race' and the 'nation-territory' had

---

34   Ibid., p. 207.
35   Medem 1943, pp. 252–3.
36   Ibid., p. 254.
37   Mill 1899, p. 27, quoted by Frankel 1984, p. 219.

been much less important than the linguistic factor, the creator of a 'profile' and a 'national individuality' among the extraterritorial minorities.[38] For the Jews, Yiddish literature had replaced a territorial identity that did not exist. In a Yiddishland shaken by secularisation, religion no longer assured the cohesion of the Jewish world, and the idea of nationality developed outside of a territorial dimension: territory was a sort of vacuum, which was filled by Yiddish literature. Language became a 'frontier' that circumscribed the Jewish life in the same way that the land defined the culture of the Polish or Ukrainian peasants.

Radicalising this approach, the Bundist propagandist David Balakan reduced the nation to language. The national question, he explained in *Die Sozialdemokratie und das jüdische Proletariat*, published in German in Czernowiz in 1905, was 'neither economic, nor political ... but uniquely a linguistic question [*bloßeine Sprachenfrage*]'.[39] The Jews formed a nation, despite being deprived of territorial homogeneity, because of their common language, spoken by eight million people. The fact that Yiddish was a mixture of German, Hebrew, and other Latin and Slavic languages was of no importance, he answered to his critics, because even English had been born out of the fusion of different languages.[40] Balakan did not exclude *a priori* the Kautskyan hypothesis of a future fusion of languages and nations – henceforth of Jewish assimilation – but in the present Yiddish was flourishing as a national language.

In similar terms, Medem's theorised 'national neutralism', which refused to make any forecast about the future of the Jews (nation or assimilation). He simply argued that history would decide and there was no need to act for or against these tendencies: 'We are neutral ... We are not against assimilation, we are against *assimilationism* [*strebung tsu assimilatsie*], against assimilation as a goal'.[41] In short, Medem recognised the national character of contemporary Jewish culture, but rejected nationalism. In his view, the distinction between nation – the feeling of belonging to a community of culture – and nationalism – the tendency to the domination of one nation over the others – was fundamental. 'Assimilationism' was only a 'nationalism of appropriation'[42] inasmuch as it implied the disappearance of the national minorities. In claiming the Jewish assimilation and criticising the 'nationalism of the Bund', the Russian Marxists only expressed their defence of a dominant (Russian) nationalism.

---

38   Quoted by Heller 1977, pp. 107–10.
39   Balakan 1905, p. 16.
40   Ibid., p. 22.
41   Medem 1943, p. 189.
42   Ibid., p. 185.

In 1904, Medem's inscribed this conception of 'national neutralism' into a broader vision of historical development as an uncontrollable 'blind process [*a blindn protses*]'.[43] 'National neutralism' probably resulted from a compromise between the nationalist current (Mill) and the assimilationist current (Kopelson) of the party.[44] Kossovsky observed that the 'neutralist' attitude allowed the Bund to avoid the pitfalls of both assimilationism and nationalism but, he concluded, in the long term it was unsustainable. A mass party like the Bund could not avoid a clear position on the future of the Jews, particularly when all its practical activity was directed against assimilation. The Bund had played a fundamental role in the development of the 'language, of the literature, of Jewish schools, of all the elements of modern Jewish culture'.[45]

In his 1910 essay, *Nationalism or Neutralism*, Medem reformulated his theory in a less fatalistic sense. He noted the continuing existence of two opposed tendencies, one toward assimilation and the other toward 'nationalisation' (*natsionalizirendige tendents*): 'Both exist and act. Which will carry the day? That depends on thousands of different cultural, political and economic factors. It depends on the combination of these factors, the rapidity with which they develop, and it is not possible to predict the rapidity of this development'.[46] Unlike the 'assimilationists', the Bund had no certainties on the future, but neutralism did not mean indifference: the impossibility of predicting the distant future of the Jews – national existence or assimilation – did not exempt it from the task of answering the problems stemming from the current existence of a Jewish nation. Moreover, this question about their own future did not concern the Jews alone, but all the modern nations. He wrote: 'The Jewish nation exists, its national life develops and strengthens itself ... It does not amount to a prediction but a fact. The national demands flourish and are at the basis of our cultural life'.[47] In this perspective, neutralism did not prevent the Bund from adopting a positive attitude toward national autonomy even if, unlike the nationalists, it did not consider the nation as a 'goal in itself' (*a tsiel far zikh*). Neutralism did not even mean 'fatalism' if the struggle for material interests and conscious action could play a role in the historic process, modifying the 'national demands' and conditioning the tendencies towards assimilation or national development.[48]

43 Ibid., p. 189.
44 See Levin 1977, p. 338.
45 Kosowski 1943, p. 136.
46 Medem 1917, p. 117.
47 Ibid., p. 119.
48 Ibid., pp. 124, 133.

Medem's theoretical elaboration had multiple sources. As we have already indicated, Austro-Marxism, whose works he had studied intensively during his exile in Switzerland, was probably the most important. There is no doubt that Karl Renner's essay *Staat und Nation* (1899), which defined nation as a 'personal association', not a 'territorial corporation' but a 'cultural and spiritual community that expressed itself through national literature',[49] deeply influenced him. Otto Bauer's classic work on the national question showed many conceptual affinities with his thought, as he openly recognised in his autobiography,[50] but it was only published in 1907, three years after his own seminal essays. On the other hand, the idea of an extraterritorial Jewish nation rooted in Yiddish language and literature had been advanced, at least from 1897, by Chaim Zhitlovsky in several works: *Why Yiddish?* (1897), *Socialism and the National Question* (1899), and *The Jewish People and Yiddish* (1904). A Bundist fellow-traveller, Zhitlovsky had defined the nation 'not (as) a natural and psychological fact, given once and for all and immutable, but (as) a cultural-historical formation (*a kulturhistorishe dersheinung*) that changes in the course of time'.[51] He had also been a pioneer among the Jewish socialists in the search for reconciliation between proletarian internationalism and the idea of a Jewish nation. Last but not least, the great Jewish historian Simon Dubnov had laid down the intellectual premises of Bundism. Medem recognised his debt toward Dubnov, but he also criticised his 'mystic' vision of the Jews as a world nation founded on a *Kulturgemeinshaft*. 'Our common history', wrote Medem, 'has transmitted to us a series of impressions that are difficult to erase. But, since that time (the period of the ancient Jewish nation) our roads have separated and we have no longer lived a common history ... Our common heritage evolves and takes different form, among its different heirs ... in the context of different cultures'.[52] He gave the example of an assimilated French Jew who no longer shared a common culture with a Polish co-religionist. Medem's Jewish nation was rooted in the *Yiddishkeit*: it was not a spiritual but a cultural and socio-historical entity. Differently from Dubnov, for whom a French Jew remained a 'member of the Jewish nation because of his birth',[53] that is as a member of a 'spiritual' community, Medem never took religion into consideration as a constitutive element of the Jewish nation. In the eyes of Dubnov, conversely, this identification between Jewish nation and *Yiddishkeit* was a form of 'linguistic

---

49   See Renner 1974.
50   Medem 1979, p. 315.
51   Zhitlovsky 1955, p. 379.
52   Medem 1917, pp. 93–4.
53   Dubnov 1961, pp. 99, 102.

chauvinism'.[54] Stressing the importance of social and economic factors in history, Dubnov had distanced himself from the spiritualist conception of Judaism that permeated the work of Heinrich Graetz, with whom he nonetheless continued to share a vision of Jewish history as an ultimately unitary phenomenon (this would lead him to write a *World History of the Jews* in the 1920s). As a Marxist, Medem had broken with such an approach. The lack of the name of Dubnov in his autobiography, nevertheless, suppresses a crucial intellectual source of his thought.

It is obvious that Bundism, focused on national cultural autonomy, could not avoid a radical conflict with Zionism. According to Medem, Zionism, even in its 'proletarian' and 'socialist' variants, was nothing but a 'national mirage', a dangerous form of Jewish nationalism.[55] In 1898, the Bund ignored the Basel Congress in which Herzl established the bases of Zionism, simply depicting it as 'utopian' and 'reactionary'.[56] In 1902, *Der yiddisher arbeter* analysed Zionism as a manifestation of 'bourgeois psychology' that conceived the nation as property (the control of a territory),[57] and two years later the Bund denounced the goal of a Palestinian settlement as a diversion from the struggle against the Tsarist regime – the real source of anti-Semitism – which inculcated a 'ghetto psychology' in the Jews.[58] The sixth Bund congress, held at Zurich in 1905, put the finishing touches on this critique by definitively condemning Zionism as a 'specific nationalist version of petty bourgeois ideology', owing to the 'utopian and adventurist' character of its territorial demands: it offered a false objective to the working class and created an obstacle to its struggle for a solution to the Jewish Question in the Diaspora, where a Jewish nation really existed. The conclusion affirmed the 'necessity' of struggling against Zionism 'in all its forms and all its nuances'.[59] The Bund could not accept that the right of Jews to determine their future should be put off to a distant future, outside Russia. They had to fight for liberation 'here and now', not in another continent, not escaping their present circumstances, and their action was inscribed in their 'being here' or *doikeyt* (*do* meaning 'here').

The critique of Zionism, nonetheless, remained a marginal task compared with the struggle against anti-Semitism. In 1910, Medem analysed this topic in

---

54   Ibid., p. 53. To the socialist (and of course, Bundist) slogan 'Workers of all countries unite!' Dubnov opposed another: 'Jews of all classes and all parties, unite!'

55   Medem 1943, p. 259.

56   See Bukhbinder 1931, p. 108, and Tobias 1972, p. 164.

57   See Mill 1949, pp. 36–9.

58   See Allg. Jüdischen Arbeiterbund 1904, p. 26.

59   Bunzl 1975, p. 158.

the *Neue Zeit*, distinguishing two principal forms of Russian anti-Semitism. In the first instance, it was a popular movement that had an economic motivation and resulted in the slogan 'don't buy from the Jews', trying to boycott Jewish trade in the Pale of Settlement.[60] Paradoxically, it was an aspect of Russian modernisation and Westernisation. Then, there was what Medem defined as 'a-Semitism' (*Asemitismus*), which reflected the hostility of the cultivated middle class towards the Jewish intellectuals.[61] Unlike the traditional anti-Judaism, modern mass anti-Semitism was opposed to assimilation. Taking a clear racist connotation, it did not demand the Russification of the Jews, but rather their exclusion from Russian society: 'Elsewhere national oppression tends toward the denationalisation of a particular ethnic group, toward incorporating it into the nation, toward eliminating its specificities. The case of the Jew is different. Not only does anti-Semitism not seek to assimilate the Jews, but it is directly opposed to assimilation'.[62] This tendency resulted in a whole set of discriminatory laws limiting the rights of Jews in the areas of residence, some professional activities and so on. In other words – and this revealed its vicious character – this new anti-Semitism acted as a policy of denationalisation: the tsarist regime did not try to impose Russian culture on the Jews but prevented them from developing their own. The Jews thus found themselves at an impasse: 'They can neither become Russian nor remain Jewish'.[63] According to Medem, Russian anti-Semitism was the tsarist reaction to the development of a Jewish 'modern cultural nation' under the impulsion of the workers' movement.

Medem was the first Marxist of his time to reject the dogma of assimilation. He stressed the national character of the Eastern European Jews and claimed cultural national autonomy for them in the framework of Diaspora, where they had developed Yiddish as a modern national language. He never denied the historical reality of the assimilation of the Jews in the West. In his eyes, the Bund was a socialist party of the Jewish workers of the Tsarist Empire, certainly not – in the manner of Poale Zion – a sort of Jewish workers' International.

4   Zionism: Ber Borokhov

Socialist Zionism appeared toward the end of the 1890s, when Nahman Syrkin published in Berne *Die Judenfrage und der Sozialistische judische Staat* (*The*

---

60   Medem 1974, p. 120.
61   Ibid., pp. 121–2.
62   Ibid., p. 123.
63   Ibid., p. 125.

Jewish Question and the Jewish Socialist State). At that moment, many socialist Zionist circles had emerged in the Tsarist Empire, as well as in the Russian Jewish émigré circles of Germany and Switzerland, which led an organisationally precarious and ideologically confused existence. In 1905, in an effort to distinguish itself from Herzl on the one hand and from the Bund on the other hand, socialist Zionism defined its own identity, which resulted in three principal currents: the Zionist-Socialist Workers Party (Syrkin, Lestschinsky, Tchernikov); the Jewish Socialist Workers party, the so-called SERP (Rosin, Zilberfarb, Ratner, Zhitlovsky); and the Poale Zion (Borokhov). Despite their discrepancies, all of them agreed on a fundamental point that radically distinguished them from the Bund: they claimed a *territorial* solution to the Jewish Question.[64] Syrkin and Lestschinsky initially denied any future to the Diaspora, which they considered as a fundamental obstacle for a *normal* national life, the source of an 'economic degeneration' that objectively impeded the existence of a modern Jewish nation. Later they abandoned this 'nihilistic' attitude and finally accepted the idea of Jewish cultural-national autonomy in a Russian federation liberated from tsarism.[65] Zhitlovsky's territorialism, on the other hand, amounted to a distant and indeterminate perspective. In the short term, however, he argued for concrete responses to the situation of the Jewish masses in Russia. Practically, this meant the creation of a *sejm*, a sort of Jewish national parliament. In other words, this orientation was a 'territorial' version of the national autonomy theorised by Medem and Dubnov.[66]

Socialist Zionism was principally rooted in the southern areas of the Pale of Settlement, notably in Ukraine, where the Bund and the Russian social democracy had a weaker presence among the Jewish workers, and it thus succeeded in filling a political vacuum. This geographical split was not accidental. The Bund was born in Lithuania and Poale Zion in the Ukraine, two regions in which Jewish culture had followed different trajectories. Vilnius was the heart of the Yiddish *Haskalah* and Odessa was the capital of the Russian-speaking Jewish enlightenment. Nearly all the leaders of the Bund emerged from Vilnius, in the heart of the *Yiddishkeit*, whereas the Jewish intelligentsia in the south of the empire was overwhelmingly Russified. There, the Jewish intellectuals were more easily confronted with a simple alternative: assimilation or Zionism.[67]

---

64   Medem 1943, p. 256. On the genesis of the different currents inside the Jewish workers' movement, see Weinstock 1984, vol. 1, pp. 238–77, and particularly the thesis already quoted by Suchecky 1986.
65   See Lestschinsky 1979, pp. 69–96.
66   See Kolatt 1977, p. 235.
67   See Mishkinski 1969, pp. 27–52.

Within socialist Zionism, however, only Borokhov could be qualified as a Marxist. Syrkin claimed a kind of vague humanistic socialism and Zhitlovsky never abandoned populism; their attitude towards Marx's ideas could be either indifferent or positive, but they never tried to participate in the Marxist debate. Borokhov was a different case, insofar as he believed himself to have found in Marxism a solution to the contradictions and blind alleys of 'bourgeois' Zionism. Up until 1904, this young intellectual from Poltava, the son of a Hebrew teacher, was not interested in the search for a symbiosis between Marxism and Jewish nationalism. He considered himself a disciple of Menachem Ussishkin, the founder of the Chibbat Zion movement and the principal antagonist of Theodor Herzl at the Sixth Zionist Congress, held at Basle in 1903.[68] Ussishkin represented the Russian current of Zionism, which was neither secular nor assimilated, and did not accept the replacement of Palestine with Uganda; his idea of a return to the 'land of the fathers' often entered into conflict with the pragmatic orientation of Herzl and Nordau.[69] The essay 'On the Question of Zionist Theory', published in early 1905 but written in 1902–3, summed up Borokhov's pre-Marxist vision of Jewish nationalism. He rejected both the Diaspora – 'It is our deep conviction that in the *galut* there is no salvation for the Jewish people'[70] – and assimilation, which did not work in the case of intermingled nations. According to Borokhov, an extraterritorial minority was despised by the hegemonic nation, as proven by the case of the converted and assimilated Jews who remained 'dirty Jews' in the eyes of the Russians. Such an assessment was justified, insofar as the virtual nonexistence of the Jews in agriculture – 'the basis of all society ... independently of the theories of the Physiocrats' – inevitably condemned them to 'complete economic degeneration as well as physical and cultural degeneration'.[71] The impoverished Jews were absorbed into the lumpenproletariat, into the 'desperate poverty of the sansculottes'. The total uselessness and negativity of the Diaspora Jews could only feed anti-Semitism, whose roots, in Borokhov's opinion, were as 'socio-psychological' as economic. It did not make sense to suppress the legal discriminations against the Jews if the real and profound causes of anti-Semitism remained untouched. Thus, the abolition of the Pale of Settlement would only have resulted in the flourishing of anti-Semitism throughout Russia. His conclusion did not differ very much from contemporary Herzelian commonplaces: 'We are foreigners and nowhere in the world do we possess the social power

---

68   On the influence of Ussishkin on Borokhov, see Frankel 1984, pp. 333–8.
69   On the debate inside the Zionist movement, see Laqueur 1976 and Vital 1982.
70   Borokhov 1984, p. 36.
71   Ibid., p. 47.

that could make us masters of our fate. We are cut off from nature and have no agriculture. All this has left us hovering in the air. Our history in the *galut* has never been shaped by our own powers, our fate has always depended on external ties'.[72] In other words, the Diaspora meant the 'economic degeneration' of the Jewish people and anti-Semitism was eternal and ineradicable, the inevitable reaction of 'normal' nations against this Jewish pathological otherness.[73] Syrkin, Herzl, Spencer, Mach and Avenarius – the empirio-critist theoreticians from whom he borrowed his psychological explanation of anti-Semitism – were merged in this first essay of the young Borokhov. Echoing Max Nordau's *Entartung* (*Degeneration*), which had just been published in German, he criticised the idea of progress as an irreversible and continuous process that would automatically lead to assimilation and the extinction of the Jews. In his eyes, the oppression of the Jews was not only the product of Russian social and cultural backwardness, but also a symptom of modernity:

> We do not rely on progress; we know that its very zealous proponents inflate its achievements out of all proportion. Progress is an important factor in the rapid development of technology, science, perhaps even of the arts, but certainly in the development of neuroses, hysteria, and prostitution. Of the moral progress of nations, of the end of the national egoism that is destroying their best – it is too soon to speak about these. Progress is a double-edged sword. If the good angel in man advances, the Satan within him advances too.[74]

Borokhov sensed through this allegorical language that scientific-technical progress was not inevitably the bearer of 'moral' and social progress, but that on the contrary it included the possibility of a modern 'degeneration' of which the Jews would be the victims. The return of the Jews to Palestine, which was not yet rationally motivated by socio-economic terms, was derived from a messianic ideal and conceived as the re-composition of an original harmony shattered by the Diaspora. For its part, the *galut* was seen, according to the Hebraic tradition, as a place of exile and a waiting for liberation. In short, Borokhov combined Nordau's idea of 'degeneration' with Nahman Syrkin's Messianic idea of redemption.[75]

---

72   Ibid., p. 48.
73   Halevi 1981, p. 185.
74   Borokhov 1984, p. 37. Nordau's successful book had been published in 1899. See Nordau 1993.
75   Syrkin 1975, p. 350. On Nachman Syrkin, see Frankel 1984, pp. 288–328 and Levin 1977, pp. 377–99.

Borokhov's first Marxist work was *Class Interests and the National Question*, published in Vilnius in 1905 in both Russian and Yiddish. This ambitious essay did not deal directly with Jewish issues, but it sketched the outlines of a Marxist theory of nation and nationalism that already contained the core of Borokhovism.[76] His starting point was the concept of 'conditions of production', which set the framework in which the productive forces of society grew and developed and in which given relations of production were consequently established. These conditions of production, which thus represented the primary base of any economic and social system, were hierarchically enumerated in the following order: *geographical* (climatic-physical); *anthropological* (race); *historical* (the development of a human community, its internal relations, and so on). The historical conditions of production, the last in this series that sometimes reminds one of (and also anticipates) Fernand Braudel's '*longue durée*', belonged to a stratified conception of historical time, which originated in the natural conditions and coalesced into a 'spiritual' and cultural legacy made of 'language, traditions, customs, worldviews'.[77] Relations of production established the division of society into classes, whereas the conditions of production separated humanity into distinct communities (peoples, nations). Social conflicts had their origin in the divorce between the productive forces and the relations of production (when the economic structure of society could no longer contain the development of the productive forces), whereas the national question emerged from the opposition between the productive forces and the conditions of production. Borokhov borrowed the concept of conditions of production from Marx, who had employed it in *Capital* in order to define the natural premises of economic life such as climate, soil fertility, underground wealth, etc. Borokhov now extended its meaning and transformed it into a pillar of his theory. Differently from Marx, for whom the conditions of production were limited to natural factors alone, Borokhov argued that there were also *historical* conditions of production (superimposed upon natural ones) among which were 'culture' and 'worldviews',[78] two categories that the author of *Capital* usually included in the ideological superstructure of society. This approach avoided a widespread form of economic determinism, but practically replaced it with a similar form of cultural determinism.

Conditions of production served as the point of departure for his definitions of the concepts of people and nation: a people corresponded with a 'society'

---

76   Najenson 1979, p. 9. See also Frankel 1984, pp. 329–63; and Perlmutter 1969, pp. 32–43.

77   Borokhov 1920, pp. 39–40.

78   Ibid., pp. 32–3.

(divided into classes) whose profile had been created by the common historic conditions of production; a nation was situated at a superior level, where a human community became conscious of its own 'common historic past'.[79] Peoples were only embryonic steps in the process of the formation of nations that presupposed a certain homogeneity of the conditions of production. Thus, Borokhov distinguished between people and nation by extending the dichotomy, established by Marx in *The Poverty of Philosophy* (1846), between the concept of 'class in itself' and that of 'class for itself', namely the distinction between class seen as a simple economic category – people who occupy the same place in the process of production – and class seen as a collective, conscious historical subject. 'Life on the basis of the same relations of production, when these conditions are harmonious for the individuals of the group', Borokhov wrote, 'produces class consciousness and the sentiment of class solidarity. Life on the basis of the same conditions of production, when these conditions are harmonious for the members of the society, produces national consciousness and the sentiment of national integration'.[80] And this feeling created by a common historical memory was nothing but nationalism, because, before being a policy or an ideology, nationalism was the natural feeling of belonging to a particular national community. In this sense, Borokhov refused to qualify nationalism as an 'anachronistic, reactionary, or traditional thing',[81] emphasising that even the proletariat expressed its own form of nationalism. During the First World War, in which Poale Zion joined the Zimmerwald movement and defended a pacifist/internationalist orientation, Borokhov reaffirmed the value of proletarian nationalism in these terms:

> This instinct of self-preservation in nations cannot be destroyed. It is rank dilettantism and sheer nonsense to demand that nations lose their identity and shake off their loyalty to themselves. The national instinct of self-preservation latent in the socialist working class is a healthy nationalism. Only international socialism based upon a realist approach to nationalism can liberate sick humanity in this capitalist era and cure society of its social and national conflicts.[82]

On this base, Borokhov distinguished between four forms of nationalism: a) the nationalism of landowners, attached to the land, the source of their wealth; b)

---

79   Ibid., p. 42.
80   Ibid., p. 44.
81   Ibid., p. 48.
82   Borokhov 1984, p. 166.

the nationalism of the bourgeoisie, for whom territory was only a necessary base for the conquest of the world market; c) the nationalism of the middle class, which attributed to territory the value of a 'consumer market'; d) finally, the nationalism of the proletariat, a class settled on a territory conceived as a place of work.[83] Defined first as the feeling of belonging to a particular human community, nationalism divided then into a plurality of aspirations and conceptions linked to the division of society into classes. Borokhov concluded that a positive form of nationalism could be found 'only among the progressive elements of the oppressed nations'.[84] Nonetheless, the fundamental feature always present in his definition of nation and nationalism was *territory*. On this point, he differentiated himself as much from Medem, who was accused of ignoring the 'material base' of the national problem, as from Austro-Marxism.[85] At the same time, Borokhov shared his stress on territory – the irreplaceable 'material base' of the nation – with both Kautsky and Stalin. Differently from the Bund, which identified the Jewish nation with the *Yiddishkeit*, stressing its origins and the historical peculiarities that distinguished it from most Western European nations, Kautsky, Stalin, and Borokhov *naturalised* nations by explaining them through a rigid deterministic causality (geographical, economic, cultural, psychological, etc.).[86]

In 'Our Platform' (1906), Borokhov approached the Jewish Question as a national 'anomaly' linked to the Diaspora. Extraterritorial nations had to adapt themselves to conditions of external production that they could not control. Deprived of a material base (territory), they were transformed into alien bodies inside exterior social formations. When, thanks to the development of the productive forces, society could assume directly the functions that had remained until then the prerogative of a 'foreign' minority, the latter became an obstacle to the flowering of the 'indigenous' people and, consequently, was rejected as a 'superfluous' element. Anti-Semitism, in other words, was the product of an ineluctable historical law.[87]

Assimilation had been an active tendency at the time of the transition from feudalism to capitalism, when the Jews exercised an essential socio-economic function as market agents and could play a role in a continent not yet divided into developed nations. The great exodus of the Jews toward Eastern Europe took place when the rise of capitalism in the West meant there was no further

---

83   1920, p. 67.
84   Ibid., p. 82.
85   Borokhov 1920, pp. 169–70.
86   On this similarity between Stalin and Borokhov see Kolatt 1977, p. 240 and Finzi 1985, p. 61.
87   Borokhov 1920, pp. 116–17.

need for their services. Before, their profession had distinguished them from the rest of the population, but in the modern world their social parasitic character isolated them and prevented their assimilation. Thus, the Jews developed a national consciousness without disposing of the necessary material conditions to live like other nations. According to Borokhov:

> During the first period of industrial capitalism, the factor of assimilation was largely dominant in Jewish life. The industrial revolution brought down the walls of the ghetto, opening to the Jews the broad space of free competition. The epoch of the decisive collision between capitalism and feudalism was, at the same time, the golden age of Jewish assimilation. However, a little later, an implacable corrective of individual specialization, national specialization, made its appearance, and assimilation began to give way to isolation. All the Jewish assimilationists are basically utopians and swim against the real current of the Jewish historical dynamic. The growing national specialization does not assimilate the Jew, but, on the contrary, nationalizes him.[88]

In 'Our Platform', Borokhov interpreted both anti-Semitism and Jewish nationalism as historical tendencies that condemned the idea of assimilation as illusory, but he still defined the Jewish nation *negatively*, by its lack of a territory (a characteristic common to the whole Jewish Diaspora). He never indicated what the Jewish national identity, this consciousness of a 'common historic past', was concretely made of. In 1906 Borokhov had not yet discovered the values of the *Yiddishkeit* and was hardly concerned to distinguish between the assimilated Jews of the West and those of Eastern Europe who led a national life. In the light of his deterministic Marxism, the Bund's politics appeared 'undoubtedly reactionary'[89] and Medem's theory of national neutralism was summed up in a single phrase: *Asylum ignorantiae*.[90]

Two years later, however, Borokhov had changed his mind. He began to write in Yiddish, the *mame loshn*, and in 1915 he published an important *History of Yiddish Literature*. Gradually his conception of the Jewish nation became charged with a positive cultural content, linked primarily to language. Different from a Yiddish defender like Zhitlovsky, he did not hold Hebrew in contempt, continuing to attribute a significant 'spiritual' function to the sacred language (*loshn kdush*), but now he saw Yiddish as the mirror of Jewish national life and

---

88   Ibid., p. 135.
89   Ibid., pp. 169–70.
90   Ibid., p. 164.

considered the development of philological research as a necessary task for legitimating it among the modern national languages. In Borokhov's view, Yiddish and Hebrew – the two languages of the Jewish nation – were not incompatible but complementary and capable of enriching each other, like two 'Siamese brothers'. As he wrote in his *History of Yiddish Literature*, 'Hebrew created our historic personality in time, Yiddish in the world'.[91]

After discovering Yiddish, Borokhov circumscribed his conception of the Jewish nation within linguistic borders, thus significantly reducing his discrepancy with Medem and the Bund. 'The Western Jews', he wrote in 1911, 'do not participate in the essentially collective life of our people. That is why they can only accept, among the current Jewish ideologies, unconditional assimilation or an abstract and passive Zionism. The problems of a collective national life, of its development in the Diaspora, almost do not exist for the Western Jew'.[92] Zionism, in other words, had become a fight for the Jews of Eastern Europe, a combat in which the colonisation of Palestine could coexist with cultural autonomy in the Tsarist Empire: '*galut* and *Zion* each represent one goal in itself',[93] Borokhov emphasised, recognising that the Poale Zion and the Bund could share the same struggle 'for the civil and national emancipation of the Jews'.[94]

In spite of its tremendous role in building a modern national culture, the Jewish proletariat remained structurally weak, and its exclusion from mechanised industry was the fundamental cause of its political impotence. Jewish workers who went on strike could neither paralyse the economy nor significantly affect social life. Without a territorial unity, a Jewish national economy could not exist, and that deprived the political action of the workers of a 'strategic base'.[95] In 'Our Platform', Borokhov depicted the Jewish proletariat by the allegorical image of a 'chained Prometheus who, furious and impotent, plucks the feathers of the eagle that eats at his heart'.[96] This did not prevent him, in *The Economic Development of the Jewish People* (1916) – a series of articles published in the New York daily *Der Yidisher Kempfer* – from criticising the theory of the 'economic degeneration' of the Jewish Diaspora elaborated by Jakob Lestschinsky. Of course, the Jewish workers were almost totally excluded from agriculture

---

91 Borokhov 1966, p. 180. On Borokhov as philologist and historian of Yiddish literature, see Robin 1984, pp. 106–7.
92 Borokhov 1928, p. 163.
93 Ibid., p. 283.
94 Ibid., p. 220.
95 Borokhov 1920, pp. 156–9.
96 Ibid., p. 160.

and large-scale industry, and, at the same time, concentrated in the 'final stages of production'.[97] They did not produce machines but only consumption commodities, within economic sectors that were the most distant from the 'land', and these anomalies condemned the Jewish economy to a pariah condition, as a free floating 'air economy [*Luftwirtschaft*]'.[98] Referring to the Aristotelian distinction between 'natural function' and 'human function', he observed that in the Russian Empire, where 70 to 80 percent of the economically active citizens lived from 'nature' (agriculture and primary stages of production: mining, timber, metallurgy, building ...), the same percentage of Jews worked in the 'latter stages of production' (carpentry, chemicals, fabrication of leather and paper, but above all clothing, food, and so on). Insofar as this tendency grew rapidly, the structural weakness of the Jewish proletariat became endemic: 'Marx demonstrated that the machine replaces the worker and that variable capital is replaced by constant capital. But inasmuch as Jewish labor, as we have seen, is fully employed in the production of variable capital, it follows that it is increasingly expelled from production and replaced by non-Jewish labor'.[99]

Mass emigration was the inevitable consequence of the expulsion of the Jews from industry. In the United States, France, and England they vaguely foresaw a concrete solution to their growing impoverishment, but emigration was a tramp when the same economic anomaly reappeared in the country in which they settled. Borokhov gave the example of the United States, where the Jewish workers experienced 'a much more unilateral development than in Russia ... and were concentrated exclusively in clothing'.[100] The United States did not break the fatal law of the Diaspora: deprived of a territory of their own, even in America, the Jews had to adapt themselves to a body of 'external conditions of production', which perpetuated their national anomaly and oppression. Because large-scale industry remained closed to the Jews in the advanced capitalist countries, Borokhov explained, they should emigrate to the economically backward countries, where they could 'occupy immediately a dominant position' through the expropriation of a territory, the 'strategic base' on which to build an independent national economy. Jewish immigration was a spontaneous, 'immanent' process that had to be oriented, planned and transformed

---

97   Borokhov 1966, p. 192.
98   Ibid., p. 194. In 1906, Alexander Lampert criticised Borokhov's tendency to consider as belonging to the proletariat only the industrial workers and concluded that the weakness of the Jewish working class did not lie in the lack of a Jewish national economy but in national oppression and anti-Semitism. See Lampert 1905–6, pp. 804–13.
99   Borokhov 1966, p. 200.
100   Ibid., p. 191.

into a 'movement of colonisation'. In Borokhov's view, this was the only way to redress the 'inverted pyramid' of Jewish society. Reestablishing an organic link, cut for two thousand years, between the nation and the land, meant a Jewish return to agriculture and the primary sectors of production.

Why, then, Palestine? Borokhov tried to justify this choice with rational rather than theological arguments. As a semi-agricultural country, Palestine presented the ideal economic conditions for the Zionist colonisation, and furthermore offered some cultural advantages non-existent in other countries. Its inhabitants were the 'direct descendants of the people of Judea and of Kahan, with a small addition of Arab blood';[101] they were scarcely different from Sephardic Jews and their level of cultural development prepared them to encounter the European Jewish colonists. Their culture allowed them to integrate into a modern economy, but not to resist assimilation by the 'superior' Western culture: 'The population of Eretz Israel', he wrote in 'Our Platform', 'will adopt the new economic and cultural model of the country. The indigenous people will assimilate economically and culturally to those who will have assumed the leadership of the development of the productive forces'.[102] Borokhov despised all the partisans of Jewish assimilation in Europe but, at the same time, he considered the assimilation of the Arabs in Palestine as an obvious and 'progressive' tendency. In this field, his conceptions did not differ very much from those of Herzl, the author of *Der Judenstaat*, who proposed to transform Palestine into an outpost of Western civilisation and against the barbarism of Asia.[103] In 1916, Borokhov eulogised the militiaman (*shomer*) forced to defend himself against the attacks of his 'semi-barbarous' (*halb-wildn mentshn*) neighbours.[104] In spite of his criticism of 'bourgeois' Zionism, he shared with Herzl and Nordau the 'vision of the non-European world as a space to be colonized' (Maxime Rodinson).[105] The idea of a multi-ethnic and culturally pluralist society – the kernel of Medem's thought – was incompatible with Borokhov's conceptual categories: whereas in Russia the Jewish minority represented a national anomaly that needed to be overcome, in a Jewish Palestine the Arab culture would become a national anomaly.

---

101   Quoted in Frankel 1984, p. 341.
102   Borokhov 1920, p. 271.
103   According to Jakob Taut, 'Borokhov never speaks of Arabs, but only of "natives", who possess neither culture nor nation ... Like Herzl, he thought that these people without culture should adhere to the superior culture of the Zionist society and should finally be assimilated'. See Taut 1986, p. 51.
104   Borokhov 1928, p. 269.
105   Rodinson 1981, p. 142.

Unlike Nahman Syrkin, who considered the realisation of Zionism and the struggle for socialism as two aspects of the same process, Borokhov did not avoid collaboration with the Jewish bourgeoisie. As the planning of a spontaneous migratory movement, Zionist colonisation had to combine two distinct moments, one 'constructive' and the other 'liberating'. The bourgeoisie could have accomplished the first one (*di shafende momenten*) in developing the productive forces of the country, which meant concentrating capital and the labour force; the proletariat would have realised the second one (*die befreiende momenten*) in leading the global process of colonisation.[106] In this perspective, Borokhov also defended the policy of a Zionist diplomacy for recognition of the Jewish right to colonise Palestine. He envisaged, then, the creation of a Jewish national state (or, at least, political-territorial autonomy) in the framework of a capitalist Palestine. The struggle for national liberation was a democratic revolution carried on by a social coalition between the 'progressive' bourgeoisie and the proletariat. This is why the Bund accused the Poale Zion of replacing the international class solidarity of the proletariat with Jewish interclass solidarity, and the legitimate national demands of the Jewish workers with a bourgeois nationalist programme.[107]

Moreover, whereas he admitted a 'constructive' collaboration with the Jewish bourgeoisie in Zionist colonisation, Borokhov rejected any possible encounter between the Jewish and non-Jewish proletariat. The danger, he wrote, was not represented 'by big foreign capital (large-scale industry) but by the foreign proletarianisation of the country'.[108] In short, the Jewish proletariat was the subject of a process of colonisation based on either the assimilation (indigenous Palestinians) or the exclusion of the non-Jewish population (Arab neighbours). Palestine, with its 90,000 square kilometres, he wrote in 1917, was 'sufficient territory to accommodate Jews and Arabs'.[109] Differently from 'cultural' Zionists such as Martin Buber or A'had ha Am (Asher Ginsberg), however, Borokhov never imagined a bi-national Palestine. In his eyes, Arabs represented a secondary obstacle to Zionism. He referred to Palestine as *Eretz Israel* (Land of Israel), an appellation completely foreign to the Bundists. Socialist Zionism did not escape the blind alley of European colonialism.

---

106   Borokhov 1920, p. 311.
107   Cf. Rosin 1908–9, pp. 29–34.
108   Borokhov 1928, p. 274.
109   Ibid., pp. 276–7.

The Jews and the Russian Revolution (1917–37)

The fall of tsarism in March 1917 was greeted by Russian Jews as an event that marked the end of their suffering and the beginning of a new era of liberation. One of the first measures adopted by the provisional government was the suppression of the anti-Semitic legislation in force under the old regime: a total of 650 laws limiting the civic rights of the Jewish population, as Trotsky noted in his *History of the Russian Revolution*.[1] The Jews remained somewhat mistrustful, however, toward the October Revolution, because it was centred in Petrograd, far from the Pale of Settlement, and was the product of a 'historical bloc' – the industrial proletariat and the Russian peasants – to whom they were largely alien. The Soviet decree that distributed the land to the peasants was of no interest for the Jews, urbanised and traditionally not involved in agricultural activities. Moreover, the Soviets of Petrograd and Moscow barely had a real existence for the Jewish workers and artisans of Vilnius and Bialystok. This was the Jewish paradox at the core of the Russian Revolution. On the one hand, the Jews appeared as the true architects of the Revolution and were denounced by the newspapers all over the world as conspirers who had overthrown the Tsarist regime: in April 1917, almost half of the members of the Petrograd Soviet bureau were Jews; on 23 October, five out of the twelve members of the Bolshevik Central Committee that decided to take power were Jews.[2] For years, an international anti-Semitic campaign presented the Russian Revolution as a Jewish 'plot'. On the other hand, the Pale of Settlement remained at the margins of this revolutionary wave.

In June 1918, Zionists won the elections in the Jewish community councils (*kehillot*), followed by the Bund, the principal force on the left, whose eighth national conference (December 1917) had condemned the October Revolution. *Arbeiter Shtime*, the Bund's weekly, denounced Lenin's 'coup' as nothing but 'insanity'.[3] The Bolsheviks had ignored the 'Jewish street' and now their policies faced widespread scepticism among the Russian Jews, not to speak of the open

---

1 See Trotsky 2008, p. 643.
2 Slezkine 2004, p. 175. Before the Revolution of 1917, the Jews represented between one-third and one-fourth of the Central Committee of both the Menshevik and the Bolshevik parties. See Budnitskii 2012, p. 55.
3 Budnitskii 2012, p. 65.

opposition expressed by most Jewish political parties.[4] In 1918, the People's Commissariat of Nationalities – led by Stalin – established a Jewish section. Its leader was Simon Dimanshtein, an old Bolshevik who spoke Yiddish – he had received the title of rabbi before becoming an atheist Marxist – but had never participated in Jewish political life. To make up for such serious limits, he asked for the collaboration of Samuel Agurskj, a Socialist Jew just returned from the United States. The first Communist party magazine in Yiddish, the weekly *Wahreit* (*Truth*), appeared in March 1918, six months after the revolution, and rapidly became a daily, changing its title to *Der Emess* (*Truth*, a Yiddish term of Hebrew rather than German origin). The publication of a Yiddish newspaper raised numerous difficulties – because of the lack of Yiddish journalists – and most articles were translated from Russian.[5] In October 1918, Dimanshtein created the *Evsektsiia*, the Jewish section of the Communist party, in order to win over the 'Jewish street' to the proletarian dictatorship. Rapidly, the *Evsektsiia* took charge of the Soviet government's policy on the Jewish affairs.

During the civil war, between 1918 and 1921, the Russian Jews gradually shifted from an attitude of mistrust, indeed hostility, to substantial support for the Soviet regime. The most important source of this change was the anti-Semitism of the counter-revolution. A wave of extremely violent pogroms swept throughout Ukraine, which in 1917 had been an experimental ground for Jewish cultural national autonomy. Initially, most Jewish parties supported the government of Petliura (where the 'territorialist' Socialist Zilberfarb took the ministry of Jewish affairs) but they progressively joined the Soviet regime during the following years.[6] Anti-Semitism always had been a pillar of the ideology and culture of the Russian army and quickly became – in an even more radicalised form – the banner of the Whites. The armies of Kolchak, Denikin and Wrangel made very extensive use of anti-Semitism as a weapon in their struggle against the Soviet regime. Ukraine was the scene of 2,000 pogroms, affecting around a million Jews and leaving between 75,000 and 150,000 victims.[7] According to several scholars, the pogroms of 1918–20 were qualitatively different from the previous waves of tsarist anti-Semitism of the 1880s and 1905–6: not only was the number of their victims incomparably higher, but also their propaganda turned into an open appeal to massacre. They took the form

---

4 Sloves 1982, p. 24. In 1917, the Bund had more than ten times the number of the Jews within the Bolshevik party; see Budnitskii 2012, p. 80.
5 See Weinstock 1986, vol. 3, p. 32.
6 See Sloves 1982, p. 37.
7 See Gitelman 1972, pp. 160–3.

of a modern military campaign carefully planned and ideologically implemented, in which several scholars have seen a precedent of the Holocaust.[8]

The identification of the new revolutionary power with the Jews enormously sharpened the old prejudices widespread among the Russian peasants, especially when the Bolsheviks attacked the religious symbols of tsarism. In April 1922, Maxim Gorky wrote to his friend Scholem Asch:

> The reason for the current anti-Semitism in Russia is the tactlessness of the Jewish Bolsheviks. The Jewish Bolsheviks, not all of them but some irresponsible boys, are taking part in the defiling of the holy sites of the Russian people. They have turned churches into movies theaters and reading rooms without considering the feelings of the Russian people. The Jewish Bolsheviks should have left such things to the Russian Bolsheviks.[9]

In this desperate situation, the Jewish population saw in the Red Army a chance for salvation. Some of the latter's units also took part in pogroms, as Isaac Babel testifies in *Red Cavalry*, but in most cases this concerned troops who had already fought with Denikin and then switched to the other side. Trotsky punished three regiments accused of having participated in pogroms and attempted by every means to stop such events from recurring.[10] Thereafter, many Jews – even those who had been most hostile to the revolution and to Bolshevism – enrolled in the Red Army. In such a dramatic context, the Soviet regime stood up for the Jews and displayed an unshakable will to struggle against anti-Semitism. The election of Iakov Sverdlov, a Bolshevik leader of Jewish origin, to the defacto head of the Russian SFSR appeared as a declaration of war against anti-Semitism. Tsarism had been replaced by a revolutionary regime that elected a Jew as its supreme representative: nobody could remain indifferent to such a metamorphosis. In July 1918, a decree of the Council of People's Commissars signed by Lenin condemned anti-Semitism and the pogroms 'as a mortal danger for the entire revolution, as a menace to the interests of the workers and the peasants' and called on 'the laboring masses and socialist Russia to combat them with all their strength'. The decree ordained that all the provincial soviets 'take the strongest measures to uproot the anti-Semitic movement' and added that 'the pogromists and all those who foment the pogroms' were

---

8   Budnitskii 2012, p. 274, and Laqueur 1965, p. 115.

9   Quoted in Slezkine 2004, p. 186.

10   See Sloves 1982, pp. 164–7.

outside the law.[11] Anti-Semitism was no longer fought as a specifically Jewish problem but as a state problem, intertwined with the very survival of the revolution. On the one hand there was the counter-revolution, which massacred the Jews; on the other hand, the Soviets, who made Emancipation their symbol and adopted legislation against anti-Semitism. Faced with such options, the choice of the Russian Jews was very easy. According to Oleg Budnitskii, 'for the Jews, the choice between the Reds and the Whites gradually evolved into a choice between life and death'.[12]

The Soviet regime gradually conquered the Jewish intelligentsia. The building of a new state apparatus was sown with obstacles, for the most politicised sector of the working class was engaged in the military effort and the old civil servants boycotted the new authorities. There remained the Jews: a vast reservoir of intellectual energies that Tsarism had always repressed and excluded. The revolution transformed this layer of pariahs, humiliated and persecuted by the former regime, into an elite called upon to play a role of the highest importance in the construction of socialism. The Jews entered the state apparatus, universities, and liberal professions on a massive scale. In 1927, ten years after the revolution, they made up 1.8 percent of the total population of the USSR but represented 10.3 percent of the civil servants in the Moscow public administration, 22.6 percent in the Ukraine and 30 percent in Byelorussia.[13] It was an emblematic example of the application of the principle of 'positive discrimination' on an ethnic basis – the first steps of what has been called an 'affirmitive action empire'.[14]

Finally, the shift of the intelligentsia quickly modified the attitude of Jewish socialism towards the Bolsheviks. The October Revolution led to a profound crisis inside the Jewish workers' movement in which significant currents sympathetic to Bolshevism emerged. In 1919 the foundation of the Communist International polarised the most radical tendencies of the Jewish left and began the process of splits and fusions that culminated in 1921 with the integration of most of the left Jewish organisations into the *Evsektsiia*. The Bund divided between a social democratic current (Medem, Abramovich) and the partisans of the Bolshevik Revolution, who founded a Ukrainian 'Communist Bund' (*Kombund*) in 1919. In its eleventh national conference that took place in Minsk on the same year, the Bund declared: 'the Red Army is our army'.[15]

---

11   See Sloves 1982, p. 294.

12   Budnitskii 2012, p. 405.

13   Sloves 1982, p. 45.

14   Zaslavsky 1985, p. 66, and Martin 2001.

15   Budnitskii 2012, p. 274.

Led by Moshe Rafes and Aleksandr Chemerisky, the Bund proclaimed its support for the Soviet regime, launched an appeal to all Jewish workers to join the Red Army and asked to enter the Comintern as a national and autonomous organisation of the Jewish proletariat. Essentially, it wanted to join the Third International without renouncing its programme of Jewish national autonomy. Once more, Bundist federalism entered into conflict with Bolshevik centralism and the members of the Bund were compelled to join the Communist party individually.[16] The socialist Zionists and the SERP followed the same path: in 1917, they merged to form the United Jewish Workers Socialist party, known as the *Farainikte*; in 1919, they created a Communist Alliance (*Komunistishe Farband*) with the Bund in Ukraine and Byelorussia; finally, they merged with the *Evsektsiia* in 1921. In spite of the opposition of the *Evsektsiia*, both the Bund and the Poale Zion created their own battalions within the Red Army.[17] The Poale Zion also split in 1920 between a social democratic right prepared to adhere to the official Zionist Congress, and a communist left that struggled in vain to be admitted to the Comintern without renouncing its Zionist orientation. The militants of Poale Zion organised a regiment that bore the name of Borokhov in the Red Army, but they were unable to join the Communist party and maintain their Zionist identity.[18] Shaken by ideological conflicts and organisationally weakened, the Jewish workers' movement was finally absorbed by the Bolshevik party.

During its first ten years, the Soviet regime applied to a considerable extent the projects of national autonomy that the Austro-Marxists and the Bund had elaborated at the beginning of the century.[19] Paradoxically, the People's Commissar for National Affairs was Stalin, who had mercilessly condemned the 'nationalism' of Otto Bauer and the 'Zionist' idea of a Jewish national culture in his famous study of 1913. Stalin's elaboration of a 'leninist' nationalities policy in the 1920s was in some ways a strange reversal from the tenor of Bolshevik thought up to this point: complex questions of geopolitical strategy and state administration led to the paradox of a universalist state aggressively promoting national particularism. This line, however, was rooted in the idea of 'national in form, socialist in content' – there was no perceived contradiction between

---

16   See Bunzl 1975, pp. 136–8.

17   Budnitskii 2012, pp. 362–83. On the Poale Zion units of the Red Army, see also Nedava 1971, p. 112.

18   On the dissolution of the Poale Zion left into the Communist party, see Weinstock 1984–6, vol. 3, pp. 58–67. On this failed attempt to merge Bolshevism and Zionism, see Gurevitz 2009.

19   See Rodinson 1968, p. 139.

the valorization of culturo-linguistic identity and the goal of internationalist assimilation. Indeed, invigorating the linguistic and educational institutions of each of the Soviet Union's 192 recognized linguistic and national entities was seen as a logical step on the path to their eventual 'withering away'.[20]

The *Evsektsiia* was the instrument of this empirical Soviet orientation toward Jewish cultural national autonomy. The new regime made a considerable effort to improve the status of Yiddish, which remained the mother tongue of 70.4 percent of Soviet Jews in 1926. Just after the revolution, Yiddish gained the status of an official language in the Ukraine and Byelorussia. Yiddish literature was subsidised and encouraged; libraries, newspapers, magazines, publishing houses, and Yiddish theatres sprang up.[21] At the beginning of the 1930s there were 339 Yiddish schools in Byelorussia and 831 in the Ukraine (in Kiev a university institute was created that rivalled the YIVO in Vilnius). Writers such as I.L. Peretz, Sholom Aleichem, and Mendele M. Sforim were introduced into school textbooks. Yiddish literary production experienced a veritable cultural flourishing: 238 titles were published in 1928, rising to 668 in 1933, with a total print run of 2.5 million copies (for a Soviet Jewish population of about three million).[22]

However, in an extreme expression of an attitude already implicit in the theory of the Bund, the *Evsektsiia* was responsible for closing down Hebrew schools and publications: the repression of religion was the necessary condition for building a modern Jewish (Yiddish) nation, cut off from its tradition and history. Along with Hebrew, both Zionism and Orthodox Judaism were banned. The *Evsektsiia* shaped Jewish cultural life by establishing a kind of enlightened despotism, applying its emancipatory and revolutionary measures with authoritarian and bureaucratic methods.[23]

While lauding the efforts made by the Soviets to emancipate the Jews from their age-old oppression, Joseph Roth saw in 1927 the limits of the Russian Revolution in the Jewish world. He speculated on whether the Bolsheviks had really understood the nature of the Jewish Question, given their desire to create a modern Jewish nation completely separated from its past and its historic identity, of which religion was an irreplaceable element. In his opinion, the revolution had never considered

---

20   Slezkine 1994. I thank Nicholas Bujalski for suggesting this point.
21   See Moss 2009.
22   See Robin 1984, p. 190.
23   See Weinstock 1984–6, vol. 3, p. 37.

the old question, the most important: are the Jews a nation like the others? Is it possible to consider as a 'people', independently of its religion, a people which has conserved itself in Europe over thousands of years solely because of its religion and its exceptional situation? Is it possible, in this specific case, to separate nationality from the church? Is it possible to transform into peasants men with intellectual interests rooted for some generations, to inculcate a mass psychology into men endowed with a strong individuality?[24]

Eradicating Hebrew from Jewish culture meant in the final analysis to 'de-historicise' it:[25] the recognition of Yiddish engendered a modern Jewish nation deprived of its soul and its historical identity. The attitude of the Bolshevik power, nevertheless, should not be separated from a much broader transformation of the Jewish world after the Russian Revolution. In the 1920s, the social context from which the *Yiddishkeit* had been born – the Jewish economy of the Pale of Settlement – no longer existed. During the civil war, the pogroms had transformed hundreds of thousands of Jews into displaced persons and exiles, while war communism had suppressed Jewish trade and the intelligentsia had become integrated within the state apparatus, and a significant part of the Jewish population had turned into proletarians and civil servants. During the 1930s, this tendency only increased. In 1939, almost 87 percent of the Jews of the USSR lived in urban areas and they formed significant minorities in the biggest cities of the country like Moscow (6 percent), Leningrad (5.2 percent), Kharkov (15.6 percent) and Kiev (26.5 percent).[26] There was no longer a *shtetl*, a 'Jewish street' where Yiddish – a people's language before it became a literary one – was vibrant and daily enriching itself. In the new Russia, Yiddish had become a language of culture, but the *Yiddishkeit* that had been its original source had disappeared. Jewish culture was supposed to be 'Yiddish in form and socialist in content', but, as Zvi Gitelman has put it, the Soviet regime had reduced 'Jewish nationality to the denationalized Jewish language'.[27]

In the 1930s, Stalinism led to the restoration of Great Russian nationalism and the end of any form of Jewish cultural autonomy. Yiddish schools, theatres, newspapers and publishing houses were finally closed.[28] In 1930 the *Evsektsiia*

---

24   Roth 1985, p. 70.
25   See Sloves 1982, p. 197. On the repression of Hebrew literature in the Soviet Union, see also
      Gilboa 1978, pp. 226–41.
26   Slezkine 2004, p. 217.
27   Gitelman 1972, p. 501.
28   Brossat and Klingberg 1983, p. 263.

was suppressed and, in the course of the bloody repression that followed the Moscow trials, nearly all its leaders were executed as 'Trotskyists' and 'Bundist-Trotskyists.' Already, toward the end of the 1920s, Stalin had employed anti-Semitic arguments in the struggle against the Left Opposition (which included many Jews and was also strongly represented in the *Evsektsiia*). The construction of 'socialism in one country' had no need of the support of revolutionary Jews, who suddenly became 'rootless cosmopolitans'. In 1937, Trotsky openly accused Stalin of fomenting a new wave of anti-Semitism in the USSR: 'If Stalin', he wrote, 'has organised trials in Moscow where the Trotskyists are accused of having poisoned the workers, it is not difficult to imagine what obscene depths the bureaucracy will stoop to in the far-off corners of the Ukraine or Central Asia'.[29] In fact, anti-Semitism was a very marginal aspect of the Great Terror, but the repression of the Yiddish culture was inscribed into a general wave of Russification of the national minorities of the USSR.[30]

While during the immediate post-revolutionary period the idea of nationality was still slightly disarticulated from the concept of territory, by 1928 Stalin's definition of nation from his 1913 essay would receive fulfilment for the Jews in the establishment of the Jewish Autonomous Oblast' in Birobidzhan. As Dimanshtein wrote in his 1935 essay "An Answer to the Question of Whether the Jews Constitute a Nation in the Scientific Sense":

> By acquiring their own territory, their own statehood, the toiling Jews of the USSR received a crucial element that they had lacked before and that made it impossible for them to be considered a nation in the scientific sense of the term. And so it happned that, like many other Soviet nationalities completing the process of national consolidation, the Jewish national minority became a nation as a result of receiving its own national administrative entity in the Soviet Union.[31]

Despite these triumphalist words, Birobidzhan represented the end, not the beginning, of the drive for Jewish national autonomy in the USSR. In reality, the *Evsektsiia* did not support the project of settling a Jewish colony in this desert region of Siberia, larger than Belgium and already inhabited. Rather it favoured the creation of agricultural colonies in Crimea, and remained attached to an extraterritorial conception of Jewish nationality. The decision to colonise Biro-

---

29   Trotsky 1970. See also Mandel 1995, ch. 10.
30   According to Yuri Slezkine, 'the Jews, who were not numerous among non-elite victims, were underrepresented in the Great Terror as a whole'. See Slezkine 2004, p. 273.
31   Slezkine 1994, pp. 444–445.

bidzhan was taken in 1928 by the Soviet government (the Commissariat of Defense and the Academy of Agriculture) without any prior consultation with the Jewish population. Behind this decision lay a strategic consideration – the need to establish a forward post capable of containing Japanese expansionism in the Far East – which took no account of national or socio-economic factors. After the Japanese occupation of Manchuria in 1931, the process of construction of Jewish Birobidzhan was intensified. Kalinin, then president of the USSR, stressed the importance of building a Jewish national homeland by arguing that territorial concentration was a necessary condition for the national preservation of the Jewish people:

> We have many Jews among us, but they possess no state identity. They are the sole nationality of the USSR, three million souls, which does not have its own state. I believe that the creation of the autonomous region constitutes, in our conditions, the only means of normal state evolution for this nationality. I consider that, in ten years, Birobidzhan will be the most significant, if not the only guardian of national and socialist Jewish culture.[32]

The reality was quite different: between 1928 and 1933, out of some twenty thousand Jews who migrated to Birobidzhan, just over eight thousand decided to stay there; when the Jewish autonomous regime was proclaimed in 1934 – a state entity according to the Soviet constitution – less than 20 percent of the population was Jewish.[33] In 1937, the regional administration reverted to the use of the Russian language alone and the new president, M. Koteles – brought in to replace Liberberg, who had just been executed as a Trotskyist – did not know Yiddish. The Jewish state of the Soviet Union was no more than a fiction.

---

32   Quoted by Robin 1984, p. 225.
33   See Schwarz 1951, p. 178.

CHAPTER 6

Gramsci and the Jewish Question

The Jews barely figure in Gramsci's writings. In prison, he read and even partly translated Marx's *Zur Judenfrage*,[1] but Jewish history never became an object of investigation for the Italian Marxist. He devoted to this topic solely some fragmentary observations in his 1932 correspondence with his sister-in-law, Tatiana Schucht, who had told him of her impressions of a film dealing with Polish anti-Semitism during the First World War. Furthermore, these references were confined to the Jewish Question in Italy, a country where political emancipation and cultural assimilation appeared as irreversible achievements (the fascist regime's 'race laws', which followed the alliance with Nazi Germany, were introduced only in 1938, one year after Gramsci's death).[2]

The founder of *L'Ordine nuovo* was not himself Jewish. According to his own account, he spent his childhood in Sardinia, where the Jews existed only in the popular imagination rather than in everyday life. In some passages on folklore, he evoked the contradictory meanings that the word 'Jew' had among the Sardinian shepherds and peasants: the *Giudeo* who had been responsible for the killing of Christ, the 'compassionate Nicodemus' who had helped Mary to bring her son down from the cross and also the *Marranu*, a vaguely contemptible figure. But he added that unlike, for example, the anti-Semitic Cossacks, the Sardinians 'did not distinguish between Jews and other men'.[3] Gramsci became more familiar with Jewish matters after his marriage to Julca Schucht, whose mother was Jewish, and during the long periods he spent in Moscow and Vienna[4] where he worked for the Communist International. Thus, even though his scattered notes fall outside the framework of the Marxist debate investig-

---

1   Marx's text is included on the list of works read by Gramsci during his imprisonment. See Gramsci 1975, vol. 4, p. 3063.

2   See De Felice 2001; Sarfatti 2006; Collotti 2003; Matard-Bonucci 2006.

3   Gramsci 1973, p. 506; Gramsci 1994, vol. 2, p. 86.

4   In a letter to Tatiana of 13 September 1931, Gramsci tells an anecdote about his stay in Vienna, when he lived by 'an old superstitious petty bourgeois woman' who, before accepting him as a tenant, asked him if he was Jewish or Roman Catholic. When he left Vienna, he gave his room to a Ukrainian Jew, explaining to the old anti-Semitic lady that she was the wife of a diplomat. In his letter, he referred to 'a Frenchman' – probably Victor Serge, with whom he worked in Vienna for the Comintern – who had explained to him that 'as much as they hate Jews, the petty bourgeois will grovel before diplomats'. See Antonio Gramsci 1973, p. 169; Gramsci 1994, vol. 2, p. 71.

ated in this book, they remain interesting insofar as they reveal the vision of a Western Marxist for whom the Jewish Question was a matter of intellectual reflection rather than everyday politics. Additionally, Gramsci is an outstanding figure of inter-war Marxism. It is possible to check, through his writings, the extent to which the paradigm of assimilation achieved a kind of normative value in Marxist thought. In spite of his radically anti-positivistic conception of Marxism as a 'philosophy of praxis', which did not fit in easily with Kautsky and Lenin's evolutionism, he did not criticise the dogma of Jewish assimilation as the natural outcome of historical development.

Different from a commonplace of his time, well represented in Italy by Cesare Lombroso, Gramsci refused to consider the Jews in terms of race or nation. During the First World War, he published in the newspaper of the Socialist party, *Avanti!*, a strong criticism of the anti-German League, whose nationalist propaganda depicted the war as a conflict between antagonistic races. Gramsci's target was a Piedmont lawyer of Jewish origin, Cesare Foà, who had defended a racial conception of the nation in the pages of *Riscossa italica*. In Gramsci's view, 'When one speaks of Italic revenge, one implicitly puts the question of stock, of blood'.[5] He defined the Italian character (*italianità*) as the sentiment of belonging to a community of culture (established primarily by language) marked by a 'cosmopolitan' imprint and completely foreign to any form of racial determinism. He argued that Italians owed their ethnic origin to various, and not merely 'Italic' antecedents. On the basis of the single racial criteria, the Jews could not be considered as Italians, any more than the Ligurians, the Sardinians and so on. Sharpening his polemical tone, Gramsci argued that 'if Italy was to remain Italic, that is Roman, they [the Jews] would be slaves, or the managers of brothels for the dregs of society'.[6] In other words, if the Jews had been emancipated and had become citizens in every respect, it was because the Italian nation, in its process of historical formation, had gone beyond the narrow racialist idea which Foà defended. Socialism had transcended tiresome controversies over race and rejected all forms of nationalism: 'We are absolutely not anti-Semitic. Karl Marx was a Semite: very many of our comrades, and, among them, some of the most active and the most intelligent are Semites. But socialism has gone beyond questions of race and blood'.[7] In 1931, he wrote that 'outside of anthropology and the study of prehistory', the racial problem did not arouse the slightest interest in him.[8] In the *Prison Notebooks*

---

5   Gramsci 1958, p. 97.
6   Ibid., p. 98.
7   Ibid., p. 97.
8   Gramsci 1973, p. 506; Gramsci 1994, vol. 2, p. 86.

he sometimes employed the German expression 'sordidly Jewish' [*schmützig jüdisch*], referring to Croce's concept of 'passion', which had in his view a certain analogy with the concept of 'egoism' developed by Marx in his *Theses on Feuerbach*.[9] This insouciant language certainly shows how widespread and banal anti-Semitic stereotypes were in Italy at the beginning of the 1930s – under a still 'philo-Jewish' fascism – but, in a letter to his wife in March 1932, he used the same term – 'sordidly Jewish' – while making it clear that he had no intention of using it in an anti-Semitic sense.[10]

In a later letter, Gramsci interpreted the Jewish Question in more traditional Marxist terms. For example, he denied the status of nation to the Jews, repeating the arguments already developed by Kautsky and Stalin: namely, the lack of economic, cultural, linguistic, territorial, and state unity that had characterised the Jewish Diaspora for centuries.[11] His letter echoed Stalin's *Marxism and the National Question* (1913), which he certainly knew. In other letters, the reference to Marx was explicit:

> Marx wrote that the Jewish question no longer exists since Christians have all become Jews by assimilating what was the essence of Judaism, i.e., speculation, and that the solution of the Jewish question will occur when all of Europe is freed from speculation, that is, from Judaism in general.[12]

Gramsci shared this general Marxist assessment on assimilation, but he did not hesitate to recognise the right of Jewish communities to 'cultural autonomy' (in language, schooling, and so forth) and even 'national autonomy', where they 'in one fashion or another inhabited a definite territory'. The ritual acceptance of Marxist orthodoxy coexisted, then, with the recognition of the living character of the Jewish culture. Gramsci probably did not know the conflict that had raged between the Bund and the Bolsheviks, and his positive attitude toward Jewish cultural autonomy cannot be interpreted as an attitude of sympathy towards the Bund or other currents of Eastern European Jewish socialism.[13] He

9   See Gramsci 1975, vol. 2, p. 977, vol. 3, p. 1569; Gramsci 1995, p. 439. In his *Theses on Feuerbach* (1845), Marx distinguished two concepts in the work of the author of *The Essence of Christianity*: on the one hand, 'theoretical attitude as the truly human attitude', and on the other hand, 'practice', which was 'understood and fixed only in its dirtily Jewish form of appearance'. See Marx 1994, vol. 2, p. 99.

10 Gramsci 1973, pp. 598–9; Gramsci 1994, vol. 2, p. 156.

11 Gramsci 1973, p. 501; Gramsci 1994, vol. 2, pp. 82–3.

12 Gramsci 1973, ibid., p. 505; Gramsci 1994, vol. 2, p. 85.

13 In 1916, Gramsci considered the 'territorial idea of fatherland' as completely foreign to the proletariat. See Gramsci 1960, p. 258.

probably referred to the Soviet debate of the late 1920s on the development of Yiddish culture and the colonisation of Crimea (and, later, Birobidzhan), which Gramsci certainly knew of during his time in Moscow.

However, this observation remained isolated and was not developed, insofar as the paradigm of assimilation prevails in Gramsci's writings. His vision of Jewish assimilation as an ineluctable process, nonetheless, was deduced from an analysis of Italian history rather than from a universal historical schema (like in Kautsky). The *Prison Notebooks* include some critical remarks on a famous study by Arnaldo Momigliano devoted to the history of the Italian Jews.[14] In Momigliano's view, the assimilation process of the Italian Jews perfectly corresponded with that of the other regional minorities, like, for example, the inhabitants of Piedmont, Lombardy, Latium, Sicily, and so on. In other words, Momigliano perceived the Jewish assimilation as an aspect of the process of formation of an Italian national consciousness and not as the integration of the Jews in an already accomplished national community. This amounted to a major difference with the experience of most European countries, where assimilation had allowed the entry of the Jews into pre-existing nations. Gramsci shared this analysis, which coincided with his vision of cosmopolitanism as a crucial feature of Italian national unification, and thought it also explained the weakness of anti-Semitism in modern Italy (at least in comparison to the other European countries, from France to Russia). He added that Italian national consciousness had been born from the dialectical transcendence of the particular forms of feudalism in the Peninsula: 'municipal particularism and Catholic cosmopolitanism'. The affirmation of a secular spirit and the struggle against Catholicism had contributed toward the 'nationalising' of the Jews, which inevitably led to their 'casting aside their Jewishness' (*nel loro disebreizzarsi*).[15]

Different from Russia, Germany, Austria, or even France, anti-Semitism in Italy was neither a political strategy nor a widespread hostility toward the Jews, but rather the vestige of religious prejudices in popular language and mentality. In the *Prison Notebooks*, Gramsci pointed out that, for the peasant, the words 'Christian' and 'man' were synonymous ('I am not a Christian!' 'Then, what are you, some kind of beast?') and he observed that 'in some countries, where Jews

---

14   Gramsci 1975, vol. 3, pp. 1800–1; Gramsci 1995, pp. 102–4. Momigliano's review of Cecil Roth's book *Gli ebrei a Venezia* (Rome, 1930), is now included in Momigliano 1987, pp. 237–40. For a critical analysis of Momigliano and Gramsci's interpretation, see Sofia 1991, pp. 342–57, and Levis-Sullam 2007, pp. 59–82.

15   Gramsci 1975, p. 1801; Gramsci 1995, p. 104.

are unknown, it is or was believed that they had a tail or the ears of a swine or some other animal attribute'.[16] In a 1931 letter to Tatiana, Gramsci reaffirmed the absence of a Jewish Question in Italy, which he attributed to the completion of the process of assimilation:

> there hasn't been any anti-Semitism in Italy for some time: Jews can become ministers (and even prime minister like Luzzati) and generals in the army; marriages between Jews and Christians are very numerous, especially in the cities and not only in the lower classes but also between young ladies of the aristocracy and Jewish intellectuals. In what way does an Italian Jew (save for a small minority of rabbis and old bearded tradi- tionalists) differ from another Italian of the same class? He is much more different from a Polish or Galician Jew of the same class.[17]

Gramsci emphasised the almost complete disappearance of anti-Semitism in Italy. In his opinion, the treaty between the Catholic Church and the fascist regime in 1929 implied no discriminatory measures against the Jewish com- munity. To his friend Piero Sraffa, who did not completely share this point of view, he responded that the situation of unfrocked priests, condemned by the Lateran treaty to become true 'pariahs', was much worse than that of the Jews.[18] However, in a 1932 letter, he reverted to the conception of anti-Semitism as pop- ular hostility toward the Jewish usurer. Here, anti-Semitism was perceived as a socio-economic phenomenon, where the religious element was only super- ficial and accessory. Hatred for the usurer was a generalised social practice of which anti-Semitism represented only a particular variant. 'In Georgia', he wrote,

> the Armenians were moneylenders and the Armenians were the 'Jews' of Georgia. In Naples, when there is a mood of rebellion in the air, the police stand guard before the popular pawnbrokers' offices because the fury of the populace turns against them; if these offices were run by Jews and not by Saint Gennaro's faithful there would be anti-Semitism in Naples, just as there is in part of the Casale, Lomellina, and Alessandria areas, where the Jews are the land brokers and always show up when there is a 'mis- fortune' in the family and one has to sell or practically give away one's

---

16   Gramsci 1975, pp. 2082–3; Gramsci 1995, pp. 29–30.

17   Gramsci 1973, p. 496; Gramsci 1994, vol. 2, p. 79.

18   Gramsci 1973, p. 570; Gramsci 1994, vol. 2, pp. 136–7.

assets at bargain prices. But here too, where no one is intent on stirring up trouble, such feelings never go beyond modest limits.[19]

This letter reproduces – with more anthropological than historical arguments – a 'classical' vision of anti-Semitism. In a previous letter of 1931, Gramsci analysed the religious dimension of the problem, explaining that the hostility toward the Jews was not only the product of their economic function, but also a religious mentality, linked to the age-old domination of Christianity. Discrimination and oppression by the Catholic Church, and not the economic role of the Jews, were then at the root of segregation and the true source, in Gramsci's view, of Jewish otherness in history. He considered the French Revolution and the uprisings of 1848 as turning points in the history of the Jews in Europe, insofar as they shut down the ghettos and opened a new era of emancipation. Gramsci wrote:

> The Jews were freed from the ghetto only after 1848 and had remained in the ghetto or in any event segregated from European society for almost two thousand years and not of their own accord but due to outside imposition. From 1848 on the process of assimilation in the Western countries has been so rapid and thoroughgoing that one is entitled to think that only imposed segregation prevented their complete assimilation in the various countries if until the French Revolution the Christian religion had not been the sole 'state culture' which in fact demanded the segregation of the religiously obstinate Jews (at the time; now no longer because they pass from Judaism to pure and simple deism or atheism). In any case, it should be noted that many characteristics that are supposedly determined by race are instead due to the ghetto life imposed in different forms in various countries, so that an English Jew has almost nothing in common with a Jew from Galicia.[20]

This passage contains two traditional arguments from the Marxist debate, which Kautsky and Bauer had long since systematised: first, Gramsci did not see the Jews as the bearers of a distinct culture – the Jew in himself – but only as the mirror of an external attitude of hostility, a product of anti-Semitism; second, he identified modernity with Jewish assimilation, inasmuch as its advent implied the progressive elimination of feudality, the secularisation of

---

19   Gramsci 1973., p. 591; Gramsci 1994, vol. 2, pp. 152–3.
20   Gramsci 1973, p. 501; Gramsci 1994, vol. 2, pp. 82–3.

culture and, consequently, the political emancipation of the Jews. These observations were fundamentally similar to Kautsky's analysis, but were deduced from Italian history. Writing in a country where anti-Semitism always had been a privileged field of Catholic propaganda, Gramsci stressed its the religious dimension.

The *Prison Notebooks* also contain a conception of the Jews as a cosmopolitan group playing a role in international relations. Gramsci attributed to 'religion' and to other 'international formations', among which he mentioned Freemasonry, the Rotary Club, diplomacy and the Jews, the function of maintaining a peaceful coexistence between competing states and a solution of their conflicts. According to Gramsci, these 'international formations' belonged to the category of the 'intellectuals' whose specific task was to 'mediate between extremes'.[21] This conception does not seem incompatible with the definition of the Jews as a caste, which, nonetheless, had for Gramsci an intellectual character and not a purely economic character (the Jewish caste). In the *Prison Notebooks*, he used the concept of caste in order to define the role of the Church, which had exercised a monopoly of culture and education throughout the Middle Ages (thus amounting to an intellectual caste).[22] In a passage concerning the privileges granted to Catholicism by the Lateran treaty, Gramsci employed an analogy from Shakespeare's *Merchant of Venice*, defining the Church as 'a Shylock even more implacable than the Shakespeare's character',[23] but all the evidence indicates that this was a literary artifice, not a historical comparison between the Church and the Jews as castes.

Investigating sources drawn from Italian history and cultural anthropology, Gramsci reformulated the canonical Marxist approach to the Jewish Question, which identified emancipation with assimilation and analysed anti-Semitism as a historical anachronism. Writing from a fascist jail, Gramsci did not perceive the rise of National Socialism at the end of Weimar Germany, nor the premises of a fascist (not Catholic) anti-Semitism, which became official law just one year after his death. His path was original, but his conclusions were as blind as those of Bauer and Kautsky: in his eyes, anti-Semitism was a vestige of the past, not a possible face of modernity.

---

21   Gramsci 1975, vol. 3, p. 1585; Gramsci 1995, pp. 104, 147.
22   See Portelli 1974, p. 14.
23   See Gramsci 1975, vol. 1, p. 497; Gramsci 1995, p. 68.

CHAPTER 7

From Weimar to Auschwitz: Anti-Semitism and the German Left

The Weimar Republic was born in the middle of a deep economic and political crisis, under the double shock of a terrible defeat and the fall of the values on which the German Empire had been built. In this context, nationalism immediately transformed the Jews into a useful scapegoat, depicting them as responsible for the military collapse (the famous Jewish 'backstab'), uncontrollable inflation, the loss of 10 percent of German territories and a significant part of its population, and finally the humiliation inflicted by the Treaty of Versailles. Thus the Jews – who had been genuine patriots since August 1914 – suddenly became a group of 'traitors' who had conspired with the enemies for preparing the German defeat and now were profiting from the financial catastrophe that afflicted the country. They were immediately identified with the new democratic regime, by definition 'anti-German'.[1] The Weimar Republic embodied the triumph of a hated liberal modernity in which ballots replaced the traditional values of German *Kultur*, always defended by the army and the military caste. Foreigners to the *Volk*, the Jews had contributed to destroying Germany by plotting against it from inside and now they tried to control the new Republic's institutions. Beginning in 1919, a new wave of Anti-Semitism spread in Germany, penetrating the middle-class that had already been struck by the economic crisis and inspiring both conservative nationalists and the 'republicans by reason' (*Vernunftrepublikaner*) who remained attached to the regime of Wilhelm II in their hearts.[2]

Of course, this nationalistic reaction focused on the leaders of the revolution. In January 1919, Rosa Luxemburg became the Berlin Spartacist insurrection's most charismatic figure as well as its martyr; a few months later, Paul Levi became the secretary of the new Communist party; Kurt Eisner was the President of the Bavarian Republic born in November 1918; after his death, Munich became the capital of a Soviet republic in which many Jewish intellectuals – from Eric Mühsam to Ernst Toller, from Gustav Landauer to Eugene Leviné – played a leading role until its bloody repression by the *Freikorps* in the spring-

---

1   Mosse 1964.
2   Cf. Weitz 2007; and Peukert 1989.

© KONINKLIJKE BRILL NV, LEIDEN, 2019 | DOI:10.1163/9789004384767_010

time of 1919.[3] In short, in the eyes of the conservatives, the Jews incarnated the Bolshevik danger that threatened Germany and embodied the 'negative identity' of a wounded nation: the myth of 'Judeo-Bolshevism' was born. In 1930, at the beginning of the second and final stage of the Weimar crisis, this anti-Semitic wave took the form of National Socialism. Rejected by radical nationalism, Prussian conservatism, and even the confessional parties – notably the Catholic *Zentrum* – the Jews identified themselves with an agonised Republic. The army had always been anti-Semitic, as well as the university; both the civil servants' trade unions and the students' associations were among the first segments of the German society to be Nazified.[4] In 1922, the assassination of Walther Rathenau, the minister of Foreign Affairs, symbolised the violent rejection of any Jewish presence inside German institutions.[5] In such a context, the left remained virtually the only political defence for the Jews. But in reality, as we have seen in Chapter 7, it was hardly prepared to fulfil this crucial task.

Just as the German left in the nineteenth century had ignored the anti-Semitic propaganda of Richard Wagner, Heinrich von Treitschke and Houston Stewart Chamberlain, under the Weimar Republic it did not pay attention to *Mein Kampf*. Hitler represented a form of 'redemptive anti-Semitism' that broke with the traditional hatred of the Jews. Of course, both Édoaurd Drumont and Chamberlain shared with the Nazis the view of the Jews as a dangerous and corrupting 'race', but their goal was to exclude, to discriminate, and eventually to persecute; not to destroy. Nazi anti-Semitism, on the contrary, was charged with a new apocalyptic strength that took an almost religious dimension, thus becoming a sort of emancipating fight, carried on with the ardour of faith. Saul Friedländer has reconstituted the trajectory of this anti-Semitism fuelled by *völkisch* ideology, conservative nationalism, reactionary neo-romanticism, Christian-German mythologies and biological racism: an explosive ideological mixture whose roots came back to the Wagnerian circle of Bayreuth and whose radicalism was powerfully sharpened by the Russian Revolution and the defeat of November 1918.[6] Of course, the extreme consequences of this new form of anti-Semitism were not perceivable before the Second World War, but such changes did not affect the Weimar left. Insofar as social Darwinism had deeply pervaded – notably with Kautsky – the culture of German social democracy, neither eugenics nor biological racism appeared as dangers to left culture. In general, both the SPD and the KPD neglected Nazi anti-Semitism and reduced

---

3   See Angress 1971, pp. 137–315.
4   Cf. Niewyk 1980.
5   Cf. Volkov 2012, ch. 7.
6   Friedländer 1997, ch. 3.

it to a minor problem, an accessory phenomenon, a pure rhetorical tool: in short, a useful façade to hide the real class nature of Hitler's ideology. Insofar as Nazism did not wish to put capitalism into question, it would necessarily find an agreement with the Jewish bourgeoisie. The satirical writings of Kurt Tucholsky, who depicted as 'farce' the anti-Semitic eructation of the Nazi meetings, mirrored such blindness.[7] In 1930, one day after the first great Nazi electoral breakthrough, the most popular German left weekly, *Die Weltbühne*, reassured its readers by saying that it was not necessary to take Hitler too seriously and that there was no need to pack any suitcases.[8]

1 The KPD: from the 'Schlageter Line' to the 'Third Period'

In its early days, the KPD reduced the Jewish Question to a 'class' question. In a propaganda pamphlet against anti-Semitism published at the beginning of the 1920s, an anonymous propagandist explained: 'For us, there are in the world only two peoples, two classes: the workers and the parasites, the owners and those who possess nothing ... For us, there are neither Christians nor Jews, neither Germans nor Russians, neither French nor British! For we Communists, there are only the Capitalists and the exploited. The Christian usurer seems to us as odious as the Jew, Stinnes as much so as Rothschild'.[9] The fundamental antagonisms of society annulled all differences of a national or religious type. In 1931, this abstract form of internationalism, which dominated the culture and political horizon of the left during the Weimar Republic, was perfectly summed up in Brecht's play 'The Round Heads and The Pointed Heads' (*Die Rundköpfe und die Spitzköpfe*), where the Nazis and the Jewish bourgeoisie both found themselves allied.[10]

'National-Bolshevism', born in 1920 out of the attempt to unify the revolutionary left and pan-Germanist reaction in the struggle against the Treaty of

---

7 See Knütter 1977, p. 148.

8 Mosse 1971, 16/1, pp. 123–51.

9 Spartakus n.d., p. 9. The pamphlet indicates as editor the peasant section of the KPD. If the position of the KPD tended toward this crude internationalism, it should not be forgotten that the attitude of social democracy was much more ambiguous. During the revolutionary crisis of 1919–20, the SPD-dominated government did not hesitate to exploit the argument of 'Bolshevik Jews' – then widespread in reactionary circles – to repress the Spartakist revolt. In 1919 the Prussian social democratic government organised internment camps in which *Ostjuden* were kept prior to their expulsion. See Aschheim 1982, pp. 238–40.

10 Jay 1986, p. 87.

Versailles, was not radically rejected by the KPD. Some isolated attempts to integrate racism with Marxist theory were quickly denounced and their authors expelled, but the party leadership showed an ambiguous attitude towards *völkisch* nationalism.[11] The response of the German communists to the French occupation of the Ruhr was the 'Schlageter line', theorised by Karl Radek in 1923. In a famous speech, he celebrated the memory of Leo Schlageter, a Nazi who had been shot after carrying out a sabotage action in the occupied Ruhr, with the following words: 'The fate of this martyr of German nationalism should not be passed over in silence nor treated with contempt ... Schlageter, this courageous soldier of the counter-revolution, deserves to be honored by us, soldiers of the revolution'.[12] Radek identified Germany, a great power under military occupation, with a semi-colonial country and came close to equating pan-Germanism with the political movement of an oppressed nation.[13] In short, instead of opposing the nationalist wave sweeping the country, the KPD adopted a nationalist rhetoric focused on national liberation. On this basis, it did not reject a 'dialogue' with the Nazis: Radek debated with Möller van der Bruk, one of the most popular representatives of the 'Conservative Revolution', and the communist newspaper, *Rote Fahne*, published the interventions of Count von Reventlow. The frontier between Marxism and the *völkisch* ideology was becoming more and more blurred.

In the framework of the 'Schlageter line', the KPD also adopted several very ambiguous positions on anti-Semitism. The most notorious example was a speech by Ruth Fischer, the secretary of the KPD, to the nationalist students of Berlin in 1923, whose anti-Semitic demagogical tone was explicit: 'The German Reich can only be saved if you recognize, gentlemen of the populist side, that you must struggle in collaboration with the masses organized by the KPD. Whoever struggles against Jewish capital ... is already a class fighter, even if he does not know it ... Shoot down the Jew-capitalists, hang them from the lampposts, crush them!'[14] Some days later, Hermann Remmele gave a similar speech in Stuttgart: 'I understand easily how anti-Semitism can be born. It is enough to go to the cattle markets and abattoirs of Stuttgart to see how the cattle merchants, for the most part Jews, sell their animals at almost any price, so long as the butchers of Stuttgart go home with empty hands for the very simple reason that they do not have enough to pay the price that is asked of

11   See Knütter 1977, pp. 176–83.

12   Quoted by Flechteim 1972, p. 118.

13   Frank 1979, vol. 1, pp. 287–92. On the 'Schlageter line,' see also Broué 1971, pp. 690–7, and Golbach 1973, pp. 116–25.

14   Quoted by Flechteim 1972, p. 119.

them!'[15] When a certain number of posters that combined the swastika and the Soviet star appeared in Berlin, the KPD was compelled to abandon this chauvinistic and anti-Semitic language. This turn, however, was an empirical correction rather than the expression of a convinced self-criticism. In October 1923 the last revolutionary attempt in Germany, the abortive insurrection in Hamburg, took place: a wave of repression rained down on the KPD, which, because of the temporary stabilisation of the Weimar Republic, avoided any serious discussion on the Schlageter line. The SPD, which had not hesitated to employ the *Freikorps* to crush the revolution in 1919, now stigmatised communist anti-Semitism. The social democratic newspaper, *Vorwärts*, devoted to Fischer and Radek's speeches a satirical poem titled 'The new anti-Semites', in which Sobelsohn (Radek) marched arm in arm with Count von Reventlow, Werner Scholem pondered before his mirror on his Aryan appearance and Ruth Fischer dyed her hair to converse with the nationalist students.[16] The Nazis, for their part, never seemed affected by this communist propaganda: invited to speak at a communist meeting in Stuttgart in 1923, for example, a representative of the NSDAP declared that the communists could not be national 'as long as they are led by Sobelsohn-Radek and other Jews'.[17]

In reality, the Schlageter line was put aside but not completely abandoned and, in 1930, the KPD took a new nationalist turn. Germany plunged into economic crisis and the number of unemployed soon reached the figure of six million. The Weimar Republic entered a phase of decomposition and was faced with the threat of National Socialism, which had increased its vote over two years from 800,000 to more than six million (in 1932, the NSDAP obtained more than thirteen million votes at the elections). In such a context, the new KPD leader, Ernst Thälmann, launched the slogan of the 'popular revolution', which was an obvious appeal to the *völkisch* ideology of the Nazis. Nationalist slogans went hand in hand with the theory of 'social fascism', which designated social democracy as the principal enemy of the proletariat. The KPD rejected any political alliance against the Nazis and, on several occasions, allied itself with the Nazis against the social democrats: for example, in 1931, when it supported the referendum proposed by the Nazis against the social democratic government in Prussia, calling it the 'red referendum', and in November 1932, when it organised a transport strike in Berlin with the NSDAP. The KPD had already qualified the Brüning and von Papen governments as 'fascist dictator-

---

15   Quoted by Brossat 1985, p. 32.
16   Lindenhecken 1923; this text is reproduced in full by Silberner 1983, pp. 268–9. On the
       intellectual and political trajectory of Ruth Fischer, see Kessler 2013.
17   Quoted by Dupeux 1976, p. 234.

ships' and its entire policy banalised the eventuality of a Nazi seizure of power. Thälmann even declared that a victory for Hitler would finally create the conditions for a socialist revolution in Germany.[18]

Thus, the ambiguities of the Schlageter line were not only repeated but even accentuated. In 1931, the *Rote Fahne* denounced Hitler as the saviour of the Jewish bourgeoisie: 'Hitler wishes to be the friend of everyone who owns a cashbox. Now, the man of the swastika and the open anti-Semite draws closer to the Jews; but, of course, only the rich Jews whom he wants to save from Bolshevism, as well as the capitalists to the west and the Eastern landowners'.[19] The same argument was taken up the following year, in an article titled 'The Nazis help Jewish capital!'[20] In 1931, a former officer of the *Reichswehr*, Richard Scheringer, entered the KPD and depicted it as 'authentically' nationalist by pointing to the absence of Jews on its central committee.[21]

The KPD intellectuals did not devote many efforts to analysing Nazi anti-Semitism. Otto Heller's book, *Der Untergang des Judentums* (*The End of Judaism*), published in Berlin in 1931, employed the traditional Marxist conception of anti-Semitism as a tool of the dominant class to divide the workers and mobilise the petty bourgeois masses against the proletariat.[22] The following year, however, the KPD published a brochure entitled *Kommunismus und Judenfrage*, which drew up a historical and sociological assessment on German anti-Semitism.[23] The booklet sketched a typology that identified six major components. First, the artisans and the small traders crushed by monopoly capital, who had always been anti-Semites. Second, the liberal professions (doctors, engineers, small lawyers, university teachers, and so on), which saw the Jews as competitors on a labour market affected by the economic crisis. Third, the civil servants who identified the Jews with the republic, which had destroyed the prestigious image of the state bureaucracy created under the Prussian Empire. Fourth, the employees of the private companies felt threatened by unemployment and increasingly declassed because of economic rationalisation, and gave massive support to the Nazi movement. The Jews appeared to them not only as competitors but also as bosses (above all in the case of employees of banks and commercial companies). The racism of these employees took on a class connotation, then, and they were the only proletarian layer affected by anti-

---

18   See Frank 1979, vol. 2, pp. 655–60.
19   Quoted in Silberner 1983, p. 272.
20   *Die Rote Fahne* 1932.
21   See Knütter 1977, p. 188.
22   Heller 1933, pp. 130–47.
23   Zentralkomitee der KPD 1932, pp. 272–86.

Semitism. Fifth, with its mystical conception of the soil and its vision of the *Volk ohne Raum*, Nazi propaganda could successfully attract the peasantry already suffused with the traditional perception of the Jews as moneylenders. Sixth, the students saw unemployment as their only future perspective. Nourished on the principles of pan-Germanism, they were not attracted by the left but rather by Nazism, which combined romantic nationalism with an anti-capitalist phraseology. The author of *Kommunismus und Judenfrage*, however, did not confine himself to a sociological analysis of anti-Semitism: he identified its cultural roots in the ideological backwardness of the German bourgeoisie, which had taken power through a Bonapartist or passive revolution (Bismarck) rather than by a popular (Jacobin) revolution. This lack of a bourgeois revolution also explained the delay in Jewish emancipation: unlike France, Germany had experienced a belated capitalist development without being able to completely erase the vestiges of its feudal past. Capitalism developed within Prussian absolutism, which remained a pre-modern state, as well as the culture of its aristocratic elite. Anti-Semitism was, then, only an aspect of this archaic culture that survived inside the modern, capitalist and industrialised Germany.[24] The Nazis had only transformed the hatred against the Jews into racial hatred: in an epoch when the natural sciences had replaced religion, the Jews were no longer accused of ritual murder but of 'sins against the blood' (*Sünde wider das Blut*).[25]

Prefiguring the posterior historical interpretations of Nazism as the result of a German *Sonderweg* (a special German path to modernity), this analysis was one of the most interesting produced by the German left in the Weimar years. Nonetheless, it persisted in considering anti-Semitism as the simple superstructure of an essentially economic phenomenon. The transition outlined above from traditional to 'redemptive' anti-Semitism was ignored. In other words, the KPD's analysis did not consider anti-Semitism to be a major current of modern German culture, but simply a feudal ideological legacy that corresponded, in a precise historical moment, to the interests of big capital affected by a deep economic crisis.

On the basis of this explanatory model, the KPD excluded any real conflict between Nazism and Jewish capital: Hitler must necessarily defend the interests of the big Jewish bourgeoisie. In September 1933, in the middle of Nazi 'synchronisation' (*Gleichschaltung*), *International Correspondence* – the Comintern official weekly – published a 'letter from Berlin' that contained the

---

24   Ibid., p. 281.
25   Ibid., p. 282.

following assessment: 'So far as the extermination is concerned, things are not going too badly – at least for those Jewish circles capable of paying ... The German Jews could then consider the future with hope – to the extent that they have money'.[26] The author even formulated the hypothesis that the Nazis would be obliged to defend Jewish capital against the racist reaction provoked by their propaganda. 'These theoretical attacks', he concluded, 'serve only to hide from the masses excited by anti-Semitism the horse dealing going on behind the scenes between the "chiefs" and the capitalist Jews'.[27] In line with this conception, the Nuremburg Laws of 1935 were explained as the inevitable product of the process of concentration of German capital. According to Hans Behrend, 'anti-Semitism leads in a straight line to a new concentration of capital'.[28] It was unequivocally proved, in his opinion, by the fact that certain companies whose proprietors were Jewish had been absorbed by trusts such as Siemens and Krupp. The pogroms of the notorious *Kristallnacht* in 1938 were explained once again by the Nazi regime's need to find a scapegoat for the economic crisis.[29]

After 1935, the new strategic orientation of the Comintern, the Popular Front, replaced the ultra-leftism of the 'third period' with the defence of democracy: from that point forward, the racism and anti-Semitism of Nazi Germany were qualified as a return to a medieval obscurantism which had to be fought in the name of a defence of Western civilisation. In 1937, the international communist movement organised a World Congress Against Racial Fanaticism and Anti-Semitism in Paris, which concluded with this slogan: 'Men of all nations of the world, unite for peace, justice and fraternity!'[30] Communists had become the most ardent defenders of the Enlightenment, which had been betrayed by the bourgeoisie with its complicity with fascism.

2   The 'Roofless Left'

In 1935, the seventh congress of the Comintern formulated the well-known theory of fascism as the direct expression of 'the most aggressive sectors of monopoly capitalism': a definition which neglected the problem of fascism as a mass movement as well as its anti-Semitic dimension. Outside of the Stalinised com-

---

26   Behrend 1933 1933, p. 921.
27   Ibid.
28   Behrend 1935, p. 1530.
29   W. 1938, p. 797.
30   Friede 1937, p. 940.

munist parties, some heretic Marxists produced more nuanced and sometimes insightful interpretations, but did not abandon this analytical framework. This was true of August Thalheimer, who tended to reduce fascism to a form of Bonapartism,[31] but it was also true of the writings of Ernst Bloch and Herbert Marcuse devoted to Nazi ideology. In 1934, Marcuse published an essay in the journal of the Frankfurt School in which he saw the most characteristic traits of totalitarian ideology in the conception of the charismatic leader, irrational naturalism (the romantic idealisation of a mythical prehistoric nature) and the organicism of the *Volk*.[32] Ernst Bloch's *Heritage of Our Times* (1934), rather than simply an analysis of the Nazi doctrine, was a collection of essays on the mass psychology of fascism.[33] Both Marcuse and Bloch ignored the question of anti-Semitism. For Arthur Rosenberg, anti-Semitism was essentially a sublimated form of anti-capitalism, like other forms of racism and xenophobia. 'Demagogic nationalism' needed to focus on a target: in the American South, the 'poor white' hated the black; in the Ottoman Empire, the Turk hated the Armenian; in Central and Eastern Europe, the scapegoat of nationalism had always been the Jews.[34] The Nazis had taken up this traditional form of anti-Semitism and transformed it into 'a tactic of the fascist assault group' (*die faschistische Stosstrupptaktik*). Rosenberg barely distinguished between the anti-Jewish violence of the SA and tsarist pogroms, stressing only a minor difference: in Russia, the pogroms were the work of the Black Hundreds, while in Germany they were carried out directly by the state.[35] In both countries, anti-Semitism turned the hatred of capitalism into anti-Jewish hatred: 'When the nationalist agitators unleashed their fury against Jewish usurer capital, they spread out their sails to the wind of socialism'.[36]

Daniel Guérin, author of the most significant Marxist contribution to the analysis of Nazism in the inter-war years, defended a virtually identical position. As he wrote in *Fascism and Big Business* (1936):

> Anti-Semitism exists in a latent state in the subconscious of the middle classes; throughout the nineteenth century, the petty bourgeoisie, the victim of capitalist evolution, had a tendency to render responsible for its evils the usurer and the banker, indeed the small Jewish trader. Already,

---

31   See Thalheimer 1930.
32   Marcuse 1968, pp. 3–42.
33   Bloch 2009.
34   Rosenberg 1967, p. 86. On Rosenberg and fascism, see Kessler 2003, pp. 216–28.
35   Rosenberg 1967, p. 87.
36   Ibid., p. 126.

the Frenchman Toussenel gave as a subtitle to his *Financial Feudalism*: 'The Jews, Kings of the Epoch', and wrote: 'I advise all the makers of the revolution to withdraw the bank from the Jews'. In exploiting the racist theme, fascism is assured of being applauded by the middle classes; at the same time, it preserves its financial backers from popular anger; it diverts the anticapitalism of the masses toward the Jews.[37]

Daniel Guérin had already developed this viewpoint in his reporting from Germany in 1933, where he wrote:

How can 650,000 Jews deprive 65 million Germans of work? But when things go badly, a scapegoat is needed and, to preserve from popular anger those who are truly responsible, the capitalists, Israel has been charged with every sin ... It is necessary to have understood these men of the people who are not racial theorists, who have not donned the brown shirt, to understand the profound sources of their hatred. Hitler has invented nothing; he has only listened, formulated, guessed what an outlet anti-Semitism offered to the anti-capitalism of the masses.[38]

In *Behemoth: The Structure and Practice of National Socialism* (1942), one of the most brilliant Marxist analyses of the socio-economic structure of Nazi Germany, Franz Neumann distinguished between 'non-totalitarian' and 'totalitarian' anti-Semitism, but he arrived once again at the conclusion that under the Nazi regime, racism and the anti-Jewish persecutions were only 'substitutes for the class struggle'.[39] Otto Bauer compared Nazi anti-Semitism to the social demagogy of Carl Lueger and Georg von Schönerer, which followed from the economic position occupied by the Jews within society. Hatred of the Jews, Bauer thought, was an ephemeral expedient, insofar as the eviction of the Jews from economic life would, sooner or later, lead the impoverished masses to oppose fascism itself.[40] Even Max Horkheimer, the director of the Frankfurt School exiled in New York, repeated the same arguments in a famous article titled 'The Jews and Europe' (1939). In his eyes, the Jews were only a commercial caste who, in the epoch of imperialism, became the victims of state capitalism. Nazism had replaced the archaic forms of the nineteenth-century capitalism – laissez-faire – and a totalitarian state had come to control the economic sys-

---

37   Guérin 1983b, p. 80.
38   Guérin 1983a, p. 81.
39   Neumann 1967, p. 125.
40   Bauer 1983, pp. 356–7. See also Bauer 1936.

tem in its entirety, profoundly abandoning the traditional structures of the free market. This tendency to subjugate the market inevitably led to anti-Semitism, for the Jews had always been the emblematic representatives of commercial capitalism. Thus, Nazi propaganda transformed them into the source of all the evils of society. Horkheimer integrated the conception of anti-Semitism as the 'socialism of fools' with the theory of state capitalism elaborated by Friedrich Pollock, the economist of the Frankfurt School. According to Horkheimer,

> The sphere of circulation, which was decisive for the fate of the Jews in a dual fashion, as the site of their livelihood and the foundation of bourgeois democracy, is losing its economic importance ... The Jews are stripped of power as agents of circulation, because the modern structure of the economy largely puts that whole sphere out of action. They are the first victims of the ruling group that has taken over the canceled function.[41]

This article, written as the Nazis began the 'final solution' to the Jewish Question in Europe, considers the Jews exclusively as an economic category. This was a shared approach in the Frankfurt School, first formulated by Friedrich Pollock in a 1939 report where he defined the 'liberal conditions' of the nineteenth century – both Jewish emancipation and free market economy – as a sort of 'interlude'. According to him, 'one of the main causes of the persecution of the Jewish minority in the totalitarian order is the replacement of the function of the market by governmental functions'.[42] What is remarkable – and it reveals a pre-Holocaust shared mental dispositions – is the enthusiastic reception of Horkheimer's article among many Jewish exiles.[43] A dissonant voice was Gershom Scholem. In a 1940 letter to Walter Benjamin, he criticised this economic approach. In his eyes, Horkheimer's Marxism had lost any interpretive value and was incapable of seeing the real danger embodied by Nazism, that is, the end of European Judaism. Arguing about the abolition of Jewish commerce when several million human beings had been deprived of their most elementary rights, the Frankfurt philosopher simply proved his complete inability to understand what was happening.[44]

---

41   Horkheimer 1989, p. 90. On Pollock's economic theories, see Pollock 1989, pp. 95–117; and Jay 1973, ch. 5.

42   Quoted in Wheatland 2009, p. 220.

43   On the publication and reception of Horkheimer's essay, see Jacobs 2015, pp. 44–52.

44   Benjamin, Scholem 1989, pp. 263–5. Another exception was Siegfried Kracauer, who read

According to the historian Martin Jay, the source of such a persistent and widespread incomprehension of the nature of Nazi anti-Semitism should be sought essentially in the Jewish origins of a great number of the German left political leaders and Marxist intellectuals.[45] Faced with the Nazis, who accused the left of being a Jewish creation, they were put in a real dilemma: if they acknowledged their Jewishness, this would have been understood as an implicit legitimation of the vision of communism as a Jewish plot; if they denied their origins, they could be accused of cowardice and treason (not only by the Zionists) or even of 'Jewish self-hatred'. How was this contradiction to be resolved? Repression of the problem was an easy way out: both to consider anti-Semitism as a simple demagogic tool, without trying to understand its deeper roots, and to ignore its developments and its consequences.

3   Trotsky's Warnings

The rise of Nazism in Germany led Leon Trotsky to abandon the traditional Marxist approach to the Jewish Question. In numerous articles and interviews, he openly recognised the historical failure of the assimilationist model and stressed the national character of the Eastern Jewry. In an interview given in 1937 to the Mexican Yiddish daily, *Der Weg*, he said: 'During my youth I rather leaned toward the prognosis that the Jews of different countries would be assimilated and that the Jewish Question would thus disappear in a quasi-automatic fashion. The historical development of the last quarter of a century has not confirmed this perspective'.[46] In other words, Jewish assimilation had not taken place or had not been fulfilled in Europe because of anti-Semitism.

Trotsky's writings oscillate between the vision of anti-Semitism as a form of obscurantism and irrationalism opposed to modernity and the Enlightenment, on the one hand, and the definition of Nazism as totalitarianism, the expression of modern decaying capitalism on the other. In 1933, Trotsky depicted Hitler's racism as a regression 'from economic materialism to zoological materialism'. In his opinion, Hitler had drawn inspiration from the traditional theoretical arsenal of racist thought, plagiarising the ideas of the 'diplomat and a literary dilettante' Count Gobineau. He distinguished Nazism from Italian fascism,

---

Horkheimer's essay in Paris. He later wrote: 'it appeared to me at that time, that one had to commit suicide, if that so-depressing essay was correct' (quoted in Jacobs 2015, p. 48).

45   Jay 1986, pp. 79–89.

46   *LTO*, vol. 12, p. 111. On Trotsky's rethinking of his approach to the Jewish Question, see Nedava 1972, p. 231, and Howe 1978, p. 157.

because the nationalist rhetoric of the latter remained free of anti-Semitic components (at least until 1938), but he remained vague enough in the definition of the ideological roots of Nazism. Trotsky wrote:

> To evolution, materialist thought, and rationalism – of the twentieth, nineteenth, and eighteenth centuries – is opposed in his mind national idealism as the source of heroic inspiration. Hitler's nation is the mythological shadow of the petty bourgeoisie itself, a pathetic delirium of a thousand-year Reich. In order to raise it above history, the nation is given the support of the race. History is viewed as the emanation of the race. The qualities of the race are construed without relation to changing social conditions. Rejecting 'economic thought' as base, National Socialism descends a stage lower: from economic materialism it appeals to zoological materialism.[47]

Trotsky did not discern that the 'scientific' character of biological racism – like many progressive ideas of the nineteenth century – originated in evolutionism and social Darwinism. In his view, racism was, rather, a feudal ideological vestige exhumed by a declining capitalism. As he wrote, 'not only in peasant homes but also in city skyscrapers there lives alongside of the twentieth century the tenth or the thirteenth'.[48] Fascism blocked the 'normal development of society' by raising against it an immense wall formed from the 'inexhaustible reserves ... of darkness, ignorance and savagery' from which German society had not been capable of liberating itself: 'Capitalist civilization is puking up the undigested barbarism'.[49]

In other words, Trotsky viewed as a simple juxtaposition what in reality was a fusion of feudalism and totalitarianism into a dialectic of 'reactionary modernism', the core of Nazi ideology: a peculiar amalgamation of the Counter-Enlightenment (authoritarianism, conservatism and the rejection of human rights) with scientism and a cult of technical modernity. Nazism was not a simple coexistence, but rather a dialectical interpenetration between reaction and modernity that resulted in a form of 'steel romanticism'.[50] In this article, however, Trotsky still interpreted anti-Semitism exclusively as the product of an economic conflict inside the bourgeoisie:

---

47   Trotsky 1971, p. 403.
48   Ibid., p. 405.
49   Ibid.
50   Cf. Herf 1984. On Trotsky's interpretation of Nazi anti-Semitism, see also Geras 1998, pp. 151–9, and Callinicos 2001.

Nationalism in economy comes down in practice to impotent though savage outbursts of anti-Semitism. The Nazis abstract usurious or banking capital from the modern economic system because it is of the spirit of evil: and, as is well known, it is precisely in this sphere that the Jewish bourgeoisie occupies an important position. Bowing down before capitalism as a whole, the petty bourgeois declares war against the evil spirit of gain in the guise of a Polish Jew in a long-skirted caftan, and usually without a cent in his pocket. The pogrom becomes the supreme evidence of racial superiority.[51]

But toward the end of the 1930s, Trotsky began to consider anti-Semitism from a different perspective. Now, he depicted the Jews as the first victims of a rotting capitalism that the ruling class was trying to preserve by plunging humanity into a bloodbath. Scientific, technical and industrial development, until then considered criteria of progress, was henceforth perceived in its dual nature: both as possible instrument of human liberation and as possible bearer of a modern barbarism. Thus, the fate of the Jews tended to be identified with the alternative *socialism or barbarism*. This theme was evoked in the *Transitional Program* (1938), the founding manifesto of the Fourth International, with the following words: 'Before exhausting or drowning mankind in blood, capitalism befouls the world atmosphere with the poisonous vapors of national and race hatred. Anti-Semitism today is one of the more malignant convulsions of capitalism's death agony'.[52] In May 1940, just after the outbreak of the Second World War, he reaffirmed the same idea in a more imaginative form:

In an era of aviation, telegraph, telephone, radio, and television, travel from country to country is paralyzed by passports and visas. The period of the wasting away of foreign trade and the decline of domestic trade is at the same time the period of the monstrous intensification of chauvinism and especially of anti-Semitism. In the epoch of its rise, capitalism took the Jewish people out of the ghetto and utilized them as an instrument in its commercial expansion. Today decaying capitalist society is striving to squeeze the Jewish people from all its pores: seventeen million individuals out of the two billion populating the globe, that is, less than one percent, can no longer find a place on our planet! Amid the vast expanses of land and the marvels of technology, which has also conquered the skies

---

51   Trotsky 1971, p. 405.
52   Trotsky 1977, p. 133.

for man as well as the earth, the bourgeoisie has managed to convert our planet into a foul prison.[53]

Anti-Semitism was a global phenomenon in which Trotsky recognised a kind of division of labour between fascism and liberal democracies. On the one hand, Nazi anti-Semitism represented a 'chemically pure distillation of the culture of imperialism';[54] on the other hand, he criticised the United States for refusing to open their doors to the Jews threatened by Hitler. Exiled in Mexico, the Russian revolutionary observed Hitler's Europe as the laboratory where the genocide of the Jewish people was being prepared. The victory of fascism meant 'a monstrous growth of violent anti-Semitism in all the world', not excluding the United States. Thus, it was 'possible to imagine without difficulty what await[ed] the Jews at the mere outbreak of the future world war. But even without war the next development of world reaction signifie(d) with certainty the *physical extermination of the Jews*'.[55] This change of view on anti-Semitism between 1933 and 1938 reveals a dichotomy inherent in Trotsky's thought. It amounts to a contradiction between his 'spontaneous philosophy', formed from a superficial adhesion to classical Marxism (a tradition dominated by the figures of Plekhanov and Kautsky), and his practical, that is to say non-systematised, break with any form of evolutionistic and positivistic Marxism.[56] An understanding of this contradiction makes it possible to explain his definition of fascism and anti-Semitism at first as an attempt to stop the 'wheel' of history in its course and, subsequently, as one of the possible roads taken by this same history.

With the exception of Trotsky, whose position is quite peculiar, it is possible to classify the Marxist analysis of anti-Semitism of the 1930s into two principal currents: first, as an *economic theory* that saw anti-Semitism as a mirror of the

---

53   Trotsky 1973, p. 184.

54   Ibid., p. 193.

55   Trotsky 1970a, p. 29. In a letter to Jack and Sara Weber, dated 4 February 1938, Trotsky defined anti-Semitism as 'a terrible historic convulsion of declining capitalism' and characterised as 'a negative privilege' of the Jews the fact of their being the victims of racism (as we will see later, the same phrase – 'negative privilege' – had been used by Max Weber to define the concept of the 'pariah people'). Trotsky wrote that this racist reaction threatened the Jews 'with physical extermination'. In his opinion, the only hope of salvation for the Jews lay in socialist revolution and, from this point of view, he praised the potentiality for revolt against the capitalist order residing in 'the messianic spirit' of the Jewish proletariat. The importance of this passage should be stressed because it is the only text of Trotsky's that refers to religion as one of the paths to the liberation of the oppressed (*LTO*, vol. 19, 137–8).

56   Cf. Brossat 1978, pp. 113–36.

elimination of Jewish commerce by monopoly capital (the KPD, Otto Bauer and Max Horkheimer up until 1939); second, as a *functionalist theory* that defined anti-Semitism as a substitute for the class struggle and an instrument for transforming the Jews into scapegoats (Heller, Guérin, Rosenberg, Neumann).

Retrospectively, both interpretations appear incapable of grasping the real dynamic of German anti-Semitism, which culminated in Auschwitz during the Second World War. Fundamentally, they perceived anti-Semitism as an epiphenomenon, a 'tactic' or a simple prejudice, and not as a goal in itself of Third Reich policy. As the Holocaust would clearly show, Nazi anti-Semitism did not correspond to any criteria of productive rationality.[57] Furthermore, if the Jews had been the scapegoats in the past against which any social discomfort and sufferance was turned, their total elimination excluded their being able to play this role in the future. Both interpretations are also essentially mono-causal. In the inter-war period, Marxists did not succeed in analysing anti-Semitism as a whole, as a complex historical phenomenon with socio-economic, cultural, political and psychological roots. Focusing on the economy and the crisis of capitalism, the Marxists did not see the 'syncretism' of the Nazi ideology, in which imperialism (the colonisation of Eastern Europe as a German 'vital space'), reactionary modernism (a secular crusade against the Enlightenment) and anti-Semitism (the Jews as the symbolic embodiment of the USSR) merged into a single war of conquest and extermination.[58] For these elements to lead to genocide, a particular historical context was necessary – war – but they had already been fused in National Socialism, which gave to anti-Semitism a new qualitative dimension: biological racism and radical anti-Bolshevism. Thus, Marxists persisted in considering anti-Semitism as an archaism rather than a form of reactionary modernism.

---

57   Cf. Herbert 1987, pp. 198–236.
58   Mayer 1988, and Traverso 2003.

CHAPTER 8

The Messianic Materialism of Walter Benjamin

The life and work of Walter Benjamin took place between two poles: Judaism and revolution. Though at first purely metaphysical and spiritual, from the mid-1920s onwards his revolutionary orientation took the form of historical materialism, a peculiar Marxism with a distinctly anarchistic charge; as for Judaism, he always perceived in it its messianic dimension. In fact, Benjamin neither 'swung' nor 'was torn between' these two poles; he created a bridge between Judaism and revolution and considered himself a Marxist while being at the same time profoundly Jewish. In other words, he held a 'dual' identity of which he was fully conscious and that he considered as his 'Janus face'.[1] He did not seek in Marxism the key to a sociological comprehension of the Jewish past and never attempted any 'materialist interpretation' of the Jewish Question; indeed, he was scarcely interested in that kind of debate inside the left. Unlike the Marxists of his time, he was attracted by the spiritual and religious strength of Judaism, not by its social or national aspects. Judaism did not represent for Benjamin a field to which Marxist theory could be applied, but a fundamental and irreplaceable source for the revolutionary transformation of the world.

1 German Culture and Jewishness

From his youth, Walter Benjamin possessed an acute consciousness of his own Jewishness. In 1912, at the age of twenty, he wrote: 'I am Jewish, and if I live as a conscious human being, then as a conscious Jew [*lebe ich als bewusster Jude*].'[2] Coming from a wealthy Berlin family, he discovered the spirituality of Judaism very early when he joined Gustav Wynecken's *Jugendbewegung* in opposition to his assimilated and conformist family milieu, of which he gives a critical portrait in *Berlin Childhood*.[3] For a romantic youth, rebellious and vaguely inclined towards anarchism, a partisan of school reform and contributor (under the pseudonym 'Ardor') to *Der Anfang*, the journal of the youth movement, this fascination with Judaism meant the rejection of the life-style

---

1 Scholem 1981, p. 209.

2 *GS*, vol. 2/3, p. 837.

3 Benjamin 2006.

© KONINKLIJKE BRILL NV, LEIDEN, 2019 | DOI:10.1163/9789004384767_011

and values of the German Jewish bourgeoisie (the Jewish 'parvenus', in Hannah Arendt's despising definition).[4] Born into an assimilated Jewish environment where religion was becoming less and less respected – Scholem observed that his friend's family had adopted the habit of celebrating Christmas – Benjamin discovered Judaism in his search for an identity opposed to that of his parents. He rejected the conformism of the Jewish bourgeoisie (his father was a rich art merchant), but, at the same time, he was opposed to the religious orthodoxy practised by the synagogue. Instead of rules and liturgies, Judaism represented for him a sensibility and a spiritual value.

At the turn of the twentieth century, the dominant cultural tendency in Germany was romanticism, conceived in a broad sense as a critique of industrial modernity in the name of tradition and the past, where a rationalised and mechanised system had not yet destroyed nature, where 'society' had not yet replaced the 'community' (Ferdinand Tönnies) and *Kultur* had not yet submitted to *Zivilisation*. For Benjamin, as for many other Jewish intellectuals of his generation, the rediscovery of a religious sensibility meant the rejection of the rationalisation of a 'disenchanted' world. For some of them, Judaism took the form of the *Ostjudentum*, where the *shtetl* appeared as an authentic *Gemeinschaft* (community). For example, Franz Kafka was fascinated by Yiddish theatre, and Martin Buber passionately investigated the mystic tradition of Hassidism. Benjamin was too rooted in German culture to feel a similar fascination for the Judaism of Eastern Europe. Pushed by his friend Gershom Scholem, he discovered the messianic dimension of Judaism above all through the Kabbalah. It was from Kabbalist sources that he took the concept of redemption (*Erlösung*), which runs like a red thread through his work.

Within Wyneken's youth movement – which unlike the nationalist *Wanderfogeln* was opened to the Jews – he met many Zionist students and, in 1915, established a deep friendship with Gershom Scholem. In 1913, in his correspondence with the young poet Ludwig Strauss, he had criticised political Zionism, which represented in his view a disfigurement of Judaism. He defended a 'Zionism of culture, which recognizes Jewish values everywhere and which works for their preservation'. In his eyes, the Jews represented an 'elite among the crowd of spiritual men', whereas the Zionist project for the colonisation of Palestine degraded Judaism to a banal form of nationalism, weakening its spiritual force. 'In my opinion', wrote Benjamin, 'it is useless to ask which of the two is more urgent, Jewish work in Palestine or European Jewish work. I have my roots here [*Ich bin hier gebunden*]. And, apart from that, things will go very

---

4   Arendt 2007, pp. 285–6.

badly in Europe if the intellectual energies of the Jews abandon it'.[5] There is, in this affirmation, both a demand for Jewish integration into European culture and the perception of a latent fracture between *Deutschum* and *Judentum*. The Jews should preserve this cultural unity, and, consequently, Zionism appeared to Benjamin as an abdication: the abandonment of a necessary struggle.

Benjamin's Jewishness was rooted in two major principles: first of all, the defence of the Diaspora, because the Jews had to accomplish a spiritual mission within European culture; second, a critique of political Zionism. These are, *in nuce*, the reasons why he never went to Palestine, where his friend Scholem emigrated in 1925. Forming part of the spiritual humus of German culture, Judaism could not be conceived in terms of nation or race. In a letter to Scholem in 1917, Benjamin wrote that the Zionists were similar to the anti-Semites in their conception of racial hatred as the sole possible relationship between Jews and Gentiles, and such a supposition appeared to him completely false.[6] In a previous letter to his young friend Ludwig Strauss, he had depicted the Zionists like people that 'make propaganda for Palestine and then get drunk like Germans'.[7]

This unshakeable faith in the Jewish-German symbiosis explains his mistrust for Martin Buber. In 1916, during a conversation with Scholem, Benjamin formulated a more precise critique of Zionism, affirming that it needed to free itself of three major weaknesses: the 'agricultural orientation, the racial ideology' and the idea of 'blood and experience' derived from Buber.[8] Benjamin's rejection of the agricultural myths of Zionism was self-evident: could he, the intellectual fascinated by the city (which he saw as the symbol of modernity), envisage rebuilding his life in Palestine? As for the critique of the idea of 'blood and experience', it lay in his complete rejection of any racial rhetoric. Of course, this criticism of Buber was to a large extent unjust and exaggerated. Far from being a partisan of a *völkisch* Zionism, Buber had powerfully contributed (above all through creating *Der Jude*, his journal with which Benjamin did not wish to collaborate) to the rediscovery of the romantic and mystical aspects of Judaism in opposition to the rationalist school of the *Wissenschaft des Judentums* and to the neo-Kantian philosopher Hermann Cohen, for whom Hassidism was only a form of medieval obscurantism. Through works such as *Die Legende des Baal Schem* (1908) and *Drei Reden über das Judentum* (1911), Buber created a new spiritual climate among young Jewish intellectuals; he no longer perceived Judaism as a 'religion of reason', but rather as a

---

5   *GS*, p. 838.
6   Benjamin 1978, vol. 1, pp. 152–3.
7   Ibid., p. 72. See also Eiland and Jennings 2014, pp. 46–8.
8   Scholem 1981, p. 37.

Lebensphilosophie opposed to Western modernity and rationalism. Benjamin's intellectual formation took place in the context of this reinterpretation of the Jewish tradition of which Martin Buber was one of the most convinced defenders.[9] Between them, there were probably more affinities than they thought. It nevertheless remains that in Benjamin's study of Jewish cultural heritage, Buber was a marginal source, not to be compared with the (Christian) historian of the Kabbalah, Franz Joseph Molitor, or with the philosopher of Judaism, Franz Rosenzweig, author of *The Star of Redemption* (1921). In short, Benjamin always manifested a radical opposition to Zionism as a form of Jewish nationalism. In his opinion, Judaism was neither a political category in the ordinary, completely secularised, sense of the word (Zionism), nor a lost identity to be rediscovered, but a religious category subjacent to history. There was no contradiction between his Jewishness and his ambition of becoming the Weimar Republic's most celebrated literary critic (an aspiration he probably realised at the end of the 1920s).

In 1936, *Deutsche Menschen*, a collection of articles that Benjamin had written for the newspaper *Frankfurter Zeitung* before the Nazis came to power, was published in Zurich. He conceived this book – an 'Ark' built on the Jewish model, according to the explanation he gave to his sister Dora – as a contribution towards rescuing a German culture threatened by the Nazi deluge.[10] In Benjamin's opinion, Judaism was in no way contradictory with being German. At a time when the Nazis were fiercely persecuting the Jews, Benjamin appealed to the Hebrew tradition to preserve German culture from Hitler's barbarism that wished to pervert and disfigure it. In her remembrances of Benjamin, whom she knew at the end of the 1930s, Adrienne Monnier stresses that he was 'Jewish and German; he possessed the characteristics of the two, without one appearing stronger than the other'.[11] Benjamin incarnated the Judeo-German cultural symbiosis, of which he was one of the last and greatest representatives, but he approached the Jewish tradition as a German intellectual, for whom the discovery of Judaism presupposed assimilation. As a German Jew, he saw in German culture a spiritual home, even if – unlike the assimilated Jewish intelligentsia of liberal orientation – he never considered the Prussian state as his own *Heimat*. A tireless traveller and intellectual fascinated by Paris, which he chose as his second residence and which was, after 1933, the place of his exile, he displayed a restlessness and a mobility that made him a true wandering Jew. According to Scholem, he was always conscious, in

---

9   See Kohn 1961.
10   See Scholem 1981, p. 255, and Schöne 1986, pp. 350–65.
11   See Monnier 1972, p. 70.

the same way as Kafka or Freud, of the distance that separated him as a Jewish writer from his German readers: 'They truly came from foreign parts and knew it'.[12] One could consider this retrospective judgment a little too cut and dried, inasmuch as Benjamin could not have shared the belief, formulated by his friend after the Second World War, that there had never been a Jewish-German dialogue. It remains the case nevertheless that he became more and more conscious of his role as an outsider in German society and culture. Unlike the great majority of Jewish Socialists and Communists (Rosa Luxemburg, Paul Levi, Eduard Bernstein, and so on), who were completely assimilated, he did not deny his religious identity. At the same time, he could not recognise himself in any of the various forms of Jewishness dominant in his time: neither orthodox Judaism (Samson-Raphaël Hirsch) nor liberal Judaism (Hermann Cohen), neither Zionism (Theodor Herzl or Martin Buber) nor an idealised *Ostjudentum* (Franz Kafka, Nathan Birnbaum), appeared to him as viable perspectives.

With the exception of a short period around 1935–6 – shaped by essays like *The Work of Art in the Age of Mechanical Reproduction* and *The Author as Producer* – Benjamin always drew on a religious inspiration in his works of literary criticism and philosophy. The style of his thought and the structure of his literary works were theological, as he stressed in 1931 (when he was already a Marxist) in a letter to the Swiss publisher Max Rychner: 'I have never been able to do research and think in any sense other than, if you will, a theological one, namely, in accord with the Talmudic teaching about the forty-nine levels of meaning in every passage of *Torah*'.[13] But the Judaism to which Benjamin was attached was not, of course, the ritual practised in the synagogue and had nothing to do with rabbinical orthodoxy. Nor did it amount to a 'rational' religion, according to the conception laid down in Central Europe by the *Haskalah*: Benjamin perceived Judaism essentially in its messianic dimension. Indeed, as Gershom Scholem has shown, Jewish messianism contains both a 'restoration' and a utopian current, seeking simultaneously a return to an original purity and the creation of a radically new order.[14] In this 'catastrophe theory', the coming of the Messiah takes an apocalyptic form and the redemption of humanity ushers in a utopian kingdom (a 'state of things having never yet existed') that represents at the same time the reestablishment of a lost original harmony (according to the Hebrew conception of the *Tikkun*) and the suppression of all temporal authority (the reign of God on earth as a 'paradisiac condition'). It is obvious that such a religious position could easily take on an anarchist colouring and

---

12   Scholem 1976, p. 191.
13   Benjamin 1994, p. 372.
14   See Scholem 1971, pp. 1–36.

be reconciled with a radical critique of capitalism. Benjamin remained profoundly faithful to this messianic conception (religious/libertarian/utopian) of Judaism, which pushed him to approach the analysis of all social and political problems from the angle of redemption. Before approaching Marxism, Benjamin had developed a 'metaphysical' form of anarchism – notably in his article 'The Life of the Students' (1914) or in the 'Critique of Violence' (1920–1) – which came close to that of Gustav Landauer and Ernst Bloch.[15]

2   Marxism

Benjamin came to Marxism in 1924, in Capri, thanks to the Latvian communist Asja Lacis. Why, unlike many other German Jewish intellectuals, did he become a communist only in 1924 at the end of the post-war revolutionary wave? Georg Lukács and Gustav Landauer, the authors of *Soul and Form* (1910) and *The Revolution* (1907) respectively, two essays that had strongly influenced him, passionately participated in the Hungarian and Bavarian revolutions. But Benjamin, who had opposed the war and had broken with the youth movement because of its nationalism, was not affected by these events. The Hungarian revolution appeared to him as a 'childish aberration' and a book like Ernst Bloch's *Spirit of Utopia* (1918) – simply inconceivable outside of the context of the war and revolution in Europe – probably had a stronger impact on him than the wave of post-war insurrections.[16] Indeed, up to 1924, Benjamin was completely absorbed by the German cultural tradition – he wrote his doctoral thesis on *The Concept of Art Criticism in German Romanticism* (1919) and his essay on Goethe (1922) – and showed only a superficial interest in politics (with few exceptions, like his commentaries on George Sorel's *Reflections on Violence*). It is true that for Benjamin, as Anson Rabinbach has pointed out, esoteric Messianism was a form of politics,[17] but this abstract attitude did not correspond to any political option inside Weimar Germany.

Benjamin's political radicalisation took place at a precise moment in his life and spiritual evolution, when he became conscious of his 'pariah' intellectual condition. After the great inflation of 1923, his family, with whom he had never had good relations, ceased to support him financially. In 1925, the University of Frankfurt rejected his *Habilitation*, unable to understand and accept a work as

---

15   Cf. *SW*, vol. 1, pp. 37–47, 236–52. On Benjamin's interest in Landauer see Scholem 1981, p. 16.
      On the relationship between Benjamin and Bloch, see Münster 1985, pp. 111–29.
16   See Eiland and Jennings 2014, pp. 128–9.
17   Rabinbach 1997, pp. 27–65.

innovative as the *Trauerspielbuch*. From the mid-1920s onward, Benjamin was then obliged to work as a literary critic and, plunged into material precariousness, he realised he was a member of the growing army of impoverished intellectuals of the Weimar Republic.[18] This is the context in which Benjamin turned toward politics and his romantic anti-capitalism joined Marxism. Through Asja Lacis, he met Bertolt Brecht, who became his friend and inspired his research on mass culture. Apart from Brecht, Lukács played an important role in Benjamin's understanding of Marxism. He discovered Marxism through *History and Class Consciousness*, a work published in 1923 in Berlin and immediately put on the index by the official communist movement. In 1924, he wrote to Scholem in order to inform his friend about both his relationship with Asja and his reading of Lukács's book. 'Starting from political considerations', he emphasised, Lukács had arrived at conclusions on the theory of consciousness that were 'very close' to his own.[19] In 1929, he classified *History and Class Consciousness* – together with Rosenzweig's *The Star of Redemption* – among those books that had 'remained living', defining it as 'the most organic and the most complete work of Marxist theory'.[20]

In fact, what attracted Benjamin in communism was not only its theoretical aspects, but also its 'political praxis' that he defined as an 'obligatory behavior'.[21] As Hannah Arendt stressed, Benjamin saw in Marxism a radical critique of bourgeois society, a spiritual and ethical rejection of capitalism as a social system and as a form of civilisation.[22] Benjamin became a communist in his own fashion, without rejecting his past or his intellectual trajectory, but this turn was not superficial, nor simply the adoption of a language and categories that, according to Scholem, distracted him from his true vocation.[23] Before all else, Marxism was for Benjamin the answer to a moral demand rather than a scientific discovery. He saw in it a theory of history as the history of class struggle rather than an analysis of the laws of movement of the capitalist system. 'Scientific' socialism, detached from its humanist and revolutionary dimension, in his view was equivalent to the reformist platitudes of German social democracy. It is true that Benjamin was never inclined to political activism, but he

---

18   Wolin 1982, p. 111. On this failed *Habilitation*, see Brodersen 1996, pp. 132–4, and Eiland and Jennings 2014, pp. 230–4.

19   Benjamin 1978, vol. 1, p. 355.

20   *GS*, vol. 3, p. 170.

21   Benjamin 1978, vol. 1, p. 355.

22   Arendt 1968, pp. 153–205.

23   According to Gershom Scholem, Benjamin argued like 'a theologian marooned in the realm of the profane' and translated his thought into a foreign language, that of historical materialism; see Scholem 1976, p. 187.

saw Marxism as more than an instrument of critical engagement in culture. In his eyes, communist politics was 'organized pessimism' and Marxism the historical memory of the oppressed in revolt against an age-old domination. He saw Marxism as a system of thought and a movement committed to the 'methodical and disciplinary preparation for revolution', or, in other words, as an indispensable ally of the 'radical conception of freedom' advocated by the surrealists.[24]

Benjamin integrated Marx's theory into his own system of thought without ruptures or breaks. Several scholars have distinguished different steps in Benjamin's intellectual trajectory: an initial romantic phase, shaped by an anarchist and nihilist orientation; a second phase, opened in 1926 by *One-Way Street*, marked by his discovery of Marxism; and a third moment, in which both romanticism and Marxism amalgamate with messianic Judaism. It should be stressed, however, that these steps succeeded each other in a substantial continuity, without breaks.[25] Marxism was, for Benjamin, the natural extension of his messianic and anti-capitalist romanticism, certainly not an atheist and rationalist worldview in line with the official doctrine of social democracy or communism. In his eyes, the revolutionary transformation of society, the destruction of the state and the creation of a new order – a classless, communist and self-managed society – was not in contradiction with the idea of a messianic redemption. According to Michael Löwy, communism had not replaced his old romantic anarchism, but had merged with it, creating a new and original form of thought.[26]

In Benjamin's vision of history, Jewish theology and secular Marxism were dialectically interpenetrated. In a letter to Scholem in 1926, he wrote that communist activity – a 'radical politics' – could only act 'in favor of Judaism', where it would always find an 'ally'. Thus, it was pointless to distinguish between politics and religion: 'In considering their profound nature', he emphasised, 'I do not for my part see any difference between these two observances'.[27] Inevitably, this viewpoint could only meet with incomprehension and criticism, even from his closest friends. On the one hand, Scholem, who did not understand his attempt to disguise an essentially religious thought with the language of historical materialism; on the other, Brecht, who found the writings of his friend interesting, 'despite their metaphors and their Judaism' that inevitably would

---

24   *sw*, vol. 2/1, p. 216. See also Cohen 1993.
25   See Moses 2008.
26   Löwy 2006.
27   Benjamin 1978, vol. 1, p. 425.

have been completely misunderstood.[28] As for Adorno and Horkheimer, his friends of the Frankfurt School exiled in New York, they criticised Benjamin for both a too radical Marxism and a dangerous tendency to infuse his writings with Jewish theological categories.[29]

3   Critique of Progress

Benjamin discovered Marxism in a period of setback for the revolutionary movement in Europe, just after the defeat of the 'German October' in 1923. In December 1926, he went to Moscow, where the dominant dogmatism and the gloomy atmosphere of the city, the first symptoms of Stalinist bureaucratisation, disappointed him. He wrote in his diary that there was already an air of 'restoration' in the Soviet Union.[30] Therefore, his acceptance of Marxism was critical and, so to speak, selective. What interested him about Marxism was its subversive and revolutionary dimension, of which there no longer remained any trace in social democracy. Educated by Bernstein and Kautsky, the latter conceived Marxism as a theory of evolution, in which history was a linear path toward progress and technique, its fundamental tool. This historical evolutionism and technical fetishism took into account only the domination of man over nature, without considering the human and social regression that this implied.[31] The principal error of social democracy was its illusion that it was 'swimming with the current' in identifying technical and industrial development with the general progress of humanity, without perceiving that this tendency resulted in the 'technocracy' (*die technokratische Züge*) of fascism. This critique of the fetishism of technology did not stem from conservative romanticism and the *völkisch* thought of the nineteenth and early twentieth centuries. Benjamin, for instance, did not admire Oswald Spengler, the author of *The Decline of the West* (1918). Some of Benjamin's essays, notably *The Work of Art in the Age of Mechanical Reproduction* (1936), could be read as an apologia for modern technology and the emancipatory potentialities of the machine. Nonetheless, in his acceptance of technique, he considered himself closer to Fourier (despite all his naïve limitations) than to German social democracy. In his opinion, scientific and industrial development should respect nature – which

---

28   Brecht 1996, p. 159. See also Wolin 1982, pp. 139–61, and Wizisla 2014.
29   On the relationship between Benjamin and the Frankfurt School, see Jay 1973, ch. 6.
30   See Benjamin 1986, p. 53.
31   On Benjamin's critique of the positivist Marxism of German social democracy, see Grefrath 1975, pp. 196–205.

he considered, like J. Bachofen, as a 'generous mother' – and harmonise with it instead of dominating and exploiting it. In opposition to fascism, which saw in technique a 'fetish of decadence', he suggested using scientific knowledge as a 'key to happiness'.[32] This reflection on technique was already sketched in a fragment of *One-Way Street* (1928) titled 'Towards the Planetarium'. In a typically romantic style, he opposed *Kultur* to *Zivilisation*: in Antiquity, humanity had lived in community with the cosmos, whereas in the modern world it had lost this 'cosmic experience' (*kosmische Erfahrung*) and its relation with nature was mediated by technique. However, under capitalism, where it was developed and applied exclusively for the purposes of profit, technique could no longer fulfil this intermediary role: it had 'betrayed' humankind and 'turned the bridal bed into a bloodbath'.[33] Technical progress engendered destructive forces and became an instrument of domination that could only lead to war. One of the tasks of the class struggle was then to break this negative dialectic and put technique back at the service of nature and humanity. 'If the abolition of the bourgeoisie', wrote Benjamin in another fragment of the collection, 'is not completed in an almost calculable moment in economic and technical development (a moment signaled by inflation and chemical warfare), all is lost. Before the spark reaches the dynamite, the lighted fuse must be cut'.[34] Unfortunately, social democracy was not able to distinguish between the emancipatory potential of technique and its destructive application by capitalism. With its complacent optimism, it persisted in seeing each technical innovation as a new contribution to the advent of a liberated society. As he wrote in his essay on Eduard Fuchs (1937), social democracy was prisoner to the illusions of positivism, merely admiring the development of technology; its theorists 'misunderstood the destructive side of this development because they were alienated from the destructive side of dialectics'.[35]

Benjamin summed up his criticism of vulgar positivist and evolutionist Marxism in the thirteenth of his theses 'On the Concept of History' (1940). For the social democrats, progress was universal ('of mankind itself', and not just 'advances in human ability and knowledge'), unlimited ('in keeping with an infinite perfectibility of mankind') and continuous ('something that automatically pursued a straight or spiral course').[36] According to this deterministic and teleological conception, history appeared as the advance of humanity 'through

---

32   *sw*, vol. 2/1, p. 321.
33   Benjamin 1979, p. 59.
34   Ibid, p. 80.
35   *sw*, vol. 3, p. 266.
36   *sw*, Vol. 4, p. 394.

a homogeneous, empty time'.[37] Unlike social democracy (and, *a fortiori*, the Stalinism of collectivisation and forced industrialisation), which saw history as a march of society toward progress, measured by the growth of the productive forces, Benjamin observed history as the history of class struggle and as an uninterrupted chain of violence, domination, and oppression, as the 'triumphal march' of the victors. For Benjamin, history was the march of society toward barbarism and fascism. In his celebrated allegory based on Klee's painting, *Angelus Novus*, he described the past as 'one single catastrophe, which keeps piling wreckage upon wreckage and hurls it at his feet', and the storm that carries the angel from this mountain of ruins as that which 'we call progress'.[38] This vision of history as a race toward catastrophe had some affinities with the Marxist theory of the 'collapse' (*Zusammenbruch*) of capitalism, according to which this mode of production was irreversibly doomed to break down because of its own contradictions. Benjamin was greatly affected by this anti-evolutionist version of Marxism, which he probably did not know in its original version – Rosa Luxemburg's *The Accumulation of Capital* (1912) – but rather through Lukács's *History and Class Consciousness*.[39]

In Benjamin's view, the proletarian revolution would not push history toward 'progress', but stop its movement, by breaking this chain of violence and injustice. In one of his fragments on Baudelaire (*Zentralpark*), he wrote that revolutionary action, like that carried out by Blanqui in the nineteenth century, did not 'presuppose any belief in progress' but rather the 'determination to do away with present injustice.'[40] Thus, revolution would accomplish both a secular and a messianic function: by crushing fascism and the dominant class – the 'Antichrist' – it would permit the redemption (*Erlösung*) of the past. For Benjamin, class consciousness meant the collective historical memory of the proletariat and coincided with the permanent 'remembrance' (*Eingedenken*) of the past. The class struggle was not seen solely as a 'fight for the crude and material things' but also as a protest and a revolt against the injustices of the past, as an attempt to bring out from obscurity the vanquished of history – from the slaves led by Spartacus to the martyrs of the Paris Commune – and to rescue them through political action in the present. In other words, revolution should break the continuity of history. Benjamin saw it as a 'tiger's leap into the past' that would return history to its victims.[41] In his theses, the conflict

---

37   Ibid., p. 395.
38   Ibid., p. 392.
39   See Lukács 1971. See also Radnoti 1978, p. 72.
40   *SW*, vol. 4, p. 188.
41   Ibid., p. 395.

between historical materialism and messianism is dialectically transcended in a synthesis in which, in the words of Herbert Marcuse, 'redemption is a materialist political concept: the concept of revolution'.[42]

In his preparatory notes for the theses 'On the Concept of History', Benjamin wrote that Marx had 'secularized the idea of messianic time (*messianische Zeit*)' in his conception of the 'classless society'.[43] Revolution was the 'now-time' (*Jetztzeit*) in which the oppressed past and the messianic future came together in an explosive encounter.[44] On this point, the German sociologist Christoph Hering has pertinently pointed out the striking similarity that exists between this concept of revolution as a messianic interruption of the *continuum* of history and Marx's theory – formulated in the introduction to the *Critique of Political Economy* (1859) – which characterised the revolution as the end of the 'prehistory' (*Vorgeschichte*) of humanity and the transition toward history (*Geschichte*), in which a communist society founded on the self-management of the producers would replace capitalism, based on exploitation.[45] Obviously, this meant not *to await* the coming of the Messiah, but rather *to provoke* it through the class struggle. Then, Benjamin broke with Jewish theology because, as Scholem explained, in biblical texts the messianic advent is never described as the result of the action of man.[46] For Benjamin, on the contrary, the messianic aspiration to the interruption of the course of history should lead to a materialist praxis, that is, to revolutionary action.

4   Historical Materialism and Theology

In the theses 'On the Concept of History', Benjamin evokes this fusion of Marxism with Jewish theology through the allegorical image, drawn from Edgar Allan Poe and German romantic literature, of the 'hunchback dwarf' (*buckliger Zwerg*). He described the legend of an 'automaton' that was always capable of defeating his adversaries at chess. In reality, this 'automaton', present in the form of a 'puppet wearing Turkish attire', concealed inside itself a 'hunchback dwarf' who was 'a master at chess', who directed the game and assured the victory. At the end of this thesis, Benjamin revealed the meaning of the allegory,

---

42   Marcuse 1975. P. 24. See also Löwy 2006, p. 66.
43   *GS*, vol. 1/3, p. 1231; *SW*, vol. 4, p. 401.
44   *SW*, vol. 4, p. 395.
45   See Hering 1983, p. 166.
46   Scholem 1971, p. 14.

explaining that the 'puppet called "historical materialism"' could defeat its adversaries in the chess game of history 'if it enlists the services of theology'.[47] Theology – Jewish messianism – appears in this thesis as a weapon to be used in the class struggle, a powerful tool without which Marxism, reduced by social democracy and Stalinism to an empty shell and a sort of soulless machine (an 'automaton') could not vanquish the historical enemy (fascism). One could even see theology as the necessary spiritual source for the regeneration of a Marxism that had been disfigured, inasmuch as it did not base itself on an authentic revolutionary thought but 'on something called "historical materialism"'.

By putting the little hunchback at the service of the automaton, Benjamin intended neither to 'theologise' Marxism nor to dissolve theology within it. He established no primacy between them: quite simply, he did not consider them as opposed or contradictory but as linked by a deep elective affinity. He did not conceive their union as an addition, rather as a dialectical synthesis.[48] Without such a fusion, they were doomed to impotence: historical materialism became a fetish (the 'science' of Kautsky or the Stalinist 'diamat') and theology was tragically metamorphosed into an angel carried by the storm of history, incapable of accomplishing its mission of redemption. The allegory of the automaton and the little hunchback throws some light on the famous phrase in which Benjamin admitted being inspired by scripture: 'My thinking relates to theology like the blotting pad is related to ink. It is saturated in it. Were one to go by the blotter, however, nothing of what is written would remain'.[49] Historical materialism could erase theology, but to do that it should first absorb it and then remain completely suffused with it.

According to Rolf Tiedemann, who headed the critical edition of Benjamin's works, the relation between theology and materialism remained ambiguous in the theses 'On the Concept of History', and culminated only in their reciprocal dissolution.[50] In reality, Benjamin's goal was precisely to eliminate any frontier between Marxism and messianism, in order to fuse them together in a new conception, simultaneously religious and secular, of the revolution. Influenced by Scholem and Brecht, most theological and Marxist interpretations of Benjamin share this refusal to see the unity of Marxism and theology. In the

---

47 *sw*, vol. 4, p. 389.
48 See Hering 1983, pp. 15, 21.
49 Benjamin 2002, p. 471. See Wohlfarth 1978, pp. 64–5.
50 According to Tiedemann, Benjamin tried to translate historical materialism into theology, but his attempt failed, because in his theses 'the secularized content dissolves itself and the theological idea disappears'; see Tiedemann 1975, p. 110.

first place, Benjamin was a theologian, despite the equivocal nature of a language frequently borrowed from historical materialism; in the second, he was a Marxist, despite his inability to abandon the remnants of his youthful messianism.[51] To understand the theses 'On the Concept of History', it is necessary to adopt a new approach – that, for example, of the liberation theology in Latin America – founded on the idea that Marxism and religion are not two irreconcilable entities. In the theses 'On the Concept of History', their meeting took place on a precise terrain, that of the liberation of the oppressed (of the present and the past). To understand this transcendence of the Marxism/religion antinomy, one should take into account – like Marx, Gramsci, and Bloch – the dual character of religion (both *instrumentum regni* and 'the sigh of the oppressed creature') and of Marxism (not only a 'scientific' theory of society but also a revolutionary project for the transformation of the world). Benjamin saw in religion (Jewish messianism) the hope of redemption for the oppressed and, in Marxism, the organised revolt bringing about the liberation of the proletariat. As he wrote to Scholem in the letter cited above, he could not distinguish between the two.[52]

Despite Habermas's severe judgment, according to which 'an anti-evolutionist conception of history could not be pulled down like a hood over historical materialism',[53] Benjamin drew on a tradition within Marxism in his critique of progress. Unlike Kautsky and his social democratic followers, who considered human progress the product of a natural law of social development, Marx conceived history as a contradictory movement of social formations. Along with his famous passages of *The Manifesto* that could be interpreted as an apologia for industrial progress and capitalism, he devoted many writings to criticism of the violence and inhumanity of the advent of bourgeois rule, from the primitive accumulation of capital, to colonialism and the industrial revolution. Describing the British rule in India, for example, he compared 'progress' to a 'hideous, pagan idol, who would not drink nectar but from the skulls of the slain'.[54]

The catastrophism that runs through the writings of Benjamin echoes many Marxist works written during 'explosive' historical moments like the First or Second World Wars. For example, *The Junius Pamphlet* (1916), in which Rosa

51   According to Kaiser 1975, p. 74. Paolo Pullega pushed this interpretation to its limit, considering Benjamin's theses as a radically anti-Marxist text (see Pullega 1980).

52   According to Michael Löwy, the 'different 'faces' of Benjamin are the manifestations of the same unique thought that had both a messianic and a secular expression'; see Löwy 1988, p. 159.

53   Habermas 1972, p. 207.

54   Marx 1960, p. 82. On the romantic, anti-capitalist dimension of Marx's thought see Löwy 1987, pp. 891–904.

Luxemburg put forward the slogan 'socialism or barbarism', or the writings of an *aufklärerisch* Marxist like Leon Trotsky, who, on the eve of the Second World War, evoked the possibility of a 'decline of civilisation'. In such 'explosive' historical constellations, a messianic and a rational conception of history merges in the same apocalyptic vision of the present as 'Hell'. Born within the intellectual framework of 'Western Marxism', Benjamin's messianic materialism remained quite unclassifiable. Radically hostile to the positivistic materialism of the Second International, he criticised a certain economic determinism in the thought of Marx (of whom he had only a partial knowledge), and, obviously enough, could not identify with the atheistic and *aufklärerisch* tradition in Marxism. But he remained firmly within the framework of historical materialism in his vision of the proletariat as the social force capable of understanding and transforming reality: 'The subject of historical knowledge is the struggling, oppressed class itself'.[55]

Benjamin assimilated Marxism and reinterpreted it in the light of his romantic worldview. His goal was the elaboration of a 'historical materialism that had annihilated in itself the idea of Progress [*der die Idee des Fortschritts in sich annihiliert hat*]. Just here, historical materialism has every reason to distinguish itself sharply from bourgeois habits of thought. Its founding concept is not progress but actualization'.[56] To faith in progress and the objective laws of history, he opposed the utopian image of the past as 'saved' (*gerettet*) and 'redeemed' (*erlöst*) in the classless society of the future. The aspiration of the oppressed to reconstruct the social order of the world was nourished by the memory of primitive communism, kept alive in the recesses of memory. In 1935 he defined communist utopia in these terms: 'In the dream in which each epoch entertains images of its successor, the latter appears wedded to elements of primal history [*Urgeschichte*] – that is, to elements of a classless society'.[57] The liberated society of the future was conceived as a return to the origins. According to the Kabbalistic idea of redemption – evoked by Benjamin through a quotation from Karl Kraus – 'the origin is the final goal' (*Ursprung ist das Ziel*).[58]

The communist future also implied the return to an 'original language' (*Ursprache*) common to all human beings. Benjamin conceived it as 'a kind of

---

55   *sw*, vol. 4, p. 394.
56   *gs*, vol. 5/1, p. 574; Benjamin 2002, p. 460. In his preparatory notes to the theses, Benjamin wrote that revolutions were not, as Marx thought, the 'locomotive of world history', but 'the emergency brake' in the travelling train of humankind, *gs*, vol. 1/3, p. 1232; *sw*, vol. 4, p. 402.
57   *sw*, vol. 3, pp. 33–34.
58   *sw*, vol. 4, p. 395.

Esperanto',[59] that is, a universal language capable of expressing the authenticity and harmony rediscovered by all men and women in a *Weltgemeinschaft*. Universal history, coinciding with the messianic time, should transcend the multiplicity of languages and return to the transparence of the Adamic language. In his youthful essay on the theory of language, Benjamin had evoked the myth of the Tower of Babel and the resulting confusion of languages as the consequence of original sin, through which men had offended the purity of God's name.[60] After messianic redemption, language would cease to be a 'means' of communication and recover, in accordance with its original function, the expression of its spiritual essence: the name of God.

The theses 'On the Concept of History' bear the mark of the time in which they were written. Benjamin had just been freed from a French internment camp and found himself in Paris; he was in a precarious situation, and conscious of the threat of a possible Nazi occupation. They were also written after the shock of the Soviet-German treaty, evoked in the reference to the 'politicians' who had contributed to their defeat by 'betraying their own cause'.[61] It was 'midnight in the century', when the European proletariat seemed crushed by fascism and betrayed by its own leadership. The Spanish Republic had been defeated and fascism extended its rule on the old continent. The Jews experienced a new wave of persecutions in Nazi Germany that, during the war, would end in genocide. In these circumstances, in which barbarism was no longer a dark perspective for the future but the reality of the present, a revolutionary manifesto could only be conceived as an act of faith. Benjamin's Marxism needed the principle of hope contained in religion in order to conserve all its revolutionary and subversive force. Perhaps he found in messianic theology a new version of the communist utopia betrayed by both social democracy and Stalinism.

5   Outsider

In 1927, a little after his trip to Moscow, Benjamin had definitively abandoned the idea of joining the KPD and his critical distance from the Stalinised communist movement deepened in the following years. It is known that in 1932 he had read Trotsky's autobiography and *History of the Russian Revolution* with great interest. He wrote to Gretel Adorno that not 'for some years' had he

---

59   *GS*, vol. 1/3, p. 1239.
60   *SW*, vol. 1, pp. 62–74. See Agamben 1983, pp. 65–82.
61   *SW*, vol. 4, p. 393.

'absorbed anything with such intensity, so breathtaking'.[62] In 1937, he followed with 'the greatest attention' the progress of the Moscow trials of which, as he confessed to Horkheimer, he lacked 'any key to understanding'.[63] Werner Kraft has pointed out a small nuance that distinguished the attitude of Brecht from that of Benjamin toward the Soviet Union: the first was against Stalin, the second for Trotsky.[64] Toward the end of the 1930s, Benjamin had not the least confidence in the 'orthodox' left. He declared himself totally disappointed by the French Popular Front, whose major concern had been to demobilise the powerful mass movement that carried it to power one year earlier. He wrote that the policy of the Léon Blum government, if practised by the right, would have 'provoked riots'.[65] He also denounced the policy of the Spanish Popular Front, which submitted 'revolutionary thought' to the interests of the Soviet bureaucracy and its local agents. This policy led to a 'martyrdom' that the proletariat did not suffer 'in the name of its own cause' but rather as a consequence of the 'Machiavellianism of the Russian leadership' and the 'Mammonism of the indigenous one'.[66] In 1938, summing up the content of an interview with Brecht, he said that what existed in Russia was a 'dictatorship *over* the proletariat', and expressed the desire to study more deeply the analyses of Trotsky, which aroused a 'justified suspicion' toward the USSR under Stalin.[67] Finally, in the 1940 theses 'On the Concept of History', he denounced the Soviet-German pact as a treason committed by 'politicians' who had abandoned the cause of the oppressed and submitted themselves 'to an uncontrollable apparatus'.[68]

What was singular about Benjamin was his radical exteriority to any kind of orthodoxy and conformism, religious as well as political. He was a critical Marxist and a Jewish intellectual outside of both official communism and Judaism. His multiple attempts to learn Hebrew, between 1920 and 1929, remained unfinished, and despite his friendship with Scholem he never showed the slightest interest in Jewish institutions. His attempts at collaboration with the Jewish press failed disastrously. In 1929, the editors of the *Encyclopaedia Judaica* asked him for a contribution on the Jews in German culture, but they hardly appreciated the text he submitted (*Juden in der deutsche Kultur*). The article finally appeared under Benjamin's signature, but he never considered it as a product

---

62   Benjamin 1994, p. 412.
63   Benjamin 1978, vol. 2, p. 728.
64   See Kraft1972, p. 69.
65   Benjamin 1978, vol. 2, p. 732.
66   Benjamin 1978, vol. 2, p. 747; Benjamin 1994, p. 553.
67   Benjamin 1973, p. 121.
68   SW, vol. 4, p. 393.

of his pen and qualified as 'falsification' its reworking by the editors (Nahum Goldmann and the rabbi Bruno Jacob).[69] After the Zionist magazine *Jüdische Rundschau* had mutilated his essay on Kafka in 1934, publishing a fragmentary and abridged version of it, he considered this experience as a chapter that was definitively closed. At the beginning of his exile in France, he qualified the humanitarian associations set up by 'Jewish high finance' with the goal of assisting the refugees as 'external fortresses' from which he had been able to get 'neither a centime, nor a mattress, nor a stick of wood'.[70]

This spirit of contempt for Jewish institutions probably explains his enthusiasm for Horkheimer's essay 'The Jews and Europe', published in 1939 in the *Zeitschrift für Sozialforschung* (then published in the United States). In this article, which emphasised the economistic approach to the Jewish Question, the author equated the Jews with commerce and explained Nazi anti-Semitism as a consequence of monopoly capitalism, which led to the state assuming direct control of distribution. As we have seen in a previous chapter, this article aroused the indignation of Scholem, but Benjamin greeted it favourably, and even wrote to Horkheimer to congratulate him. In his opinion, this study also contained an implicit critique of the 'complacent optimism of our leaders of the left'.[71] For Benjamin, this text did not deal with the European Jews persecuted by Nazism, but the big Jewish bourgeoisie, whom he held in profound contempt, believing that there was nothing further removed from the very essence of Judaism.

Judeo-Marxist, and liberation theologian *ante litteram*, Walter Benjamin could not be understood by his contemporaries; his destiny was a stoic form of intellectual marginality. All the evidence indicates that he was understood neither by the political Zionists, who conceived Judaism as the colonisation of Palestine, nor by the 'orthodox' Marxists, who were convinced that Judaism was no more than an obscurantist heritage of the past. Benjamin's suicide at the Spanish frontier in 1940, in a desperate attempt to escape Nazism, passed unnoticed at the time, like that of so many exiled Jews, and was known only to a few friends. Brecht wrote that his death was the first important loss inflicted by Hitler on German culture. Today, his death seems charged with an 'aura' that retrospectively illuminates his whole life. It touches us profoundly and disquiets us, like that of Trotsky, killed in Mexico in 1940 by a Stalinist agent, or that of Che Guevara, assassinated in Bolivia in 1967 by the CIA. It appears to us as

---

69   GS, vol. 2/2, pp. 807–13. On the circumstances of the publication of this article, see Tiedemann's editorial notes in GS, vol. 2/3, pp. 1520–1.

70   Benjamin 1994, p. 431.

71   Ibid., p. 622. Cf. Horkheimer 1970. On this text, see the previous chapter.

the symbol of a revolt against the barbarism of this century. There remains his work, which has left its mark in culture and projects a ray of hope in the 'homogeneous, empty time' of his epoch. He introduced into Marxism the idea that there are still many 'strait gates' through which 'the Messiah might enter.'

CHAPTER 9

The Theory of the People-Class: Abram Leon

The approach to the Jewish Question pioneered by Kautsky and Bauer found its crowning moment in the work of a young Polish Jewish intellectual who died in Auschwitz at the age of 26: Abram Leon (Wajnsztok).[1] His classic book *The Jewish Question: A Marxist Interpretation* (published posthumously in Paris in 1946, but completed in December 1942 in Brussels, under the Nazi occupation) followed the methodology of Kautsky and Bauer, developing it on the basis of a greater historical knowledge. Leon's intellectual and political itinerary explains the fusion in his work of the tradition of classical Marxism with elements borrowed from Borokhov, Medem and Zhitlovsky. His intellectual formation took place in Belgium, after a childhood spent in Warsaw in the heart of Eastern European Judaism (where he learnt, among other languages, Yiddish), and before becoming a disciple of Trotsky he had been a member of Hashomer Hatzair, the most important Zionist-socialist movement where he became acquainted with Borokhov's works. Leon criticised and ultimately rejected Zionism in a precise historical moment – on the eve of the Second World War – in which all the conquests of Emancipation seemed precarious, threatened or illusory. Thus, he tried to rethink the Jewish Question beyond Kautsky and Borokhov, and looked for a Marxism that was both anti-Zionist and anti-Stalinist.

As we have seen, in the footsteps of the young Marx, Kautsky had defined the Jews as a 'caste' and Bauer had explained their national past in terms of their role as merchants inside pre-modern societies, where production was doomed to personal consumption and not to exchange. For his part, Otto Heller had characterised the Jewish question as the whole of social-historical conditions that had led a specific ethnic group 'to transform itself from a nation into a caste'.[2] These analyses were integrated and developed by Leon in his theory of the people-class, which, though more coherent and more closely argued, was founded on the same tendency to reduce Jewish history to the socio-economic function of the Jews. Leon wrote: 'Above all the Jews constitute historically a social group with a specific economic function. They are a class, or more precisely, a people-class'.[3] According to Leon, 'The concept of class does not

---

1 On the life of Abram Leon, see Mandel 1970, pp. 15–31.
2 Heller 1933, p. 17.
3 Leon 1970, p. 74.

at all contradict the concept of people. It is because the Jews have preserved themselves as a social class that they have likewise retained certain of their religious, ethnic, and linguistic traits'.[4] One can detect in this notion of the people-class a trace of the influence of Max Weber, who had defined the Jews as a 'caste' or a 'pariah people' (*Pariavolk*) rooted in a form of 'capitalism oriented toward speculation, a capitalism of pariahs' (*Pariakapitalismus*).[5] Leon used these conceptions drawn from Weber within the framework of a Marxist typology of religions: in his view, Catholicism expressed the interests of landed property, Protestantism those of modern capitalism, whereas Judaism reflected the 'interests of a pre-capitalist merchant class'.[6]

Interpreting unilaterally Marx's famous sentence according to which the 'secret of the Jew' should not be sought in religion but in the social history of the Jews, which explained their religious specificities,[7] Leon depicted the 'people' as an outcome or an extension of the 'class'. This is obvious in his sarcastic commentary on theological anti-Judaism: 'Religion explains anti-Jewish persecutions like a soporific explains sleep'.[8] This crude materialist vision negated any autonomy of superstructural phenomena in the historic process: in Leon's definition, the Jews are simultaneously a people and a class, but all his attention is focused on the class. For example, his fairly interesting initial considerations on the history of the Jewish languages (in particular Yiddish and Judeo-Spanish) as expressions of 'contradictory tendencies' within Judaism – one to assimilation and the other to ethnic conservation – were not developed and he interpreted both anti-Semitism and assimilation as purely economic phenomena.[9] Moreover, he projected the concept of the people-class onto the whole history of the Jewish Diaspora. Assuming that 'the overwhelming majority of Jews in the Diaspora unquestionably engaged in trade',[10] he depicted two

---

4   Ibid., p. 74. During the 1930s, Trotsky defined the Soviet bureaucracy as a parasitic caste, which differed from a class because of its non-organic connection to the relations of production. Unlike a dominant class, the Soviet bureaucracy appeared to Trotsky as a transitory social excrescence, born from the social relations created by the October Revolution but not necessary to their development. This probably had a certain theoretical influence on Leon. In defining the Jews as a people-class, he emphasised the economic role played by this ethnic group in feudalism (or, more generally, pre-capitalist economy). On this concept of the bureaucratic caste, see Trotsky 1995.

5   Weber 1948, pp. 165–6. On Weber's conception of the Jews as a pariah people, see Liebeschutz 1964, pp. 41–68; Momigliano 1980, pp. 313–18; and Schluchter 1981.

6   Leon 1970, p. 76.

7   See the first chapter of this book.

8   Leon 1970, p. 182.

9   Ibid., p. 79.

10   Ibid., p. 69.

thousand years of history, from the beginning of the Diaspora until the end of the nineteenth century, as a sequence of economic steps of the people-class. Leon's periodisation of Jewish history distinguished four major phases:

a. The pre-capitalist period, which began with the dispersion and continued until the eleventh century in Eastern Europe. It was a period of economic prosperity and the cultural flourishing of Judaism. Within the Roman Empire, the Jews represented a socially differentiated urban community that drew its wealth directly or indirectly from its commercial activities. Quoting Henri Pirenne, Leon argued that, in the first centuries of the Middle Ages, 'Jew' and 'merchant' were 'synonymous terms'.[11] In the context of feudalism, a mode of production based on personal consumption rather than exchange, the economic function of the Jews was irreplaceable. They embodied the exchanges between West and East, and thus the feudal monarchies constantly sought their collaboration.

b. The period of 'medieval capitalism' and the Jewish usurer, lasting from the eleventh century to the Renaissance in Western Europe, and from around the eighteenth to the nineteenth century in Eastern Europe. According to Leon, the birth of a merchant bourgeoisie forced the Jews to turn to usury. With the first forms of capitalism and the diffusion of commodity production, the bourgeoisie took over the management of commerce, whereas the Jews now became moneylenders and lost the privileges and the protection guaranteed until then by the ruling classes. In these socioeconomic conditions, popular hostility toward the Jews increased. They were economically useless and society expelled them: the fourteenth and fifteenth centuries saw the great exodus eastward (above all to Poland) of the Western Jews, affected by the edicts of expulsion (Leon's indifference towards religious anti-Judaism made him overlook a phenomenon as significant as Marranism).

c. The period of 'manufacturing capitalism' which, in the West, stretched from the Renaissance to the nineteenth century. The development of capitalism had broken up the Jewish people-class, while society had gradually emancipated the Jews, who became assimilated within the nations among whom they lived. In Leon's view, 'Wherever the Jews were integrated into the capitalist class, there *they were likewise assimilated* ... The progress of capitalism went hand in hand with the assimilation of the Jews in Western Europe'.[12] In the East, on the other hand, the penetration

---

11   Ibid., p. 124. See Pirenne 1939, p. 250.
12   Leon 1970, p. 84.

of capitalism toward the end of the nineteenth century produced a social differentiation of the Jewish commercial caste, which led to the formation of a marginal proletariat and a mass of pariahs obliged to emigrate.

d.   The phase of imperialism, in the twentieth century. The Jews of the East remained caught between feudalism in decomposition and decadent capitalism, with the process of assimilation in crisis. They remained attached to a historically doomed economic function and they could no longer integrate themselves into society. It was this contradiction that produced modern anti-Semitism, transforming the Jews into scapegoats for the economic crisis. This also happened in the West, where the global crisis of capitalism gave a new boost to anti-Semitism: the Nazi regime turned the anti-capitalist hatred of the pauperised petty bourgeoisie against the Jews.

1   Historiographical Limitations

The Jewish Question reveals a deep historical erudition for its time, still more impressive if one considers the youth of its author (the manuscript bears the date December 1942 – Leon was then twenty-four years old) and the conditions in which he completed his study (in occupied Belgium, participating at the same time in the clandestine struggle against Nazism). The concept of 'people-class', however, has a limited interpretive value. According to Maxime Rodinson, it could be fruitfully applied to feudalism – Europe at the time of the crusades – but Leon conceived it as a universal paradigm and projected it onto the entire history of the Jewish Diaspora. The existence of the Jewish 'people-class' was historically circumscribed and could not be extended both temporally (before 1096) and spatially (outside of the Western Christian world). Rodinson sums up his critique in these terms: 'Some features belonging essentially to the period after the crusades have been unconsciously and abusively transposed into the past and extended to other cultural areas. The Jews of Antiquity, even in the Diaspora, were not particularly committed to commerce'.[13] Before the eleventh century, the European Jews were socially differentiated – in addition to traders, there were also artisans and farmers in great numbers – and were distinguishable from the surrounding population neither economically nor culturally, but only in terms of religion. For Bernard Blumenkranz, it was the crusades that marked a turning point, bringing about a veritable economic metamorphosis of Jewish life:

---

13   Rodinson 1981, pp. 89–90.

> In many ways, the eleventh century is fundamental in the history of the Jews. This is true also at the economic level. From the end of the tenth century, we can observe the abandonment by the Jews of their farming concerns. The deeds that, until then, had shown the Jews as buyers of land show them henceforth as sellers. At the same time, one observes their migration toward the towns. It should not astonish us that those Jews who moved to the towns showed a preference for commerce ... In the twelfth century, the economic conversion that had started a century before was almost completed. A man living in this century could now say with some justice that all Jews were devoted to trade.[14]

The development of a Christian merchant bourgeoisie, however, rapidly replaced the Jewish traders, who were obliged to transform themselves into usurers. Two elements favoured this turn: on the one hand, unlike the Christians, the Jews were not affected by religious restrictions (or, as Jacob Katz has shown, they were obliged to shed them);[15] on the other hand, they had ceased to be landowners because of persecution. The theory of the people-class is then relevant from the eleventh century onward. In feudal society not all Jews were traders or usurers, and moreover these latter were not all Jews: as Léon Poliakov has stressed in his *History of Anti-Semitism*, the role of the Christian usurers, the Lombards and the Cahorsins, was much more significant than that of the Jewish moneylenders.[16] Nevertheless, it is certain that at this time the whole life of the Jewish community turned around usury. It is in this period also that economic hostility toward the Jews, transformed into scapegoats for the popular hatred of usury and commerce, developed.

The historical studies have shown the limits of Leon's paradigm for around a thousand years of Jewish life in the Diaspora. It follows then that the 'secret' of the historical continuity of the Jewish question cannot be sought exclusively in the socioeconomic function of the Jews. It is obvious that this critique of Leon's theory implies a challenge to the manner in which historical materialism – from Marx to Kautsky – had interpreted Jewish history. In his introduction to the 1970 American edition of Leon's book, Nathan Weinstock enlarged the concept of people-class, even extending its application to other ethnic or national groups such as the Gypsies, the Armenians, and the Chinese

---

14   Blumenkranz 1960, pp. 20–1.
15   See Katz 1962, ch. 4.
16   See Poliakov 1981, p. 271. Jacques Le Goff has observed that the ecclesiastical ban on usury was, de facto, ignored with the approval of the clerical hierarchies (providing that form was respected); see Le Goff 1972, p. 77.

of South-Eastern Asia. According to Weinstock, before the crusades the Jews represented a 'differentiated people-class' whose social activities were globally related to an exchange economy, for the most part urban, which was managed by Jewish traders.[17] He also proposed an interpretation of Leon's theory that conceived the people-class as the product of a process of selection: those Jews who devoted themselves to trade had conserved their own group identity, whereas those who worked in non-commercial economic branches would be progressively assimilated.[18] This interpretation nuances Leon's theory according to which, as we have already seen, 'the overwhelming majority of Jews of the Diaspora unquestionably engaged in trade'.[19] However, it cannot meet the criticisms raised by Pierre Vidal-Naquet, who has pointed to the existence over several centuries of Jewish communities in India and China neither specialising in trade nor affected by anti-Semitic persecutions, and by Maxime Rodinson, who has underlined the Jewish concentration in the artisan class rather than in trade in Islamic societies.[20] Concerning Christian Europe before the eleventh century, Rodinson does not accent the economic function of the Jews but rather the peculiarities of their religion. Until the formation of feudal Europe, the Jews were a 'religion having certain characteristics of an ethnic group'.[21] They had a common origin and history, but they shared the culture of the peoples among whom they lived, whose languages they also spoke (Hebrew being maintained as a liturgical language). In the final analysis, the Jews constituted an ethnic group defined by religion. In the Diaspora, Yahweh remained the God of Israel, identified with a *people*, and it was not possible to participate in his cult without belonging at the same time to his people. In Rodinson's words, 'the conjunction in Judaism of religious and ethnic particularisms, inside pluralist societies of weak unifying force, assured its survival'.[22] In the pagan Hellenic world, in the Roman Empire before and after Christianity, and finally in the Islamic world, the Jews were a minority distinguished neither by language nor by economic role, but solely by religion. It is only from the eleventh century onwards that this group began to assume a specific economic role and to be marked, socially and culturally, by what one could define as a *negative otherness*, the product of exclusion and discrimination. This change was so profound that the rigid separation between Christians and

---

17   See Weinstock 2010, p. 44.

18   Ibid., p. 41.

19   Leon 1970, p. 69.

20   See Vidal-Naquet 1971, p. 24; Poliakov 1981, vol. 1, p. 13; and Rodinson 1981, pp. 112–13.

21   Rodinson 1981, p. 114.

22   Ibid., p. 115.

Jews which followed was not simply suffered by the latter and imposed by the former, but stemmed also from a reciprocal will for distinction. In this sense, as Louis Wirth and Jacob Katz have observed, the institution of the ghettoes from the fourteenth century onward was welcomed favourably by the Jews as a measure corresponding to their demands.[23] In their eyes, segregation appeared almost as the consequence of their social and religious differentiation from the Christian majority. Furthermore, David Ruben locates another major cause of Jewish otherness in the history of the Diaspora, namely the extraterritorial Jewish culture. The dispersion sheltered the Jews from total annihilation because, when a centre was destroyed, there always remained others that could act as poles of attraction for the persecuted and expelled Jews. In Ruben's view, 'territorialised cultures' put up a weaker resistance than the Jews towards exterior threats.[24]

Taking into account this historical debate, the theory of the people-class fatally appears both mono-causal and inspired with a form of economic determinism. Trade is not enough in order to explain the historical permanence of the Jews as a religious minority for over two millennia. Leon's theory, however, presents striking affinities with some interpretations of the Jewish Question from German sociology. Weber's definition of the Jews as a 'pariah people' pointed out their socioeconomic activity as a 'capitalism of pariahs' oriented toward speculation. Weber wrote in his *Religionssoziologie* that 'sociologically speaking, the Jews were a pariah people, which means, as we know from India, that they were a guest people (*Gastvolk*) who were ritually separated, formally or de facto, from their social surroundings'.[25] According to Weber, the fundamental difference between the Jews and the Indian castes had both a religious and a social explanation. In Hinduism, the hierarchical cast system was static, almost frozen, whereas Judaism defended the idea of liberation from exile and oppression by messianic redemption. Moreover, socially speaking, the Jews formed 'a pariah people in a world without castes'. Weber recognised, then, an economic foundation to Jewish otherness – the 'adventurer capitalism' abhorred by Protestantism – but he gave a sociological description of the Jewish pariah people that did not reduce it to trading. In his eyes, the Jews represented a minority recognisable by an ensemble of features: until emancipation, they had kept the status of strangers; they were rootless; they were economically dependent from outside; they were endogamy-oriented; and finally, they

---

23   See Katz 1962, ch. 11, and Wirth 1997.
24   Ruben 1982, p. 225.
25   Weber 1952, p. 3.

shared many 'negative privileges' (namely discriminations and bans, from the feudal ghetto up to their exclusion from certain professions in modern societies).

For Georg Simmel, the Jew was the prototype of the 'stranger' (*der Fremde*). He was not a traveller in the current sense of the term, but someone who had settled inside a community different from his own. He did not belong to the majority group, by whom he was perceived as 'other', as a 'stranger'. In most economically backward societies, Simmel concluded, the stranger often was the trader: he was almost never a landowner and had two fundamental traits, rootlessness and mobility, traditionally linked to trade. Thus, the European Jews were the 'classic example' of strangers.[26]

Differently from Leon, Weber and Simmel did not reduce the 'people' to the 'class'. After recognising an economic basis to the 'pariah' and the 'foreigner', they did not ignore the 'people.' Both of them stressed the importance of the exterior, negative perception of Jewish otherness, and thus avoided unilateral economic determinism.

2 Capitalism and Assimilation

Leon's interpretation of the historical changes that had shaped the Jewish world in the age of the transition from feudalism to capitalism started from a careful criticism of the theses of Werner Sombart. In his controversial book *The Jews and Economic Life* (1911), the German economic historian had reversed Max Weber's vision on the 'elective affinity' between capitalism and the Protestant ethic: according to Sombart, it was the Jews who had played a fundamental role in the birth of modern capitalism.[27] Weber's portrait of the ascetic, rational, productive and ethically oriented German bourgeois did not correspond to the prosaic reality of an economic system intimately shaped by the egoistic and calculating Jewish spirit. It is true that Weber had essentially reduced the contribution of Judaism to the Western economy to usury and commerce, but he posited a fundamental incompatibility between Judaism and the major trait of modern capitalism, which was for him the rational organisation of labour and of industrial production. He ascribed the lack of economic rationality in Judaism and the absence of a Jewish industrial bourgeoisie of any significant size to the *pariah* character of the Jews: on the one hand, their extraterritori-

---

26   Simmel 1964, pp. 402–408. See also Raphaël 1986, pp. 63–81.
27   See Sombart 1982.

ality hindered the creation of stable economic enterprises with fixed capital; on the other hand, their traditionalist and economically irrational religion – whose emblematic expression was the Talmud – distanced them from any form of technological innovation.[28] In Weber's view, the only significant contribution the Jews made to the development of capitalism lay in their hostility to magic that they had transmitted to Christianity. Capitalism created a rational, 'disenchanted' world in which there was no place for magic; the Jews had introduced this rejection to Western civilisation, even if they had not been able to turn it into a rational economic ethos, a task that was finally accomplished by Protestantism with its idea of salvation through ascetical economic activity in a profane sphere.

Sombart, by contrast, saw the essence of capitalism in commerce rather than in industrial production. He considered the Jews as the precursors and the quintessential representatives of modern capitalism. They invented 'the commercial machinery that moves the business life of today', gave 'the capitalistic organization its peculiar features' and 'endowed economic life with its modern spirit'.[29] According to him, the decline of Spain began with the expulsion of the Jews in 1492, whereas the economic take off of the Low Countries began with the arrival of the Spanish and Portuguese Jews persecuted by the Inquisition.[30] Writing in 1942, Leon did not discuss Weber's theses, but he did pay attention to Sombart's arguments, which reformulated in a sophisticated version the most widespread anti-Semitic stereotypes of his time: the vision of the Jews as eternal usurers and kings of finance. Leon criticised Sombart's historical (and ideological) reconstruction by re-establishing the sequence of historic events: a) the expulsion of the Jews took place at the apogee of Spanish power, without automatically provoking its decline (which came much later); b) most of the Jews expelled from the Iberian Peninsula went to the Ottoman Empire, which did not experience any significant capitalist development; c) in the Low Countries, there was a rich and dynamic Jewish bourgeoisie, whose import-

---

28   According to Weber, 'the Jews were relatively or altogether absent from the new and distinctive forms of modern capitalism, the rational organization of labour, especially production in an industrial enterprise of the factory type'. If 'the distinctive elements of modern capitalism originated and developed quite apart from the Jews', the reason lay in 'their peculiar character as a pariah people and in the idiosyncrasy of their religion'. See Weber 1978, p. 614.

29   Sombart 1982, p. 21. On this controversy, see Raphaël 1982.

30   According to Werner Sombart, 'the shifting of the economic centre from Southern to Northern Europe' was linked to 'the wanderings of the Jews'. See Sombart 1982, p. 13. David Landes depicts Sombart's theories as 'pseudo-scientific,' insofar as they try to rationalise the anti-Semitic arguments current at the time in Germany; see Landes 1974, p. 22.

ance should however not be exaggerated, inasmuch as it was too small to play a motor role in the economic development of the country; d) capitalism experienced a slow development in the countries where the Jews had settled their biggest communities, like Russia and Poland.[31] Against Sombart, Leon emphasised that it was wrong to 'regard the Jews as founders of modern capitalism. The Jews certainly contributed to the development of exchange economy in Europe, but their *specific* economic role ends precisely where modern capitalism starts'.[32]

But Leon did not accept Weber's explanation either. In his opinion, if the Jews were not at the origin of bourgeois capitalist society, this was not due to the economic irrationality of Talmudic traditionalism, but rather to the fact that usury – the principal economic activity of the Jews under feudalism – was foreign to the mode of capitalist production. The Jewish traders, who were transformed in most cases into usurers, did not create a new mode of production, but confined themselves to linking up the different atomised components of the feudal system. Their capital was not productively invested through the purchase of means of production and of labour power; it was used in order to connect forms of production they did not control. Whereas usurer capital – typically feudal – represented a form of credit for consumption, banking capital – typically bourgeois – was a form of credit for production and contributed directly to the production of surplus value. Leon quoted a passage from *Capital*, where Marx wrote:

> Both usury and commerce exploit the various modes of production. They do not create it but attack it from the outside. Usury centralizes money wealth, where the means of production are disjointed. *It does not alter the mode of production* but attaches itself to it as a parasite, and makes it miserable. It sucks its blood, kills its nerve and compels production to proceed under even more disheartening conditions ... Usurer's capital uses capital's methods of exploitation without its mode of production.[33]

This fundamental antagonism between usury and capitalism was at the origin of the economic decline of the Jews, at the time of the rise of bourgeois society. The transition from feudalism to capitalism engendered the erosion of the Jewish economic positions. If they were necessary as representatives of

---

31 Leon 1970, pp. 177–82.
32 Ibid., p. 182.
33 Ibid., p. 150.

monetary economy inside feudal society, they became useless with the generalisation of commodity production and the expansion of commerce on capitalist bases. The Jewish people-class had exhausted its function, and its cultural and religious otherness was perceived negatively. This historical impasse left only two options: either emigration to the East – favoured in the first phase of the expulsions – where economic backwardness and the survival of feudalism allowed the Jews to reproduce their function as commercial caste; or a gradual adaptation to bourgeois society, which would be endorsed by the laws of emancipation and which would culminate in assimilation. The people-class reconstituted itself in Poland, where the Jews had created a kind of 'state within a state', and dissolved itself in Western Europe. Leon considered assimilation as a kind of structural tendency, which he defined in these terms: 'Wherever the Jews cease to constitute a class, they lose, more or less rapidly, their ethnic, religious and linguistic characteristics: they become assimilated'.[34] And he added: 'So long as the economic function represented by Judaism was necessary, there was opposition to their religious assimilation, which also meant their economic assimilation. It is solely when Judaism became superfluous economically that it had to assimilate or disappear'.[35]

It was the thesis of Kautsky and Bauer, reaffirmed at the beginning of the 1930s by Otto Heller. Like Sombart, Heller considered the Jews as a fundamental element in the process of the formation of modern capitalism, but he also conceived assimilation as an economic necessity. In Heller's view, capitalism was the bearer of assimilation: 'The Jews of the West were at the very center of the formation of the modern bourgeoisie ... The dissolution of the Jewish caste is the beginning of assimilation, of fusion, of the complete dissolution of the Jews in the class whose road they had prepared'.[36] Leon used nearly the same terms to describe the situation of the Jews after the French Revolution and the Napoleonic conquests: 'In general, from the beginning of the nineteenth century, Western Judaism enters on the road of complete assimilation'.[37] This process, nevertheless, encountered major obstacles in Eastern Europe, where the penetration of capitalism produced a growing pauperisation of the Jewish community. Here, the breakup of the people-class did not favour the integration of the Jews into the new relations of production. In Poland, far from being carried on by the Jews, the formation of a modern bourgeoisie had provoked a crisis

---

34   Ibid., p. 81.
35   Ibid., p. 163.
36   Heller 1933, p. 78.
37   Leon 1970, pp. 213–14.

of Jewish commerce, which was essentially pre-capitalist. Reproducing some arguments already developed by Borokhov and Lestschinsky, Leon described the metamorphosis of the Jewish trader who, turned into craftsman and semi-artisanal worker, was excluded from big, mechanical industry and relegated to the backward economy of consumption. This marginalised Jewish proletariat appeared to Leon as a new incarnation of the people-class. Unlike the industrial working class, which came from the stratum of craftsmen and the peasantry, the Jewish proletariat was born out of a specific group charged with satisfying the needs of the Jewish trader. According to Leon,

> The Jewish artisan therefore did not work for the peasant producers, but for the merchants, the banker *intermediaries*. It is here that we must seek the fundamental cause for the specific professional structure of the Jewish proletariat and of its ancestor, Jewish craftsmanship ... Alongside of the peasant, we find the non-Jewish blacksmith artisan; close to the moneylender, we find the Jewish tailor.[38]

The Jews of Eastern Europe were in an impasse – their old economic positions were profoundly eroded and they were pushed back by an emergent capitalism – and there remained only one option: emigration to the United States and, to a lesser extent, Western Europe. This exodus, which involved around three million Jews between 1880 and 1920, was the cause, Leon argued, of a renaissance of the Jewish Question in the West. The access to production and the urban concentration of the immigrants, as well as the anti-Semitic reaction provoked by their arrival, led to an ephemeral reconstitution of the old Jewish nation. Leon saw the development of Yiddish literature, theatres, and schools as a transitory phenomenon that was destined to disappear after a generation, when the economic 'normalisation' of the Jews would inevitably bring about their cultural assimilation. Big cities, for example, initially fostered a Jewish national renaissance, but in the end they were strong elements of assimilation. The basis of this national regeneration of Judaism seemed then precarious to Leon:

> Emigration, at first a powerful obstacle to assimilation and a 'nationalisation' factor of the Jews, rapidly changes into an instrument of fusion of the Jews with other peoples. The concentration of Jewish masses in the great cities, which thus became a sort of 'territorial base' for the Jewish

---

38   Ibid., p. 210.

nationality, cannot long impede the process of assimilation. The atmosphere of the great urban centres constitutes a melting pot in which all
national differences are rapidly wiped out.[39]

Like Lenin, Leon expressed an unconditional and enthusiastic support for
the theory of the *melting pot*. This confidence in the assimilatory virtues of
the Western metropolises was combined, in Leon's work, with a significant
silence on the forms taken by the Jewish national renaissance in Eastern Europe
between 1880 and the Second World War. He had analysed in depth the economic crisis that shook the Jewish communities of Eastern Europe, but he did
not recognise their cultural vitality. Two phenomena which were situated at the
heart of the life of the *Ostjudentum* in the first half of the century – the formation of a Jewish workers' movement and the birth of a modern Yiddish literature – were totally absent from his analysis. This silence concerning the cultural
milieu from which he emerged inscribes him into Deutscher's category of 'non-
Jewish Jews'. Even if Belgium, where he spent his formative years, implied an
exterior relation to the *Yiddishkeit*, Yiddish seems to have been his maternal
language (in his book, he quotes Dubnov, Lestschinsky and Zhitlovsky, and he
undoubtedly was familiar with Borokhov). Leon's attitude, however, was coherent with his theory of the people-class: if the Jews no longer existed as a 'class'
how could they continue to exist as a 'people'? And how could they create a
modern national culture?

Thanks to assimilation, in Western Europe the Jewish people had disappeared, but not the Jew. In other words, emancipation had dissolved the Jewish
nation, but it had not erased anti-Semitism and the Jew remained an outsider,
a 'stranger' (Simmel), either a *pariah* or a *parvenu*, according to the typology of
the emancipated Jew advanced by Hannah Arendt.[40]

According to Leon, the Western European model of assimilation had a universal, structural character.[41] He vigorously defended a vision of assimilation
inherited from the Enlightenment, which did not interpret the entry of the
Jews into the modern world as a process of secularisation and acculturation,
but quite simply as the ineluctable disappearance of Jewishness.

---

39   Ibid., p. 224.
40   See Arendt 2007, pp. 275–97.
41   According to Milton M. Gordon, structural assimilation implies the disappearance of the
        ethnic group as a particular entity, whereas cultural assimilation or acculturation implies
        only a change of its identity; see Gordon 1964, pp. 70, 81.

3   Anti-Semitism

Leon wrote his book during the Second World War, as the German armies spread across Europe. His manuscript bore the date of December 1942, on the eve of Stalingrad. In the middle of this catastrophe, which would envelop him, Leon emphasised the modern character of anti-Semitism. In his eyes, anti-Semitism was not a feudal vestige: rather, a quintessential expression of the twentieth century, an age in which the 'progress of technology and of science becomes the progress of the science and the technique of death', in which 'the development of the means of production is nothing but the growth of the means of destruction'.[42]

There was a considerable difference between Nazi anti-Semitism and its historical ancestors. According to Leon, Treitschke in Berlin, Lueger in Vienna, and the Dreyfus affair in Paris were the transitional answers of Western European conservatism to emancipation and Jewish immigration from the Tsarist Empire. Differently from these episodic outbreaks of anti-Semitic fever, Nazi anti-Semitism was rooted in the historic crisis of capitalism that transformed the Jews into the scapegoats of a decaying social system. In Leon's view, Anti-Semitism resulted from the conflict between big monopoly capital and the 'commercial speculative capital that was principally Jewish capital' and fulfilled a social function, inasmuch as it allowed the bourgeoisie to turn against the Jews the anti-capitalist radicalisation of the middle class affected by the crisis: 'By the myth of "Jewish capitalism", big business endeavored to divert and control the anti-capitalist hatred of the masses for its own exclusive profit'.[43] Thus, fascist and Nazi anti-Semitism resurrected a ghost from the past; it was a deeply anachronistic phenomenon at a time when the Jews had ceased to be a distinct economic and cultural group.

Abroad, anti-Semitism took on a racist tinge and acted as a covering ideology for Nazi expansionism. In this case, the struggle for the conquest of foreign markets made the 'international Jew' the enemy of the 'Germanic race', uniquely for the purposes of 'syncretism', to harmonise the exterior racism and the interior anti-Semitism:

> Just as it is necessary to cast the different classes into *one single race*, so is it also necessary that this 'race' have only a single enemy: 'the interna-

---

42   Leon 1970, p. 226.
43   Ibid., p. 23.

tional Jew'. The myth of race is necessarily accompanied by its 'negative'; the anti-race, the Jew.[44]

In a passage that has some striking affinities with Horkheimer and Adorno's *Dialectic of Reason*, Leon qualified anti-Semitism as an attempt made by decaying capitalism to project onto the Jews its own negativity. In reality, the negative myth of Judaism only reflected the repulsive aspects of fascism. As Leon puts it:

> At the present time, capitalist society, on the edge of the abyss, tries to save itself by resurrecting the Jew and the hatred of the Jews. But it is precisely because the Jews do not play the role that is attributed to them that anti-Semitic persecution can take on such an amplitude. Jewish capitalism is a myth; that is why it is easy to defeat it. But, in vanquishing its 'negative', racism at the same time destroys the foundations for its own existence. In the measure that the phantom of 'Jewish capitalism' disappears, capitalist reality appears in all its ugliness.[45]

In Eastern Europe, despite the decomposition of the people-class, the Jews remained a socially distinct and particularly vulnerable ethnic group, insofar as they were victims of imperialism and still suffered the consequences of the decline of feudalism. Anti-Semitism could then draw on a traditional economic hostility toward the Jews, which had never been extinguished. In the developed capitalist countries of Western Europe, by contrast, anti-Semitism affected Jews who had been emancipated and assimilated for generations. This amounted for Leon to an 'apparent' paradox. The Jews could become the scapegoats of the social malaise only at a time when they were no longer 'necessary', where they could no longer fulfil the role that anti-Semitic propaganda attributed to them. In other words, Anti-Semitism was the dialectical product of Western civilisation, the same civilisation that had granted civic rights to the Jews: the *Aufklärung* had suppressed the Jew as an economic entity only to transform him definitively into a social pariah. Once the walls of the ghetto were destroyed, there emerged a new, invisible barrier, which re-established a separation between Jews and Gentiles. In the eyes of the anti-Semite, emancipation rendered Jewish otherness still more dangerous because it was now hidden and intangible. It was not by chance that modern anti-Semitism was born in Central Europe immediately after emancipation.

---

44   Ibid., p. 239.
45   Ibid., pp. 238–9.

4   Solutions

In line with a classical Marxist conception, Leon considered Zionism as a 'petty bourgeois' nationalist movement, born at the end of the last century under the impact of the Russian pogroms and the Dreyfus affair. It appeared on the European scene as the incarnation of a nationalist ideology that Theodor Herzl had constructed around the myth of an eternal anti-Semitism. According to Leon, the Zionist movement was condemned to an insoluble contradiction. On the one hand, the historical crisis of capitalism created the conditions for its birth (anti-Semitism) and, on the other hand, it prevented its realisation: in an era of the decline of the productive forces and the total submission of the planet to a few imperialist powers, the idea of industrialising Palestine and creating a Jewish national state there seemed to Leon a naïve utopia. Nonetheless, Leon did not exclude the creation of a Jewish state in Palestine under British control. This was the sole existing possibility for developing Zionist colonisation, in a region where the conflict between the Jewish settlers and the indigenous Arab population continued to grow.[46]

But Leon considered Zionism a reactionary movement, above all because of its views on Palestine, at a time when the Jewish Question had turned to tragedy and needed an immediate solution in Europe, in the Diaspora. In his opinion, the attempt to give the Jews a 'spiritual or political homeland' was foremost diversionary, when the task of the moment was to 'save Judaism from annihilation'. He put the question in the following terms:

> But in what way will the existence of a little Jewish state in Palestine change anything in the situation of the Polish or German Jews? Admitting even that all the Jews in the world were today Palestinian citizens, would the policy of Hitler have been any different? One must be stricken with an incurable juridical cretinism to believe that the creation of a small Jewish state in Palestine can change anything at all in the situation of the Jews throughout the world, especially in the present period.[47]

The World Zionist Organization did little during the inter-war period to build a movement of struggle against Nazism (it even attempted to convert Nazi anti-Semitism into a pro-Zionist option) and tried to prevent any form of emigration of German Jews not directed toward Palestine. Moreover, Nazism threatened

---

46   Ibid., pp. 251–3.
47   Ibid., p. 253.

even the Palestinian Jews. The British army, not the *kibbutzim*, saved them in halting the German offensive at El Alamein. A different outcome to the war in Africa would not have spared the Jews of Jerusalem and Tel Aviv from genocide.[48]

However, it should be repeated that Leon's opposition to Zionism went well beyond a simple condemnation of its practical impotence in the face of Nazism. He rejected Zionism as an illusory response, in historical terms, to the Jewish Question. Capitalist society was shaken by a profound overall crisis which challenged a whole form of civilisation: in this context, the Zionist idea of a Promised Land where the Jewish people, the foremost victims of this crisis, would be able to remain sheltered from the general catastrophe, was a dangerous illusion: the solution of the Jewish Question implied the abolition of capitalism.

On this point, Leon echoed Trotsky. As we have seen, the coming to power of the Nazis in Germany had led the Russian revolutionary to renounce his former assimilationism. In 1937, he had unambiguously recognised the existence of a modern Jewish nation in an interview with a Mexican Yiddish daily newspaper: 'The Jews of different countries have created their press and developed the Yiddish language as an instrument adapted to modern culture. One must therefore reckon with the fact that the Jewish nation will maintain itself for an entire epoch to come'.[49] Trotsky rejected Zionism, saying that the Jewish question could not find a positive solution 'within the framework of rotting capitalism and under the control of British imperialism', but he affirmed the necessity of a 'territorial solution' that socialism should assure to the Jewish people. One can recognise without difficulty in this argument an allusion to the Soviet experience of Birobidzhan, which Trotsky denounced as a 'bureaucratic farce' for the way in which it had been carried out, but which he accepted in principle.[50] Finally, in a 1937 article, he adopted an agnostic attitude toward the future of the Jews. Obviously, he excluded the possibility of a 'forced assimilation' inside a socialist democracy, but at the same time he left open the question of whether the Jews would assimilate naturally or if, on the contrary, they would opt for the creation of an 'independent republic'.[51] In a historical perspective, his approach was open but, in the present, Trotsky was convinced of the necessity of a national solution to the Jewish problem and was conscious of

48   See Arendt 2007, pp. 343–74; and Diner 1985, p. 46.
49   *LTO*, vol. 12, p. 111.
50   *LTO*, vol. 13, p. 297.
51   *LTO*, vol. 12, pp. 350–1.

the impasse into which assimilation had entered. This theme was present in all his writings on Jewish affairs from 1934 onwards.

This approach marked, even if only marginally, Leon's work, which indeed ended with the conclusion that the solution to the Jewish Question could not be conceived as a binary option: assimilation or territorial concentration. The Jews should exercise their right to self-determination, 'but socialism must give the Jews, as it will to all peoples, the possibility of assimilation as well as the possibility of having a special national life'.[52] Employing almost the same terms (probably unconsciously) as Vladimir Medem's theory of 'national neutralism', Leon said that socialism would confine itself, in this area, to 'letting nature take its course'.[53]

In spite of its vagueness about the forms that an eventual Jewish national existence would take in a post-capitalist society (an existence which would not necessarily be linked to a territorial concentration), this assumption was quite contradictory with Leon's previous analyses, which presented assimilation as the natural culmination of the dissolution of the people-class. Indeed, Leon himself recognised the incompatibility between the concept of the people-class and the perspective of a Jewish national renaissance under socialism, when he suggested that a 'national solution' to the Jewish Question would probably only be a 'preface' to assimilation. It was a strange conclusion, in which Leon recognised implicitly that the Jews had the possibility of remaining a 'people' even after having ceased to be a 'class'. In short, he relativised his theory. This contradiction mirrored the impasse of classical Marxism during the Second World War: Leon was the last representative of the traditional vision of assimilation as a historical tendency and culmination of 'progress'; he completed his work precisely at the moment in which the Holocaust was destroying the conquests of Jewish emancipation.

---

52   Leon 1970, p. 264.
53   Ibid., p. 265.

CHAPTER 10

Post-war Marxism and the Holocaust

The fundamental reason for the lack of a Marxist debate on the causes, forms and consequences of the destruction of the European Jews is the Holocaust itself. It showed the limits of pre-war theoretical and political disputes, and at the same time brutally put them to an end by destroying the people who had been at issue. The post-war cultural and political context contributed neither to an examination of this break nor to filling the theoretical void. During the 1940s and 1950s Marxism became an essential component of anti-fascist culture, in which the Jewish tragedy was reduced to a marginal aspect of the gigantic conflict that had ravaged Europe. The defeat of Nazism, the Red Army's advance into Central Europe and the impressive growth of Communist parties in countries where they had played a leading role in the Resistance all encouraged a return in the immediate post-war period to a philosophy of progress. This left hardly any room for thinking through the catastrophe. Marxism was thus characterised by its *silence* on Auschwitz. How could one pay attention to the 'little difference' at a moment when history, having cleared away a mountain of corpses, seemed to have reached its happy ending? When its spirit seemed to be incarnated by a 'liberator' advancing triumphantly, no longer on a white horse as Napoleon appeared to Hegel at Jena, but in command of a Soviet tank?[1] This silence has lasted up until our own times. Eric J. Hobsbawm, to give only one example, opens his balance sheet of the twentieth century by noting the striking 'regression' in this century from the level of civilisation considered as permanently attained in the Western world during the century from the Congress of Vienna in 1815 to the eve of 1914. He observes 'the rising curve of barbarism after 1914', reminding us that torture and the killing of civilian populations had officially been abolished throughout Western Europe by the early twentieth century, but he devotes only a few marginal lines to the Nazi extermination camps.[2] In short, Marxism has proved no exception to the blindness of European culture in face of the civilisational break epitomised by Auschwitz.

As we have seen, Leon Trotsky and Walter Benjamin managed to break with the general tendency and showed remarkable clear-sightedness about the consequences that the war could have for the fate of European Jewry. In 1938,

---

1   According to a statement by Alexandre Kojève, quoted in Niethammer 1989, p. 77.

2   Hobsbawm 1996, p. 49. The word Auschwitz does not appear in his book. On the reasons for this well-remarked absence, see Hobsbawm 1997, pp. 88–9.

© KONINKLIJKE BRILL NV, LEIDEN, 2019 | DOI:10.1163/9789004384767_013

Trotsky predicted that a new conflict would lead to 'physical extermination' of the Jews. In 1940, in his famous theses 'On the Concept of History', Benjamin sketched the outlines of a new vision of the past in which the idea of catastrophe replaced the myth of progress. The two approaches were radically different – Trotsky was an atheist revolutionary and rigorously rationalist, while Benjamin was a Jewish thinker in search of a synthesis between historical materialism and messianic redemption – but their conclusions significantly converged. Trotsky forcefully announced the gravity of the imminent danger; Benjamin developed the philosophical categories capable of recognising and thinking through the laceration of Auschwitz. The Russian exile seemed almost to translate into political terms the idea preached by the German Jewish critic, of no longer conceiving of revolution as the 'locomotive' of history but rather as the 'emergency brake' necessary to halt the rush towards catastrophe. Both would be carried off by the barbarism of the century, victims respectively of Stalinism and of National Socialism.[3] It is the heirs of these two figures who would renew the Marxist debate on the Jewish Question after the war. Like Trotsky and Benjamin, nevertheless, even their inheritors were marginal intellectuals in exile or escapees from the Nazi genocide whose analyses remained practically unknown at the time.

Thinking the Holocaust with Marxist categories would be the attempt, starting from different but parallel approaches, of the Frankfurt School and of Ernest Mandel. Horkheimer and Adorno developed in their *Dialectic of Enlightenment* (1947) certain themes that were present in Benjamin's 'Theses'. Shortly after the war other philosophers affiliated with the Institute for Social Research or situated at its periphery, such as Leo Löwenthal, Herbert Marcuse and Gunther Anders, made Auschwitz the starting point for their critique of modern civilization. Ernest Mandel, a Belgian Marxist of Jewish origin, was the friend and comrade of Abram Leon, like Leon had been arrested, but unlike Leon had succeeded in escaping from a work camp in Germany. Mandel's work undoubtedly contains the most coherent attempt to interpret the Jewish genocide in the light of classical Marxism, and in this way developed further Trotsky's approach.

We must nonetheless take note of a gap of roughly four decades between the Frankfurt School's works, written at the end of the war, and Mandel's, which date essentially from the late 1980s. Once again, as with Trotsky and Benjamin, these two currents of thought followed separate roads without ever crossing paths. There is no doubt that the impossibility of their meeting had largely to

---

3   Traverso 1997, pp. 697–705.

do with what Perry Anderson pointed out as one of the trademarks of Western Marxism – its withdrawal into philosophy and aesthetics – and what Martin Jay presented as one of the essential characteristics of Frankfurt School Marxism: its radical separation from the organised workers' movement.[4] This isolation enabled it, on the one hand, to preserve its autonomy and originality, but condemned it, on the other hand, to a gradual loss of any social anchorage.

With the remarkable exception of Herbert Marcuse, Frankfurt School Marxism (and notably its radical version represented by Gunther Anders, the most interesting of its 'fellow travellers') seemed to take on a more and more antiutopian dimension. Ultimately, it based itself on a paradigm that we could call, at the antipodes from Ernst Bloch, the 'principle of despair' (*das Prinzip Verzweiflung*). Anders replaced Ernst Bloch's ontology of the *not yet* (*Noch-Nicht-Sein*) with an anti-Utopia of waiting for annihilation (*noch-nicht-Nichtsein*), which turned him into a kind of Heideggerian Marxist.[5] Its radical critique of civilisation went together with an attitude of despair, scepticism and a tragic feeling of impotence (to the point of opposing student protest movements, as Adorno and Horkheimer would do in 1968). Mandel, by contrast, developed a critical theory of society that was inseparable from a political project that located its subject in the exploited classes. His Marxism was utopian, generous and constantly on the look-out for turning points or 'bifurcations' in history that might be transformed into revolutionary breaks. Mandel reached his zenith as a political thinker in the period after May 1968. The neoliberal outcome of the 1989–91 crisis of the Soviet bloc failed to break his spirit. His trajectory was thus very much distinct from that of Adorno and Anders. The only element that they shared despite everything was a rejection of Stalinism.

1   The Frankfurt School

Walter Benjamin had already cleared the way for Frankfurt School intellectuals to think about the Jewish genocide, by affirming the necessity of developing a new form of historical materialism 'that has annihilated within itself the idea of progress'.[6] Following in Benjamin's footsteps, the effort to rethink history in the wake of Auschwitz was undertaken by Adorno and Horkheimer towards the end of the war in their *Dialectic of Enlightenment*. A chapter of this work, drafted with the help of Leo Löwenthal in 1943–4, is devoted to analys-

---

4   See Anderson 1976, and the concluding chapters of Jay 1973.
5   See Bloch 1986 and Liessman 1993, p. 92.
6   Benjamin 1999, p. 460.

ing anti-Semitism. The Final Solution is presented there as the paradigm of a barbarism towards which the whole trajectory of Western civilisation, characterised as a process of the 'self-destruction of Enlightenment' (*Selbstzerstörung der Aufklärung*), has converged.[7] The emancipatory potentialities of Enlightenment humanist rationalism, Adorno and Horkheimer explain, have gradually but inexorably given way to an instrumental, blind, and power-hungry rationality. Like Benjamin in his allegory of the angel of history, they seem to turn upside down the positivist vision of a long, linear, automatic human development towards progress, seeing in National Socialism the terminus of the Western world's course. Auschwitz unveils the destructive dimension of *Aufklärung*, which has now revealed itself in place of Hegel's Absolute Spirit to be the true content of history.[8]

This break with the philosophy of progress is still incomplete – and in this sense less radical than Benjamin's – inasmuch as Horkheimer and Adorno present Nazism as 'the reversion of enlightened civilization into barbarism' (*Rückkehr der aufgeklärte Zivilisation zur Barbarei*).[9] This could be interpreted literally as a regression towards the past, rather than as the emergence of a modern 'barbarism' founded on the material structures, ideologies and mentalities of industrial civilisation.[10] Formulas common in Adorno's and Horkheimer's work, such as 'progress is reverting to regression',[11] only make more dialectical a vision of history incapable of breaking with the idea that history moves – alternately forwards and backwards – along a diachronic, linear axis. Resting on the foundation of Hegel and Marx, Adorno's and Horkheimer's critical approach merged ideas from Weber, Benjamin and Freud into a coherent synthesis. The power of a work like *Dialectic of Enlightenment*, conceived and published in exile, would only be perceived much later when it was republished in Germany towards the end of the 1960s, but its influence would then be lasting. Herbert Marcuse radicalised this approach in *Eros and Civilization* (1954), whose introduction no longer presents 'concentration camps, mass exterminations, world wars, and atomic bombs' as a 'relapse into barbarism', but rather as 'the unrepressed implementation of the achievements of modern science, technology, and domination'.[12] For Gunther Anders, author of *Die Antiquier-*

---

7   Horkheimer and Adorno 2002, p. xiv.

8   See Connerton 1989, p. 114.

9   Horkheimer and Adorno 2002, p. xix.

10   According to Michael Löwy and Eleni Varikas, Adorno carried out a 'dialectical reassessment of the notion of progress', without however 'clearing it off his conceptual horizon'; see Löwy and Varikas, 1993, pp. 53, 59.

11   Horkheimer and Adorno 2002, p. XVIII.

12   Marcuse 1955, p. 4.

theit des Menschen (1956 and 1980), far from plunging humanity back into ancestral barbarism, Auschwitz and Hiroshima herald the arrival of a new era for the human species, which has now become 'obsolete' in a world dominated by technology and thus susceptible to being totally wiped out.[13] In the gas chambers of Auschwitz and Treblinka, Jews and Gypsies were eliminated by industrial methods, in the same way that a machine can 'treat' its raw material (*Rohstoff*). Hiroshima, Anders emphasises, demonstrated that all of humanity can be annihilated, that the Apocalypse has stopped being a prophetic vision and become a wholly concrete threat. In this era in which the Jewish tragedy and the atomic bomb have revealed a danger for our existence on earth, any distinction between ontology and ethics seems out of date. The task of the liberator that formed the horizon of socialism since Marx's time is now coming to coincide with a 'conservative' task, aiming at preserving the planet and the human species. Anders thus defines his political commitment as that of an 'ontological conservative'.[14] The Heideggerian matrix of such an approach is clearly tangible, but differently from his German mentor, his ontology of technology did not result in a trivialisation of the gas chambers: it rather engendered a radical critique of capitalism.[15] His work doubtlessly expresses the most consistent effort to rethink Marxism under the dark light of Auschwitz. He claims less to 'explain' the extermination camps than to make them the starting point for a radical critique of the existing social order and for a project of human and social liberation.

Adorno's, Marcuse's and Anders's approaches run counter to those who tried to see National Socialism as the culmination of a centuries-old attempt (begun just after and in reaction to the French revolution) at the 'destruction of Reason' (in Georg Lukács's terms).[16] Marxism after Marx had largely renounced the critique of civilisation begun by Rousseau, Fourier and Blanqui, in order to celebrate 'progress'. But Auschwitz showed that many institutions common to modern society, traditionally interpreted as fruits of 'progress', could be the antechambers to hell.[17] The emergence of modern science and the strengthening of the state monopoly on violence – seen by the European cultural tradition from Thomas Hobbes to Norbert Elias as two hallmarks of the civilising process – were essential conditions for the Final Solution, for its ideology (bio-

---

13   Anders 1985.
14   Anders 1984, p. 319. See also Anders 1987.
15   See Heidegger 1993.
16   Lukács 1981.
17   On the romantic dimension of Marxism, see Löwy 1993. Marxists' abandonment of the critique of industrial modernity is noted and criticised in Bloch 1991.

logical racism) as well as its industrial and bureaucratic rational structures. Unveiling this paradox of civilisation was one of the Frankfurt School's most important contributions. In taking up Marx's radical critique of bourgeois civilisation once more, it carried out a break within Marxist thought. A work such as *Dialectic of Enlightenment* shows that at the origins of this theoretical break lay the laceration of history that took place in the Nazi extermination camps.[18] This rupture took place within the Frankfurt School itself as well, even though those who made it did not draw its full consequences. At the beginning of the war its members (Friedrich Pollock, for example) were still analysing National Socialism as a form of 'monopoly capitalism' and defending an entirely traditional Marxist vision of anti-Semitism. This was the case with Horkheimer's article 'The Jews and Europe' (1939) already mentioned in Chapter 8 and of a work like *Behemoth* (1942), in which Franz Neumann explicitly ruled out the possibility of the Nazi genocide:

> The internal political value of Anti-Semitism will, therefore, never allow a complete extermination of the Jews. The foe cannot and must not disappear; he must always be held in readiness as a scapegoat for all the evils originating in the socio-political system.[19]

Anti-Semitic bigotry would lose its *raison d'être* if it ever destroyed the object of its hatred, he thought. After the Final Solution, these analyses were clearly inadequate, though this by no means eliminates the value of a work like *Behemoth*, whose analysis of the Nazi system of rule would provide the starting point for one of the main historians of the destruction of the European Jews, Raul Hilberg.[20] Nonetheless, *Dialectic of Enlightenment* marked a turning point in this respect. Horkheimer and Adorno's starting point in 1944 was that total extermination *is possible*. By contrast, it is the Utopia of an emancipated world that seems after Auschwitz to have been banished or everlastingly tarnished. Having recognised the fracture of civilisation that took place at Auschwitz, the Frankfurt School's members from that time on seemed to see it as irreversible. The Holocaust had in their eyes put an end to the historical dialectic based on class

---

18   Among the Frankfurt School writings marked by the Holocaust, in addition to *Dialectic of Enlightenment*, we can mention here the first fragments (1944) of Adorno 2005, and Löwenthal 1946.

19   Neumann 1967, p. 125. For an overall analysis of the Frankfurt School's changing approach to anti-Semitism, see Jay 1986, Schäfer 1994, and especially Jacobs 2015.

20   See Hilberg's autobiography, in which he fully acknowledges his debt to Franz Neumann, whose student he had been in New York at the end of the war: Hilberg 1996, pp. 62–6.

struggle, and brought to light a negative dialectic of domination that had no room left in it for an emancipatory Utopia. Marxism, they seemed to conclude, could recognise the Holocaust only at the price of self-mutilation.[21]

2   Ernest Mandel

The idea that the categories of classical Marxism might be incapable of providing an explanation of the Jewish genocide never troubled Ernest Mandel's mind. He was 22 years old at the Liberation, and his faith in the revolutionary potential of the industrial working class was unshakable. He had not lived through the war in exile like Adorno and Anders, but in Belgium and Germany. In Antwerp he was active in the Resistance, quickly becoming a leader of its Trotskyist current. He was arrested twice, and managed to escape each time. Interned in a work camp in Germany, he came into contact with guards who had been members of the Social Democratic and Communist parties and succeeded in convincing them to help him escape.[22] His audacity saved him from being deported to Auschwitz. This was the first time he showed his irrepressible calling as an 'enlightener'. Germany remained in his eyes, as for all communists educated politically between the wars, much less the country of executioners than the country of Rosa Luxemburg and the heartland of European revolution. In 1946, in an afterword to the first edition of Abram Leon's work *The Jewish Question*, the young Mandel tried to analyse the Jewish genocide. He did not use the word, which had just been coined and was not yet in current use, but he did cite the figure of five million victims. 'The human imagination can hardly conceive concretely the meaning of this number', he wrote.[23] In his opinion, the absurdity of the tragedy was only a surface appearance, since it was the product of 'a world in torment'. Although any explanation seemed 'to fall short of the full horror of the reality' in the face of the ghettos, mass executions, gas chambers and ovens, he warned against the temptation of seeing it as 'a sudden, unique catastrophe' in history. True, the Jews had been 'hit harder than any other people', but it must not be forgotten that their destruction took place

---

21   Marcuse did not share this resignation (nor did Anders). On the conflict between Marcuse and Horkheimer and Adorno in 1969, see Wiggershaus 1995, pp. 631–6. It is worth remembering that when the students of Frankfurt occupied the Institute for Social Research in 1968, they renamed it the 'Walter Benjamin Institute'.

22   See Ali 1999. On Mandel's commitment in the Belgian Resistance, double arrest, deportation, and escape, see Jan Stuje 2009, pp. 16–41.

23   Mandel 1970.

at a time when the whole human race had nearly fallen into a bottomless pit. The war had threatened to carry off 'everything that twenty centuries of civilization had slowly accumulated', as its 60 million victims bore witness.[24] The genocide of the Jews, he said, only 'pushed to the point of paroxysm the barbarism of imperialism's customary methods in our time', above all the methods of colonial massacre.[25] The atomic bombing of Hiroshima and Nagasaki showed that Nazism had no monopoly on violence directed at innocent victims; and Mandel did not fail to express concern – rightly, but using rather unfortunate, excessive expressions – about the fate in store for Germans expelled from territories occupied by the Red Army.[26] Mandel's text ends by reaffirming the classic dichotomy between pessimism of the intellect – 'humanity has travelled a long road since it was up in arms over the fate of the victims of the Crimean War'[27] – and an unshakable optimism of the will: 'We have no reason to despair of the human race's destiny'.[28] At the time, the young Mandel saw the Jewish genocide as an *imperialist crime*, doubtless one of the most terrible ones in the context of a war that had surpassed all the horrors known previously to the human race, but certainly not as a *unique event*. He did not see it as *qualitatively different* from colonial massacres and the traditional violence of the capitalist system of domination.

Mandel would wait 40 years after the publication of this text before writing once more on the subject. The occasion was provided in 1986 by the publication of his book on the Second World War, then again in 1988 by a colloquium in Brussels on Nazi totalitarianism, and finally by the enormous impact of the German 'historians' controversy' (*Historikerstreit*). During the decades that separated his first 1946 text from the rest, he devoted several studies to the problem of fascism, but without paying any particular attention to its anti-Semitic dimension.[29] Far from being exceptional, this silence shaped the historical studies on

---

24   Mandel 1970, p. 1.

25   Ibid., p. 11.

26   He even went so far as to write, 'The death trains have set off again, in the opposite direction and with a different human cargo' (Ibid., p. 11). When in 1947 Heidegger made a similar analogy in his letters to Marcuse, the latter decided to break their dialogue; see Marcuse 1998.

27   Germain 2010, p. 11.

28   Ibid., p. xii.

29   See in particular Mandel 1974. By contrast his book *Trotsky* includes a very short reference to Trotsky's 1938 prediction of the extermination of the Jews during a new world war; see Mandel 1979, p. 103. The change of perspective seems obvious in his last book on the Russian revolutionary, in which Mandel devotes a whole chapter to the Jewish question; see Mandel 1995, ch. 10.

fascism until the 1970s. Post-war historians shared with Marxists of the 1930s a model of European fascism in which National Socialism was only a German variant and its anti-Semitic dimension occupied only a marginal place. The scholarly and public discussion on the historical singularity of the Holocaust took place in Western Germany only in the 1980s.[30] So it was in a context marked by the entrance of Jewish memory onto the public stage – along with numerous media events, from 'Holocaust denial' to the German *Historikerstreit* and Claude Lanzmann's film *Shoah* – that Mandel felt the need to revisit the issue of the Holocaust. In the intervening years his point of view had changed and his analyses had become much more nuanced. In his writings in this last period, Mandel did not hesitate to recognise the uniqueness of the Jewish genocide. The 'deliberate and systematic killing of six million men, women and children simply because of their ethnic origin', he wrote, can only be understood as a 'unique' event in history – though this does not mean that we cannot explain it, still less that we cannot compare it with others.[31] The extermination of the European Jews was the culmination of a long series of eruptions of violence that have flared up throughout the history of imperialism, and which had already led to other mass murders and even fully-fledged genocides, as with the indigenous inhabitants of the Americas. The Jews' dehumanisation by Nazism was not without historical precedent: something similar had occurred on a vast scale as early as the Middle Ages with the persecutions of heretics and witches, and then in the modern world of blacks and colonised peoples. The uniqueness of the Jewish genocide, therefore, did not consist in the Nazis' greater inhumanity when compared with their European forbears, nor in the specific nature of their anti-Semitism.[32] At the foundations of Hitler's ideology lay a form of biological racism which, systematised as early as the nineteenth century by Social Darwinism, was widespread in all Western countries, beginning with France (from Gobineau to Vacher de Lapouge). One of the basic texts of Nazi anti-Semitic politics, *The Protocols of the Elders of Zion*, which vulgarised the myth of an international Jewish conspiracy, was of Russian origin, Mandel recalled.[33]

Parallel to his critique of Eurocentric approaches that isolate Auschwitz from racism and colonial oppression, Mandel rejected the mystical cult of the

---

30   For a synthesis of the historiographical debate on Nazism, see Kershaw 2000.

31   Mandel 1986, p. 92. See also Mandel 1999, and Mandel 1991, p. 209.

32   Mandel 1999.

33   Ibid. This line of argument shows a certain affinity with Arendt 1976, in which she quotes Burke, Gobineau and the ideologues of nineteenth-century colonialism (above all French and British) as forerunners of Nazism. But Arendt's name almost never appears in Mandel's writings.

Holocaust. The Jewish genocide must be treated historically; its specificity can only be seen clearly on the basis of an analytical approach of a comparative type. In this perspective, this crime seems much less like the outcome of age-old Judeophobia than as a paroxysm resulting from the modern violence deployed by imperialism against peoples judged to be 'inferior', 'subhuman' or inassimilable. In *The Meaning of the Second World War* Mandel wrote:

> Traditional semi-feudal and petty-bourgeois anti-Semitism led to pogroms, which were to the Nazi murderers what knives are to the atom bomb. The seeds of the gas chambers resided in the mass enslavement and killing of Blacks via the slave trade, in the wholesale extermination of the Central and South American Indians by the *conquistadors*. In such cases, the term genocide is fully justified ...[34]

The unique character of the destruction of the Jews was not linked to the nature of the Nazis' anti-Semitic hatred, which was not qualitatively different from other forms of racism that were very widespread at the time inside as well as outside Germany. The Gypsies, for example, were victims of genocide comparable to the Jews. Furthermore, Nazi policies reduced Slavic peoples to the status of slaves. This meant for Mandel that other forms of extermination on a mass scale make the Final Solution much more a *paradigmatic* crime than an absolutely unique one. The uniqueness of this genocide does not have to do with the nature of the executioners, Mandel added. Moreover, responsibility for this crime was shared quite widely in Hitler's Europe. The – direct and indirect – German 'implementers' accounted for only 50–60 percent of an army of functionaries, bureaucrats, policemen, soldiers, ideologues and industrialists, which represented practically every sector of society and operated both inside and outside the Third Reich. On the other hand, the great majority of them did not have the mentality of sadistic criminals or racist fanatics. True, this motive was present, but it was relevant only to a small minority of enthusiastic Nazis. The psychology of the great mass of those complicit in the Final Solution was that of 'accessories' to the crime, who carried out tasks sometimes out of cowardice, sometimes out of calculation and more often out of habit, preferring not to ask questions about the consequences of their actions. This was the mentality of the traditional dominant classes in Germany, founded on values such as 'honour', 'loyalty', 'patriotism' and 'fulfilment of duty'.[35] The top

---

34   Mandel 1986, p. 90. See also Losurdo 1996, ch. 5.
35   Mandel 1991, p. 223.

civil servants, diplomats, industrialists and engineers who made their contribution to the work of extermination by carrying out organisational, planning and management tasks identified more with these traditional values than with the murderous slogans of Nazi propaganda. In other words, Nazism was not an inexplicable eruption of fierce, irrational hatred that suddenly sent the normal course of history off the rails. Hitler's Germany simply pushed to an extreme the violence inherent in capitalist society and imperialism. For Mandel, '*this* tendency, which fashioned the extermination of Europe's Jews as its end result, is in no way unique (*ist keinesweg einmalig*)'.[36] Seen from this perspective, the Jewish genocide was not incomparable, still less 'unique'. Postulating the paradigmatic character of this crime is the only responsible way, on an ethical and political level, to interpret it, since the social, economic and psychological conditions that made it possible did not disappear with the Third Reich. Modern society is not immune to the danger of a repetition, perhaps in other forms and with other targets, of a horror comparable to the death camps. Auschwitz's uniqueness consisted, according to Mandel, in the fusion realised in Nazi Germany between modern racism (*völkisch* ideology founded no longer on religious prejudice but on racial biology) and the destructive technology of a developed industrial society. If the unique character of the Jewish genocide was due to this tragic constellation, then its explanation carries with it a warning for the future. Until now this fatal intersection of racist hatred and industrial modernity has taken place only in Germany in the exceptional circumstances of Nazism and war, but nothing guaranteed that it could not recur one day elsewhere.

The strength of *The Meaning of the Second World War* lies in its vision of war as a dialectical totality. Mandel realised something remarkable, merging the investigation of military events and socio-economic structures with a global assessment of the *meaning* of the Second World War in the history of capitalism and Western civilisation. He articulated contingencies and long-term tendencies, linked military strategies to their economic bases and to the extraordinary technological changes engendered by the war, and finally connected the ideologies of its actors with the great cleavages of modernity: Enlightenment versus counter-Enlightenment, emancipation against imperialism, socialism or barbarism. In his vision, the Second World War was a plurality of intertwined conflicts: a war between great powers for international hegemony, a defensive war of the USSR against Nazi aggression, a liberation war of the European countries occupied by the Axis forces, a civil war between anti-fascism and collabora-

---

36   Ibid., p. 239.

tionism, and a war of the colonised countries against imperialism that in China turned into a socialist revolution. Analysing the different but correlated dimensions of this war, Mandel analyzed the Nazi violence and the atomic bomb, pointing out both their similarities and their discrepancies, and connecting them with the legacy of Western imperialism and racism. He depicted the historical background of the Holocaust, but his analysis remained as general and abstract as Horkheimer's and Adorno's diagnosis of the 'self-destruction of Enlightenment'.

A few years after Mandel's book, Arno J. Mayer, a Marxist-inspired historian of Princeton University, suggested a new interpretation of the Holocaust as a crucible of different but merging tendencies embodied by National Socialism: the destruction of the USSR as a communist state and the colonisation of Eastern Europe viewed as a German 'vital space' (*Lebensraum*). At the intersection between these two tendencies, the Jews became a privileged target of Nazi violence. In the eyes of Hitler, there was no difference between the demolition of the USSR, the colonial conquest of the Slavic world and the extermination of the Jews: they merged into the same war.[37]

3   Capitalism and the Holocaust

The Final Solution thus seemed to Mandel to confirm one of the major traits of contemporary Western economies – a hybrid of organisation with anarchy, of extremely detailed planning of each segment with an overall chaos completely out of control. He had analysed this paradox in his most ambitious theoretical work, *Late Capitalism* (1975), by developing a concept of rationality which he acknowledged as the brainchild of Max Weber and Georg Lukács. Seen from this angle, Auschwitz was a deadly example of the combination of 'partial rationality' (*Teilrationalität*) and 'global irrationality' (*Gesamtirrationalität*) typical of advanced capitalism.[38]

Here Mandel's analysis paralleled that of Herbert Marcuse, who had earlier described the 'one-dimensional' society of neo-capitalism as one whose 'sweeping rationality ... is itself irrational'.[39] This perception of the Jewish genocide as a synthesis of partial rationality (the administrative and industrial system of the death camps) and 'global irrationality pushed to its logical

---

37   Mayer 1988.
38   Mandel 1978; Mandel 1991, p. 225.
39   Marcuse 1964, p. XIII.

conclusion' (the murderous madness of destroying a people) also resembled Adorno's and Horkheimer's approach, in which the 'self-destruction of reason' completed by Nazism was made possible by an extreme radicalisation of the instrumental rationality of the modern world. But this affinity should not be interpreted as a causal relationship: Mandel and the Frankfurt School philosophers did not belong to the same intellectual current. It was rather a convergence starting from two different methodological approaches. The diagnosis is the same, but the analyses proceed along different paths. For Mandel the instrumental rationality of capitalism explains the *form* but not the *causes* of the genocide. In his book on *Late Capitalism* he reproached Adorno with failing to see that technology cannot be applied independently of human will and a more general historical context:

> Auschwitz and Hiroshima were not products of technology but of *relationships of social forces* – in other words, they were the (provisional) terminus of the great historical defeats of the international proletariat after 1917.[40]

How could Germany become the site of this murderous synthesis between racism and industry? The idea of a 'guilt' inscribed in national history, even in the German 'soul', was so foreign to his way of thinking that Mandel never even took the trouble of refuting it, either in its more noble versions (the 'metaphysical' guilt theorised by Karl Jaspers) or in its more current forms (particularly common in Europe in the 1950s and resurrected today by Daniel Goldhagen).[41] The explanation that Mandel proposed was at bottom no more than a Marxist version of the classical theory of a *deutsche Sonderweg* (exceptional German road).[42] Interpreting German history as an *exception* is quite problematic, inasmuch as it implies a *norm* of transition to modernity that is quite difficult to define (the French revolution is not such a norm).[43] It does, however, emphasise the contradictions of a modernisation process that, without being unique – similar processes took place in several countries, from Italy to Japan – nonetheless remains distinct. The weakness of the liberal tradition, delayed national unification, the weight of militarism, the influence of Prussian elites of feudal pedigree, and finally the lack of a colonial empire: all these elements contrib-

---

40   Mandel 1978, p. 506.
41   Jaspers 1947; Goldhagen 1996.
42   For a synthesis of this discussion, see Kocka 1988, pp. 3–16.
43   See Blackburn and Ely 1984.

uted to giving German imperialism a particularly aggressive and expansion-
ist character. This tendency, already manifest under the Wilhelmine Empire,
would be accentuated by the Nazi regime. From Bismarck to Hitler, German
expansionism was the product of a specific interconnection between the backwardness of the nation's political forms and the dynamism of its economic
development. The historic defeat of the bourgeois revolution in Germany –
from the crushing of the Peasant War during the Reformation until the defeat of
the 1848 revolution – combined with impressive industrial growth, and made
Germany after its unification in 1871 Europe's main economic power.[44] German
militarism was the fruit of this specific linkage between an upsurge of irrepressible productive forces inside the country's borders and the preservation
in its society of pre-capitalist-type mentalities. National Socialism thus carried
out a unique fusion between the most advanced industrial modernity and the
most reactionary obscurantism. During a colloquium held in Salzburg in 1990,
Mandel cited Ernst Bloch in order to explain the 'non-synchronism' or 'non-
contemporaneity' (*Ungleichzeitigkeit*) of ideology and society under the Third
Reich, a regime characterised by 'thirteenth-century survivals in the middle
of the twentieth century'. This vision was entirely consistent with Trotsky's
approach, in which Nazism represented a form (to use Norman Geras's particularly illuminating definition) of 'undigested barbarism'.[45]

This combination explains one of Nazism's constituent elements – its singular mixture of the archaic and the modern – which has led many historians
to present it as the heir of the 'Conservative Revolution', if not as the expression of a particular variant of 'reactionary modernism'.[46] Anti-Semitism was
exactly the right link that made a connection possible in the Nazi worldview
between past and future: an integration of technology and industry at the
heart of a reactionary ideology that set out to erase the heritage of the Enlightenment and resuscitate the values of an ancestral, Teutonic Germany. Once
the Jews were eliminated, capitalism would be productive (German industry)
rather than parasitic ('Judaised' finance); cities would regain the splendour of
classical Antiquity by becoming monuments to eternal Germany rather than
breeding places of (Jewish) cosmopolitanism; and technology could regain
its creative function after being put in service of the (Aryan) community and
reclaimed from the impersonal, corrupting mechanisms of (Jewish) society. In
other words, this form of anti-Semitism enabled a revolt against modernity to

---

44   Mandel 1991, pp. 240–1.
45   Geras 1998, p. 152.
46   See Dupeux 1992; Sieferle 1995; and Herf 1984, particularly ch. 8.

have recourse to the resources of *Zivilisation*. A comparable vision can be found in the studies of the Frankfurt School which characterise Nazism as a 'revolt of nature' channelled by technology.[47]

Inscribed into the logic of reactionary modernism – a conservative revolt against modernity that used the destructive means offered by modernity itself as an attempt to incorporate *Zivilisation* into *Kultur* – the Holocaust can be analysed through Marx's categories. Moishe Postone has acutely observed that the features generally attributed to the Jews by modern anti-Semitism – abstractness, intellectualism, extraterritoriality, mobility, universalism, etc. – perfectly correspond to 'the value dimension of the social forms analyzed by Marx'.[48] Thereafter, the Nazi war against the Jews took the form of a struggle against capitalism, not capitalism as a socio-economic system but capitalism as a social abstraction. In the Nazi worldview, Postone explains

> The Jews were not seen merely as *representatives* of capital (in which case anti-Semitic attacks would have been much more class-specific). They became the *personifications* of the intangible, destructive, immensely powerful, and international domination of capital as a social form. Certain forms of anti-capitalist discontent became directed against the manifest abstract dimension of capital, in the form of the Jews, because, given the antinomy of the abstract and concrete dimensions, capitalism appeared that way – not because the Jews were consciously identified with the value dimension. The 'anti capitalist' revolt was, consequently, also the revolt against the Jews. The overcoming of capitalism and its negative social effects became associated with the overcoming of the Jews.[49]

This analysis inspired by *Capital*'s theory of commodity fetishism is probably the most interesting and convincing attempt to elaborate a Marxist interpretation of Nazi anti-Semitism, but Mandel was probably too marked by his *concrete* experience of war and deportation to think of National Socialism as a form of *abstract* anti-capitalism. He certainly felt closer to Trotsky's vision of Nazi anti-Semitism as 'undigested barbarism'. This interpretation, however, tends to present Nazi violence – and in the final analysis the Jewish genocide – as the result of a fatal combination in which it was the archaic element (ancestral savagery) that unleashed an uncontrollable, murderous violence in the middle of the twentieth century. We could conclude from this that a completely modern,

---

47   See above all Horkheimer 1992, ch. 3, and Lunn 1985, pp. 238–41.
48   See Postone 1980, p. 108.
49   Ibid., p. 112.

secularised society would have nothing to fear from such eruptions of violence. The thesis of Nazi Germany's incomplete, contradictory modernization (*deutsche Sonderweg*) would thus appear to be a simple variant of the traditional conception of the Holocaust as the expression of society's lapse into pre-modern barbarism: Hitler as a modern Torquemada who suddenly came to power in an industrial society. There is doubtless a kernel of truth in this thesis – Arno J. Mayer describes the Final Solution as a 'secular crusade' of modern times[50] – but it has the major disadvantage of neglecting the modern dimension of Nazi ideology, anchored in racial biology and Social Darwinism and elaborated and systematised by an army of doctors, criminologists, psychologists, geneticists, physicists, ethnologists and anthropologists, who had very little to do with Luther's or the Catholic Inquisitors' worldview.[51] It also neglects the mentality and practices of the 'accessories'. Mandel had already stressed that these 'accessories' were neither obscurantist nor fanatical but banally 'modern', that is, typical of any society subjected to bureaucratic administration and 'legal-rational' government in the Weberian sense.[52]

In a footnote to his essay on the historians' debate, Mandel criticised the thesis of the German historian Ulrich Herbert, who emphasised the primacy of a racist worldview over any consideration of an economic kind in the Nazi policy of extermination. Mandel argued by contrast that as the deepening conflict made the mass of prisoners of war, while growing in number, no longer overabundant but wholly inadequate, racial elimination was subordinated to 'extermination through work' (*Vernichtung durch Arbeit*).[53] In fact, while it is true that the whole process of destruction of the Jews was marked by a constant tension between extermination and exploitation, each advocated by a different sector of the ss and Nazi regime, it seems difficult to deny that the conflict was resolved in the end in favour of extermination. The historian Raul Hilberg has emphasised the fundamentally anti-economic character of the genocide. He points out that the industrialist Krupp had asked Himmler not to deport the Jewish workforce employed in industry. In the General Government of Poland, 300,000 workers out of one million were Jews; in the textile sector, which was restructured in order to produce German shoes and uniforms for Germany, 22,000 out of 22,700 were Jews. The decision to eliminate the ghettos in the spring of 1942 had catastrophic economic consequences, which Governor General Frank did not fail to report to Berlin. 'The Polish Jews were annihilated in a

50   Mayer 1988, pp. 35, 12.
51   See Olff-Nathan 1993, and Biagioli 1992.
52   See Bauman 1989.
53   Mandel 1991, p. 225. Cf. Herbert 1987.

process in which economic factors were truly secondary', Hilberg concludes.[54] The economic and military irrationality of the deportation of the Hungarian Jews in the spring of 1944, not to mention that of the Jews of Corfu, needs no emphasis.

Mandel's approach led him to ignore a distinction in all his writings that has become almost universally recognised by historians, between Nazi *concentration camps* and *extermination camps*. Concentration camps were created for prisoners of war, political prisoners and 'anti-socials', while extermination camps were reserved for the Jews and, to a lesser extent, the Gypsies. Auschwitz – which was not only a deportation centre (Auschwitz I) and a killing centre (Birkenau), but also a centre of industrial production (Buna-Monowitz) – combined the two, as did Majdanek. But other camps, like Treblinka, Chelmno and Sobibor, were devoted exclusively to annihilating the European Jews. In other words, the racist worldview was not one aspect among others, but a genuine 'fixed point of the system'.[55] It was impossible for the classical Marxism that Mandel identified with to acknowledge this primacy of ideology over economics in the destruction of the Jews. This confirms the lag and limits that have held back the Marxist tradition and constrained its capacity to take account of *non-class* based forms of oppression: national, racial, religious or sexual.

Mandel grasped a fatal interconnection at the heart of the Final Solution between racism and industrial modernity, between capitalism's partial rationality and overall irrationality, but he could not admit that this genocide was determined 'in the final analysis' by ideology, despite the material interests (and military priorities) of German imperialism. For him this meant making too big a concession to the idea of the 'primacy of politics' in the history of the Third Reich (an idea for which he had already criticised the historian Tim Mason)[56] and stretching the axioms of historical materialism to an excessive degree. In fact the 'counter-rationality' of the extermination of the Jews and of the Gypsies constitutes a challenge for any historical account of Nazism, not

---

54   Hilberg 1985, vol. 2, pp. 527, 529, 542.

55   See Herbert 1987, p. 236, and Browning 1992, p. 76. See the thesis of the 'economic rationality' of the Holocaust in Aly and Heym 2002. On this book, originally published in Germany in 1988, see the critical essays collected in Schneider 1991. For a further development of this debate, see Aly 2008, and Tooze 2006.

56   Mandel 1974, p. 49. Cf. Mason 1966. The thesis of the 'primacy of the political' in National Socialism goes back to the Frankfurt School economist Friedrich Pollock. See Pollock 1941, and Schäfer 1994, pp. 61–71. For a reappraisal of Tim W. Mason's approach in the interpretation of the Holocaust, see Callinicos 2001.

just for the categories of classical Marxism.[57] The vision of the Holocaust as
a function of the class interests of big German capital – this is the interpretive criterion 'in the final analysis' of all Marxist theories of fascism – is not
defensible.[58] Trapped in this dead end, East German historians – not always
ideologues; sometimes genuine historians – enclosed a complex reality inside
pre-established categories. This approach was bound to end up both making
the Jewish genocide banal and discrediting Marxism itself by reducing it to a
form of economic determinism.[59] Despite his affirmed anti-dogmatism, Mandel did not avoid a certain oversimplification of reality and even arrogance. The
survivors, even those as stubbornly rationalistic as Jean Améry and Primo Levi,
were suspicious of this kind of reductionist analysis. In Améry's eyes, 'all the
attempts at economic explanations, all the one-dimensional interpretations
that claim that German industrial capital, fearing for its privileges, financed
Hitler, are absolutely meaningless for an eyewitness'. Despite his desire to 'make
clear' (*erklären*) his experience, Auschwitz remains for him 'a dark riddle' (*ein
finisteres Rätsel*).[60] Primo Levi's opinion is essentially the same: Auschwitz is
for him 'a black hole' (*un buco nero*). Current interpretations of anti-Semitism
did not satisfy him. Not that they seemed false, but they were 'limited, incom-
mensurable with and out of proportion to the events they were supposed to
clarify'.[61]

As the last great figure of post-war classical Marxism, Mandel was an heir
of the Enlightenment. His internationalism was rooted as much in the tradition of Jewish cosmopolitanism as in a universalism that was almost naturally
transmitted to Marxism by Enlightenment culture. In the face of Nazi barbar-

---

57   According to Dan Diner, this counter-rationality of Nazism, culminating in the system of
      extermination camps – factories whose product was death rather than value – is what
      makes it problematic to equate the Holocaust with the crimes of Stalinism. Though death
      was one of the essential characteristics of the gulag, it was not its *goal*. See Diner 2000.

58   See Callinicos 2001, p. 403 and Milchman 2003, p. 104.

59   See Kwiet 1976, pp. 173–98. Towards the end of the 1970s, a French extreme-left sect, cre-
      ated by former followers of Antonio Bordiga, around the bookshop La Vieille Taupe (Old
      Mole), pushed this economic determinism to the point of denying the Holocaust. Aus-
      chwitz, they argued, was a work camp following the criteria of capitalist exploitation, so
      it cannot have been created exclusively in order to kill human beings, without producing
      profit. This argument probably reveals the remains of an old left-wing anti-Semitic tradi-
      tion that has quite old roots in France, from Alphonse de Toussenel to Proudhon. In light of
      this extreme, anti-Semitic conclusion, the weakness of Marxist thinking about the Holo-
      caust seems all the more serious. See Bihr 1997. For more in general on Holocaust denial,
      see Vidal-Naquet 1992.

60   Améry 1980, p. viii.

61   Levi 1997.

ism, his response was that of a rationalist humanist. Socialism for him meant 'more and not less reason'; in other words, 'an increase in conscious control over human destiny and over history'.[62] The questions posed by critical theory about the tragic fate and inner paradoxes of Western rationalism – questions whose roots go back to Max Weber, which would be taken up again by Adorno and Horkheimer and eventually radicalised by Gunther Anders – were never considered seriously by the Fourth International's theorist.

Mandel replaced the philosophy of progress that had inspired classical Marxism – from Kautsky to Trotsky – with an *anthropological optimism* of humanist and rationalist pedigree.[63] He would always emphasise the fusion in Marxism between its 'scientific' dimension and its ethical tension, held from Marx's time forward in unsteady balance on a tightrope between the temptation of scientism and radical humanism.[64] He wrote, for example, that the struggle against oppression is justified on the ethical level, apart from any rational consideration. The fight against domination and injustice is an elementary ethical duty, binding to Marxists as a Kantian categorical imperative: 'Resistance against inhuman relations', he wrote evoking the Warsaw ghetto uprising, 'is a human right and a human duty'.[65] This ethical impulse and revolutionary humanism were at the origins of Mandel's commitment to the Resistance during the war and to all the battles of his activist life. While this generosity demands our admiration, it cannot resolve Marxism's paradoxes when faced with the 'black hole' of Auschwitz. Mandel pertinently dismissed as obscurantist a view of the Jewish genocide as by definition an incomprehensible, inexplicable and indescribable event (in the style of Elie Wiesel or Claude Lanzmann), but that does not make his own explanation any more satisfactory. Marxism's difficulties in dealing with the extermination of the Jews are at bottom shared by contemporary historical research. In a fragment published after his death, Isaac Deutscher, like Mandel a Jewish Marxist educated in Trotsky's school, wrote:

> To a historian trying to comprehend the Jewish holocaust the greatest obstacle will be the absolute uniqueness of the catastrophe. This will be not just a matter of time and historical perspective. I doubt whether even in a thousand years people will understand Hitler, Auschwitz, Majdanek, and Treblinka better than we do now. Will they have a better historical

---

62   Mandel 1991, p. 228.
63   See Löwy 1999.
64   See Bensaïd 2009.
65   Mandel 1990, p. 173.

perspective? On the contrary, posterity may understand it all even less than we do ... Perhaps a modem Aeschylus and Sophocles could cope with this theme: but they would do so on a level different from that of historical interpretation and explanation.[66]

---

66   Deutscher 1968, pp. 163–4. Other Marxist-inspired scholars came to a similar conclusion. See for instance Mason 1993, p. 282.

Conclusion

The history of the Marxist debate on the Jewish Question is the history of a misunderstanding. Classical Marxism was incapable of comprehending the nature of anti-Semitism, or of recognising the Jewish aspiration to a distinct separate identity. Actually, it shared this misconception with all intellectual and political currents that belonged to the tradition of Enlightenment, from democratic liberalism to Zionism. Modernity meant the assimilation of the Jews, from Moscow and Warsaw to Berlin and Vienna, not to speak of Paris, where the Republic had transformed them into *Israélites*. The specifically Jewish response to the crisis of assimilation at the turn of the twentieth century, Zionism, was equally useless. The movement founded by Theodor Herzl succeeded in colonising Palestine and, after the war, in building a state there, thus creating a Palestinian national question. During the entire first half of the century, Zionism rejected the Diaspora without giving any fruitful response to anti-Semitism in Europe, where a Jewish Question really existed, and Palestine was not a secure haven for the European Jews threatened by Nazism (less secure in any case than the United States, which the armies of Rommel never tried to invade and toward which the World Zionist Organization sought to prevent Jewish immigration). In contrast to liberalism (the defence of the status quo) and Zionism (the 'normalisation' of the Jewish people), socialism offered to the Jews a universalistic project conceived as the path to social and political liberation for all the oppressed, beyond states and national frontiers. This explains the enormous attraction that Marxism exerted on the Jewish world.

Its theoretical approach could be summarised as follows:

a. The religious, ethnic, and cultural features of the Jews emerged from the socioeconomic function they were supposed to play from Antiquity up until the rise of capitalism: commerce. Thus, the Jews were a caste or a 'people-class';

b. Anti-Semitism meant social backwardness and was a propaganda weapon used by the dominant class to divert the anti-capitalist feelings of labouring masses and the petty bourgeois layers. When anti-Semitism arose in Germany during the inter-war years, it was explained as the expression of decaying capitalism;

c. In an economically and culturally advanced society, anti-Semitism would disappear, in the same way as any other form of feudal obscurantism and the Jewish commercial caste would wither away. Jewish cultural otherness would thus lose its material foundation;

© KONINKLIJKE BRILL NV, LEIDEN, 2019 | DOI:10.1163/9789004384767_014

d. Jewish emancipation in Western Europe was a historical paradigm: assimilation was a necessary step in the evolution of any civil society and measured its advancement toward Progress;

e. Assimilation was ineluctable and the Jews of Eastern Europe had no future as a nation: the Jewish Question was a national question of the past, not of the present;

f. Zionism was a Jewish nationalist reaction to anti-Semitism and diverted the Jewish proletariat from the class struggle in the Diaspora toward the illusory goal of colonising Palestine. Until 1929, almost nobody foresaw the national conflicts that Zionist colonisation could create in Palestine (among the rare exceptions were Kautsky, the Palestinian Communist party from its beginnings, and, on the Zionist side, Martin Buber and Chaim Zhitlovsky).

This tendency was dominant, but not the only one. Marxism was a varied current of thought: on each of the points enumerated above, one can find exceptions or different approaches. The Judeo-Marxists (Medem, Borokhov) saw the national dimension of the Jewish Question in the Tsarist Empire; Trotsky, Rosa Luxemburg, Abram Leon, and the philosophers of the Frankfurt School (Horkheimer) came to consider anti-Semitism as an eminently modern phenomenon, no longer a feudal residue but a manifestation of backward capitalism, rooted both 'in objective social relations and in the consciousness and unconsciousness of the masses'.[1] This fundamental cleavage separated the partisans of assimilation (Bauer, Kautsky, Lenin, Leon) from those who recognised the national character of the Jews of Eastern Europe (Medem, Borokhov). The latter, in their turn, were divided between the defenders of national autonomy in the Diaspora and the builders of a Jewish state in Palestine. Thus, the assimilation/nationality dialectic was at the heart of this debate. On the one hand Kautsky, for whom Judaism was a residue of the Middle Ages in modern society; on the other Chaim Zhitlovsky, who did not understand why the Jews should be considered as '4 percent of somebody else' when they were 100 percent of themselves.[2] As Isaac Deutscher observed: 'As Marxists, we tried theoretically to deny that the Jewish labor movement had an identity of its own, but it had it all the same. It was quite obvious that in that Jewish labor movement the intellectual found his role and did not have to go to the trouble of defining it. From the Jewish working class in Eastern Europe came the efflorescence of Yiddish literature.'[3]

---

1   Horkheimer and Adorno 1985.
2   Quoted in Suchecky 1986, p. 98.
3   Deutscher 1968, p. 45.

The Jewish Question reveals the blindness of Marxism to the significance of both religion and the nation in modern world. Insofar as Judaism – a millennial religion – was reduced to the superstructure of an urban commercial caste, the transformation of religious anti-Judaism into modern racial anti-Semitism was incomprehensible. Of course, the Jewish Question had multiple dimensions that transcended religion (a form of religious determinism symmetrical to Marxist economic determinism is a common feature of Jewish historiography, from Heinrich Graetz to Simon Dubnov, from Salo I. Baron to Léon Poliakov) but the eclipse of the latter had fatal implications. Replacing religion with economy, Marxism reset the Jewish Question in 'materialist' terms and reformulated a mono-causal historical interpretation. Indeed, Yosef Haym Yerushalmi's remark that 'the Jewish past unfolds before the historian not as unity but, to an extent unanticipated by its nineteenth century predecessors, as multiplicity and relativity',[4] reminds us of the necessity of an approach capable of integrating multiple elements. In fact, religion is a factor as important as the economy to the understanding of Jewish history and, even accepting the theory of the people-class, it remains that the 'people' – Jewish social otherness – preceded and outlived the class. In the wake of the radical Enlightenment, Marxist thinkers perceived religion as synonymous with obscurantism and as an instrument for the enslavement of the oppressed. The subversive potentialities of faith, the 'hot currents' of religious thought (Ernst Bloch), completely escaped those Marxists who interpreted Jewish history. Almost nobody, in this debate, saw Judaism as the indispensable ally of materialism in the chess game of history (to employ Benjamin's image). For them, Judaism, like anti-Semitism, was a 'prejudice' to transcend. For the Judeo-Marxists, in particular, it was necessary to build a modern Jewish nation, freed from religion: from whence an uncanny coexistence of the Messianic idea, which suffused the struggle of the proletariat, and the atheism of the socialist intelligentsia in the Yiddishland.

A similar limit concerned the theorising of the nation. Marxists were haunted by the search for an 'objective' – sometimes normative – definition of the national phenomenon: they located the constitutive elements of the nation in the economy, language, territory, and so on, often forgetting to take into account its subjective dimension, that is the consciousness a group possesses of forming a community of culture, united by a collective destiny. Indeed, the nation is a dialectical totality where, above all among oppressed peoples, subjective identity is at least as significant as other 'objective' elements (the existence of a national market and so on). It was precisely this classical Marxist

---

4   Yerushalmi 1982, ch. 4.

approach that the Judeo-Marxists, in particular the Bundists, put into question. They detached the nation from territory, and dialectically conceived internationalism as a synthesis of universalism and of national liberation, of cosmopolitanism and of recognition for the cultural specificities of the national
minorities. Fundamentally, the Bundist project of cultural national autonomy
already included the idea of a disassociation of citizenship and nationality. It
also prefigured what is today currently defined as 'identity politics', even if this
genealogy is not recognised in the existing literature on this topic.

The Jewish Question also reveals a blindness of classical Marxism toward
forms of domination not directly related to the class structure of society, such
as national, but also racial and gender oppression. There is a striking analogy
between the Jewish Question and the Woman Question. As a general rule,
the German and Russian Socialists confined themselves, according to Annik
Mahaim, 'to posing the problems of women workers almost exclusively in terms
of class and hardly ever of sex'.[5] For them, the liberation of women would be
realised under socialism, but the question did not directly concern the everyday
struggles of the workers' movement. Women were considered as a sector of the
proletariat, and not as an object of specific oppression. Moreover, the rejection
of the concept of Jewish nationality and the critique of Jewish socialism corresponded to the opposition to feminism and the very idea of an autonomous
movement for women's liberation. With some rare exceptions, women could
play a role in the workers' movement as militants devoted to the cause of the
proletariat, but not as representatives of an oppressed sex. Rosa Luxemburg
appeared, in this sense, as an emblematic figure, who had succeeded in becoming a leader of the socialist movement at the price of a dual self-negation: both
of her Jewishness and her womanness.[6] This applies too for homosexuality. In
the pages of the Viennese *Arbeiterzeitung*, an extremely ambiguous attitude to
the Jewish Question (refusal to struggle against anti-Semitism, denunciation
of the 'Judaised' finance and press) was often accompanied by an outright
condemnation of homosexuality, which led Karl Kraus to conclude that the
word 'comrade' (*Genosse*) could certainly not derive from the verb 'to enjoy'
(*geniessen*).[7] But the roots of this attitude are not to be found exclusively in
the prudishness and bourgeois morality of the Habsburg Empire. Despite the

---

5 See Mahaim 1979, p. 80.
6 Christel Neusüss detects a Jewish dimension, although subterranean, in her critique of the
   organisational (bureaucratic-centralist and to a certain extent 'patriarchal') structure of German social democracy. See Neusüss 1986, pp. 91–9. On Rosa's belonging to two oppressed
   groups – Jews and women – see Ettinger 1979, pp. 129–42.
7 See Cases 1985, p. 180.

decriminilization of homosexuality, in the Soviet Russia of the 1920s – that is, before Stalinism – it was common to consider gay and lesbian relations as abnormal, and the sexual revolution claimed by Alexandra Kollontai did not run more than a few years.[8] In Germany, the gay movement led by Magnus Hirschfeld had conflicting relations with the Communist Party.[9] Classical socialist thought never succeeded, in general, in conceiving the struggle for the equality of the oppressed also as the struggle for gender equality, the recognition of their right to be different. Russian Marxists offered a rigid choice to national minorities – self-determination (state separation) or assimilation – which often transformed the struggle for equality into the attempt to transcend all national difference. Indeed, the entire Jewish culture of Eastern Europe at the turn of the century – from politics (Medem, Zhitlovsky) to history (Dubnov), from sociology (Lestschinsky) to literature (Peretz, Aleichem, Asch) to painting (Chagall) – was the affirmation of a Jewish identity in the Diaspora. Indeed, Judeo-Marxism belonged to the category, coined by Hannah Arendt, of 'conscious pariahs' who struggled for the recognition of their otherness by inscribing it in the framework of the 'national and social liberation' of all the oppressed of Europe.[10] The Jewish representatives of Russian, German or Austrian Marxism were, then, also outsiders, impelled to revolt by their own social marginality, but not 'conscious pariahs'. There is something profoundly Jewish in the fate of Trotsky (Lev Davidovitch Bronstein), who wrote all his great works in exile and was condemned to a permanent wandering because of his political stance: but, as Hans Meyer has pointed out, he lived his whole life as 'comrade Shylock' without ever being conscious of it.[11]

Finally, the Marxist debate on the Jewish Question shows the tragic illusions of a teleological vision of history. Behind the Marxist conception of assimilation and anti-Semitism, there was an idea of progress in which history was envisaged as a linear development, an inevitable improvement of humanity, the evolution of society following natural laws and the development of the productive forces under capitalism growing inevitably closer to the advent of the socialist order. In 1890, Engels wrote that economic development rendered laughable and anachronistic any form of anti-Semitism. Socialists and communists cultivated this illusion for fifty years, until the Holocaust demonstrated that economic development and technical progress might not necessarily correspond to human and social improvement. History could be a march towards

---

8 See Healey 2001.
9 See Dose 2014.
10 See Arendt 2007, p. 283.
11 See Mayer 1983, p. 369.

catastrophe as well as progress: it was necessary to resist the 'storm' and not promulgate the illusion of 'swimming with the tide'. As Detlev Claussen has pointed out, the Holocaust throws a new light on the 'relation of civilized society with barbarism'.[12]

After the Second World War, both Stalinism and National Socialism had uprooted, along with its actors, the Marxist debate on the Jewish Question, but some isolated thinkers 'sublated' the old discrepancies. Max Horkheimer and Theodor Adorno analysed the Holocaust as the quintessential expression of totalitarianism, the outcome of Western civilisation, whereas Ernest Mandel connected Nazi anti-Semitism with the long history of colonialism and imperial violence against non-Europeans. Finally, Moishe Postone elaborated a Marxist theory of the Holocaust as a violent solution to the explosive contradiction of commodity fetishism – anti-Semitism as a murderous rebellion against capitalism as a 'social abstraction' – which is a coherent complement to Marx's *Capital*. All of them had abandoned any illusion of historical teleology.

There were, of course, Marxists who had sounded the alarm before them: Rosa Luxemburg, who perceived the alternative between 'socialism or barbarism' and felt an 'air of Kishinev' in the nationalist convulsions of Germany in 1915; Trotsky, who predicted in 1938 the physical extermination of the Jews as a result of a new world war; Walter Benjamin, who wrote in 1940 that before a victory of fascism, 'even the dead would not be safe'. Their voices remained isolated, but they expressed a sharp consciousness of the crisis of their time.

---

12   Claussen 1987, p. 10.

Glossary

Aliyah Jewish emigration to Palestine. Two waves can be broadly distinguished before the birth of Israel; the first from 1881 to 1903, the second from 1903 to 1914.

Aufklärung The Enlightenment in German-speaking countries.

Black Hundreds Russian ultra-nationalist groups which arose in 1905 around pro-monarchistic, ethnic Russiphilic, and anti-semitic programs; responsible for numerous pogroms.

Cheder Traditional Jewish primary school.

Duma The Russian parliament created after the 1905 revolution.

Eretz Israel Palestine ('land of Zion' in Hebrew).

Evsektsiia The Jewish section of the Communist party of the Soviet Union (1918).

Fellah Arab peasant.

Galut The Diaspora ('exile' in Hebrew).

Goy A non-Jew.

Haskalah The Jewish Enlightenment. Emerging in Germany in the second half of the eighteenth century with Moses Mendelssohn, this intellectual movement began to spread through Eastern Europe in the second half of the nineteenth century, taking a 'romantic', national form.

Hassidism Popular religious movement, marked by a strong mystical imprint, born in Eastern Europe in the middle of the eighteenth century.

Kehile The highest body, at the local level, of the traditional Jewish community (plural *kehilloth*). Among its functions were social assistance, the raising of taxes, and education.

Khevere Jewish workers' mutual-aid society (plural *khevroth*).

Luftmensh 'Air Person', Yiddish word to designate Jews who were poor, unemployed or obliged to live by their wits.

Maskil Partisan of the *Haskalah* (plural *maskilim*).

Narodnik Supporter of the Russian populist movement (from Russian *narod*, people).

Obshchina The Russian peasant commune.

Ostjudentum The German name for Eastern European Jewry.

Pale of Settlement Created by Catherine II in 1794, it designated the regions in which the settlement of Jews was permitted. It included most of modern-day Poland, Lithuania, Belarus, Bessarabia, and the Ukraine.

Pogrom Anti-Semitic uprising, often leading to the massacre of the Jews (from the Russian *gromit'*, 'to destroy').

Shabbat The Jewish Saturday.

Shoah 'Destruction' in Hebrew: the Holocaust, the genocide of the European Jews during the Second World War.

Shtetl 'Village' in Yiddish: the Jewish village in Eastern Europe (plural *shtetlakh*).

Yeshiva   Higher school of Talmudic studies.

Yiddish   The language spoken by the Jews of Eastern Europe.

Yiddishkeit   The Jewish culture in Yiddish.

YIVO   Yiddish Scientific Institute (*Yiddisher Wisenshaftleker Institut*).

Chronology

1844   Karl Marx, 'On The Jewish Question', *Deutsch-Französisiche Jahrbücher*. This essay claims the emancipation of the Jews, but it shares with the 'Young Hegelians' (Feuerbach, Bauer, Hess) a conception of Judaism as a religion of money and egoism.

1847   Foundation of the Communist League in London.

1848–9   Revolutions in France, Germany, Austria, Hungary, Poland, and Italy. Friedrich Engels analyses the Jewish problem in the light of his theory of 'peoples without history' in a series of articles appearing in the *Neue Rheinische Zeitung*.

1853–6   Arthur Gobineau, *Essay on the Inequality of the Human Races*, the first formulation of modern racist theory. Heinrich Graetz begins his *History of the Jews*, one of the major works of the school of the *Wissenschaft des Judentums* (the science of Judaism).

1862   Moses Hess, *Rome and Jerusalem*, a theoretical forerunner of Zionism.

1863   Insurrection for Polish independence.

1867   Karl Marx, *Capital* (vol. 1).

1867–71   The Emancipation of the Jews in Germany, Austria, Hungary, and Italy.

1871   Paris Commune.

1873   Wilhelm Marr, *Der Sieg des Judentums über das Germanentum* (*The Victory of Judaism over Germanity*), the birth of modern anti-Semitism in Germany.

1875   Unification of German social democracy.

1876   Aaron Lieberman, *Appeal to Jewish Youth* (in Hebrew), the first expression of Jewish socialism. He participates in the creation of Jewish revolutionary circles in London and Vilnius.

1880   *Berlinerstreit* (the dispute of Berlin). a debate between conservative anti-Semites (Heinrich von Treitschke) and progressive liberals (Theodor Mommsen).

1881   The assassination of Tsar Alexander II, which is followed by a wave of pogroms throughout the Russian Empire. The beginning of Jewish emigration from Eastern Europe toward the United States and Western Europe.

1882   Leo Pinsker, *Autoemanzipation* (in German), This essay marks the beginning of Russian Zionism. In Geneva, Plekhanov, Zasulich and Aksel'rod create the Emancipation of Labor group, the first expression of Russian Marxism.

1886   Eduard Drumont, *la France juive* (*Jewish France*), the most widespread work of French anti-Semitism.

1889   Foundation of the Austrian social democracy (SPÖ) under the leadership
        of Victor Adler. The Second International is founded in Paris.

1890   Kautsky, 'Das Judentum', *Die Neue Zeit*. Franz Mehring, 'Anti-und Philose-
        mitisches', *Neue Zeit*.

1891   The Brussels congress of the Second International rejects, under the pres-
        sure of Victor Adler, a motion opposing anti-Semitism presented by the
        American delegate Abraham Cahan. According to Adler, it was necessary
        that socialism should not appear as a 'Jewish' movement.

1892   Demonstration of Jewish workers on May Day in Vilnius. The Polish Social-
        ist party (PPS) is created in Paris.

1893   August Bebel, 'The Social Democracy and Anti-Semitism'. Foundation of
        the Social Democracy of the Kingdom of Poland and Lithuania (SDKPiL)
        led by Rosa Luxemburg, Leo Jogiches and Adolf Warski.

1894-8 Dreyfus affair in France. Bernard Lazare, *L'Antisémitisme, son histoire et ses
        causes* (*Anti-Semitism, Its History and Its Causes*).

1896   Theodor Herzl, *Der Judenstaat*, which marks the birth of modern political
        Zionism.

1897   First Zionist Congress at Basel. In New York, Abraham Cahan founds the
        Yiddish socialist daily *Forverts*. The Bund (General Jewish Labor Bund of
        Lithuania, Poland and Russia) is created in Vilnius. Simon Dubnov, *Letters
        on Old and New Judaism*, which contains the first elaboration of a theory
        of Jewish national autonomy. Karl Lueger, the anti-Semitic leader of the
        Austrian social Christians, is elected mayor of Vienna. Sergej Njewsorow,
        'Der Zionismus', *Sozialistische Monatshefte*. Chaim Zhitlovsky translates the
        Communist Manifesto into Yiddish.

1898   Foundation of Russian social democracy (RSDLP) under the leadership of
        Lenin and Iulii Martov. Nakhman Syrkin, 'The Jewish Question and the Jew-
        ish Socialist State' *Deutsche Wort*, the manifesto of Russian socialist Zion-
        ism. Chaim Zhitlovsky writes the first Marxist critique of Zionism, 'Zionism
        and Socialism', *Der yidisher Arbeter*.

1899   Brünn congress of Austrian social democracy, marked by a debate on na-
        tional autonomy. Karl Renner (Synopticus), *State and Nation*.

1900   August Chamberlain, *Die Grundlagen der zwanzigsten Jahrhundert* (*The
        Foundations of the Twentieth Century*), the 'classical' work of racist anti-
        Semitism.

1901   The fourth congress of the Bund at Bialystok adopts a programme that
        defines the Russian Jews as a nation.

1903   Kishinev pogrom. The Russian social democracy holds its second con-
        gress, which leads to the split between Bolsheviks (Lenin) and Menshev-
        iks (Martov), the latter followed by the Bund. In the Bolshevik journal

Iskra, Lenin criticises the Bund's 'nationalism' and organisational federalism.

1904   Vladimir Medem, *The Social Democracy and the National Question* (in Russian and Yiddish). This text marks the birth of Judeo-Marxism.

1905   Revolution in Russia, followed by wave of pogroms. The *Okhrana*, the tsarist secret police, fabricates the *Protocols of the Elders of Zion*. The Zionist socialist movement crystallises into three distinct currents: the Zionist-Socialist Workers Party (Syrkin), which asks for territorial Jewish autonomy; the Jewish Socialist Workers party (Zhitlovsky), which advocates national autonomy; the Poale Zion (Borokhov), which is in favour of the Jewish colonisation of 'Palestine'. The Bund's fifth congress definitively adopts a programme of cultural national autonomy for the Jews of Russia.

1906   Borokhov, 'Our Platform' (in Russian and Yiddish), the most significant attempt to integrate Zionism into Marxist theory. The Bund joins the RSDLP.

1907   Otto Bauer, *The Question of Nationalities and the Social Democracy.*

1908   International conference at Czernowitz where Yiddish is proclaimed the 'national language of the Jewish people.' Karl Kautsky, *Nationality and Internationalism.* Rosa Luxemburg, *The National Question and Autonomy.* She rejects the demand for Polish independence, criticises the national programme of the Bund, and considers Jewish assimilation as an irreversible historical tendency.

1910   Vladimir Medem, *Nationalism or Neutralism.* Karl Kautsky, *The Origins of Christianity.*

1911   Werner Sombart, *The Jews and Modern Capitalism.*

1912   Otto Bauer, 'The conditions of national assimilation', *Der Kampf.*

1913   Beilis trial in Kiev (the last European trial for ritual murder). Josef Stalin, *Marxism and the National Question.* Lenin, 'Critical Notes on the National Question', *Prosveshchenie.*

1914   First World War. Leon Trotsky analyses the Beilis Affair in the *Neue Zeit.*

1915   Zimmerwald Conference. The Jewish workers' movement adopts, in its entirety, a pacifist orientation.

1916   Ber Borokhov, 'The Economic Development of the Jewish People', *Der yidisher kaempfer.*

1917   Russian Revolution. The Provisional Government proclaims Jewish emancipation and suppresses tsarist anti-Semitic legislation. The first volume of Marx's *Capital* is published in Yiddish. In the name of the British government, Lord Balfour supports the creation of a Jewish 'national homeland' in Palestine.

1918–20   Civil war in Russia. The White Guards unleash waves of pogroms, above all in the Ukraine. The great majority of the Jews rally to the Soviet regime. In

1918 the Jewish section of the Bolshevik party, the *Evsektsiia*, is created in Moscow. The different components of Jewish socialism are drawn into the Russian Revolution and the Third International through a process of splits and fusions. Most of them join the *Evsektsiia*. The Bund continues to exist in Poland. The emancipation of the Jews of the Soviet Union produces a flourishing of Yiddish culture (literature, theatre, cinema, etc.). The revolution in Germany begins the collapse of the empire. The German Communist party (*Spartakusbund*) is created in Berlin in December 1918.

1919   In Berlin, the Freikorps violently repress the Spartakist insurrection. Rosa Luxemburg and Karl Liebknecht are murdered. Defeat of the Soviet republics in Bavaria and Hungary, in which numerous Jewish intellectuals play a leading role (Eisner, Landauer, Leviné, Lukács, Kun ...). The Third International is launched in Moscow.

1920   Foundation of the National Socialist movement (NSDAP).

1922   Assassination of the (Jewish) minister of foreign affairs of the Weimar Republic, Walter Rathenau.

1923   Attempted putsch by Hitler in Munich.

1925   Adolf Hitler, *Mein Kampf*. Birth of the YIVO in Vilnius.

1928   Creation of a Jewish Autonomous Oblast' at Birobidzhan in the Soviet Union. The Poale Zion is banned in the Soviet Union. Stalin uses anti-Semitic arguments in the struggle against the Left Opposition inside the CPSU.

1929   Emile Vandervilde, *The Land of Israel. A Marxist in Palestine*, a report sympathetic to Zionism. Foundation of the Jewish agency for the development of immigration into Palestine, where about 220,000 Jewish colonists now live (between 1880 and 1929, more than 3.5 million Jews emigrated from Central and Eastern Europe to Western Europe and the United States).

1930   Rise of National Socialism in Germany.

1931   Alfred Rosenberg, *The Myth of the Twentieth Century*, a manifesto of Nazi anti-Semitism. Otto Heller, *Der Untergang des Judentums*, a Stalinist rewriting of Kautsky's interpretation of the Jewish Question. Naum Abramovich Bukhbinder, *History of the Jewish Workers' Movement in Russia* in Yiddish.

1932   Resolution of the Central Committee of the German Communist party on anti-Semitism. The Nazi party receives 37.8 percent of the popular vote at the German elections. The risk of a seizure of power by the Nazi movement is minimised by the KPD, which concentrates its attacks on the social democracy, denounced as 'social fascist'.

1933   Hitler takes power. Leon Trotsky, 'What is National Socialism?'.

1934   Herbert Marcuse, 'The Struggle Against Liberalism in the Totalitarian View of the State', *Zeitschrift für Sozialforschung*.

1935   Promulgation of the Nuremburg Laws against the Jews. Gramsci finishes his *Prison Notebooks*. Ernst Bloch, *Heritage of Our Times*.

1936   Arab revolt against Zionist colonisation in Palestine. Arthur Rosenberg, *Fascism as a Mass Movement*; Daniel Guérin, *Fascism and Big Business*, two Marxist works that analyse the rise of German anti-Semitism.

1937   Leon Trotsky, *Thermidor and Anti-Semitism*.

1938   *Anschluß*: Austria is incorporated into the Third Reich. A wave of pogroms takes place in Germany (*Kristallnacht*). Italian fascism promulgates anti-Semitic laws (*leggi sulla razza*). Rise of anti-Semitism in Poland. Trotsky launches an appeal to the American Jews for a general mobilisation against anti-Semitism, which raises the threat of the 'physical extermination of the Jews'.

1939   German-Soviet treaty of non-aggression; beginning of the Second World War. Max Horkheimer, 'The Jews and Europe', *Zeitschrift für Sozialforschung*, then published in the United States.

1940   German occupation of France, Belgium and the Netherlands. The Vichy regime of Marshal Pétain promulgates anti-Semitic legislation. Creation of the first ghettos in occupied Poland. Walter Benjamin, theses 'On the Concept of History'.

1941   Nazi Germany starts its aggression against the USSR. Beginning of the Holocaust. Strike of Amsterdam workers against the deportation of Jews in occupied Holland. The Jewish Antifascist Committee is created in Moscow. At the end of the year, the NKVD arrests its founders, the leaders of the Polish Bund Victor Alter and Henryk Erlich. They will be executed the following year.

1942   During the Wannsee (Berlin) conference, the Nazi leaders decide on the 'Final Solution' (*Endlösung*) of the Jewish Question. Franz Neumann, *Behemoth*, an analysis of the Nazi social and political system. The gas chambers are activated in the Nazi extermination camps.

1943   German defeat at Stalingrad. The Warsaw ghetto insurrection is the final act of the Jewish workers' movement in Europe. Shmuel Zygelboim, representative of the Bund in the Polish government in exile, commits suicide in London to protest against the 'passivity with which the world looks on and accepts the extermination of the Jewish people'.

1945   End of the Second World War.

1945   Jean-Paul Sartre, *Anti-Semite and Jew*.

1946   Abram Leon, *The Jewish Question: A Marxist Interpretation*, published post-humously in Paris. Marek Edelman, *The Ghetto is Fighting*, a report for the Bund (Yiddish) of the insurrection of the Warsaw ghetto. In New York, the Jewish Antifascist Committee publishes the *Black Book*, edited by Ilya

Ehrenburg and Vasily Grossman, which describes the Holocaust in Poland and the USSR.

1947   Max Horkheimer and Theodor W. Adorno, *Dialectic of Enlightenment*.

1948   Proclamation of Israel. Beginning of the first Israeli-Arab war. Herbert Marcuse interrupts his correspondence with Martin Heidegger, started one year before, because of Heidegger's comparison of the expulsion of Eastern Germans to the Holocaust.

1949   In the USSR there begins an anti-Semitic campaign against 'rootless cosmopolitanism'. Paul Massing, *Rehearsal for Destruction: A Study of Political anti-Semitism in Imperial Germany*.

1952   Georg Lukács, *The Destruction of Reason*, which analyses National Socialism as the outcome of a particular German irrationalism.

1955   Herbert Marcuse, *Eros and Civilization*, which interprets the Holocaust and the atomic bomb as expressions of the human irrationality of late capitalism.

1956   Günther Anders, *Die Antiquiertheit des Menschen* (*The Obsolescence of Man*), which analyses the Holocaust through Marx's and Heidegger's critique of modern technology.

1962   The anti-Zionist Marxist group Matzpen is created in Israel.

1967   Second Israeli-Arab War.

1968   Isaac Deutscher, *The Non-Jewish Jew*.

1969   Nathan Weinstock, *Zionism: False Messiah*.

1975   John Bunzl, *Klassenkampf in der Diaspora*.

1986   Ernest Mandel, *The Meaning of the Second World War*. Moishe Postone, 'Anti-Semitism and National Socialism'. Jakob Taut, *Judenfrage und Zionismus*.

Bibliography

Abbreviations

CW   Marx, Engels, *Collected Works*, London: Lawrence & Wishart, 1975–2005, 50 vol.

DK   *Der Kampf*

DNZ   *Die Neue Zeit*

GS   Walter Benjamin, *Gesammelte Schriften*, Rolf Tiedemann, Hermann Schweppenhäuser (eds), Frankfurt: Suhrkamp, 1991, 7 vol.

JSS   *Jewish Social Studies*

LBIYB   *Leo Baeck Institute Year Book*.

LCW   Lenin, *Collected Works*, Moscow: Progress Publishers, 1960–70, 45 vol.

LTO   Léon Trotsky, *Œuvres*, Pierre Broué (ed.), Grenoble: ILT, 1978–1987, 24 vol.

MEW   Marx, Engels, *Werke*, Berlin: Dietz Verlag 1956–90, 43 vol.

SM   *Sozialistische Monatshefte*

SW   Walter Benjamin, *Selected Writings*, Michael Jennings (ed.), Cambridge, Mass.: Harvard University Press, 2003–6, 4 vol.

References

Achcar, Gilbert (ed.), 1999, *The Legacy of Ernest Mandel*, London: Verso.

Adler, Victor 1929, *Aufsätze, Reden und Briefe*, Vienna: Verlag der Wiener Volkbuchhandlung, 11 vol.

Adorno, Theodor W. 2005 [1950], *Minima Moralia: Reflections on a Damaged Life*, London: Verso.

Agamben, Giorgio 1983, 'Lingua e storia. Categorie linguistiche e categorie, storiche nel pensiero di Benjamin', in Fabrizio Desideri (ed.), *Walter Benjamin. Tempo storia linguaggio*, Rome: Editori Riuniti, pp. 65–82.

Ali, Tariq 1999, 'The luck of a crazy youth', in Gilbert Achcar (ed.), *The Legacy of Ernest Mandel*, London: Verso, pp. 217–24.

Allg. Jüdischen Arbeiterbund (ed.) 1904, *Die Tätigkeit des Allgemeinen Jüdischen Arbeiterbundes in Litauen, Polen und Rußland ('Bund') nach seinem V. Parteitag. Bericht für dem Intern. Sozialistischen Kongreß in Amsterdam*, Geneva.

Aly, Götz 2006, *Hitler's Beneficiaries: Plunder, Racial War, and the Nazi Welfare State*, New York: Metropolitan Books.

Aly, Götz and Susanne Heym 2002 [1988], *Architects of Annihilation: On the Logic of Destruction*, Princeton: Princeton University Press.

Améry, Jean 1980 [1966], *At the Mind's Limits: Contemplations by a Survivor on Auschwitz and its Realities*, Bloomington: Indiana University Press.

Anders, Günther 1987 [1979], 'Wenn ich verzweifelt bin, was geht's mich an?', in *Das Gunther Anders Lesebuch*, edited by Mathias Greffrath, Zurich: Diogenes, pp. 287–328.

Anders, Günther 1985, *Die Antiquiertheü des Menschen. I. Uber die Seele im Zeitalter der zweiten industriellen Revolution*, Munich: C.H. Beck.

Anderson, Perry 1976, *Considerations on Western Marxism*, London: New Left Books.

Andreucci, Franco 1979, 'La diffusione e la volgarizzazione del marxismo', *Storia del marxismo, Il marxismo nell'età della Seconda Internazionale*, Turin: Einaudi, vol. 2, pp. 6–58.

Andreucci, Franco 1979b, 'La questione colonial e l'imperialismo', *Storia del marxismo*, Turin: Einaudi, vol. 2, pp. 865–93.

Angress, Werner T. 1971, 'Juden im politischen Leben der Revolutionszeit', in *Deutsches Judentum in Krieg und Revolution 1916–1923*, edited by W. Mosse and A. Paucker, Tübingen: J.C.B. Mohr, pp. 137–315.

Anin, Maxim 1908, 'Ist die Assimilation der Juden möglich?' *SM*, XII, 14, no. 10, pp. 614–19.

Anin, Maxim 1909, 'Probleme der jüdische Arbeitersleben', *SM*, XIII, 1, no. 4, pp. 231–5.

Anin, Maxim 1911, 'Was will die jüdische Sektion in der sozialistischen Internationale?' *SM*, XV, 1, no. 6, pp. 396–401.

Arendt, Hannah 1968, 'Walter Benjamin, 1892–1940', *Men in Dark Times*, New York: Harcourt, Brace, pp. 153–205.

Arendt, Hannah 1976 [1951], *The Origins of Totalitarianism*, New York: Harcourt Brace.

Arendt, Hannah 2007 [1944], 'The Jew as Pariah: A Hidden Tradition', *The Jewish Writings*, New York: Schocken Books: 275–97.

Arvon, Henri 1978, *Les Juifs et l'idéologie*, Paris: Presses Universitaires de France.

Aschheim, Steven 1982, *Brothers and Strangers. The East European Jew in Germany and German Jewish Consciousness 1800–1923*, Madison: University of Wisconsin Press.

Ascher, Alexander 1965, 'Pavel Axelrod: A Conflict Between Jewish Loyalty and Revolutionary Dedication', *Russian Review*, XXIV, no. 3, pp. 149–65.

Aubet, Maria-José 1977, *Rosa Luxemburg y la questiòn nacional*, Barcelona: Editorial Anagrama.

Austerlitz, Friedrich 1900–01, 'Karl Lueger', *DNZ*, XIX/2, no. 28, pp. 36–45.

Avineri, Shlomo 1964, 'Marx and the Jewish Emancipation', *Journal of the History of Ideas*, vol. 25, no. 3, pp. 445–50.

Avineri, Shlomo 1968, *The Social and Political Thought of Karl Marx*, New York: Cambridge University Press.

Baioni, Luciano 1984, *Kafka e l'ebraismo*, Turin: Einaudi.

Balakan, David 1905, *Die Sozialdemokratie und das jüdische proletariat*, Czernowitz: H. Pardini, K.K. Universitäts-Buchhandlung.

Barkai, A. 1970, 'The Austrian Social Democracy and the Jews', *Wiener Library Bulletin*, vol. 24, no. 1, pp. 31–40; no. 2, pp. 16–21.

Baron, Salo 1964, *The Russian Jews under Tsars and Soviets*, New York: Macmillan.

Battistrada, Franco 1982, *Marxismo e populismo*, Milan: Jaca Book.

Bauer, Bruno 1958 [1843], *The Jewish Problem*, New York: Hebrew Union College.

Bauer, Otto 1910–11, 'Sozialismus und Antisemitismus', *DK*, IV, no. 2, pp. 94–5.

Bauer, Otto 1975–80, *Gesamtausgabe*, Vienna: Europa-Verlag, 9 vol.: vol. 1: 'Die Nationalitätenfrage und die Sozialdemokratie' [1907]; vol. 8: 'Galizische Parteitage' [1912]; 'Die Bedingungen der nationalen Assimilation' [1912].

Bauer, Otto 1936, *Zwischen zwei Weltkriegen?*, Bratislava: Eugen Prager Verlag.

Bauer, Otto 1983 [1938], 'War and Fascism', in *Marxists in Face of Fascism. Writings by Marxists on Fascism from the Inter-War Period*, edited by David Beecham, Manchester: Manchester University Press.

Bauman, Zygmunt 1989, *Modernity and the Holocaust*, Cambridge: Polity Press.

Bebel, August 1906, *Sozialdemokratie und Antisemitismus*, Berlin: Buchandlung Vorwärts.

Behrend, Hans 1933, 'L'intégration des Juifs allemands dans l'État', *La Correspondance Internationale* (13), nos. 75–6.

Behrend, Hans 1935, 'L'antisémitisme conduit à la domination renforcée des trusts (lettre d'Allemagne)', *La Correspondance Internationale* (15), nos. 104–5.

Benjamin, Walter 2002–6, *Selected Writings*, edited by Michael W. Jennings, Cambridge, Mass.: Harvard University Press, 4 vol. [*SW*]: vol. 1: 'The Life of Students' (1914), pp. 37–47; 'On Language as Such and on the Language of Man' (1916), pp. 62–74; 'Critique of Violence' (1921), pp. 236–52; vol. 2/1: 'Surrealism: The Last Snapshot of the European Intelligentsia' (1929), pp. 207–21; 'Theories of German Fascism' (1930), pp. 312–21; vol. 3: 'Paris, the Capital of the Nineteenth Century' (1935), pp. 32–49; 'Eduard Fuchs: Collector and Historian' (1937), pp. 260–302; vol. 4: 'Central Park' (1940), pp. 161–99; 'Paralipomena to "On the Concept of History"' (1940), pp. 401–11; 'On the Concept of History' (1940), pp. 389–400.

Benjamin, Walter 1973, *Understanding Brecht*, London: New Left Books.

Benjamin, Walter 1978, *Briefe*, edited by Gershom Scholem, Theodor W. Adorno, Frankfurt: Suhrkamp, 2 vol.

Benjamin, Walter 1979, *One-Way Street and Other Writings*, Introduction by Susan Sontag, London: New Left Books.

Benjamin, Walter 1986, *Moscow Diary*, edited by Gary Smith, Cambridge, Mass.: Harvard University Press.

Benjamin, Walter 1994, *Correspondence 1910–1940*, translated by M.R. and E.M. Jacobson, Chicago: University of Chicago Press.

Benjamin, Walter 2002, *The Arcades Project*, trans. Howard Eiland and Kevin McLaughlin, Cambridge, Mass.: Harvard University Press.

Benjamin, Walter 2006, *Berlin Childhood Around 1900*, translated by Howard Eiland, Cambridge, MA: Harvard University Press.

Benjamin, Walter and Scholem, Gershom 1989, *Correspondence 1932–1940*, trans. Gary Smith and André Lefevre, New York: Schocken Books.

Bensaïd, Daniel 1990, *Walter Benjamin, sentinelle messianique à la gauche du possible*, Paris: Plon.

Bensaid, Daniel 2006, '"Zur Judenfrage": Une critique de l'émancipation politique', in Karl Marx, *Sur la Question juive*, Paris: La fabrique, pp. 7–30.

Daniel Bensaïd 2009 [1995], *Marx for Our Times: Adventures and Misadventures of a Critique*, London: Verso.

Berdiaeff, Nicolas 1975, *Christianisme, Marxisme. Conception chrétienne et conception marxiste de l'Histoire*, Vendôme: Le Centurion.

Berding, Helmut 1988, *Moderner Antisemitismus in Deutschland*, Frankfurt: Suhrkamp.

Berlin, Isaiah 1980, 'Benjamin Disraeli, Karl Marx, and the Search for Identity' (1970), *Against the Current: Essays in the History of Ideas*, New York: Viking Press, pp. 317–60.

Bernstein, Eduard 1893, 'Das Schlagwort und der Antisemitismus', *DNZ*, XI, 2/35, pp. 228–37.

Bernstein, Eduard 1897, 'Die Deutsche Sozialdemokratie und die türkischen Wirren', *DNZ*, XV, 1/4, pp. 108–16.

Bernstein, Eduard 1913–14, 'Die Schulstreit in Palästina', *DNZ*, XXXII, 1/20, pp. 744–52.

Bernstein, Eduard 1916, 'Vom Patriotismus der Juden', *Die Friedens-Warte* 18, no. 8–9.

Bernstein, Eduard 1917, *Von den Aufgaben der Juden im Weltkriege*, Berlin: Erich Reiß Verlag.

Bernstein, Eduard 1921, 'Jews and German Social Democracy' in *Rehearsal for Destruction: A Study of Political Anti-Semitism in Imperial Germany*, edited by Paul Massing, New York: Harper & Brothers, pp. 322–9.

Biagioli, Mario 1992, 'Science, modernity and the Final Solution', in *Probing the Limits of Representation: Nazism and the 'Final Solution'*, edited by Saul Friedländer, Cambridge, MA: Harvard University Press, pp. 185–205.

Bihr, Alain and Daeninckx, Didier (eds) 1997, *Négationnistes: Les chiffoniers de l'histoire*, Paris: Syllepse/Golias.

Birnbaum, Pierre 1996, *The Jews of the Republic: A Political History of State Jews in France from Gambetta to Vichy*, Stanford: Stanford University Press.

Birnbaum, Pierre 2004, *Géographie de l'espoir. L'exil, les Lumières, la désassimilation*, Paris: Gallimard.

Blackburn, David and Geoff Ely 1984, *The Peculiarities of German History*, Oxford: Oxford University Press.

Bloch, Ernst 2009 [1934], *Heritage of Our Times*, Cambridge: Polity Press.

Bloch, Ernst 1986 [1938–47], *Principle of Hope*, Cambridge, MA: MIT Press.

Blumenkranz, Bernard 1960, *Juifs et Chrétiens dans le monde occidental 430–1096*, La Haye: Mouton.

Bölich, Walter (ed.) 1965, *Der Berliner Antisemitismusstreit*, Frankfurt: Sammlung Insel.

Borkenau, Franz 1956, *Karl Marx*, Frankfurt: Fischer.

Borojov, Ber 1979, *Nacionalismo y lucha de clases 1905–1917*, Mexico: Ediciones de Pasado y Presente/Siglo XXI Editores.

Borokhov, Ber 1920, *Pueli tsiun shrift*, New York: Pueli tsiun farlag.

Borokhov, Ber 1928, *Geklibene shriftn*, New York: Yidish-natsionaler arbeter farband.

Borokhov, Ber 1966, *Shprakh forshung un literatur geshikte*, Tel Aviv: I.L. Peretz farlag.

Borokhov, Ber 1984, 'On the Question of Zionist Theory' (1905), *Class Struggle and the Jewish Question: Selected Essays in Marxist Zionism*, edited by Mitchell Cohen, New Brunswick: Transaction Books, pp. 35–50.

Bourdet, Yvon 1971, *Dictionnaire biographique du mouvement ouvrier international*, vol. 1, *Autriche*, Paris: Éditions ouvrières.

Braunthal, Julius 1965a, *Victor und Friedrich Adler. Zwei Generationen Arbeiterbewegung*, Vienna: Verlag der Wiener Volksbuchhandlung.

Braunthal, Julius 1965b, 'The Jewish Background of Victor and Friedrich Adler', *LBIYB*, vol. 10, pp. 269–79.

Brecht, Bertolt 1996, *Journals 1934–1955*, New York: Routledge.

Bronner Eric, and Kellner, Douglas M. (eds) 1989, *Critical Theory and Society: A Reader*, New York: Routledge.

Brossat, Alain 1978, 'Une chasse à l'ours mouvementée en compagnie de Léon Davidovitch Trotsky (Théorie révolutionnaire et philosophie spontanée chez Trotsky)', *Critique communiste*, no. 25.

Brossat, Alain 1985, 'Le PC allemand face aux nazis (1923–1933)', *Critique communiste*, no. 39.

Brossat, Alain and Klingberg, Sylvia 1983, *Le Yiddishland révolutionnaire*, Paris: Balland.

Broué, Pierre 1971, *Révolution en Allemagne 1917–1923*, Paris: Éditions de Minuit.

Browning, Christopher 1992, *The Path to Genocide*, New York: Cambridge University Press.

Brunazzi, Mario and Fubini, Anna Maria 1985 (eds.), *Gli ebrei orientali dall'utopia alla rivolta*, Milan: Edizioni di Comunità.

Brym, Robert J. 1978, *Jewish Intelligentsia and Russian Marxism*, London: Macmillan.

Buber, Martin 1967, *Der utopische Sozialismus*, Cologne: Hegner Verlag.

Budeiri, Musa 2010 [1980], *The Palestine Communist Party 1919–1948: Arab and Jew in the Struggle for Internationalism*, Chicago: Haymarket.

Budnitskii, Oleg 2012, *Russian Jews Between the Reds and the Whites 1917–1920*, Philadelphia: University of Pennsylvania Press.

Buhle, Paul 1987, *Marxism in the USA: Remapping the History of the American Left*, London: Verso.

Bukhbinder, Naum 1931, *Di geshikte fun yidisher arbeter-bavegung in Rusland*, Vilne: Farlag Tomor.

Bulthaup, Peter (ed.) 1975, *Materialen zu Benjamin Thesen 'Über den Begriff der Geschichte'*, Frankfurt: Suhrkamp.

Bunzl, John 1975, *Klassenkampf in der Diaspora*, Vienna: Europaverlag, 1975.

Bunzl, John, *Der lange Arm der Erinnerung. Jüdisches Bewußtsein Heute*, Vienna: Böhlau Verlag.

Callinicos, Alex 2001, 'Plumbing the Depths: Marxism and the Holocaust', *The Yale Journal of Criticism*, vol. 14/2, pp. 385–414.

Carlebach, Julius 1978, *Karl Marx and the Radical Critique of Judaism*, London: Routledge & Kegan Paul.

Cases, Cesare 1985, *Il testimone secondario. Saggi e interventi sulla cultura del Novecento*, Turin: Einaudi.

Chasanowich, Leon 1914, 'Ziele und Mittel des sozialistischen Zionismus', *SM*, no. 15.

Claussen, Detlev 1987, *Grenzen der Aufklärung. Zur gesellschaftlichen Geschichte des modernen Antisemitismus*, Frankfurt: Fischer.

Cohen, Margaret 1993, *Profane Illuminations: Walter Benjamin and the Paris of Surrealist Revolution*, Berkeley: University of California Press.

Collotti, Enzo 2003, *Il fascism e gli ebrei. Le leggi razziali in Italia*, Rome: Laterza.

Connerton, Paul 1989, *The Tragedy of Enlightenment: An Essay on the Frankfurt School*, Cambridge, Mass.: Cambridge University Press.

Cornu, Auguste 1958, *Karl Marx et Friedrich Engels*, Paris: Presses Universitaires de France, 2 vol.

Davis, Horace B. 1967, *Nationalism and Socialism: Marxism and Labor Theories of Nationalism to 1917*, New York: Monthly Review Press.

Deak, Istvan 1968, 'Budapest and the Hungarian Revolution', *Slavonic and East European Review*, vol. 46, no. 106, pp. 129–40.

De Felice, Renzo 2001 [1993], *The Jews in Fascist Italy*, New York: Enigma Books.

Della Pergola, Sergio 1983, *La trasformazione demografica della diaspora ebraica*, Turin: Loescher.

Derrida, Jacques 1993, 'Circumfession', in *Jacques Derrida*, edited by Geoffrey Bennington, Chicago: Chicago University Press.

Derrida, Jacques 1994, *Specters of Marx*, New York: Routledge.

Deutscher, Isaac 1968, *The Non-Jewish Jew and Other Essays*, Introduction by Tamara Deutscher, London: Oxford University Press.

Diner, Dan 1985, 'Percezione e identità. Considerazioni storico-psicologiche sul sionismo e sull'Olocausto', in Brunazzi and Fubini 1985, pp. 45–51.

Diner Dan 2000, *Beyond the Conceivable: Studies on Germany, Nazism, and the Holo-*

caust, Berkeley: University of California Press: 'Rationality and Rationalization: An Economist Explanation of the Final Solution', pp. 138–59; 'Nazism and Stalinism: On Memory, Arbitrariness, Labor, and Death', pp. 187–200.

Dinse, Helmut and Sol Liptzin 1978, *Einführung in die jiddische Literatur*, Stuttgart: Metzler.

Draper, Hal 1977, 'Marx and the Economic-Jew Stereotype', *Marx's Theory of Revolution*, New York: Monthly Review Press, vol. 1, pp. 591–608.

Dubnov, Simon 1961, 'Letters on Old and New Judaism' (1897–1907), *Nationalism and History: Essays on Old and New Judaism*, Cleveland: Meridian Books – The Jewish Publication Society of America.

Dupeux, Louis 1976, *'National-Bolchevisme' en Allemagne sous la République de Weimar, 1919–1923*, Lille: Champion.

Eiland, Howard and Michael W. Jennings 2014, *Walter Benjamin: A Critical Life*, Cambridge, MA: Harvard University Press.

Ellenbogen, Wilhelm 1899, 'Der Wiener Antisemitismus', *SM*, vol. 5, no. 9, 418–25.

Emmanuel, B. 1895, 'Über den Zionismus', *DNZ*, 13/2, pp. 599–603.

Epler, Ernst 1986, 'Tu es Juif ...', in Ruth Beckermann (ed.), *Vienne, rue du Temple. Le quartier juif 1918–1938*, Paris: Hazan, pp. 74–81.

Ertel, Rachel 1982, *Le Shtetl. La bourgade juive de Pologne*, Paris: Payot.

Ettinger, Elizbieta 1979, 'Comrade and Lover: Rosa Luxemburg's Letters to Leo Jogiches', *New German Critique*, no. 17, pp. 129–42.

Farber, Samuel 2014, 'Deutscher and the Jews', *New Politics*, XIV, no. 4, pp. 83 sq.

Feuer, Lewis S. 1972, 'The Conversion of Karl Marx's Father', *Jewish Journal of Sociology* 14/2, pp. 149–66.

Fetscher, Irving (ed.) 1974, *Marxisten gegen Antisemitismus*, Hamburg: Hoffmann und Campe.

Feuerbach, Ludwig 1881, *Essence of Christianity*, London: Trübner.

Finzi, Roberto 1981, 'Una anomalia nazionale: la "questione ebraica"', in *Storia del marxismo*, edited by Eric Hobsbawm, Turin: Einaudi, vol. 3/2, pp. 897–936.

Finzi, Roberto 1983, 'La storia in cammino: Marx, Engels e la questione nazionale', *Critica marxista*, no. 5, pp. 129–40.

Finzi, Roberto 1985, 'Il movimento operaio e la questione ebraica', in Brunazzi and Fubini 1985, pp. 52–64.

Fishman, David E. 2005, *The Rise of Modern Yiddish Culture*, Pittsburg: University of Pittsburg Press.

Flechteim, Ossip K. 1972, *Le Parti communiste allemand (KPD) sous la République de Weimar*, Paris: Maspero.

Fontenay, Elisabeth de 1973, *Les figures juives de Marx*, Paris: Galilée.

Frank, Pierre 1979, *Histoire de l'Internationale communiste, 1919–1943*, Paris: La Brèche, 2 vol.

Frankel, Jonathan 1981, *Prophecy and Politics, Socialism, Nationalism and the Russian Jews 1862–1917*, New York: Cambridge University Press.

Freud, Sigmund 2005 [1930], *Civilization and its Discontents*, New York: Norton.

Friede, H. 1937, 'Le premier congrès mondial contre le fanatisme raciste et l'antisémitisme', *La Correspondance Internationale* (17), no. 40.

Friedländer, Saul 1997, *Nazi Germany and the Jews: I. The Years of Persecution, 1933–1939*, New York: Harper Collins.

Frölich, Paul 2010 [1939], *Rosa Luxemburg*, Chicago: Haymarket Books.

Gay, Peter 1975, 'Encounter with Modernism: German Jews in German Culture 1888–1914', *Midstream* 21, no. 2, pp. 23–65.

Gay, Peter 2001 [1968], *Weimar Culture: The Outsider as Insider*, New York: Norton.

Geras, Norman 1998, 'Marxists Before the Holocaust', *The Contract of Mutual Indifference: Political Philosophy after the Holocaust*, London: Verso, pp. 139–70.

Gerschenkon, Alexander 1965, 'Lo sviluppo economico nella storia della cultura russa dell'Ottocento', *Il problema storico dell'arretratezza economica*, Turin: Einaudi.

Getzler, Israel 2003, *Martov: A Political Biography of a Russian Social Democrat*, Cambridge: Cambridge University Press.

Gilboa, Yehoshua A. 1978, 'Hebrew Literature in the USSR', in *The Jews in the Soviet Union since 1917*, edited by Lionel Kochan, Oxford: Oxford University Press, pp. 226–41.

Gilman, Sander 1986, *Jewish Self-Hatred: Anti-Semitism and the Hidden Language of the Jews*, Baltimore: The Johns Hopkins University Press.

Gitelman, Zvi 1972, *Jewish Nationality and Soviet Politics. The Jewish Sections of the CPSU, 1917–1930*, Princeton: Princeton University Press.

Golbach, Marie-Luise 1973, *Karl Radek und die deutsch-sowietischen Beziehungen 1918–1923*, Bonn-Bad Godesberg: Verlag Neue Gesellschaft.

Goldhagen, Daniel J. 1996, *Hitler's Willing Executioners: Ordinary Germans and the Holocaust*, London: Little, Brown.

Goldmann, Lucien 1963, 'Pour une approche marxiste des études sur le marxisme', *Annales*, vol. 18, no. 1, pp. 114–18.

Goldscheider, Calvin and Alan Zuckerman 1986, *The Transformation of the Jews*, Chicago: University of Chicago Press.

Goldsmith, Emanuel S. 1987, *Modern Yiddish Culture: The Story of the Yiddish Language Movement*, New York: Shapolsky Publishers.

Gordon, Milton M. 1964, *Assimilation in American Life: The Role of Race, Religion and National Origins*, New York: Oxford University Press.

Gramsci, Antonio 1958, *Scritti giovanili 1914–1918*, Turin: Einaudi.

Gramsci, Antonio 1996, *Prison Letters*, London: Pluto Press.

Gramsci, Antonio 1973, *Lettere dal carcere*, Turin: Einaudi.

Gramsci, Antonio 1975, *Quaderni del carcere*, edited by Valentino Gerratana, Turin: Einaudi, 4 vol.

Gramsci, Antonio 1994, *Letters from Prison*, edited by Frank Rosengarten, New York: Columbia University Press, 2 vol.

Gramsci, Antonio 1995, *Further Selection from the Prison Notebooks*, edited by Derek Boothman, Minneapolis: University of Minnesota Press.

Green, Nancy 1985, 'Socialist Anti-Semitism, Defense of a Bourgeois Jew and Discovery of the Jewish Proletariat: Changing Attitudes of French Socialists Before 1914', *International Review of Social History*, vol. 30, no. 3, pp. 374–99.

Green, Nancy 1986, *The Pletzl of Paris: Jewish Immigrants Workers in the Belle Epoque*, New York: Holmes & Meier.

Greffrath, Krista R. 1975, 'Der historische Materialist als Dialektischer. Zum Motiv der Rettung in Walter Benjamin Thesen "Über den Begriff der Geschichte"', in Bulthaup 1975, pp. 193–230.

Grunfelf, Fredric V. 1979, *Prophets Without Honor: Freud, Kafka, Einstein, and their World*, New York: Holt.

Guérin, Daniel 1983a [1934], *La peste brune*, Paris: Maspero.

Guérin, Daniel 1983b [1936], *Fascisme et grand capital*, Paris: Maspero.

Gurevitz, G.B. 1974, 'Un cas de communisme national en Union Soviétique: le Poalé-Zion, 1918–1928', *Cahiers du monde russe et soviétique*, vol. 5, no. 3–4, pp. 333–61.

Guttmann, Julius 1973, *Philosophies of Judaism*, New York: Schocken.

Habermas, Jürgen 1972, 'Bewußtmachende oder rettende Kritik: die Aktualität Walter Benjamins', in Unseld 1972, pp. 173–224.

Häcker, S. 1895, 'Über den Zionismus', *DNZ*, XIV/2, pp. 759–61.

Halevi, Ilan 1981, *Question juive. La tribu, la loi, l'espace*, Paris: Éditions de Minuit.

Hanstein, Ulrich 1969, *Sozialismus und nationale Frage in Polen. Die Entwicklung der sozialistischen Bewegung in Kongrepolen von 1875 bis 1900 unter besonderer Berücksichtigung der Polnischen Sozialistischen Partei (PPS)*, Cologne: Bökhau Verlag.

Haupt, Georges 1974, 'Les marxistes et la question nationale: histoire du problème', in Haupt, Löwy, and Weill 1974, pp. 9–61.

Haupt, Georges and Marie, Jean-Jacques (eds.) 1969, *Les bolcheviks par eux-mêmes*, Paris: Maspero.

Haupt, Georges and Madeleine Rebérioux 1967, *La Deuxième Internationale et l'Orient*, Paris: Cujas.

Haupt George and Claudie Weill 1974, 'Marx et Engels devant le problème des nations', *Cahiers de l'ISEA* 8, no. 10, pp. 1431–86.

Haupt, Georges, Löwy, Michael and Weill, Claudie (eds.) 1974, *Les marxistes et la question nationale 1848–1914*, Paris: Maspero.

Haupt, Georges 1980, 'Dynamisme et conservatisme de l'idéologie: Rosa Luxemburg à l'orée de la recherche marxiste dans le domaine national', *L'historien et le mouvement social*, Paris: Maspero, pp. 293–341.

Heidegger, Martin 1993 [1954], 'The Question Concerning Technology', *Basic Writings*, David Farrell Krell (ed.), New York: Harper Collins, pp. 307–42.

Hellige, Hans Dieter 1979, 'Generationskonflikt, Selbsthaß und die Enstehung antikapitalistischen Positionen in Judentum', *Geschichte und Gesellschaft*, vol. 5, no. 4, pp. 476–518.

Heller, Klaus 1977, *Revolutionärer Sozialismus und nationale Frage. Das Problem des Nationalismus bei russischen und jüdischen Sozialdemokraten und Sozial-revolutionären im Russischen Reich bis zur Revolution 1905–1907*, Frankfurt: Peter Lang.

Heller, Otto 1933, *La fin du judaïsme*, Paris: Rieder.

Herbert, Ulrich 1987, 'Arbeit und Vernichtung. Oekonomisches Interesse und Primat der "Weltanschauung" im Nationalsozialismus', in Dan Diner (ed.), *Ist der Nationalsozialismus Geschichte?*, Frankfurt: Fischer, pp. 198–236.

Herf, Jeffrey 1984, *Reactionary Modernism: Technology, Culture, and Politics in Weimar and the Third Reich*, New York: Cambridge University Press.

Hering, Christoph 1983, *Die Rekonstruktion der Revolution. Walter Benjamins messianischer Materialismus in der Thesen 'Über den Begriff der Geschichte'*, Frankfurt: Peter Lang.

Hertz, Y.Sh. (ed.) 1960, *Di geshikte fun Bund*, New York: Farlag Unser Tsait, 2 vol.

Hess, Moses 1921 [1841], 'Über das Geldwesen', *Sozialistische Aufsätze (1841–1847)*, Berlin: Welt Verlag, p. 179 sq.

Hess, Jonathan M. 2002, *Germans, Jews and the Claims of Modernity*, New Haven: Yale University Press.

Hilberg, Raul 1985, *The Destruction of the European Jews*, New York: Holmes and Meier, 3 vol.

Hilberg, Raul 1996, *The Politics of Memory: The Journey of a Holocaust Historian*, Chicago: Ivan R. Dee.

Hirsch, Helmut 1963, 'Marxiana judaica', *Cahiers de l'ISEA*, n. 7, pp. 5–52.

Hobsbawm, Eric J. 1973, 'Intellectuals and the Class Struggle', *Revolutionaries: Contemporary Essays*, New York: Pantheon Books, pp. 245–65.

Hobsbawm, Eric J. 1979, 'La cultura europea e il marxismo', in *Storia del marxismo*, vol. 2, *Il marxismo nell'età della Seconda Internazionale*, Turin: Einaudi, pp. 62–108.

Hobsbawm, Eric J. 1996, *The Age of Extremes: The Short Twentieth Century 1914–1991*, New York: Vintage Books.

Hobsbawm, Eric J. 1997, 'Commentaires', *Le Débat*, no. 93, pp. 88–9.

Hobsbawm, Eric J. 2011, 'The Influence of Marxism 1880–1914', *How to Change the World: Tales of Marx and Marxism*, London: Little, Brown, pp. 211–60.

Horkheimer, Max 1992 [1947], *Eclipse of Reason*, New York: Continuum.

Horkheimer, Max and Theodor W. Adorno 1985 [1949], 'Introduction' to Massing 1985, pp. V–VIII.

Horkheimer, Max 1989 [1939], 'The Jews and Europe', in Bronner and Kellner 1989, pp. 77–94.

Horkheimer, Max and Theodor W. Adorno 2002 [1947], *Dialectic of Enlightenment: Philocophical Fragments*, Stanford: Stanford University Press.

Howe, Irving 1976, *World of Our Fathers: The Journey of the East European Jews to America and the Life They Found and Made*, New York: Schocken Books.

Howe, Irving 1978, *Trotsky*, London: Fontana.

Jacobs, Jack 1992, *On Socialists and 'The Jewish Question' After Marx*, New York: New York University.

Jacobs, Jack 2015, *The Frankfurt School, Jewish Lives, and Anti-Semitism*, New York: Cambridge University Press.

Jaspers, Karl 1957, *The Question of German Guilt*, New York: Dial Press.

Jay, Martin 1973, *The Dialectical Imagination. A History of the Frankfurt School and the Institute of Social Research, 1923–1950*, Boston: Little, Brown.

Jay, Martin 1986, *Permanent Exiles. Essays on Intellectual Migration from Germany to America*, New York: Columbia University Press: 'Anti-Semitism and the German Left', pp. 79–89; 'The Jews and the Frankfurt School: Critical theory's analysis of anti-Semitism', pp. 90–100.

Kaiser, Gerhard 1975, 'Walter Benjamins "Geschichtsphilosophischen Thesen"', in Bülthaup 1975, pp. 43–76.

Kampe, Norbert 1985, 'Akademisierung der Juden und Beginn eines studentischen Antisemitismus', in *Jüdisches Leben*, edited by Wolfgang Dreßen, Berlin: Verlag Aesthetik und Kommunikation, pp. 10–23.

Kampmann, Wanda 1981, *Deutsche und Juden*, Frankfurt: Fischer.

Karady, Victor and Kemeny, Istvan 1978, 'Les Juifs dans la structure de classe en Hongrie', *Actes de la recherche en sciences sociales*, no. 22, pp. 25–59.

Katz, Jacob 1962, *Exclusiveness and Tolerance: Studies in Jewish-Gentile Relations in Medieval and Modern Times*, New York: Schocken Books.

Katz, Jacob 1973, *Out of the Ghetto: The Social Background of Jewish Emancipation, 1770–1870*, Cambridge: Harvard University Press.

Katz, Jacob 1982, 'The Term "Emancipation": Its Origin and Historical Impact', *Zur Assimilation und Emanzipation der Juden*, Darmstadt: Wissenschaftliche Buchgesellschaft, pp. 99–123.

Kautsky, Karl 1887, 'Die moderne Nationalität', *DNZ*, 5/10, pp. 442–51.

Kautsky, Karl 1899, 'Un mot de Kautsky', *La Petite République*, 24 July.

Kautsky, Karl 1890, 'Das Judentum', *DNZ*, VIII, pp. 23–30.

Kautsky, Karl 1902–3, 'Das Massaker von Kishineff und die Judenfrage', *DNZ*, XXI, 2/36, pp. 303–9.

Kautsky, Karl 1908, 'Nationalität und Internationalität', *Erganzungshefte zur Neuen Zeit*.

Kautsky, Karl 1910, *Der Ursprung des Christentums*, Stuttgart: Dietz Verlag.

Kautsky, Karl 1917, *Die Befreiung der Nationen*, Stuttgart: Dietz Verlag.

Kautsky, Karl 1921, *Rasse und Judentum*, Stuttgart: Dietz Verlag.

Kazdan, H.S. 1960, 'Der Bund biz dem finftn tsuzamenfor', in Hertz 1960, vol. 1, pp. 107–279.

Kenig, Eddy 1976, *Lénine et les Juifs de Russie. Contribution à l'étude des conceptions de Lénine sur la question juive*, Paris: Centre d'études et de recherches marxistes.

Kessler, Mario 1993, *Antisemitismus, Zionismus und Sozialismus. Arbeiterbewegung und jüdische Frage im 20. Jahrhundert*, Maniz: Decaton.

Kessler, Mario 1994, *Zionismus und internationale Arbeiterbewegung 1897 bis 1933*, Berlin: Akademie Verlag.

Kessler, Mario 2003, *Arthur Rosenberg: Ein Historiker im Zeitalter der Katastrophen (1889–1943)*, Cologne: Böhlau.

Kessler, Mario 2013, *Ruth Fischer: Ein Leben mit und gegen Kommunisten (1895–1961)*, Cologne: Böhlau.

Kershaw, Ian 2000, *The Nazi Dictatorship: Problems and Perspectives of Interpretation*, New York: Oxford University Press.

Khalidi, Rashid 2010, *Palestinian Identity: The Construction of Modern National Consciousness*, New York: Columbia University Press.

Kiel, Mark 1970, 'The Jewish Narodnik', *Judaism*, no. 19, pp. 295–310.

Knepper, Paul 2013, 'Lombroso and Jewish Social Science', in *The Cesare Lombroso Handbook*, edited by P. Knepper, P.J. Istehede, New York: Routledge, pp. 171–86.

Knütter, Hans-Helmut 1977, *Die Juden und die deutsche Linke in der Weimarer Republik 1918–1923*, Düsseldorf: Droste Verlag.

Kocka, Jürgen 1988, 'German history before Hitler: The debate about the German *Sonderweg*', *Journal of Contemporary History* vol. 23, no. 1, pp. 3–16.

Kohn, Hans 1961, *Martin Buber: sein Werk und seine Zeit*, Stuttgart: Melzer.

Kolatt, Israel 1977, 'Zionist Marxism', in *Varieties of Marxism*, edited by Shlomo Avineri, The Hague: Martinus Nijhoff, pp. 227–70.

Kosowski, Wladimir 1943 [1928], 'Wladimir Medem un di natsionale frage', in Medem 1943.

Kraft, Werner 1972, 'Über Walter Benjamin', in Unseld 1972, pp. 59–69.

Kriegel, Annie 1977, *Les Juifs et le monde modern*, Paris: Éditions du Seuil.

Künzli, Arnold 1969, *Karl Marx. Eine Psychographie*, Vienna: Europaverlag.

Kwiet, Konrad 1976, 'Historians of the German Democratic Republic on anti-Semitism and persecution', *LBIYB*, vol. 21, no. 1, pp. 173–98.

Ignatieff, J. 1893, 'Russisch-jüdische Arbeiter über die Judenfrage', *DNZ*, XI, 1, pp. 175–9.

Israel, Jonathan 2001, *Radical Enlightenment: Philosophy and the Making of Modernity 1650–1750*, New York: Oxford University Press.

Lamm, Hans 1969, *Karl Marx und das Judentum*, Munich: Max Hüber Verlag.

Lampert, Alexander 1905–6, 'Der Poalei-Zionismus. Eine neue Strömung im russischen Judentum', *DNZ*, XXIV, 1, pp. 804–16.

Landes, David 1974, 'The Jewish Merchant: Typology and Stereotypology', *LBIYB*, Vol. 19, pp. 11–24.

Laqueur, Walter 1965, *Russia and Germany*, London: Little, Brown, 1965.

Laqueur, Walter 1976, *A History of Zionism*, New York: Schocken Books.

Lazitch, B. and Drachovich, M. 1973, *Biographical Dictionary of the Comintern*, Stanford: Hoover Institution Press.

Lazare, Bernard 1969, *L'antisémitisme. Son histoire et ses causes*, Paris: Documents et Témoignages.

Le Goff, Jacques 1972, *Marchands et banquiers au Moyen Age*, Paris: Presses universitaires de France.

Lenin 1976 [1913], *Critical Notes on the National Question*, Moscow: Progress Publishers.

Leon, Abram 1970 [1950], *The Jewish Question: A Marxist Interpretation*, New York: Merit Publishers.

Lerner, Warner 1970, *Karl Radek: The Last Internationalist*, Stanford: Stanford University Press.

Leslie, Esther 2000, *Walter Benjamin: Overpowering Conformism*, London: Pluto Press.

Leslie, Esther 2007, *Walter Benjamin*, London: Reaktion Books.

Lessing, Theodor 1984 [1930], *Der jüdisches Selbsthaß*, Munich: Matthes & Seiz.

Lestschinsky, Jakob 1979, 'Nos revendications nationales' (1905), *Pluriel-Débat*, no. 20, pp. 69–96.

Levi, Primo 1997, 'Buco nero di Auschwitz', *Opere*, edited by Marco Belpoliti, Turin: Einaudi, vol. 2, pp. 1321–4.

Levin, Nora 1977, *While Messiah Tarried: Jewish Socialist Movements 1871–1917*, New York: Schocken Books.

Levis-Sullam, Simon 2007, 'Arnaldo Momigliano e la 'nazionalizzazione parallela:' autobiografia, religion, storia', *Passato e Presente*, vol. 25, no. 70, pp. 59–82.

Liebeschutz, Hans 1964, 'Max Weber Historical Interpretation of Judaism', *LBIYB*, Vol. 9, no. 1.

Liebknecht, Wilhelm 1899, 'Nachträgliches zur "Affaire"', *Die Fackel*, no. 18, pp. 1–10; no. 19, pp. 1–12.

Liessman, Konrad-Paul 1993, *Günther Anders*, Hamburg: Junius Verlag.

Lindenhecken, D. 1923 [23 August], 'Die neuen Antisemiten', *Vorwärts*.

Lombroso, Cesare 1894, *Der Antisemitismus und die Juden im Lichte der modernen Wissenschaft*, Leipzig: Georg Wigand's Verlag.

Low, Alfred 1958, *Lenin on the Question of Nationality*, New York: Bookman Associates.

Löw, Raimund (ed.) 1984, *Der Zerfall der 'Kleinen Internationale.' Nationalitätenkonflikte in der Arbeiterbewegung des alten Österreich 1889–1914*, Vienna: Europaverlag.

Löwenthal, Leo 1946, 'Terror's atomization of man: The crisis of the individual', *Commentary*, no. 1, pp. 1–8.

Löwith, Karl 1949, *Meaning in History. The Theological Implications of the Philosophy of History*, Chicago: University of Chicago Press.

Löwy, Michael 1970, *La théorie de la révolution chez le jeune Marx*, Paris: Maspero.

Löwy, Michael 1974, 'Le problème de l'histoire: remarques de théorie et de méthode', in Haupt, Löwy, Weill 1974, pp. 370–91.

Löwy, Michael 1981a, 'Marx and Engels: Cosmopolites', *Critique*, no. 14, pp. 5–12.

Löwy, Michael 1981b, *Uneven and Combined Development. The Theory of Permanent Revolution*, London: Verso Edition.

Löwy, Michael 1981c, 'Messianisme juif et utopies libertaires en Europe centrale (1905–1923)', *Archives de Science Sociales des Religions* 51, no. 1, pp. 5–47.

Löwy, Michael 1985, 'Le messianisme romantique de Gustav Landauer', *Archives de Sciences Sociales des Religions*, 60, no. 1, pp. 55–66.

Löwy, Michael 1987, 'The Romantic and Marxist critique of modern civilization', *Theory and Society*, no. 16, pp. 891–904.

Löwy, Michael 1988, *Rédemption et utopie: Le Judaïsme libertaire en Europe central*, Paris: Presses Universitaires de France.

Löwy, Michael 1992, *Redemption and Utopia: Jewish Libertarian Thought in Central Europe: A Study in Elective Affinity*, Stanford: Stanford University Press.

Löwy, Michael 1993, *On Changing the World: Essays in Political Philosophy, from Karl Marx to Walter Benjamin*, Atlantic Highlands, NJ: Humanities Press.

Michael Löwy, 'Ernest Mandel's Revolutionary Humanism', in Achcar 1999, pp. 24–37.

Löwy, Michael 2004, *Franz Kafka. Rêveur insoumis*, Paris: Stock.

Löwy, Michael 2006, *Fire Alarm: Reading Walter Benjamin's 'On the Concept of History'*, London: Verso.

Löwy, Michael 2013, *La cage d'acier. Max Weber et le marxisme wébérien*, Paris: Stock.

Löwy, Michael and Eleni Varikas 1993, ''L'esprit du monde sur les ailes d'une fusée:' la critique du progrès chez Adorno', *Revue des Sciences Humaines*, no. 229, pp. 47–60.

Losurdo, Domenico 1996, *Il revisionismo storico: Problemi e miti*, Bari: Laterza.

Lukács, Georg 1971, *History and Class Consciousness: Studies in Marxist Dialectics*, Cambridge, MA: MIT Press.

Lukács, Georg 1981 [1954], *The Destruction of Reason*, Atlantic Highlands, NJ: Humanities Press.

Lunn, Eugene 1985, *Marxism and Modernism: Lukács, Brecht, Benjamin, Adorno*, London: Verso.

Luxemburg, Rosa 1963 [1918], 'Fragment über Krieg, nationale Frage und Revolution', *Die Russische Revolution*, Frankfurt: Europäische Verlagsanstalt.

Luxemburg, Rosa 1950, *Briefe an Freunde*, Hamburg: Europäische Verlagsanstalt.

Luxemburg, Rosa 1970, *La crise de la Social-démocratie*, Brussels: La Taupe, 1970.

Luxemburg, Rosa 1971, 'Affaire Dreyfus et cas Millerand. Réponse à une consultation internationale', *Cahiers de la Quinzaine*, no. 11 (1899), in Rosa Luxemburg, *Le socialisme en France 1898–1912*, Paris: Belfond.

Luxemburg, Rosa 1972, 'Die Krise in Frankreich', *Sächsische Arbeiter-Zeitung* (29 October 1898), *Gesammelte Werke*, Berlin: Dietz, vol. 1/1.

Luxemburg, Rosa 1974, 'Diskussion' (1910); 'Rufzüg auf der ganzen Linie' (1910); 'Nach dem Pogrom' (1910), respectively in Fetscher 1974, pp. 141–50; pp. 136–40; pp. 127–35.

Luxemburg, Rosa 1976, *The National Question: Selected Writings*, New York: Monthly Review Press.

Luxemburg, Rosa 2013, *The Letters of Rosa Luxemburg*, London: Verso.

Magris, Claudio 1979, *Joseph Roth e la tradizione ebraico orientale*, Turin: Einaudi.

Mahaim, Annik 1979, 'Les femmes et la social-démocratie allemande', in *Femmes et mouvement ouvrier*, edited by A. Mahaim, A. Holt, and J. Heinen, Paris: Éditions la Brèche.

Mandel, Ernest 1970 [1946], 'Introduction' and 'A Biographical Sketch of Abram Leon', in Leon 1970, respectively pp. 1–11 and pp. 15–31.

Mandel, Ernest 1974, *Du fascisme*, Paris: Maspero.

Mandel, Ernest 1978, *Late Capitalism*, London: Verso.

Mandel, Ernest 1979, *Trotsky: A Study in the Dynamic of His Thought*, London: Verso.

Mandel, Ernest 1980, *Trotsky*, Paris: Maspero.

Mandel, Ernest 1986, *The Meaning of the Second World War*, London: Verso.

Mandel, Ernest 1990, 'Die zukünftige Funktion des Marxismus', in *Das verspielte 'Kapital?' Die marxistische Ideologie nach dem Scheitern des realen Sozialismus*, edited by Hans Spatzenegger Salzburg: Verlag Anton Pustet, pp. 171–86.

Mandel, Ernest 1991, 'Zum Historikerstreit: Ursprung, Wesen, Einmaligkeit und Reproduzierbarkeit des Dritten Reiches', *Der zweite Weltkrieg*, Frankfurt: ISP Verlag, pp. 209–45.

Mandel, Ernest 1995, 'Trotsky and the Jewish Question', *Trotsky as Alternative*, London: Verso, pp. 146–56.

Mandel, Ernest 1999 [1990], 'Material, Social, and Ideological Preconditions for the Nazi Genocide', in *The Legacy of Ernest Mandel*, edited by Gilbert Achcar, London: Verso, pp. 225–31.

Mannheim, Karl 1936 [1921], *Ideology and Utopia: An Introduction to the Sociology of Knowledge*, New York: Harcourt.

Marcuse, Herbert 1964, *One-Dimensional Man*, Boston: Beacon Press.

Marcuse, Herbert 1955, *Eros and Civilization: A Philosophical Inquiry into Freud*, Boston: Beacon Press.

Marcuse, Herbert 1968 [1934], 'The Struggle Against Liberalism in the Totalitarian View of the State', *Negations*, Boston: Beacon, pp. 3–42.

Marcuse, Herbert 1975, 'Revolution und Kritik der Gewalt. Zur Geschichtsphilosophie Walter Benjamins', in Bülthaup 1975, pp. 23–7.

Marcuse, Herbert 1998 [1947], 'Heidegger and Marcuse: A Dialogue in Letters', *Technology, War and Fascism*, edited by Douglas Kellner, New York: Routledge, pp. 261–7.

Marienstras, Richard 1977, *Etre un peuple en diaspora*, Paris: Maspero.

Marx, Karl 1951, *Capital*, Moscow: Progress, vol. 3.

Marx, Karl 1953, *Grundrisse der Kritik der politischen Ökonomie*, Berlin: Dietz Verlag.

Marx, Karl 1960, *On Colonialism*, Moscow: Progress.

Marx, Karl 1973, *Foundations of the Critique of the Political Economy: Rough Draft*, London: Penguin Books.

Marx, Karl 1994 [1843], 'On the Jewish Question', *Early Political Writings*, edited by Joseph O'Malley and Richard A. Davis, Cambridge, UK: Cambridge University Press, pp. 28–56.

Marx, Engels 1956–90, *Werke* [MEW]: Marx, 'Zur Judenfrage' (1843), vol. 1; Marx, Engels, 'Die heilige Familie' (1844), vol. 2; Marx, Engels, 'Die deutsche Ideologie' (1845), vol. 3; Marx, Engels, 'Manifest der kommunistischen Partei' (1848), vol. 4; Engels, 'Neue Teilungs Polen' (1848), vol. 5; Engels, 'Posen', 'Der magyarische Kampf' (1848), vol. 6; Marx, Engels, 'Revolution und Konterrevolution in Deutschland' (1849), vol. 8; Engels, 'Über Antisemitismus' (1890), vol. 22; Marx, 'Das Kapital' (1867), vol. 23.

Marx, Karl and Friedrich Engels 1956 [1845], *The Holy Family*, London: Lawrence & Wishart.

Marx, Karl and Friedrich Engels 2012 [1848], *The Communist Manifesto*, London: Verso.

Marrus, Michael R. 1981, *The Politics of Assimilation: The French Jewish Community at the Time of the Dreyfuss Affair*, Oxford: Oxford University Press.

Mason, Tim 1966, 'Das Primat der Politik', *Das Argument*, no. 41, pp. 473–94.

Mason, Tim W. 1993, *Social Policy in the Third Reich*, Oxford: Berg.

Massara, Massimo (ed.) 1972, *Il marxismo e la question ebraica*, Milan: Edizioni del Calendario.

Martin, Terry 2001, *The Affirmitive Action Empire: Nations and Nationalism in the Soviet Union, 1923–1939*, Ithaca, NY: Cornell University Press.

Mayer, Arno J. 1988, *Why Did the Heavens Not Darken? The Final Solution in History*, New York: Pantheon Books.

Mayer, Arno J. 2008, *Plowshares into Swords: From Zionism to Israel*, London: Verso.

Mayer, Hans 1983, *Outsiders: A Study of Life and Letters*, Cambridge: MIT Press.

Massing, Paul 1985 [1949], *Vorgeschichte des politischen Antisemitismus*, Frankfurt am Main: Syndikat/EVA.

Matard-Bonucci, Marie-Anne 2006, *L'Italie fasciste et la persecution des Juifs*, Paris: Perrin.

McLellan, David 1970, *Marx Before Marxism*, London: Macmillan.

Medem, Vladimir 1917, *Zichroines un artiklen*, Warsaw: Verlag Yidish.

Medem, Vladimir 1943, *Tsum tswantsikstn yartsayt*, New York: American Representation of the General Jewish Workers' Union of Poland.

Medem, Wladimir 1974 [1910], 'Der moderne Antisemitismus in Rußland', in Fetscher 1974, pp. 120–5.

Medem, Vladimir 1979, *Memoirs: The Life and Soul of a Legendary Jewish Socialist*, New York: KTAV.

Meghnagi, David 1985, 'Una società di paria e di "luftmenshn", Gli ebrei dell'est, la questione ebraica e il socialismo ebraico. Considerazioni storicopsicologiche', in Brunazzi and Fubini 1985, pp. 172–84

Mehring, Franz 1891, 'Anti- und Philosemitisches', *DNZ*, IX/2, pp. 585–8.

Mehring, Franz 1923, *Aus dem literarischen Nachlaß von Karl Marx und Friedrich Engels*, Berlin-Stuttgart: Dietz.

Mehring, Franz 2003 [1936], *Karl Marx: The Story of His Life*, London: Routledge.

Mendel, Hersch 1982, *Mémoires d'un révolutionnaire juif*, Grenoble: Presses Universitaire de Grenoble.

Mendelsohn Ezra 1983, *The Jews of East-Central Europe Between the World Wars*, Bloomington: Indiana University Press.

Mendelsohn, Ezra (ed.) 1997, *The Essential Papers on the Jews and the Left*, New York: New York University Press.

Menes, Abraham 1955, 'The Jewish Socialist Movement in Russia and Poland (1870–1897)', *The Jewish People. Past and Present*, New York: Jewish Encyclopedic Handbooks, pp. 355–68.

Merchav, Peretz 1976, 'Jüdische Aspekte in der Einschätzung von Rosa Luxemburg', in *Juden und jüdischen Aspekte in der deutschen Arbeiterbewegung*, edited by W. Grab, Tel Aviv: Institut für deutsche Geschichte, pp. 185–201.

Meszaros, Istvan 1970, *Marx's Theory of Alienation*, London: Merlin Press.

Michels, Robert 1957 [1911], *Soziologie des Parteiwesens in der modernen Demokratie*, Stuttgart: Alfred Kröner Verlag.

Milchman, Alan 2003, 'Marxism and the Holocaust', *Hitstorical Materialism*, vol. 11/3, pp. 97–120.

Mill, John 1946–9, *Pionirn un boiern*, New York: Farlag Der Veker, 2 vol.

Mishkinski, Moses 1969, 'Regional Factors in the Formation of the Jewish Labor Movement in Tsarist Russia', *YIVO Annual of Jewish Social Science* 14, pp. 27–52.

Misrahi, Robert 1972, *Marx et la question juive*, Paris: Gallimard.

Momigliano, Arnaldo 1980, 'A Note on Max Weber Definition of Judaism as a Pariah Religion', *History and Theory*, Vol. 19, no. 3, pp. 313–18.

Momigliano, Arnaldo 1987b, *Pagine ebraiche*, Turin: Einaudi.

Monnier, Adrianne 1972, 'Ein Porträt Walter Benjamins', in Unseld 1972.

Montefiore, Simon Sebag 2008, *Young Stalin*, New York: Vintage.

Moses, Stéphane 2008, *The Angel of History: Benjamin, Rosenzweig, Scholem*, Stanford: Stanford University Press.

Moss, Kenneth B. 2009, *Jewish Renaissance in the Russian Revolution*, Cambridge: Harvard University Press.

Mosse, George L. 1964, *The Crisis of German Ideology*, New York: Schocken.

Mosse, George L. 1971, 'German Socialists and the Jewish Question in the Weimar Republic', *LBIYB*, 16/1, pp. 123–51.

Mosse, George L. 1978, *Toward the Final Solution: A History of European Racism*, New York: Howard Fertig.

Mosse, Werner 1976, 'Die Juden in Wirtschaft und Gesellschaft', in *Juden in Wilhelminischen Deutschland 1890–1914*, edited by Werner Mosse and Arnold Paucker, Tübingen: J.C.B. Mohr.

Mosse, Werner 1987, *Jews in German Economy: The German-Jewish Economic Elite 1820–1935*, New York: Oxford University Press.

Münster, Arno 1985, 'Ernst Bloch et Walter Benjamin: *Éléments d'analyse d'une amitié difficile*', *Figures de l'utopie dans la pensée d'Ernst Bloch*, Paris: Aubier, pp. 111–30.

Najenson, José Luis 1979, 'Marxismo y question nacional en el pensamiento de Borojov', in Borojov 1979, pp. 7–51.

Nedava, Joseph 1971, *Trotsky and the Jews*, Philadelphia: Jewish Publication Society of America.

Nettl, Peter 1966, *Rosa Luxemburg*, London: Oxford University Press, 2 vol.

Neumann, Franz 1967 [1944], *Behemoth: The Structure and Practice of National Socialism 1933–1944*, London: Frank Cass.

Neusüss, Christel 1986, 'Patriarcat et organisation du parti. Rosa Luxemburg critique des idées de ses comilitants masculins', in *Rosa Luxemburg aujourd'hui*, edited by Gilbert Badia and Claudie Weill, Paris: Presses universitaires de Vincennes, pp. 91–100.

Niethammer, Lutz 1989, *Posthistoire: Ist die Geschichte zu Ende?*, Hamburg: Rowohlt.

Niewyk, Donald 1980, *The Jews in Weimar Germany*, Manchester: Manchester University Press.

Njewsorow, S. 1897, 'Der Zionismus', *SM*, 3/12, pp. 645–51.

Nordau, Max 1993 [1899], *Degeneration*, Lincoln: University of Nebraska Press.

Olff-Nathan, Josiane (ed.) 1993, *La science sous le Troisième Reich*, Paris: Seuil, 1993.

Parinetto, Luciano 1980, 'Introduzione', in Karl Marx, *Sulla religion*, Florence: La Nuova Italia, 1980, pp. 9–121.

Patkin, Alexander 1947, *The Origins of the Russian-Jewish Labour Movement*, Melbourne: Chesire.

Perlmutter, A. 1969, 'Dov Ber Borokhov: A Marxist Zionist Ideologist', *Middle Eastern Studies* 5, no. 1, pp. 32–43.

Pernerstorfer, Engelbert 1916–17, 'Zur Judenfrage', *Der Jude*, vol. 1, pp. 307–15.

Pfabigan, Alfred 1986, 'Die austromarxistische Denkweise', in *Der Austromarxismus. Eine Autopsie*, edited by R. Löw, Si Mattl, and A. Pfabigan, Frankfurt: ISP Verlag, pp. 102–13.

Peukert, Detlev J. 1989, *The Weimar Republic*, London: Penguin Books.

Pinson, K.S. 1945, 'Arkadi Kremer, Vladimir Medem, and the Ideology of the Jewish Bund', *JSS*, vol. 7, no. 3, pp. 233–64.

Pirenne, Henri 1939, *Mohammed and Charlemagne*: New York: Norton.

Poliakov, Léon 1981, *Histoire de l'antisémitisme*, Paris: Calmann-Lévy, 2 vol.

Pollak, J. 1897–8, 'Der politische Zionismus', *DNZ*, XVI, 1, pp. 596–600.

Pollock, Friedrich 1941, 'Is National Socialism a new order', *Zeitschrift für Sozialfoschung/Studies in Philosophy and Social Science*, no. 9, pp. 200–25.

Pollock, Friedrich 1989 [1939], 'State Capitalism: Its Possibilities and Limitations', in Bronner, Kellner 1989, pp. 95–118.

Portelli, Hugues 1974, *Gramsci et la question religieuse*, Paris: Anthropos.

Postone, Moishe 1980, 'Anti-Semitism and National Socialism', *New German Critique*, no. 19, pp. 97–115.

Pullega, Paolo 1980, *Commento alle 'Tesi di filosofia della storia' di Walter Benjamin*, Bologna: Cappelli.

Pulzer, Peter J. 1988, *The Rise of Political Antisemitism in Germany and Austria*, Cambridge: Harvard University Press.

Rabinbach, Anson 1997, 'Between Enlightenment and Apocalypse: Benjamin, Bloch and Modern German Jewish Messianism', *In the Shadow of Catastrophe: German Intellectuals Between Apocalypse and Enlightenment*, Berkeley: University of California Press, pp. 27–65.

Radnoti, Sandor 1978, 'Benjamin's Politics', *Telos*, no. 37, pp. 63–81.

Raphaël, Freddy 1982, *Judaïsme et capitalisme. Essai sur la controverse entre Max Weber et Werner Sombart*, Paris: Presses Universitaires de France.

Raphaël, Freddy 1986, 'L'étranger et le paria dans l'oeuvre de Max Weber et de Georg Simmel', *Archives de Sciences Sociales des Religions*, 61, no. 1, pp. 63–81.

Rappoport, Charles 1951, 'The Life of a Revolutionary Émigré (Reminiscences)', *YIVO Annual of Jewish Social Studies*, vol. 6, pp. 106–36.

Ratner, Markus 1911, 'Die nationale Autonomie und das jüdische Proletariat', *SM*, vol. 17, no. 21, pp. 1333–42.

Renner, Karl [Synoptikus] 1974 [1899], 'État et nation', in Haupt, Löwy, and Weill 1974, pp. 212–29.

Robin, Régine 1984, *L'amour du yiddish. Ecriture juive et sentiment de la langue 1830–1930*, Paris: Editions du Sorbier.

Rodinson, Maxime 1968, 'Le marxisme et la nation', *L'Homme et la société*, no. 7.

Rodinson, Maxime 1981, *Peuple juif ou problème juif?*, Paris: Maspero.

Rosdolsky, Roman 1965, 'Workers and Fatherland: A Note on a Passage in *The Communist Manifesto*', *Science and Society*, 29, no. 3, pp. 330–7.

Rosdolsky, Roman 1979 [1948], *Zur nationalen Frage. Friedrich Engels und das Problem der 'geschichtslosen' Völker*, Berlin: Olle & Wolter.

Rosenberg, Arthur 1930, 'Treitschke und die Juden', *Die Gesellschaft*, vol. 7, no. 7, pp. 78–83.

Rosenberg, Arthur 1967 [1936], 'Der Faschismus als Massenbewegung', in *Faschismus und Kapitalismus. Theorien über die sozialen Ursprünge und Funktion des Faschismus*, edited by Wolfgang Abendroth, Frankfurt: Europäische Verlaganstalt-Europaverlag, pp. 75–141.

Rosenthal, E. 1944, 'Trends of the Jewish Population in Germany 1910–1939', *JSS*, vol. 6, no. 3, pp. 233–74.

Die Rote Fahne 1931 [15 November], 'Hitler proklamiert Rettung reicher Juden'.

Rotenstreich, Nathan 1959, 'For and Against Emancipation: The Bruno Bauer Controversy', *LBIYB*, 4, pp. 3–36.

Roth, Joseph 1984, 'Das Autodafé des Geistes' [1933], *Berliner Saisonberich. Reportagen und journalistischen Arbeiten 1920–1939*, by Joseph Roth, Cologne: Kiepenheuer & Witsch, pp. 381–91.

Roth, Joseph 1985 [1926], *Juden auf Wanderschaft*, Cologne: Kiepenheuer & Witsch.

Rozenblit, Marsha 1983, *The Jews of Vienna: Assimilation and Identity*, Albany: State of New York University Press.

Rubel, Maximilien 1957, *Karl Marx. Essai de biographie intellectuelle*, Paris: Marcel Rivière.

Ruben, David 1982, 'Marxism and the Jewish Question', *The Socialist Register*, London: Merlin Press, pp. 205–37.

Runes, Dagobert D. 1960, *A World Without Jews*, New York: Philosophical Library.

Sand, Shlomo 1984, 'Sorel, les Juifs et l'antisémitisme', *Cahiers Georges Sorel*, 2: 7–36.

Sarfatti, Michele 2006, *The Jews in Mussolini's Italy: From Equality to Persecution*, Madison: University of Wisconsin Press.

Schäfer, Michael 1994, *Die Rationatität des National sozialismus: Zur Kritik philosophischer Faschismus theorien am Beispiel der Kritischen Theorie*, Veinheim: Bekz-Athenäum.

Scheidemann, Philip 1905–6, 'Wandlungen des Antisemitismus', *DNZ*, XXIV, 22, pp. 632–6.

Scherrer, Jutta 1976 and 1977, 'Intelligentsia, Religion, Révolution. Premières manifestations d'un socialisme chrétien en Russie 1905–1907', *Cahiers du monde russe et soviétique*, vol. 17, no. 4, pp. 427–66; and vol. 18, nos. 1–2, pp. 5–32.

Schluchter, Wolfgang (ed.) 1981, *Max Webers Studie über das antike Judentum*, Frankfurt: Suhrkamp.

Schneider, Wolfgang (ed.) 1991, *'Vernichtungspolitik:' Eine Debatte über den Zusammen-*

hang von Sozialpolitik und Genozid im nationalsozialistischen Deutschland, Hamburg: Junius Verlag.

Scholem, Gershom 1971, 'Toward an Understanding of the Messianic Idea in Judaism', *The Messianic Idea in Judaism and Other Essays on Jewish Spirituality*, New York: Schocken Books, pp. 1–36.

Scholem, Gershom 1976, 'Jews and Germans', *On Jews and Judaism in Crisis: Selected Essays*, New York: Schocken Books, pp. 61–4.

Scholem, Gershom 1981, *Walter Benjamin: The Story of a Friendship*, New York: Schocken Books.

Schöne, Albrecht 1986, ''Diese nach jüdischem Vorbild erbaute Arche': Walter Benjamins Deutsche Menschen', in *Juden in der deutschen Literatur*, edited by Stefan Moses and Albrecht Schöne, Frankfurt: Suhrkamp, pp. 350–65.

Schumacher, Horst and Feliks Tych 1966, *Julian Marchlewski-Karski. Eine Biographie*, Berlin: Dietz Verlag.

Schwarz, Solomon 1951, *The Jews in the Soviet Union*, Syracuse: Syracuse University Press.

Shapiro, Leonard 1961, 'The Role of the Jews in the Russian Revolutionary Movement', *Slavonic and East European Review*, 9, no. 94, pp. 148–67.

Shanin, Theodore (ed.) 1984, *Late Marx and the Russian Road*, London: Routledge & Kegan Paul.

Shukman, Harold 1970, 'Lenin's Nationalities Policy and the Jewish Question: A Contribution to the Lenin Centenary', *Bulletin on Soviet and East European Jewish Affairs*, no. 5, pp. 43–50.

Silberner, Edmund 1949a, 'Was Marx an anti-Semite?', *Historia Judaica*, 11, no. 1, pp. 3–52.

Silberner, Edmund 1949b, 'Friedrich Engels and the Jews', *JSS*, vol. 11, no. 4, pp. 323–42.

Silberner, Edmund 1962, *Sozialisten zur Judenfrage. Ein Beitrag zur Geschichte der Sozialismus vom Anfang des 19. Jahrhunderts bis 1914*, Berlin: Colloquium Verlag.

Silberner, Edmund 1983, *Kommunisten zur Judenfrage. Zur Geschichte von Theorie und Praxis des Kommunismus*, Opladen: Westdeutscher Verlag.

Simmel, Georg 1964 [1908], 'The Stranger', in *The Sociology of Georg Simmel*, edited by Kurt H. Wolf, New York: The Free Press, pp. 402–8.

Slezkine, Yuri 1994, 'The USSR as a Communal Apartment, or How a Socialist State Promoted Ethnic Particularism', *Slavic Review* 53:2.

Slezkine, Yuri 2004, *The Jewish Century*, Princeton: Princeton University Press.

Sloves, Henri 1982, *L'État juif de l'Union soviétique*, Paris: Les Presses d'Aujourd'hui.

Snyder, Timothy 2010, *Bloodlands: Europe Between Hitler and Stalin*, New York: Basic Books.

Schwarz, Solomon 1951, *The Jews in the Soviet Union*, Syracuse, NY: Syracuse University Press.

Sofia, Francesca 1991, 'Su assimilazione e autocoscienza ebraica nell'Italia liberale', *Il pensiero politico*, vol. 25, pp. 342–57.

Sombart, Werner 1982 [1912], *The Jews and Modern Capitalism*, New Brunswick: Transaction.

Sorkin, David 1987, *The Transformation of German Jewry, 1780–1840* (New York: Oxford University Press).

Spartakus n.d., *Der Jud' ist Schuld! Ein ernstes Wort an alle Kleinbauern, Häusler und Landarbeiter!*, Berlin: Frankes Verlag.

Sperber, Jonathan 2013, *Karl Marx: A Nineteenth-Century Life*, New York: Norton.

Stalin, Josef 1973, 'Marxism and the National Question' (1913), *The Essential Stalin: Major Theoretical Writings 1905–1952*, edited by Bruce Franklin, London: Croom Helm, pp. 54–84.

Steinberg, Hans Josef 1979, *Il socialismo tedesco da Bebel a Kautsky*, Rome: Editori Riuniti.

Stern, Jakob 1896–7, review of T. Herzl's book *Der Judenstaat. Versuch einer Lösung der Judenfrage*, *DNZ*, XV, 1, p. 186.

Stuje, Jan Willem 2009, *Ernest Mandel: A Rebel's Dream Deferred*, London: Verso.

Suchecky, Bernard 1986, *Sionistes-socialistes, Sejmistes et Poalej Tsion en Russie: les premières années 1900–1907*, Paris: Thèse E.H.E.S.S.

Suleiman, Susan 1995, 'The Jew in Sartre's Réflexions sur la question juive: An Exercise in Historical Reading', in *The Jew in the Text: Modernity and the Construction of Identity*, edited by Linda Nochlin & Tamar Garb, New York: Thames & Hudson, pp. 201–18.

Syrkin, Nakhman 1975, 'The Jewish Problem and the Socialist Jewish State' (1898), in *The Zionist Idea: A Historical Analysis and Reader*, edited by Arthur Hertzberg, New York: Atheneum, pp. 333–51.

Taut, Jakob 1986, *Judenfrage und Zionismus*, Frankfurt: ISP Verlag.

Thalheimer, August 1930, 'Über den Faschismus', *Gegen den Strom*, nos. 2–4.

Talmon, Jacob 1970, *Israel Among the Nations*, London: Weidenfeld & Nicolson.

Tiedemann, Rolf 1975, 'Historischer Materialismus oder politischer Messianismus? Politische Gehalte in der Geschichtsphilosophie Walter Benjamins', in Bülthaup 1975.

Tobias, Henry J. 1972, *The Jewish Bund in Russia from Its Origins to 1905*, Stanford: Stanford University Press.

Tooze, Adam 2007, *The Wages of Destruction: The Making and Breaking of the Nazi Economy*, London: Penguin Books.

Toynbee, Arnold 1974, *A Study of History: Abridgement of Volumes I–VI*, Oxford: Oxford University Press.

Traverso, Enzo 1995, *The Jews and Germany*, Lincoln: Nebraska University Press.

Traverso, Enzo 1997, 'Trotzki und Benjamin: Wahlverwandschaften', *Das Argument* no. 222, pp. 697–705.

Traverso, Enzo 1999, *Understanding the Nazi Genocide: Marxism After Auschwitz*, London: Pluto Press, 1999: 'The Blindness of the Intellectuals: Historicising Sartre's *Anti-Semite and Jew*', pp. 26–41; 'On the Edge of Understanding: From the Frankfurt School to Ernest Mandel', pp. 42–62.

Traverso, Enzo 2003, *The Origins of Nazi Violence*, New York: The New Press.

Traverso, Enzo 2016, *The End of Jewish Modernity*, London: Pluto Press.

Trotsky, Leon 1913–14, 'Die Beilis Affäre', *DNZ*, XXXII, 9, pp. 310–20.

Trotsky, Leon 1970a, *On the Jewish Question*, New York: Pathfinder Press.

Trotsky, Leon 1970b [1929], *My Life*, New York: Pathfinder Press.

Trotsky, Leon 1971a, *1905*, New York: Random House.

Trotsky, Leon 1971b [1933], 'What is National Socialism?', *The Struggle Against Fascism in Germany*, New York: Pathfinder, pp. 522–33.

Trotsky, Leon 1973, 'Manifesto of the Fourth International on the Imperialist War and the Proletarian World Revolution', *Writings 1939–40*, New York: Pathfinder Press, pp. 183–222.

Trotsky, Leon 1975 [1915], 'Nation et économie', *Pluriel-Débat*, no. 4.

Trotsky, Leon 1977 [1938], *The Transitional Program for Socialist Revolution*, New York: Pathfinder Press.

Trotsky, Leon 1980a [1903], *Report of the Siberian Delegation*, London: New Park.

Trotsky, Leon 1980b, 'The Jewish Question' (1913), *The Balkan Wars 1912–1913*, New York: Monad Press, pp. 412–20.

Trotsky, Leon 1995 [1942], *In Defense of Marxism*: New York: Pathfinder Press.

Trotsky, Leon 2008 [1932], *History of the Russian Revolution*, Chicago: Haymarket.

Trotzki, Leon 1918 [1914], *The Bolsheviki and World Peace*, New York: Boni and Liveright.

Unseld, Siegrid (ed.) 1972, *Zur Aktualität Walter Benjamins*, Frankfurt: Suhrkamp.

Venturi, Franco 1980, *Roots of Revolution: A History of the Populist and Socialist Movements in Nineteenth Century Russia*, Chicago: University of Chicago Press.

Vidal-Naquet, Pierre 1971, 'Colloque sur la conception matérialiste de la question juive', *ISRAC*, no. 5.

Vidal-Naquet, Pierre 1991, 'Le privilège de la liberté', *Les Juifs, la mémoire et le present II*, Paris: La Découverte, pp. 59–94.

Vidal-Naquet, Pierre 1992, *The Assassins of Memory*, New York: Columbia University Press.

Vidal-Naquet, Pierre 1996, 'Jewish Prism, Marxist Prism', *The Jews: History, Memory, and the Present*, New York: Columbia University Press, pp. 111–24.

Vital, David 1982, *The Origins of Zionism*, Oxford: Clarendon Press.

Volkov, Shulamit 2006, *Germans, Jews, and Antisemites: Trials in Emancipation*, New York: Cambridge University Press.

Volkov, Shulamit 2012, *Walther Rathenau: Weimar's Fallen Statesman*, New Haven: Yale University Press.

Waldenberg, Marek 1983, 'La problematica nazionale nel pensiero socialista polacco nell'età della II Internazionale', *Passato e Presente*, no. 3, pp. 81–114.

Walicki, Andrej 1969, *The Controversy over Capitalism: Studies in the Social Philosophy of the Russian Populists*, New York: Oxford University Press.

Weber, Hermann 1969, *Die Wandlung des deutschen Kommunismus. Die Stalinisierung der KPD in der Weimarer Republik*, Frankfurt: EVA, 2 vol.

Weber, Max 1952 [1921], *Ancient Judaism*, New York: The Free Press.

Weber, Max 1978 [1920], *Economy and Society*, Berkeley: University of California Press.

Weill, Claudie 1987, *L'Internationale et l'autre. Les relations interethniques dans la IIe Internationale*, Paris: Arcantère.

Weill, Claudie 1996, *Les étudiants russes en Allemagne 1900–1914. Quand la Russie frappait aux portes de l'Europe*, Paris: L'Harmattan.

Weinstock, Nathan 1970, *Zionism: The False Messiah*, London: Ink Links.

Weinstock, Nathan 1984–6, *Le pain de misère. Histoire du mouvement ouvrier juif en Europe*, 3 vols., Paris: La Découverte.

Weitz, Eric D. 2007, *Weimar Germany: Promise and Tragedy*, Princeton: Princeton University Press.

Wertheimer, Jack 1981, 'The "Unwanted Element", Eastern Jews in Imperial Germany', *LBIYB*, vol. 26, pp. 23–46.

Wheatland, Thomas 2009, *The Frankfurt School in Exile*, Minneapolis: University of Minnesota Press.

Wiggershaus, Rolf, *The Frankfurt School: Its History, Theory, and Political Significance*, Cambridge, MA: The MIT Press.

Wilson, Nelly 1978, *Bernard Lazare: Anti-Semitism and the Problems of Jewish Identity in Late Nineteenth-Century France*, New York: Cambridge University Press.

Wirth, Louis 1997 [1929], *The Ghetto*, Chicago: University of Chicago Press.

Wistrich, Robert S. 1974, 'Victor Adler: A Viennese Socialist against Philo-Semitism', *Wiener Library Bulletin*, 27, no. 32, pp. 251–62.

Wistrich, Robert S. 1976a, *Revolutionary Jews from Marx to Trotsky*, London: Harrap.

Wistrich, Robert S. 1976b, 'German Social Democracy and the Problem of Jewish Nationalism', *LBIYB*, vol. 20, pp. 109–42.

Wistrich, Robert S. 1977, 'Anti-Capitalism or Anti-Semitism? The Case of Franz Mehring', *LBIYB*, vol. 22, pp. 35–51.

Wistrich, Robert S. 1981, 'Austrian Social Democracy and the Problem of Galician Jewry 1890–1914', *LBIYB*, vol. 26, pp. 89–124.

Wistrich, Robert S. 1982, *Socialism and the Jews: The Dilemmas of Assimilation in Germany and Austria-Hungary*, London: Associated University Press.

Wizisla, Erdmut 2014, *Walter Benjamin and Bertolt Brecht: The Story of a Friendship*, New Haven: Yale University Press.

Wohlfarth, Irving 1978, 'No-Man's Land: On Walter Benjamin's "Destructive Character"',
    Diacritics, vol. 8, no. 2, pp. 64–5.

Wolfe, Bertram D. 1984, *Three Who Made a Revolution*, New York: Penguin Books.

Wolfson, Murray 1982, *Marx: Economist, Philosopher, Jew. Steps in the Development of a
    Doctrine*, London: Macmillan.

Wolin, Richard 1982, *Walter Benjamin. An Aesthetic of Redemption*, New York: Columbia
    University Press.

Yerushalmi, Yosef Hayim 1982, *Zakhor: Jewish History and Jewish Memory*, Seattle: Uni-
    versity of Washington Press.

Zeman, Z.A.B. and W.B. Scharlau 1965, *The Merchant of Revolution: The Life of Alexander
    Israel Helphand (Parvus) 1867–1924*, Oxford: Oxford University Press.

Zentralkomitee der KPD 1932, 'Kommunismus und Judenfrage', *Der Jud ist Schuld ...?
    Diskussionsbuch über die Judenfrage*, Basel: Zinnen Verlag.

Zhitlovsky, Hayim 1955, 'Der sotzializm un di natsionale frage', *Geklibene Werk*, New
    York: Cyco-bicher farlag.

Index